The **Rough Guide** to

Singapore

written and researched by

Mark Lewis

with additional contributions by

Steve Martin

ROUGH GUIDES

NEW YORK • LONDON • DELHI

Contents

Colour maps

Singapore food colour
section following p.112

Festive Singapore colour
section following p.176

◄◄ View of the CBD and the Theatres on the Bay from the *Marina Mandarin Hotel* ◄ Incense burners
outside the Wak Hai Cheng Bio Temple

Introduction to

Singapore

Singapore is certainly the handiest and most marvellous city I ever saw, as well planned and carefully executed as though built entirely by one man. It is like a big desk, full of drawers and pigeon-holes, where everything has its place, and can always be found in it.

W. Hornaday, 1885

Despite the immense changes that the twentieth century has imposed upon the tiny island of **Singapore**, natural historian William Hornaday's succinct appraisal is as valid today as it was in 1885. Since gaining full independence from Malaysia in 1965, this absorbing city-state has been transformed from a sleepy colonial backwater into a pristine, futuristic shrine to consumerism. Yet visitors prepared to peer beneath the state's squeaky-clean surface will discover a profusion of age-old buildings, and values and traditions that have survived the profound social and geographical change. Nor has this change turned the island into a drab, urban slum – even as you make your way in from the airport you'll be struck immediately by Singapore's abundance of parks, nature reserves, and lush, tropical greenery.

Singapore's **progress** over the past four decades has been remarkable. Lacking any noteworthy natural resources, its early prosperity was based on a vigorous free-trade policy, in place since 1819 when Sir Stamford Raffles first set up a British trading post here. Later, mass industrialization bolstered the economy, and today the state boasts the world's busiest container port (in terms of total shipping tonnage), minimal unemployment, and a super-efficient infrastructure. Almost the entire population has been moved from unsanitary kampungs (villages) into new apartments, and the

◀ Carving at the Sri Mariamman Temple

average per capita income is over S$40,000 (US$24,200: World Bank estimate). Yet none of this was achieved without considerable compromise – indeed, the state's detractors claim it has sold its soul in return for prosperity.

Put simply, at the core of the Singapore success story is an unwritten bargain between its **government** and population that critics describe as soft **authoritarianism**. The loss of a certain amount of personal freedom has been accepted in return for levels of affluence and comfort that would have seemed unimaginable thirty years ago. But as the nation's youth (who don't remember a time before the improvements they take for granted) begin to find a voice, public life should become increasingly, if gradually, more liberal and democratic.

Whatever the political ramifications of the state's economic success, of more relevance to its millions of annual visitors (9 million in 2005) is that improvements in living conditions have resulted in a steady loss of the state's **heritage**, with historic buildings and streets bulldozed to make way for shopping centres. Singapore undoubtedly lacks the personality of some Southeast Asian cities, but its reputation for being sterile and sanitized is unfair. Shopping on state-of-the-art Orchard Road is undoubtedly a major draw for many tourists, but elsewhere can still be found the dusty temples, fragrant medicinal shops, and colonial buildings of old Singapore, neatly divided into historical enclaves.

▼ The Sim Lim Square Technology Mall

Much of the city's fascination springs from its **multicultural population**: of the 3.55 million permanent residents, approximately 77 percent are ethnic Chinese, whose shops, restaurants and temples are

5

Singlish

Upon first hearing the machine-gun rattle of Singaporean English, or Singlish, you could easily be forgiven for thinking you're listening to a language other than English. Pronunciation is so staccato that many words are rendered almost unrecognizable – especially monosyllabic words such as "cheque" and "book", which together would be spoken "che-boo". In contrast, in two-syllable words the second syllable is lengthened, and stressed by a rise in tone: ask a Singaporean what they've been doing, and you'll variously be told "wor-king", "shop-ping", and "slee-ping".

But it's the unorthodox rhythms of phrasing that make Singlish so memorable. Conventional English syntax is twisted and wrung, and tenses and pronouns discarded. If you ask a Singaporean if they've ever seen Michael Jackson, you might be answered "I ever see him", while enquiring whether they've just been shopping might yield "go come back already".

Responses are almost invariably reduced to their bare bones, with single-word replies often repeated for stress. Request something in a shop and you'll hear "have, have", or "got, got". Suffixes and exclamations drawn from Malay, Hokkien and English complete this patois, the most distinctive being "lah", as in "okay lah", and "so cheap one lah" (which translates as "this is really inexpensive, isn't it?").

If Singlish still has you totally baffled, you might try raising your eyes to the heavens, and crying either "ay yor" (with a drop of tone on "yor") or "Allama" – both expressions of annoyance or exasperation.

found across the island; fourteen percent are ethnic Malay; and eight percent are ethnic Indians, with the remainder made up of other ethnic groups. This diverse mix textures the whole island, and often turns a ten-minute walk into what seems like a hop from one country to another. One intriguing by-product of this ethnic melting pot is **Singlish**, or Singaporean English, a patois that blends English with the speech patterns, exclamations and vocabulary of Chinese and Malay. Another is the amazing range of mouthwatering **cuisines** on offer in the city. Inevitably, the greatest emphasis is on Chinese, Malay and Indian foods, but your trip to Singapore will give you the opportunity to sample Thai, Vietnamese, and any number of other Asian specialities.

▼ Singapore's symbol: the Merlion

What to see

The diamond-shaped island of Singapore is 42km from east to west and 23km from north to south, making it compact enough to be explored exhaustively in just a few days. The state's central or downtown districts lie within a three-kilometre radius of the mouth of the river and although MRT lines and buses do run between these districts (see MRT system map at the back of the book), you might prefer to explore the whole area on foot. Downtown Singapore is probably where you'll spend most of your time, but the rest of the island has its attractions too – the super-efficient bus and underground train networks link the city centre with the suburbs to the north, east and west, and there's even the chance to take a ride on a **cable car**. While exploring always bear in mind that you're in the tropics: apply sunscreen and stay out of the midday sun. And beware, strolling through the remaining pockets of old Singapore entails negotiating uneven five-foot ways (the covered pavements that front Singapore's old shophouses) and yawning storm drains.

Ever since Sir Stamford Raffles first landed on its northern bank in 1819, the area around the **Singapore River**, which strikes into the heart of the island from the south coast, has formed the hub of the city. North of the river, and forming the core of downtown Singapore is the **Colonial District**, around whose public buildings and lofty cathedral the island's British residents used to promenade. The Colonial District has a cluster of buildings that recall the days of early British rule: Parliament House, the Cathedral, the Supreme Court, the Cricket Club and, most famously, **Raffles Hotel**. Further west, **Fort Canning Park** provides a welcome splash of green to the high-rise landscape and offers several attractions, including the **Singapore History Museum**. From here, it's a five-minute stroll to the eastern end of **Orchard Road**, the main shopping area in the city, and a metropolis of retail malls and shopping centres. South, across the river, the monolithic towers of the **Financial District** cast their long shadows over the city.

Each of Singapore's three **ethnic enclaves** has its own distinct flavour, ranging from the aromatic spice stores and gaudy Hindu temples of **Little India**, to the tumbledown back streets of **Chinatown**, where it's still possible to happen upon calligraphers and fortune-tellers. Visitors to

Historical roots: the layout of Singapore

The basic skeleton plan of Singapore's central streets and districts has changed little since the British assembled it in the first half of the nineteenth century. Modern Singapore's founder, **Sir Stamford Raffles**, established the Padang as the nucleus of European life as early as 1819, and the trappings of colonial rule – government building, court house, church – were constructed around it in subsequent decades.

Elsewhere, "native divisions or campongs" were established. An 1823 map of Singapore shows **Chinatown** and the **Arab quarter** in the positions they occupy now. By the late 1820s, Indian immigrants were starting to gravitate towards the brick kiln and livestock industries that were developing along Serangoon Road – the spine of today's **Little India**.

The south bank of the Singapore River was clawed back from the swamp that covered it in 1823, to form the site of modern-day Raffles Place. This was the earliest example of a trend towards **land reclamation** that has substantially remoulded the coastline and contours of Singapore, and which still continues. To appreciate just how much of modern Singapore lay underwater a century ago, turn to the map of Central Singapore at the back and check out how far from the sea Beach Road and Telok Ayer ("Watery Bay") Street are, today.

the **Arab Quarter** can browse stores stacked with fine cloths and silks, to the accompaniment of the otherworldly wail of the muezzin's call to prayer at the **Sultan Mosque**.

The area **north** of downtown Singapore is the island's suburban heartland, and home to a grid of vast new towns; but it's here that you'll also find the state's last remaining pocket of primary rainforest, the **Bukit Timah Nature Reserve**, and the splendid **Singapore Zoological Gardens**. In addition to Singapore's industrial zone and port, the **west** of the island boasts a clutch of good theme parks, most notably **Jurong BirdPark**, and **Haw Par Villas** – a mind-boggling hybrid of eastern mythology and Disneyland kitsch.

▲ Outside the Thian Hock Keng Temple, Chinatown

Aside from a museum recalling the infamous jail near **Changi Village**, where so many soldiers lost their lives in World War II, the **east** of Singapore features some of Singapore's best **seafood restaurants**, set behind long stretches of sandy beach.

Over fifty **islands and islets** lie within Singaporean waters, all of which can be reached with varying degrees of ease. The best day-trips, however, are to **Sentosa**, the island amusement arcade linked to the south coast by causeway and cable car; and to **Pulau Ubin**, off the east coast, whose inhabitants continue to live a kampung life long since eradicated from the mainland.

▼ Night time on Clarke Quay

▼ Peranakan houses on Koon Seng Road

When to go

Singapore is just 136km north of the equator, which means that you should be prepared for a hot and sticky time whenever you go. Temperatures are uniformly high throughout the year, but it's the region's humidity levels that make the heat really uncomfortable – a good downpour is the only thing that clears the air. Be prepared for rain during your stay – November and December are usually the coolest, and the wettest, months, but rain can fall all year round. On average, June, July and August record the lowest annual rainfall. Otherwise, the only other consideration is the possibility of coinciding with one of the island's many festivals (see p.177 and the *Festive Singapore* colour insert), of which the liveliest and most extensive is Chinese New Year.

Singapore climate

	Jan	Feb	Mar	Apr	May	Jun	Jul	Aug	Sep	Oct	Nov	Dec
Average daily temperature												
max (°C)	31	32	32	32	32	32	31	31	31	31	31	30
max (°F)	88	90	90	90	90	90	88	88	88	88	88	86
min (°C)	21	22	23	23	23	23	22	22	22	22	22	22
min (°F)	70	72	73	73	73	73	72	72	72	72	72	72
Average rainfall												
mm	146	155	182	223	228	151	170	163	200	199	255	258

things not to miss

Unless you're in town for a while it's not possible to see everything Singapore has to offer in one trip. What follows is a selective taste of the city-state's highlights – its best museums, most atmospheric restaurants and most vibrant neighbourhoods. Arranged in five colour-coded categories, you can browse through to find the very best things to see, do and experience. All highlights have a page reference to take you straight into the Guide, where you can find out more.

01 A trip to the Theatres on the Bay Page 57 • Singapore's spectacular new arts centre offers a full range of Western and Oriental cultural treats.

02 **Chinatown** Page **69** • Chinatown has been extensively redeveloped in recent years and its once characterful shophouses rendered improbably perfect, but if you venture into the tumbledown back streets it's still possible to happen upon traditional customs, trades and crafts. Lively most of the year, it really comes alive during Chinese New Year.

03 **The Thian Hock Keng Temple** Page **74** • Gilt altars, Eastern deities, chanting monks, praying worshippers and incense smoke – stroll into the courtyard and soak up the atmosphere.

04 **Bukit Timah Reserve** Page **99** • An incongruous but pristine pocket of primary rainforest, slap bang in the middle of twentyfirst-century Singapore.

05 Breakfast with the animals
Page **144** • You've heard of a chimp's tea party – now try orange juice (and bananas, of course) with an orang utan.

06 A cable car to Sentosa
Page **124** • Never mind bussing it across the causeway, this is the most fun approach to Singapore's pleasure island.

07 Changi Prison Museum
Page **112** • A hushed and moving memorial to the horrors perpetrated in Singapore during World War II.

08 An Orchard Road shopping spree
Page **65** • Think Oxford Street, think 5th Avenue, think Champs-Elysées: shopping centres and famous brands enough to test even the most confirmed shopaholic.

09 A Singapore Sling at Raffles Hotel
Page **59** • No trip is complete without an obligatory glass of this famous cherry brandy cocktail, created by 1920's bartender, Ngiam Tong Boon's, and best sipped in the Bar & Billiards Room.

13

10 Chilli crab on the East Coast Page

115 • Fresh crabs tossed in a fiery and lip-smackingly tasty chilli sauce, eaten overlooking the South China Sea. Roll your sleeves up and get stuck in – but don't wear a white shirt.

12 A walk down Serangoon Road Page 90 • Sensual overload:
colourful sarees, aromatic spice-grinding shops, fortune-telling parrots and jasmine garlands.

11 Evening prayer at the Sultan Mosque Page 96 •
The muezzin's wailing call to prayer floats hauntingly on the warm evening air.

13 Standing in Raffles Place looking up at the skyline Page 83 •
Ground-level vertigo: look up for long, and you'll swear Singapore's immaculate skyscrapers are bowing towards one another to form a roof above you.

14 **Arab Quarter** Page **96** • With its mosques, cafés and shops, this vibrant area frames a perfect snapshot of Malay life and culture.

15 **Bumboats and bikes**
Page **113** • Taking a bumboat and then hiring a bike is the perfect way to explore some of Singapore's outlying areas, such as the East Coast Parkway or sleepy Pulau Ubin.

17 **Clubbing at Zouk** Page **170** • Some of the world's most happening DJs guest at Singapore's hippest nightspot, set in a converted warehouse beside the river.

16 **Satay** See **Singapore food colour section** • Satay is a staple of Malay cooking, just one of the amazing range of mouth-watering cuisines on offer in the city.

18 **Evening on Boat Quay** Page **85** • Al fresco dining at its best: bars and restaurants galore, whose reflected lights dance on the waters of the Singapore River.

19 **The view from the Swissôtel's City Space**
Page **58** • From the *City Space* bar at the top of the *Swissôtel*, pictured here, you can see as far as Malaysia to the north, and Indonesia to the south.

20 **Timithi at Sri Mariamman Temple** Page **77** • No surprise in multicultural Singapore, a Hindu temple in Chinatown and the venue for the annual fire-walking festival.

Basics

Basics

Getting there

The easiest and quickest way to get to Singapore is to fly, and with Singapore being one of the world's main air hubs finding a flight should be relatively straightforward.

Generally speaking, booking a scheduled ticket direct with the airline is the most expensive way to fly. You can usually cut costs considerably by booking through a specialist flight agent – either a consolidator or a discount agent. **Consolidators** buy up large blocks of tickets to sell on at a discount. They don't normally impose advance purchase requirements (although in busy periods you'll want to book ahead to be sure of getting a seat), but they often charge very stiff fees for date changes; note also that airlines generally won't alter tickets after they've gone to a consolidator, so you can make changes only through the consolidator. **Discount agents** also deal in blocks of tickets off-loaded by the airlines, and may in addition offer special student and youth fares and a range of other travel-related services such as travel insurance, rail passes, car rentals, tours and the like.

Reliable flight agents are listed on the pages that follow. Alternatively, consult the ads in the Sunday newspaper travel sections. Occasionally you'll turn up better deals by calling the **airlines** direct (be sure to ask about seasonal promotions).

Discount **travel clubs**, offering money off air tickets, car rental and the like, are an option if you travel a lot. Most charge annual membership fees.

A further possibility is to see if you can arrange a **courier flight**, although you'll need a flexible schedule, and preferably be travelling alone with very little luggage. In return for shepherding a parcel through customs, you can expect to get a deeply discounted ticket, though you'll probably also be restricted in the duration of your stay.

If you want to see more of Southeast Asia on your trip to Singapore you could consider buying an **open-jaw** ticket which allows you, for example, to fly into Bangkok, travel overland to Singapore and then fly home from there. There's also the option of a **round-the-world ticket** (RTW), if Singapore is just one stop on a longer itinerary. Some travel agents can sell you an "off-the-shelf" RTW ticket that will have you touching down in about half a dozen cities (Singapore is on many itineraries); these tickets can also be tailored to your needs, though this is apt to be more expensive. If you're not too pushed for time you could also consider flying to another **Southeast Asian gateway**, such as Bangkok, and travelling by air or overland from there.

Additionally, an increasing number of **package holidays** are available, including fly-drive deals and city breaks. Although usually not the cheapest way of travelling, these can be worthwhile if your time is limited.

Online travel agents

Many airlines and discount travel websites offer you the opportunity to book your tickets **online**, cutting the cost of agents and middlemen. Good deals can often be found through discount or auction sites, as well as through the airlines' own websites.

Online booking agents and general travel sites

ⓦ **travel.yahoo.com** Incorporates a lot of Rough Guide material in its coverage of destination countries and cities across the world, with information about places to eat, sleep, etc.
ⓦ **www.cheapflights.com** Flight deals, travel agents, plus links to other travel sites.
ⓦ **www.cheaptickets.com** Discount flight specialists.
ⓦ **www.etn.nl/discount.htm** A hub of consolidator and discount agent Web links, maintained by the non-profit European Travel Network.
ⓦ **www.expedia.com** Discount air fares, all-airline search engine and daily deals.

ⓦ **www.flyaow.com** Online air travel info and reservations site.

ⓦ **www.gaytravel.com** Gay online travel agent, offering accommodation, cruises, tours and more.

ⓦ **www.hotwire.com** Bookings from the US only. Last-minute savings of up to forty percent on regular published fares. Travellers must be at least 18 and there are no refunds, transfers or changes allowed. Log-in required.

ⓦ **www.lastminute.com** Offers good last-minute holiday package and flight-only deals.

ⓦ **www.priceline.com** Name-your-own-price website that has deals at around forty percent off standard fares. You cannot specify flight times (although you do specify dates) and the tickets are non-refundable, non-transferable and non-changeable.

ⓦ **www.skyauction.com** Bookings from the US only. Auctions tickets and travel packages using a "second bid" scheme. The best strategy is to bid the maximum you're willing to pay, since if you win you'll pay just enough to beat the runner-up regardless of your maximum bid.

ⓦ **www.travelocity.com** Destination guides, hot Web fares and best deals for car rental, accommodation and lodging as well as fares. Provides access to the travel agent system SABRE, the most comprehensive central reservations system in the US.

ⓦ **www.travelshop.com.au** Australian website offering discounted flights, packages, insurance and online bookings.

Flights from the UK and Ireland

There are regular daily flights to Singapore from Britain and connecting flights from Ireland to all major British airports. Singapore Airlines, British Airways, Qantas and Virgin Atlantic all offer **direct** flights out of London, a journey time of twelve to thirteen hours. Many other scheduled airlines offer **indirect** flights, which typically touch down at their own national hubs, and maybe elsewhere, en route to the final destination. These flights take longer (16–22 hours), but work out cheaper. Add-on costs from other British airports are around £60 return to London.

There are no non-stop flights from **Ireland** to Singapore; airlines will quote you through-fares via British airports. Alternatively, you could take advantage of the cheap airfares between Ireland and Britain and pick up an onward flight from London with another airline.

Discounted return **fares** start from around £380 for non-stop flights and £280 for indirect in low season, but you should be prepared to add to that a couple of hundred pounds in the high-season months of July, August and December. The cheapest tickets will be with airlines such as KLM (via Amsterdam), Finnair (via Helsinki), Pakistan International Airlines (via Karachi), Turkish Airlines (via Istanbul), Thai International (via Bangkok), Gulf Air (via Bahrain), Kuwait Airways, or Aeroflot (via Moscow and Dubai).

The cheapest **round-the-world tickets** start from around £700 in low season (departing Jan–June & Sept to early Dec). A typical one-year open ticket could depart from and return to London, taking in, say, Singapore, Bangkok, Bali, Sydney, Auckland, Tahiti, Los Angeles and New York, allowing you to cover the Singapore–Bangkok and Los Angeles–New York legs overland. STA, usit Now and Trailfinders all specialize in RTW tickets.

Open-jaw tickets, which allow you to fly into one airport and out of another without having to retrace your steps, are calculated in different ways by different airlines, but you can expect to pay at least the highest of the two return fares you are combining. Flying into Bangkok and out of Singapore, reckon on around £500, although it's well worth shopping around for deals on these tickets. For details of the overland sector see "Getting there from Southeast Asia", p.26.

If you're considering a **courier flight**, contact the International Association of Air Travel Couriers UK (☎0800/0746 481, ⓦwww.aircourier.co.uk), which acts as a courier agent for lots of companies.

Airlines in the UK and Ireland

Aer Lingus ☎0845/08 44444, Rep Ireland ☎0818/365 000; ⓦwww.aerlingus.ie.
Aeroflot ☎020/7355 2233, ⓦwww.aeroflot.co.uk.
bmibaby ☎0870/264 2229, Rep Ireland ☎01/236 6130; ⓦwww.bmibaby.com.
British Airways ☎0845/773 3377, Rep Ireland ☎1800/626 747; ⓦwww.ba.com.
British Midland ☎0870/607 0555, Rep Ireland ☎01/4073036; ⓦwww.flybmi.com.
EasyJet ☎0870/600 0000, ⓦwww.easyjet.com.
Finnair ☎0870/241 4411, Rep Ireland ☎01/844 6565; ⓦwww.finnair.com.

Fly less – stay longer! Travel and climate change

Climate change is a serious threat to the ecosystems that humans rely upon, and air travel is the fastest-growing contributor to the problem. Rough Guides regard travel, overall, as a global benefit, and feel strongly that the advantages to developing economies are important, as is the opportunity of greater contact and awareness among peoples. But we all have a responsibility to limit our personal impact on global warming, and that means giving thought to how often we fly, and what we can do to redress the harm that our trips create.

Flying and climate change

Pretty much every form of motorized travel generates CO_2 (the main cause of human-induced climate change) but planes are far and away the worst offenders, not just because of the sheer distances they allow us to travel, but because they release a selection of greenhouse gases high into the atmosphere. The statistics are frightening: two people taking a return flight between Europe and the US will contribute as much to climate change as an average household's gas and electricity over a whole year.

Fuel-cell and other less harmful types of plane may emerge eventually. But until then, there are really just two options for concerned travellers: to reduce the amount we travel by air (take fewer trips – stay for longer!), and to make the trips we do take "climate neutral" via a carbon offset scheme.

Carbon offset schemes

Offset schemes run by climatecare.org, carbonneutral.com and others allow you to make up for some or all of the greenhouse gases that you are responsible for releasing. To do this, they provide "carbon calculators" for working out the global-warming contribution of a specific flight (or even your entire existence), and then let you contribute an appropriate amount of money to fund offsetting measures. These include rainforest and other indigenous reforestation, and initiatives to reduce future energy demand – often run in conjunction with sustainable development schemes.

Rough Guides, together with Lonely Planet and other concerned partners in the travel industry, are supporting a carbon offset scheme run by climatecare.org. Please take the time to view our website and see how you can help to make your trip climate neutral.

ⓦ **www.roughguides.com/climatechange**

Go ⓣ 0870/607 6543, ⓦ www.go-fly.com.
Gulf Air ⓣ 0870/777 1717, ⓦ www.gulfairco.com.
KLM ⓣ 0870/507 4074, ⓦ www.klm.com.
Kuwait Airways ⓣ 020/7412 0006, ⓦ www.kuwait-airways.com.
Lufthansa ⓣ 0845/7737747, Rep Ireland ⓣ 01/844 5544; ⓦ www.lufthansa.co.uk.
Malaysia Airlines (MAS) ⓣ 0870/607 9090, Rep Ireland ⓣ 01/676 1561; ⓦ www.mas.com.my.
Pakistan International Airlines ⓣ 020/7499 5500, ⓦ www.piac.com.pk.
Qantas ⓣ 0845/774 7767, ⓦ www.qantas.co.uk.
Royal Brunei Airlines ⓣ 020/7584 6660, ⓦ www.bruneiair.com.
Ryanair ⓣ 0871/246 0000, Rep Ireland ⓣ 0818/303 030; ⓦ www.ryanair.com.
SAS Scandinavian Airlines ⓣ 0845/607 2772, Rep Ireland ⓣ 01/844 5440; ⓦ www.scandinavian.net.

Singapore Airlines ⓣ 0870/608 8886, Rep Ireland ⓣ 01/671 0722; ⓦ www.singaporeair.com.
SriLankan Airlines ⓣ 020/8538 2000, ⓦ www.srilankan.lk.
Thai International ⓣ 0870/606 0911, ⓦ www.thaiair.com.
Turkish Airlines ⓣ 020/7766 9300, ⓦ www.turkishairlines.com.
Virgin Atlantic Airways ⓣ 01293/747 747, ⓦ www.virgin-atlantic.com.

Discount flight and travel agents in the UK and Ireland

Apex Travel Rep Ireland ⓣ 01/241 8000, ⓦ www.apextravel.ie. Specialists in flights to Far East and other long-haul destinations.
Bridge the World ⓣ 0870/444 7474, ⓦ www.bridgetheworld.com. Specializing in

round-the-world tickets, with good deals aimed at the backpacker market.

Flightbookers ☎0870/010 7000, ⓦwww .ebookers.com. Low fares on an extensive selection of scheduled flights.

Joe Walsh Tours Rep Ireland ☎01/676 0991, ⓦwww.joewalshtours.ie. General budget fares agent.

North South Travel ☎01245/608 291, ⓦwww .northsouthtravel.co.uk. Friendly, competitive travel agency, offering discounted fares worldwide – profits are used to support projects in the developing world, especially the promotion of sustainable tourism.

STA Travel ☎0870/1600 599, ⓦwww.statravel .co.uk. Worldwide specialists in low-cost flights and tours for students and under-26s, though other customers welcome.

Trailfinders London ☎020/7628 7628, ⓦwww .trailfinders.co.uk; Rep Ireland ☎01/677 7888, ⓦwww.trailfinders.ie. One of the best-informed and most efficient agents for independent travellers.

Travel Bag ☎0870/890 1456, ⓦwww.travelbag .co.uk. Discount flights to the Far East.

usit Now Rep Ireland ☎01/602 1600, Northern Ireland ☎028/9032 7111; ⓦwww.usitnow.ie. Student and youth specialists.

Packages and organized tours

There is a range of **package holidays** and **organized tours** available to Singapore, and the main operators are listed below; all also offer trips further afield into Malaysia and beyond. For **city breaks**, five nights in Singapore, including flights but with room-only accommodation in a three-star hotel, cost around £650 (£850 in high season), rising to £900–1100 for two weeks.

Specialist operators can also arrange itineraries which include a ride on the extremely swish **Eastern and Oriental Express** train between Singapore and Bangkok (see p.26 for more details).

Several companies offer **multi-centre packages** to Singapore and other Southeast Asian destinations. For example, a ten-night stay in Singapore and Thailand's Phuket Island should cost around £750, including return flight and accommodation in three-star hotels.

Specialist tour operators in the UK and Ireland

Abercrombie & Kent Travel ☎020/7730 9600, ⓦwww.abercrombiekent.com. Top-of-the-range, tailor-made cruises and tours.

Bales Worldwide ☎0870/241 3208, ⓦwww .balesworldwide.com. Tailor-made trips incorporating the Eastern and Oriental train journey from Singapore to Bangkok.

British Airways Holidays ☎0870/442 3820, ⓦwww.baholidays.co.uk. Five-night city breaks starting from £700.

Eastern and Oriental Express ☎020/7805 5100, ⓦwww.orient-express.com. Tours based around one of the most exclusive train journeys in the world.

Kuoni Travel ☎01306/742888, ⓦwww.kuoni .co.uk. Tailor-made tours in Southeast Asia, plus Singapore city breaks.

Magic of the Orient ☎0117/311 6050, ⓦwww .magic-of-the-orient.com. Offers a two-week Singapore & Vietnam Highlights tour for £1500, plus swish seven-night stays at the Fullerton.

Qantas Holidays ☎0870/567 3464, ⓦwww .qantas-holidays.co.uk. Stylish Singapore holidays flying business class and staying at Raffles.

Silverbird Travel ☎020/8875 9090, ⓦwww .silverbird.co.uk. Tours pair Singapore up with Malaysian and Thai islands.

Thomas Cook Holidays ☎0173/3417 100, ⓦwww.thomascook.com. Good selection of flight-and-board holidays and city breaks.

Tradewinds Worldwide Holidays ☎0870/751 0003, ⓦwww.tradewinds.co.uk. Lush multi-centre trips to Singapore plus the Maldives, or Thailand.

Flights from the US and Canada

With strong competition between a large number of carriers, Singapore is one of the cheapest Southeast Asian destinations to reach **from North America**.

Singapore is roughly halfway around the world from the **east coast** of the USA, which means that whether you plan on flying east or west you're going to have a long flight with at least one stopover. The eastbound (transatlantic) route is more direct and a bit faster – about 21 hours' total travel time – which makes it cheaper than flying west. From the **west coast**, it's faster and cheaper to head west (over the Pacific) – Los Angeles to Singapore takes as little as nineteen hours – although flying via Europe may suit your itinerary better and doesn't cost much more.

Airfares from North America to Southeast Asia are highest from around early June to late August, and again from early December to early January. All other times are considered low season. The price difference between high season and low season is about $200–300 on a typical round-trip fare, but bear in mind that you will have to make your reservation further in advance during the high season. Remember that flying on weekends ordinarily adds about $100 to the round-trip fare; price ranges quoted below assume midweek travel.

Singapore Airlines offers the most frequent departures, with **direct flights** originating in New York (eastbound via Frankfurt or Amsterdam), Los Angeles/San Francisco (westbound via Tokyo, Taipei or Hong Kong) and Vancouver (westbound via Seoul). However, **indirect flights** on other airlines – or a combination of airlines – might not actually add much time to your journey, and if you go through a consolidator you might be able to get a free stopover each way. The airlines that fly to Singapore are too numerous to list here: see opposite for some of the major carriers.

If you're planning to **travel in several Asian countries**, consider making Hong Kong or Bangkok your first stop; you'll save about $200 over the fare to Singapore and from Bangkok you can travel overland by train to Singapore – see "Getting there from Southeast Asia" (p.26).

From **New York**, you'll pay $750 direct round-trip in low season, but as much as $1100 in high season; from **Los Angeles**, **San Francisco** or **Seattle**, $800/$1100; from **Toronto** or **Montréal**, CDN$2200/$2500; and from **Vancouver**, CDN$2000/$2400.

If Singapore is only one stop on a longer journey, you might want to consider buying a **round-the-world ticket (RTW)**. Plan for between $1300 and $1500 for a RTW ticket travelling for example New York–Hong Kong–Singapore–(overland on your own)–Bangkok–Delhi–London–New York.

Most airlines operating in this part of the world offer so-called **Circle Pacific** fares, allowing four (or sometimes more) stopovers in the course of a round trip between North America and Asia or Australasia. However, fares for these deals can approach $2000 – not very economical unless you have some really obscure stopovers in mind, and plan to travel right across Australia as well. Otherwise, you'll probably find it's cheaper to have a discount travel agent put together a ticket with your intended stops.

A further possibility is a **courier flight**. Courier flights to Singapore come up regularly, but most departures are from Los Angeles – figure on paying around $300, maybe less if it's a last-minute deal. Contact the Air Courier Association (Ⓣ1-800/282-1202, Ⓦwww.aircourier.org) or the International Association of Air Travel Couriers (Ⓣ308/632-3273, Ⓦwww.courier.org), both of which levy a modest membership fee before they'll arrange flights for you.

Airlines in the US and Canada

Air Canada Ⓣ1-888/247-2262, Ⓦwww.aircanada.ca.
Air France US Ⓣ1-800/237-2747, Ⓦwww.airfrance.com; Canada Ⓣ1-800/667-2747, Ⓦwww.airfrance.ca.
British Airways Ⓣ1-800/247-9297, Ⓦwww.british-airways.com.
British Midland Ⓣ1-800/788-0555, Ⓦwww.flybmi.com.
Cathay Pacific Ⓣ1-800/233-2742, Ⓦwww.cathay-usa.com.
EVA Airways Ⓣ1-800/695-1188, Ⓦwww.evaair.com.
Finnair Ⓣ1-800/950-5000, Ⓦwww.finnair.com.
Gulf Air Ⓣ1-800/FLY-GULF, Ⓦwww.gulfairco.com.
Japan Air Lines Ⓣ1-800/525-3663, Ⓦwww.japanair.com.
Korean Airlines Ⓣ1-800/438-5000, Ⓦwww.koreanair.com.
Lufthansa US Ⓣ1-800/645-3880 Canada Ⓣ1-800/563-5954; Ⓦwww.lufthansa-usa.com.
Malaysia Airlines Ⓣ1-800/552-9264, Ⓦwww.mas.com.my.
Northwest/KLM Airlines domestic Ⓣ1-800/225-2525, international Ⓣ1-800/447-4747, Ⓦwww.nwa.com, Ⓦwww.klm.com.
Pakistan International Airlines Ⓣ1-800/221-2552 or 212/760-8484, Ⓦwww.piac.com.pk.
Philippine Airlines Ⓣ1-800/435-9725, Ⓦwww.philippineairlines.com.
Singapore Airlines Ⓣ1-800/742-3333, Ⓦwww.singaporeair.com.
SriLankan Airlines Ⓣ1-877/915-2652, Ⓦwww.srilankan.lk.
Thai Airways International Ⓣ1-800/426-5204, Ⓦwww.thaiairways.com.
United Airlines domestic Ⓣ1-800/241-6522, international Ⓣ1-800/538-2929, Ⓦwww.ual.com.

Agents, consolidators and travel clubs in the US and Canada

Air Brokers International ☎1-800/883-3273, ⊛www.airbrokers.com. Consolidator and specialist in round-the-world and Circle Pacific tickets.

Airtreks.com ☎1-877-AIRTREKS or 415/912-5600, ⊛www.airtreks.com. Round-the-world and Circle Pacific tickets. The website features an interactive database that lets you build and price your own round-the-world itinerary. Also does Asian overland connections.

Educational Travel Center ☎1-800/747-5551 or 608/256-5551, ⊛www.edtrav.com. Student/youth discount agent.

SkyLink US ☎1-800/AIR-ONLY or 212/573-8980, Canada ☎1-800/SKY-LINK, ⊛www.skylinkus.com. Consolidator.

STA Travel US ☎1-800/781-4040, Canada ☎1-888/427-5639, ⊛www.sta-travel.com. Worldwide specialists in independent travel; also student IDs, travel insurance, car rental, rail passes etc.

TFI Tours ☎1-800/745-8000 or 212/736-1140, ⊛www.lowestairprice.com. Consolidator.

Travel Cuts Canada ☎1-800/667-2887, US ☎1-866/246-9762; ⊛www.travelcuts.com. Canadian student-travel organization.

Worldtek Travel ☎1-800/243-1723, ⊛www.worldtek.com. Discount travel agency for worldwide travel.

Packages and organized tours

Packages to Singapore can include five-star city breaks, sightseeing excursions and opulent splendour aboard the Eastern and Oriental Express train. Inevitably, these packaged journeys are more expensive and less spontaneous than they would be if done independently, but for the traveller with more money than time they offer a convenient and hassle-free experience.

The **Eastern and Oriental train journey** between Bangkok and Singapore (see p.26 for more information) is the ultimate in luxury: tours start at $600 and invariably throw in several days' worth of side trips along with the two-night train journey.

Note that your local travel agent should be able to book any tour for you at no additional cost. For a list of North American tour companies, see opposite.

Tour operators in the US and Canada

Abercrombie & Kent ☎1-800/323-7308 or 630/954-2944, ⊛www.abercrombiekent.com. De luxe tours built around the Eastern and Oriental Express.

Absolute Asia ☎1-800/736-8187, ⊛www.absoluteasia.com. Luxury, multi-centre trips to Southeast Asia, including Singapore and Malaysia.

Adventure Center ☎1-800/228-8747 or 510/654-1879, ⊛www.adventurecenter.com. Hiking and "soft adventure" specialists that include Singapore in Southeast Asian itineraries.

Adventures Abroad ☎1-800/665-3998 or 360/775-9926, ⊛www.adventures-abroad.com. Small-group adventure tours taking in Malaysia and other spots in Southeast Asia.

Cox & Kings ☎1-800/999-1758, ⊛www.coxandkingsusa.com. Top-notch company offering Singapore stopovers in its Southeast Asian schedules.

Eastern and Oriental Express ☎1-866/674-3689, ⊛www.orient-express.com. Tours based around one of the most exclusive train journeys in the world.

Globus ☎1-866/755-8581, ⊛www.globusjourneys.com. Features Singapore in its Asia Medley and Asia Selection schedules.

Pacific Bestours ☎1-800/272-1149, ⊛www.bestour.com. Custom-built city breaks with city tours.

Pleasant Holidays ☎1-800/742-9244, ⊛www.pleasantholidays.com. City breaks and fly-drives.

Vacationland ☎1-800/245-0050, ⊛www.vacation-land.com. Extensive range of city breaks, fly-drives, regional tours, sightseeing add-ons, plus golf itineraries.

Flights from Australia and New Zealand

Singapore is one of the main stops on the way from Australasia to Europe, so there are plenty of airlines and routes to choose from. Direct flights are not always the cheapest and it's well worth taking advantage of a **stopover** en route – Asian airlines fly via their home base giving you a perfect opportunity to explore a bit more of the area. If you want to visit Singapore as part of a wider trip there are several good-value options worth considering such as: an **open-jaw ticket** that allows you to fly you into one country and out of another, and travel overland in between; multi-stop **Circle Asia** fares; **round-the-world** (RTW) tickets; or flying somewhere else first – such as Thailand,

Malaysia or Indonesia – and continuing **overland** from there. For example, you could take the train from Malaysia (Kuala Lumpur to Singapore takes only six hours – see "Getting there from Southeast Asia", p.26 for details).

Fares to Southeast Asian destinations are very competitive, so whatever kind of ticket you're after it's best to shop around. The flight agents listed opposite can fill you in on all the latest deals and any special limited offers. If you're a student or under 26, you may be able to get a discounted fare; STA is a good place to start.

Fares are seasonally rated, with prices for flights usually higher during Christmas and New Year and mid-year periods; generally high season is mid-May to end-August and December to mid-January, shoulder March to mid-May and September to mid-October and low the rest of the year – with a difference of around A/NZ$200–300 between each. Airfares from east coast Australian gateways are all pretty much the same (common rated on most airlines, with Qantas providing a shuttle service to the point of departure); Perth and Darwin are A$100–200 cheaper. From New Zealand you can expect to pay NZ$150–300 more from Christchurch and Wellington than from Auckland.

Malaysian Airlines (MAS), Singapore Airlines, Royal Brunei, Qantas and Garuda all have regular services **from Australia** to Singapore. On the whole, fares to Singapore from Brisbane, Sydney or Melbourne and Cairns are roughly between A$600 low season and A$800 high season for a single and A$900–1200 for a return depending on which airline you choose. But the real bargains are often with Middle Eastern airlines keen to fill flights for the leg to Singapore before they head for home.

From New Zealand, Air New Zealand, British Airways, Garuda, Qantas, Singapore Airlines and Malaysia Airlines, among others, fly to Singapore, with fares starting at NZ$750 low season and NZ$1000 high season for a single and NZ$1200–1500 for a return.

Airlines in Australia and New Zealand

Air New Zealand Australia ℡13 24 76, ⓦwww.airnz.com.au; New Zealand ℡0800/737 000, ⓦwww.airnz.co.nz.

British Airways Australia ℡1300/767 177, New Zealand ℡0800/274 847 or 09/356 8690; ⓦwww.britishairways.com.

Egypt Air Australia ℡02/9232 6677, ⓦwww.egyptair.com.eg.

Finnair Australia ℡02/9244 2299, New Zealand ℡09/308 3365; ⓦwww.finnair.com.

Garuda Indonesia Australia ℡02/9334 9970, New Zealand ℡09/366 1862; ⓦwww.garuda-indonesia.com.

Gulf Air Australia ℡02/9244 2199, New Zealand ℡09/308 3366; ⓦwww.gulfairco.com.

Lufthansa Australia ℡1300/655 727, ⓦwww.lufthansa-australia.com; New Zealand ℡09/303 1529, ⓦwww.lufthansa.com/index_en.html.

Malaysia Airlines Australia ℡13 26 27, New Zealand ℡0800/777 747; ⓦwww.malaysiaairlines.com.my.

Qantas Australia ℡13 13 13, ⓦwww.qantas.com.au; New Zealand ℡0800/808 767, ⓦwww.qantas.co.nz.

Royal Brunei Airlines Australia ℡07/3017 5000, ⓦwww.bruneiair.com; no NZ office.

Scandinavian Airlines (SAS) Australia ℡1300/727 707, New Zealand agent: Air New Zealand ℡09/357 3000; ⓦwww.scandinavian.net.

Singapore Airlines Australia ℡13 10 11, New Zealand ℡0800/808 909; ⓦwww.singaporeair.com.

Thai Airways Australia ℡1300/651 960, New Zealand ℡09/377 0268; ⓦwww.thaiair.com.

Discount flight agents in Australia and New Zealand

Flight Centre Australia ℡13 31 33 or 02/9235 3522, ⓦwww.flightcentre.com.au; New Zealand ℡0800/243 544 or 09/358 4310, ⓦwww.flightcentre.co.nz. Large chain of discount flight specialists.

STA Travel Australia ℡1300/733 035, ⓦwww.statravel.com.au; New Zealand ℡0508/782 872, ⓦwww.statravel.co.nz. Worldwide specialists in "learning travel", with low-cost flights for students and under-26s; other customers also welcome.

Student Uni Travel Australia ℡02/9232 8444, ⓦaustralia@backpackers.net. Specialists in student and backpacker deals.

Trailfinders Australia ℡02/9247 7666, ⓦwww.trailfinders.com.au. Australian branch of large UK-based independent travel specialists.

Packages and organized tours

Package holidays to Singapore are numerous and good value, especially if you just want a relaxing break around the pool. As well as flights and accommodation, most companies also offer a range of itineraries that take in the major sights and activities. Bookings are usually made through travel agents who carry a wide selection of brochures for you to choose from. An organized tour is worth considering if you're after a more energetic holiday, have ambitious sightseeing plans and limited time, are uneasy with the language and customs or just don't like travelling alone.

City stays, **fly-drive** options and **coach tours** are offered by a whole host of operators through your travel agent; most of these can also arrange add-on trips to resort islands, cruises from Singapore, air passes, rail travel and can book accommodation in regional Malaysia. Extended journeys from Singapore cater to all tastes – from those in search of thrills and adventure to those who simply prefer to tour in a group. Most of the specialists listed below can organize activities that may be difficult to arrange yourself such as whitewater rafting, diving, cycling and trekking.

Most organized tours don't include airfares from Australasia.

MAGIC
OF THE ORIENT

SINGAPORE
tailor-made for you by specialists

Magic of the Orient
Tel: 0117 311 6050
www.magicoftheorient.com
Email: info@magicoftheorient.com

Specialist tour operators in Australia and New Zealand

Abercrombie & Kent Australia ☎ 1300/851 800, New Zealand ☎ 0800/441 638; ⓦ www
.abercrombiekent.com.au. Upmarket tours of Southeast Asia including travel on the Eastern and Oriental Express (see below).

Adventure World Australia ☎ 02/8913 0755, ⓦ www.adventureworld.com.au; New Zealand ☎ 09/524 5118, ⓦ www.adventureworld.co.nz. Agents for a vast array of international adventure travel companies.
Intrepid Travel Australia ☎ 1300/360 667, ⓦ www.intrepidtravel.com. Small-group tours with the emphasis on cross-cultural contact and low-impact tourism.
San Michele Travel Australia ☎ 02/9299 1111 or 1800/22 22 44, ⓦ www.asiatravel.com.au. Long-running Southeast Asia specialist, with customized rail

Eastern and Oriental Express

If you've got money to burn, there's no more luxurious way to cover the 1900km between Bangkok and Singapore than on the sumptuous **Eastern and Oriental Express** (ⓦ www.orient-express.com), a trip that tries to re-create the pampered days of the region's colonial past. Departing once or twice weekly from Bangkok (and Singapore), the Express takes 41 hours to wend its unhurried way between the two cities, stopping at Butterworth, Ipoh and KL en route. At Butterworth, passengers disembark for a whistle-stop tour of Penang by bus and trishaw. On board, guests enjoy breakfast in bed, lunch, tea and dinner, all served by attentive Thai and Malaysian staff in traditional or period garb. There are two bars (one in the observation carriage at the rear of the train), as well as two luxurious restaurant cars serving Western and Oriental cuisine of a high standard; fortune-tellers, Chinese opera singers and musicians keep you entertained. Guests are encouraged to dress up lavishly for the occasion, and the trip is very popular with honeymooners.

tours throughout the region, as well as city breaks, sightseeing trips and cruises out of Singapore. **Silke's Travel** Australia ☏ 1800/807 860, or 02/8347 2000, ✉ silke@silkes.com.au. Specially tailored packages for gay and lesbian travellers.

Getting there from Southeast Asia

If you are not too restricted by time, it can work out cheaper to get a flight to another Southeast Asian city and then continue your journey from there.

For rock-bottom airfares, check into the region's **"low cost airlines"**. Airfares can be as little as one fifth of regular fares, but of course along with the savings you forfeit some conveniences, including the option to change dates or flight times free of charge. Travel agents are unlikely to be of any help since they don't book these airlines

– bookings are made online. You will have to be at the airport early to ensure you get a seat and don't expect any kind of inflight service. The best bets are Singapore's Tiger Airways (🌐 www.tigerairways.com) and Malaysia's Air Asia (🌐 www.airasia.com).

It's obviously longer, but more scenic, to travel **overland** by train from Bangkok – the main line runs down the west coast of Malaysia and ends in Singapore. Unrest in southern Thailand is sometimes a problem and the railway has been targeted. It's a good idea to check the current situation before booking a train journey through southern Thailand.

From Thailand

It's possible to take a series of buses to Singapore from Bangkok, but with the advent of the region's low-cost airlines, only a glutton for punishment would do this long haul by bus. Taking a train is a more comfortable option if you are set on seeing the scenery. Trains depart from Bangkok's Hualamphong station (book at least a day in advance at the station ticket office, or check out ⓦ www.railway.co.th/Eng/) several times a day for Hat Yai, where the line divides. One daily train goes south via the Malaysian border town of Padang Besar to Butterworth. From there you can board a train for Kuala Lumpur and Singapore.

Besides the low-cost airlines mentioned earlier, there are several daily non-stop flights from Bangkok on Thai Airways to Singapore, as well as one daily from Hat Yai. From Phuket, there's one direct flight daily on Singapore's Silk Air (ⓦ www.silkair.com), and there's one direct flight daily from Koh Samui on Bangkok Airways (ⓦ www.bangkokair .com). Tickets are available from travel agents in Bangkok or can be booked online.

From Indonesia

There are daily Garuda flights from Jakarta to Singapore and Denpasar, Bali, to Singapore. From other Indonesian regions you'll need to take an internal flight to Jakarta or Denpasar first. In addition, ferries run through the day from Pulau Batam in the Riau archipelago (accessible by plane or boat from Sumatra or Jakarta) to Singapore – a thirty-minute trip; £10/US$17).

From Malaysia

Regular flights connect the major Malaysian airports with Singapore (£50/US$88 from KL with MAS), and there are four trains a day from Kuala Lumpur. Buses link Singapore with all large towns and cities in peninsular Malaysia and represent the most affordable means of reaching the city-state. From KL expect to pay the equivalent of £10/US$17.

Red tape and visas

B

BASICS | Red tape and visas

British citizens, and those of the Republic of Ireland, the United States, Canada, Australia and New Zealand, don't need a visa to enter Singapore. Regulations change from time to time, though, so check with the embassy before departure. You'll normally be stamped in for fourteen days, although you can be given one month on request.

Extending your stay for up to three months is perfectly possible, at the discretion of the Immigration Department extensions beyond three months are not unknown, but are less common. If you have any problems with extending your stay, there's always the option of taking a bus up to Johor Bahru, across the border in Malaysia, and then coming back in again.

Singaporean embassies and consulates abroad

Australia 17 Forster Crescent, Yarralumla, Canberra, ACT 2600 ☎ 02/6273 3944.
Canada Suite 1820, 999 Hastings St, Vancouver, BC V6C 2W2 ☎ 604/669-5115.
Indonesia Block X/4 Kav No. 2, Jalan H.R. Rasuna Said Kuningan, Jakarta 12950 ☎ 021/520 1489.
Ireland Contact UK embassy.
Malaysia 209 Jalan Tun Razak, Kuala Lumpur 50400 ☎ 03/2161 6277.

New Zealand 17 Kabul St, Khandallah, Wellington, PO Box 13-140 ☎ 04/479 2976.
UK 9 Wilton Crescent, London SW1X 8SP ☎ 020/7235 9852.
USA 3501 International Place NW, Washington, DC 20008 ☎ 202/537-3100; 231 East 51st St, New York, NY 10022 ☎ 212/223-3331.

Customs

Upon entry from anywhere other than Malaysia you can bring into Singapore one litre each of spirits, wine and beer duty-free; duty is payable on all tobacco. There are no restrictions if you're coming from Malaysia. For up-to-the-minute customs information, go to ⊛ www.customs.gov.sg.

Many goods for sale in Singapore are duty-free, including electronic and electrical items, cosmetics, cameras, clocks, watches, jewellery, and precious stones and metals, but you should bear in mind how much you are allowed to import into your own country with you free of charge.

Information, websites and maps

The Singapore Tourism Board (STB) maintains five Tourist Information Centres, including one at each arrivals terminals at Changi Airport. The main office is at Tourism Court, 1 Orchard Spring Lane (daily 8am–10pm; toll-free ☎1-800/736 2000). The other is at Plaza Singapura Mall, 68 Orchard Road (daily 10am–10pm; ☎63329298).

A number of publications offer "what's on" listings and recommendations. A handful of these, including *Uniquely Singapore*, are available free at hotels all over the island, but best of all are *8 Days* magazine, which is published weekly and costs $1.50, and the newer *I-S*, a free paper published fortnightly.

Singapore tourist offices abroad

Australia 47 Yoek St, Sydney, NSW 2000 ☎02/92890 2888.
New Zealand 18 Ronwood Ave, Manukau, Auckland ☎09/262 3393.
UK lst floor, Carrington House 126–130 Regent St, London W1B 5JX ☎0207/437 0033.
USA 1156 Avenue of the Americas, Suit 702, New York, NY 10036 ☎212/302-4861; 4929 Wilshire Blvd, Suite 510, Los Angeles CA 90010 ☎323/677-0808.

Useful websites

Ⓦ **afterdark.hotspots.com** Ratings and reviews of Singapore's latest nightspots.
Ⓦ **straitstimes.asia1.com.sg** The *Singapore Straits Times* on the Internet.
Ⓦ **www.ehotelsingapore.com** Good hotel reservation service with lots of travel information.
Ⓦ **www.expatsingapore.com** A definitive guide to life in Singapore.
Ⓦ **www.getforme.com** An excellent portal to all things Singaporean, from local cuisine to info for backpackers.
Ⓦ **www.gov.sg** The offical website of the Singapore government.
Ⓦ **www.makansutra.com** Quirky website maintained by the foodies who annually publish the *Makansutra Food Guide to Singapore*; fascinating essays about cultural and culinary facets of eating out in Singapore.

Ⓦ **www.sg** Maintained by the Ministry of Information, a mine of useful practical and cultural information.
Ⓦ **www.talkingcock.com** The best (and only) satirical website out of Singapore.
Ⓦ **www.the-inncrowd.com** All kinds of up-to-the-minute info about what to do in Singapore as well as how best to get there.
Ⓦ **www.visitsingapore.com** The Singapore Tourism Board's official site, featuring tour planner, attractions, current events, a virtual "tour" of the island and an accommodation search by price range.

Maps

The best available **map** of Singapore Island is the 1:22,500 Nelles *Singapore*, though the *Singapore Street Directory*, from all Singapore bookshops, is essential if you have to rent a car.

Map outlets

In the UK and Ireland

Blackwell's Map and Travel Shop 50 Broad St, Oxford OX1 3BQ ☎01865/793 550, Ⓦmaps.blackwell.co.uk.
Easons Bookshop 40 O'Connell St, Dublin 1 ☎01/858 3881, Ⓦwww.buy4now.ie/eason.
Heffers Map and Travel 20 Trinity St, Cambridge CB2 1TJ ☎01865/333 536, Ⓦwww.heffers.co.uk.
Hodges Figgis Bookshop 56–58 Dawson St, Dublin 2 ☎01/677 4754, Ⓦwww.hodgesfiggis.com.
The Map Shop 30a Belvoir St, Leicester LE1 6QH ☎0116/247 1400, Ⓦwww.mapshopleicester.co.uk.
National Map Centre 22–24 Caxton St, London SW1H 0QU ☎020/7222 2466, Ⓦwww.mapsnmc.co.uk.
Newcastle Map Centre 55 Grey St, Newcastle-upon-Tyne NE1 6EF ☎0191/261 5622.
Ordnance Survey Ireland Phoenix Park, Dublin 8 ☎01/802 5300, Ⓦwww.osi.ie.

Ordnance Survey of Northern Ireland Colby House, Stranmillis Ct, Belfast BT9 5BJ ☎ 028/9025 5755, ⓦ www.osni.gov.uk.

Stanfords 12–14 Long Acre, London WC2E 9LP ☎ 020/7836 1321, ⓦ www.stanfords.co.uk.

The Travel Bookshop 13–15 Blenheim Crescent, London W11 2EE ☎ 020/7229 5260, ⓦ www .thetravelbookshop.co.uk.

In the US and Canada

Adventurous Traveler.com US ☎ 1-800/282-3963, ⓦ adventuroustraveler.com.

Book Passage 51 Tamal Vista Blvd, Corte Madera, CA 94925 ☎ 1-800/999-7909, ⓦ www .bookpassage.com.

Distant Lands 56 S Raymond Ave, Pasadena, CA 91105 ☎ 1-800/310-3220, ⓦ www.distantlands.com.

Elliott Bay Book Company 101 S Main St, Seattle, WA 98104 ☎ 1-800/962-5311, ⓦ www .elliottbaybook.com.

Globe Corner Bookstore 28 Church St, Cambridge, MA 02138 ☎ 1-800/358-6013, ⓦ www.globecorner.com.

Map Link 30 S La Patera Lane, Unit 5, Santa Barbara, CA 93117 ☎ 1-800/962-1394, ⓦ www .maplink.com.

Rand McNally US ☎ 1-800/333-0136, ⓦ www .randmcnally.com. Around thirty stores across the US; dial ext 2111 or check the website for the nearest location.

The Travel Bug Bookstore 2667 W Broadway, Vancouver V6K 2G2 ☎ 604/737-1122, ⓦ www .travelbugbooks.ca.

World of Maps 1235 Wellington St, Ottawa, Ontario K1Y 3A3 ☎ 1-800/214-8524, ⓦ www .worldofmaps.com.

In Australia and New Zealand

The Map Shop 6–10 Peel St, Adelaide, SA 5000 ☎ 08/8231 2033, ⓦ www.mapshop.net.au.

Mapland 372 Little Bourke St, Melbourne, Victoria 3000 ☎ 03/9670 4383, ⓦ www.mapland .com.au.

MapWorld 173 Gloucester St, Christchurch ☎ 0800/627 967 or 03/374 5399, ⓦ www .mapworld.co.nz.

Money, banks and costs

Singapore is one of the more expensive Asian cities, especially for accommodation. The city affords few savings for special groups – senior citizens do not get reductions, although an ISIC card might occasionally pay dividends for students. However, you will find that bargaining is a way of life throughout Singapore, especially when shopping or renting a room for the night; it's always worth trying to haggle, though note that you don't bargain for meals. Most tourist attractions offer discounted entrance fees for children.

Currency

The currency is the Singapore dollar, written simply as $ and divided into 100 cents. Notes are issued in denominations of $1, $2, $5, $10, $20, $50, $100, $500, $1000 and $10,000; coins are in denominations of 1, 5, 10, 20 and 50 cents, and $1. The current exchange rate is around $2.80 to £1 and $1.60 to US$1. All prices given in the guide are in Singapore dollars, unless otherwise stated.

Costs

If money is no object, you'll be able to take advantage of hotels, restaurants and shops as sumptuous as any in the world. On the other hand, with budget dormitory accommodation in plentiful supply, and both food and internal travel cheap in the extreme, you could survive on less than £10/US$17 a day. Upgrading your lodgings to a private room in a guesthouse, eating in a restaurant and having a beer or two gives a more realistic daily budget of £25/US$44 a day.

Banks

Singapore **banking hours** are generally Monday to Friday 9.30am–3pm and Saturday 9.30am–12.30pm, outside of which you'll have to go to a moneychanger in a shopping centre, or to a hotel. Major banks represented include the Overseas Union Bank, the United Overseas Bank, the OCBC, the Development Bank of Singapore, Standard Chartered Bank, Hong Kong Bank and Citibank. No black market operates in Singapore, nor are there any restrictions on carrying currency in or out of the state. This means that rates at moneychangers are as good as you'll find in the banks.

Travellers' cheques and cards

Although they are the traditional way to carry funds, **travellers' cheques** are no longer the cheapest nor the most convenient option – bank cards are better (see below). That said, they do offer safety against loss or theft, and can be cashed at Singaporean banks, licensed moneychangers and some hotels, upon presentation of a passport. Some shops will even accept travellers' cheques as cash. Either sterling or US dollar cheques are acceptable in Singapore; but check with your bank for the latest advice before you buy.

The usual fee for travellers' cheque sales is one or two percent, though this fee may be waived if you buy the cheques through a bank where you have an account. It pays to get a selection of denominations. Make sure you keep the purchase agreement and a record of cheque serial numbers safe and separate from the cheques themselves. In the event that cheques are lost or stolen, the issuing company will expect you to report the loss forthwith to their office in Singapore; most companies claim to replace lost or stolen cheques within 24 hours.

Credit cards are a very convenient way of carrying funds. They are widely accepted in mid-range and upmarket hotels, shops and restaurants throughout the region, but beware of the illegal surcharges levied by some establishments – check before you buy something with a card that there's no surcharge; if there is, contact your card company and tell them about it.

Cards can be used either in ATMs or over the counter. Mastercard, Visa and American Express are accepted just about everywhere, but other, lesser known cards may not be recognized, so check with your card issuer before you travel. Remember that all cash advances are treated as loans, with interest accruing daily from the date of withdrawal; there may be a transaction fee on top of this. However, you may be able to make withdrawals from ATMs in Singapore using your debit card, which is not liable to interest payments, and the flat transaction fee is usually quite small – your bank will be able to advise on this. Make sure you have a personal identification number (PIN) that's designed to work overseas.

A compromise between travellers' cheques and plastic is **Visa TravelMoney**, a disposable pre-paid debit card with a PIN that works in all ATMs that take Visa cards. You load up your account with funds before leaving home, and when they run out, you simply throw the card away. You can buy up to nine cards to access the same funds – useful for couples or families travelling together – and it's a good idea to buy at least one extra as a back-up in case of loss or theft. There is also a 24-hour toll-free customer assistance number (☎800-110-0344). The card is available in most countries from branches of Thomas Cook and Citicorp. For more information, check the Visa website at ⊛usa.visa.com/personal/cards/prepaid/visa_travel_money.html.

Youth and student discounts

Once obtained, various official and quasi-official **youth/student ID cards** soon pay for themselves in savings. Full-time students are eligible for the International Student ID Card (ISIC, ⊛www.isiccard.com), which entitles the bearer to special air, rail and bus fares and discounts at museums, theatres and other attractions. For Americans there's also a health benefit, providing up to $3000 in emergency medical coverage and $100 a day for sixty days in the hospital, plus a

24-hour hotline to call in the event of a medical, legal or financial emergency. The card costs £7 in the UK or online.

You only have to be 26 or younger to qualify for the International Youth Travel Card, which costs US$22/£7 and carries the same benefits. Teachers qualify for the International Teacher Card, offering similar discounts and costing £7, US$22, CDN$16, A$16.50 and NZ$21. All these cards are available in the US from Council Travel, STA, Travel Cuts (see p.24); in Australia and New Zealand from STA (see p.25) or Campus Travel; and in the UK from CTS Travel (@www.ctstravel .co.uk) and STA.

Several other travel organizations and accommodation groups also sell their own cards, good for various discounts. A university photo ID might open some doors, but is not as easily recognizable as the ISIC cards. However, the latter are often not accepted as valid proof of age, for example in bars or liquor stores.

Wiring money

Having money wired from home using one of the companies listed opposite is never convenient or cheap, and should be considered a last resort. It's also possible to have money wired directly from a bank in your home country to a bank in Singapore, although this is somewhat less reliable because it involves two separate institutions. If you go this route, your home bank will need the address of the branch bank where you want to pick up the money and the address and telex number of the Singapore head office, which will act as the clearing house; money wired this way normally takes two working days to arrive, and costs around £25/$45 per transaction.

Money-wiring companies

Thomas Cook US ☎1-800/287-7362, Canada ☎1-888/823-4732, Great Britain ☎01733/318 922, Northern Ireland ☎028/9055 0030, Republic of Ireland ☎01/677 1721, @www.thomascook .com.

Travelers Express MoneyGram US ☎1-800/955-7777, Canada ☎1-800/933-3278, UK ☎0800/018 0104, Republic of Ireland ☎1850/205 800, Australia ☎1800/230 100, New Zealand ☎0800/262 263, @www.moneygram.com.

Western Union US and Canada ☎1-800/325-6000, Australia ☎1800/501 500, New Zealand ☎0800/270 000, UK ☎0800/833 833, Republic of Ireland ☎1800/395 395, @www.westernunion .com.

Insurance

Since there are no reciprocal agreements between Singapore and any other country, the cost of medical services must be borne by the visitor. Consequently, it's essential to arrange travel insurance before you leave home, which will cover you for medical expenses incurred, as well as for loss of luggage, cancellation of flights and so on.

Before paying for a new policy, however, it's worth checking whether you are already covered: some all-risks home insurance policies may cover your possessions when overseas, and many private medical schemes include cover when abroad. In Canada, provincial health plans usually provide partial cover for medical mishaps overseas, while holders of official student/teacher/youth cards in Canada and the US are entitled to meagre accident coverage and hospital in-patient benefits. Students will often find that their student health coverage extends during the vacations and for one term beyond the date of last enrolment.

After exhausting the possibilities above, you might want to contact a specialist travel insurance company, or consider the travel insurance deal we offer (see box, below). A typical travel insurance policy usually provides cover for the loss of baggage, tickets and – up to a certain limit – cash or cheques, as well as cancellation or curtailment of your journey. Most of them exclude so-called dangerous sports unless an extra premium is paid. Many policies can be chopped and changed to exclude coverage you don't need – for example, sickness and accident benefits can often be excluded or included at will. If you do take medical coverage, ascertain whether benefits will be paid as treatment proceeds or only after return home, and whether there is a 24-hour medical emergency number. When securing baggage cover, make sure that the per-article limit – typically under £500 – will cover your most valuable possession. If you need to make a claim, you should keep receipts for medicines and medical treatment, and in the event you have anything stolen, you must obtain an official statement from the police.

Health

The levels of hygiene and medical care in Singapore are higher than in much of the rest of Southeast Asia, and with any luck, the most serious thing you'll go down with is a cold or an upset stomach. Tap water is drinkable throughout the island and all food for public consumption is prepared to exacting standards. Drinking excessive amounts of alcohol is a more likely cause of diarrhoea than the food you may eat, as in a tropical climate your tolerance level is likely to be much lower than it would be at home.

Travellers unused to tropical climates periodically suffer from **sunburn** and **dehydration**. The easiest way to avoid this is to restrict your exposure to the sun, use high-factor sunscreens, wear dark glasses to protect your eyes and wear a hat. You should also drink plenty of water and, if you do become dehydrated, keep up a regular intake of fluids; weak black tea and clear soups are useful for mineral salts, and rehydration preparations such as Dioralyte, available from pharmacies, also do the trick. The DIY version is a handful of sugar with a good pinch of salt added to a litre of water, which creates roughly the right mineral balance. Even if you aren't suffering, it's worth supplementing your daily water intake with the odd can of isotonic drink, which replaces the minerals lost through perspiration.

Heat stroke is more serious: it is indicated by a high temperature, dry red skin and a fast pulse and can require hospitalization. To prevent **heat rashes**, **prickly heat** and **fungal infections**, use a mild antiseptic soap and dust yourself with medicated talcum powder, which you can buy throughout Singapore.

Medical services are excellent, with staff almost everywhere speaking good English and using up-to-date techniques. **Pharmacies** are well stocked with familiar brand-name drugs; pharmacists can also recommend products for skin complaints

For a list of hospitals, clinics and pharmacies in Singapore, turn to the "Directory", pp.196–197. In a medical emergency, dial ☏995.

or simple stomach problems, though if you're in any doubt, it always pays to get a proper diagnosis. Opening hours are usually Monday to Saturday 9.30am–7pm. **Private clinics** are found throughout the city – your hotel or the local tourist office will be able to recommend a good English-speaking doctor. A visit costs around $25, not including the cost of any prescribed medication. Don't forget to keep any receipts for insurance claim purposes.

The spectre of **SARS** visited Singapore in early March 2003, but the island was quickly declared free from the disease. For further information on this and also for updates on **Avian flu** (which has been found in farmed birds in the surrounding countries in Southeast Asia) check out the WHO website ⓦwww.who.int/en or any of the sites on p.36.

Inoculations

There are no inoculations required for visiting Singapore, although the immigration authorities may require proof of a yellow fever vaccination (administered within the last ten years) if you're arriving from an endemic country.

However, it's a wise precaution to visit your doctor or local immunization clinic no later than four weeks before you leave to check that you are up to date with your polio, typhoid, tetanus and hepatitis A inoculations.

If you are travelling on from Singapore to other destinations in Southeast Asia, it is likely that you will require further protection, particularly against malaria. Singapore is malaria-free, but you must start taking any course of tablets one week before you plan to move on.

Medical resources for travellers

Websites

ⓦ **health.yahoo.com** Information on specific diseases and conditions, drugs and herbal remedies, as well as advice from health experts.

ⓦ **www.fitfortravel.scot.nhs.uk** UK NHS website carrying information about travel-related diseases and how to avoid them.

ⓦ **www.istm.org** The website of the International Society for Travel Medicine, with a full list of clinics specializing in international travel health.

ⓦ **www.tmvc.com.au** Contains a list of all Travellers' Medical and Vaccination Centres throughout Australia, New Zealand and Southeast Asia, plus general information on travel health.

ⓦ **www.tripprep.com** Travel Health Online provides an online-only comprehensive database of necessary vaccinations for most countries, as well as destination and medical service provider information.

In the US and Canada

Canadian Society for International Health 1 Nicholas St, Suite 1105, Ottawa, ON K1N 7B7 ☏ 613/241-5785, ⓦ www.csih.org. Distributes a free pamphlet, "Health Information for Canadian Travellers", containing an extensive list of travel health centres in Canada.

International Association for Medical Assistance to Travellers (IAMAT) 417 Center St, Lewiston, NY 14092 ☏ 716/754-4883, ⓦ www .iamat.org, and 40 Regal Rd, Guelph, ON N1K 1B5 ☏ 519/836-0102. A non-profit organization supported by donations, it can provide climate charts and leaflets on various diseases and inoculations.

MEDJET Assistance ☏ 1-800/9MEDJET, www .medjetassistance.com. Annual membership program for travellers ($175 for individuals, $275 for families) that, in the event of illness or injury, will fly members home or to the hospital of their choice in a medically equipped and staffed jet.

Travelers Medical Center 31 Washington Square West, New York, NY 10011 ☏ 212/982-1600. Consultation service on immunizations and treatment of diseases for people travelling to developing countries.

In the UK and Ireland

British Airways Travel Clinics 156 Regent St, London W1 (Mon–Fri 9.30am–5.15pm, Sat 10am–4pm, no appointment necessary; ☏ 020/7439 9584); 101 Cheapside, London EC2 (hours as above, appointment required; ☏ 020/7606 2977); ⓦ www.britishairways.com/travel/healthclinintro. Vaccinations, tailored advice from an online database and a complete range of travel healthcare products.

Hospital for Tropical Diseases Travel Clinic 2nd floor, Mortimer Market Centre, off Capper St, London WC1E 6AU (Mon–Fri 9am–5pm by appointment only; ☏ 020/7388 9600, ⓦ www .masta.org; a consultation costs £15 which is waived if you have your injections here). A recorded Health Line (☏ 0906/133 7733; 50p per min) gives hints on hygiene and illness prevention as well as listing appropriate immunizations.

MASTA (Medical Advisory Service for Travellers Abroad) 40 regional clinics (call ☏ 0870/606 2782 for the nearest). Also operates a pre-recorded 24-hour Travellers' Health Line (UK ☏ 0906/822 4100, 60p per min), giving written information tailored to your journey by return of post.

Travel Health Centre Department of International Health and Tropical Medicine, Royal College of Surgeons in Ireland, Mercers Medical Centre, Stephen's St Lower, Dublin 2 ☏ 01/402 2337. Expert pre-trip advice and inoculations.

Travel Medicine Services PO Box 254, 16 College St, Belfast BT1 6BT ☏ 028/9031 5220. Offers medical advice before a trip and help afterwards in the event of a tropical disease.

In Australia and New Zealand

Travellers' Medical and Vaccination Centres 27–29 Gilbert Place, Adelaide, SA 5000 ☏ 08/8212 7522, ⓔ adelaide@traveldoctor .com.au; 1/170 Queen St, Auckland ☏ 09/373 3531, ⓔ auckland@traveldoctor.co.nz; 5/247 Adelaide St, Brisbane, Qld 4000 ☏ 07/3221 9066, ⓔ brisbane@traveldoctor.com.au; 5/8–10 Hobart Place, Canberra, ACT 2600 ☏ 02/6257 7156, ⓔ canberra@traveldoctor.com.au; Moorhouse Medical Centre 9 Washington Way, Christchurch ☏ 03/379 4000, ⓔ christchurch@traveldoctor .co.nz; 270 Sandy Bay Rd, Sandy Bay Tas, Hobart 7005 ☏ 03/6223 7577, ⓔ hobart@traveldoctor .com.au; 2/393 Little Bourke St, Melbourne, Vic 3000 ☏ 03/9602 5788, ⓔ melbourne@traveldoctor .com.au; Level 7, Dymocks Bldg, 428 George St, Sydney, NSW 2000 ☏ 02/9221 7133, ⓔ sydney@traveldoctor.com.au; Shop 15, Grand Arcade, 14–16 Willis St, Wellington ☏ 04/473 0991, ⓔ wellington@traveldoctor.co.nz.

Arrival

Most people's first glimpse of Singapore is of Changi International airport, and a telling glimpse it is. Terminal 1 and 2 are connected by the Skytrain monorail, and are modern, efficient and air-conditioned – Singapore in microcosm. The "budget terminal" was recently completed and is for low-cost airlines such as Tiger Airways. Terminal 3 is under construction and is scheduled to open in 2008. Flights from the Malaysian resort island of Tioman set down at smaller Seletar airport, up in the north of the island. You might also arrive via one of the two causeways connecting Singapore to the southernmost Malaysian state Johor; or by boat from the Indonesian archipelago. Wherever you arrive, Singapore's well-oiled infrastructure means that you'll have no problem getting into the centre.

By air

Changi airport is at the far eastern end of Singapore, 16km from the city centre. As well as duty-free shops, money changing and left-luggage facilities, the airport boasts a 24-hour post office and telephone service, hotel reservations counters, day rooms, saunas, and business and Internet centres. There are also several fast-food outlets and, in Terminal One's basement, a food centre – the cheapest and most authentically Singaporean option. But the likelihood is that you'll barely get the chance to take in Changi – baggage comes through so quickly that you can be on a train, bus or in a taxi within fifteen minutes of arrival. Be sure to pick up one of the free maps and weekly *This Week Singapore* guides that the Singapore Tourism Board (STB) leaves at the airport, plus a copy of the excellent what's on magazine, *Where Singapore*.

Getting into the city from the airports

Singapore's **underground train** system (MRT – Mass Rapid Transit) now extends as far as Terminal Two of **Changi airport**, and is the most affordable means of getting into the city centre. A single to downtown City Hall is $1.40, and shouldn't take more than half an hour. From City Hall interchange, you can move on to any part of the island.

The **bus** departure points in the basements of both terminals are well signposted, but make sure you've got the right money before you leave the concourse, as Singapore bus drivers don't give change; take the #36 (every 10min, 6am–midnight; $1.60). The bus heads west to Stamford Road before skirting the southern side of Orchard Road. Ask the driver to give you a shout at the Capitol Building stop for Beach Road, or at the YMCA stop, where you need to cross over Bras Basah Park if you are staying in Bencoolen Street. Another option is to take a **MaxiCab** shuttle into town. These six-seater taxis depart every fifteen minutes, or when full, and will take you to any hotel in the city for a flat fare of $7 (children $5). MaxiCabs are equipped to take wheelchairs.

Taxis from the airport levy a $3 surcharge on top of the fare, rising to $5 at the weekend. Again, the taxi rank is well signposted, and a trip into downtown Singapore costs around $15 and takes twenty minutes. There are also **car-rental** agencies at the airport (see p.196), though you'd be advised not to travel around Singapore by car (see "Getting around", p.42). From **Seletar airport**, a taxi into town will cost around $15, plus $3 airport surcharge, but be prepared to have to make a phone booking upon landing (see telephone numbers on p.197).

By bus

Buses stop at one of three terminals in Singapore. Local buses from **Johor Bahru** (JB) in **Malaysia** arrive at Ban San Terminal at the junction of Queen and Arab streets, from where a two-minute walk along Queen Street and a left turn along Rochor Road takes you to Bugis MRT station. Buses

Finding an address

With so many of Singapore's shops, restaurants and offices located in vast high-rise buildings and shopping malls, deciphering addresses can sometimes be tricky. The numbering system generally adhered to is as follows: 02-15 means room number 15 on the second floor; 10-08 is room 8 on the 10th floor. Bear in mind that in Singapore, ground level is referred to as 01, or the first floor.

from elsewhere in Malaysia and from **Thailand** terminate at one of two sites, Lavender Street Terminal and the Golden Mile Complex. Lavender Street Terminal, at the corner of Lavender Street and Kallang Bahru, is around five minutes' walk from Lavender MRT. Bus #145 passes the Lavender Street Terminal on its way down North Bridge and South Bridge roads. From the Golden Mile, take any bus along Beach Road to Raffles City to connect with the MRT system. You'll have no trouble hailing a cab at any terminal.

By train

Trains from Malaysia end their journey at the **Singapore Railway Station** on Keppel Road, southwest of Chinatown. You haven't officially arrived in Singapore until you step out of the station – which is owned by Malaysia – as the "Welcome to Malaysia" sign above the main entrance testifies. The grounds of Singapore's rail system were sold lock, stock and barrel to the Federal Malay States in 1918, though recently the Singapore government has been buying back segments of it piecemeal. From Keppel Road, bus #97 travels past Tanjong Pagar, Raffles Place and City Hall MRT stations and on to Selegie and Serangoon

roads, or you can usually find a cab in the forecourt.

By sea

Boats from the **Indonesian island of Batam** dock at the World Trade Centre, off Telok Blangah Road, roughly 5km east of the centre. From adjacent HarbourFront MRT, the city centre is just a few stops away. Otherwise, from Telok Blangah Road, bus #97 runs to Tanjong Pagar MRT. Bus #65 goes to Selegie and Serangoon roads, via Orchard Road, or take #166 for Chinatown. Boats from the Indonesian island of **Bintan** dock at the Tanah Merah Ferry Terminal, linked by bus #35 to Bedok MRT station.

It's also possible to reach Singapore by **boat from Malaysia**. Bumboats from Kampung Pengerang on the southeastern coast of Johor moor at Changi Village, beyond the airport, from where bus #2 travels into the centre, via Geylang, Victoria and New Bridge roads. Swisher ferries from Tanjung Belungkor, also in Johor, dock at the Changi ferry terminal a little way east of Changi Village, from where you'll have to take a taxi – either all the way into town, or into Changi Village to connect with bus #2. Finally, ferries from Tioman Island dock at the Tanah Merah Ferry Terminal.

Departure

All International flights take off from Changi airport in the far east of the island – excepting flights to Malaysia's Tioman Island, which depart from Seletar airport. Boats to Malaysia and Indonesia push off from one of three points along the southern coast, and buses and trains access Malaysia via the causeway in the far north of the island. A second causeway links Tuas in the west of the island with Geylang Patah, 20km west of Johor Bahru, but trains and most buses still use the original link.

By air

There are good deals on plane tickets from Singapore to **Australia**, **Bali**, **Bangkok** and **Hong Kong**. However, if you're planning to head for either **Malaysia** or **Indonesia** by air, it might be worth going to JB (see below), across the causeway, or Batam, the nearest Indonesian island (see information on boats, below), and buying a flight from there.

Allow plenty of time for getting out to the airport (45–60min), especially during the morning and evening rush hours. The MRT runs right up to Terminal Two; and bus #36 (daily 6am–midnight; $1.50) runs frequently down Orchard Road and Bras Basah Road en route to Changi. Taxis cost $12–15.

Flights for Tioman Island in Malaysia depart from Seletar airport, for which the best approach is to take a taxi ($20–25 from downtown).

By road

The easiest way across the causeway to **Johor Bahru** is to get the #170 JB-bound **bus** from the Ban San Terminal (every 10min; 5.30am–midnight; $1.20) or the plusher air-con Singapore–Johor Express (every 10min; 6.30am–midnight; $2.40), both of which take around an hour (including border formalities) and stop at JB bus terminal. From the **taxi** rank next to the terminal, a car to JB (seating four) costs around $35. The Singapore–KL (Kuala Lumpur) Express leaves from the Ban San Terminal daily at 9am, 1pm, 5pm and 10pm (6hr; $23). For other destinations, go to either the Lavender Street Terminal or the Golden Mile Complex.

By train

You can make free seat reservations up to one month in advance of departure at the information kiosk (daily 8.30am–2.30pm & 3–7pm; ☎62225165) in the train station. There are air-conditioned trains to KL at 8am, 10.30am, 3.05pm and 10pm. These trains all stop at JB. There was also a railway "shuttle service" between Singapore and JB that was suspended in April 2006. Check the Malaysian Railway website to see if it has been reinstated, as well as to get up-to-the-minute schedule information for all Malaysian trains: ⓦwww.ktmb.com.my. For information on the **Eastern and Oriental Express** to Bangkok, see p.26.

By boat to Malaysia

From Changi point bumboats run to **Kampung Pengerang** in Johor. Boats leave when they're full (daily 7am–4pm; $6 one-way) and the trip takes 45 minutes. A newer, more reliable service departs three times daily for **Tanjung Belungkor**, also in Johor, from the new Changi Ferry terminal. Run by Cruise Ferries (☎65468518), the service takes 45 minutes and costs $22 return; check in one hour before departure. Finally, from the Tanah Merah Ferry Terminal, there's an 8.35am service (March–Oct daily except Tues & Thurs; Sun–Thurs $154 return, Fri & Sat $190 return) to **Tioman Island**. Information and tickets from Penguin Ferry Services (☎62714866). Again, check in one hour before departure.

By boat to Indonesia

Boats to **Batam** in the Riau archipelago depart at least half-hourly throughout the day from the Harbour Front Centre (7.30am–10.30pm; $16 one-way), docking at Sekupang, from where you take a taxi to Hangnadim airport for internal Indonesian flights. There are also several boats a day ($25 one-way) from the Tanah Merah Ferry Terminal to **Tanjung Pinang** on Pulau Bintan, from where cargo boats leave three times a week for Pekanbaru in Sumatra. Information and tickets are available from either Dino Shipping (☎62760668), Bintan Resort Ferries (☎65424369, ⓦwww.brf.com.sg) or Penguin Ferry Services (☎62714866, ⓦwww.penguin.com.sg). From Kijang Port, south of Tanjung Pinang, there are boat services to Jakarta.

Getting around

All parts of the island are accessible by MRT (the underground rail network) or bus, and fares are reasonable, so that there's little to be gained by renting a car. However you travel, it's best to avoid the rush hour (roughly 8–9.30am and 5–7pm) if at all possible; outside these times, things are relatively uncongested. The annually updated Transitlink Guide ($1.50), available from bus interchanges, MRT stations and major bookshops, outlines every bus and MRT route on the island in exhaustive detail. Singapore also has thousands of easily available and affordable taxis.

You're unlikely to have cause to make use of the LRT (Light Rail Transit) loop-line that links Bukit Panjang New Town to Choa Chu Kang MRT. It's a suburban feeder line, and doesn't serve any of Singapore's tourist attractions.

The MRT (Mass Rapid Transport System)

Singapore's **MRT** system was officially opened on March 12, 1988, and has been expanding ever since. A third line opened in 2003; and a new Circle Line is under construction. In terms of cleanliness, efficiency and value for money, the system is second to none – compared to London's tubes or New York's subways, anyway. Nor is there much possibility of delays owing to a passenger falling onto the line – the automatic doors dividing the platform from the track open only when trains are stationary.

The system has **three main lines**: the north–south line, which runs a vaguely horse-shoe-shaped route from Marina Bay up to the north of the island and then southwest to Jurong; the east–west line, connecting Boon Lay to Changi in the east; and the north–east line, linking the World Trade Centre on the south coast, to Punggol in the northeast of the island. Trains run every four to five minutes on average, daily from 6am until midnight. For **information**, pick up the free *MRT Handy Guide* from any station, or call the MRT Information Centre on ☎1-800/3368900 (toll-free).

A no-smoking rule applies on all trains, and eating and drinking are also outlawed. Signs in the ticket concourse seem to indicate that there is a ban on durians – not an unreasonable request if you've ever spent any length of time in a confined space with one of these pungent fruits.

Tickets and fares

Tickets cost between 60c and $1.80 for a one-way journey. Change machines will break $1 and $2 notes; larger notes can be changed at the information counter. The easiest way of getting about is to buy an **ez-link Farecard**, a stored-value card that's valid on all MRT and bus journeys in Singapore, is sold at MRT stations and bus interchanges, and shaves a few cents off the cost of each journey. There's a minimum purchase of $10 credit, and a maximum of $100; a $5 deposit is also collected. Hold the card over a reader when you pass through an MRT barrier, and the cost of each journey you make will be automatically deducted from the card; any credit on the card when you leave Singapore will be reimbursed at a Farecard outlet. The **Tourist Day Ticket** is also available for $10 from most MRT stations. The ticket allows you to take up to twelve bus or MRT rides a day, regardless of distance travelled.

Buses

Singapore's **bus network** is slightly cheaper to use than the MRT system, and far more comprehensive – there are several routes that are particularly useful for sightseeing (see box below). Two bus companies operate on the roads of Singapore: the **Singapore Bus Service (SBS Transit)** and **Trans-Island Bus Services (TIBS)**. Most buses charge distance-related **fares** ranging from 70c to $1.30 (80c–$1.60 for air-con buses).

Change isn't given, so make sure you have the correct fare. For bus-route information, call toll-free ☎1-800/2872727 (SBS) or ☎1-800/4825433 (TIBS). There are now **night buses** running along a few major routes across the island; call the hotlines above for more information.

If you are in town for a while, buy an **ez-link Farecard** (see opposite), which you hold against an electronic reader as you board and alight; your fare is automatically deducted from the stored value. Another ticket option is the **Tourist Day Ticket** (see opposite), though this is not a very cost-effective means of travel. Neither is the **Singapore Trolly**, a red tourist tram bus that plies a route between Orchard Road and the Colonial District. One day's unlimited travel is $14.90 (children $9.90); call ☎63396833 for more details.

One final option – and one kids will love – is to board the **Singapore Ducktour**, an amphibious craft dating from the Vietnam War, which provides hour-long, land- and sea-bound tours (hourly 9.30am–7.30pm; $33, children $17; ☎63333825, ⊛www.ducktours.com.sg) of the civic district and harbour. Tours start at Suntec City Mall.

Useful bus routes

Below is a selection of handy bus routes; note that many of the services from the Orchard Road area actually leave from Penang Road or Somerset Road:

#2 passes along Eu Tong Sen Street (in Chinatown) and Victoria Street (past the Arab Quarter) en route to Changi Prison and Changi Village.

#7 runs along Orchard Road, Bras Basah Road and Victoria Street; its return journey takes in North Bridge Road, Stamford Road, Penang Road and Somerset Road en route to Holland Village.

#36 loops between Orchard Road and Changi airport.

#65 terminates at the World Trade Centre, after passing down Jalan Besar, Bencoolen Street, Penang Road and Somerset Road.

#97 runs along Stamford Road to Little India, then on to Upper Serangoon Road; returns via Bencoolen Street and Collyer Quay.

#103 runs between New Bridge Road Terminal (Chinatown) and Serangoon Road (Little India).

#124 connects Scotts Road, Orchard Road and North Bridge Road with South Bridge Road and New Bridge Road in Chinatown; in the opposite direction, travels along Eu Tong Sen Street, Hill Street, Stamford Road and Somerset Road.

#139 heads past Tai Gin Road, via Dhoby Ghaut, Selegie Road, Serangoon Road and Balestier Road.

#167 passes down Scotts Road, Orchard Road and Bras Basah Road, Collyer Quay, Shenton Way and Neil Road (for Chinatown).

#170 starts at the Ban San Terminal at the northern end of Queen Street, passing Bukit Timah Nature Reserve and Kranji War Cemetery on its way to JB in Malaysia.

Taxis

There are over fifteen thousand **taxis** on the streets of Singapore, so you shouldn't have any trouble hailing a cab, day or night; they come in various colours, but are clearly marked "TAXI". All cabs are **metered**, the fare starting at $2.40 for the first kilometre and rising 10c for every 225 metres. However, there are **surcharges** to bear in mind, notably the fifty percent charged on journeys between midnight and 6am. Journeys from Changi airport incur a $5 surcharge, and there's a $6–8 surcharge for taxis booked over the phone. More confusingly still, the Singaporean government maintains an Electronic Road Pricing programme (ERP) in order to relieve congestion within the city's Central Business District (CBD) at peak times, and these electronic tolls will be reflected in your bill, depending upon the time of day.

Singapore's taxis have in-built **speed monitors**. If you hear a persistent chiming noise your driver is breaking the 80kph expressway speed limit.

On the whole, Singaporean taxi drivers are friendly, but their English isn't always good, so it's worth having your **destination written down** (in English) if you are heading off the beaten track. If a taxi displays a red destination sign on its dashboard, it means the driver is changing shift and will accept customers only if they are going in his direction. Finally, **tourists with wheelchairs** should note that TIBS Taxis (☎65558888) has wheelchair-accessible cabs in its fleet.

Renting cars and bikes

The Singapore government has introduced huge disincentives to driving in order to combat traffic congestion. If you want to drive into the CBD (see above) you'll have to buy a stored value **CashCard** to cover the electronic tolls that are now automatically levied. What's more, **parking** is expensive: you need to purchase coupons from a licence booth, post office or store. In fact, the only real reason for renting a car in Singapore is to travel up into Malaysia, and even then it's far cheaper to rent from a company based over the causeway (in JB), as Singaporean firms levy a $25 Malaysia surcharge. If you're still keen on driving in Singapore itself, rental companies are listed on p.196.

Bike rental is offered by Wheelpower, #01-09 Sunshine Plaza, 91 Bencoolen Street (daily 9.30am–7pm, $28 per day; ☎1800-238 2388). There are also rental firms along the East Coast Parkway, where the cycle track that skirts the seashore is always crowded with Singaporeans in full cycling gear. Expect to pay around $4–8 an hour for a mountain bike, and bring some form of ID to leave at the office. There are cycling trails at Bukit Timah Nature Reserve; Biker & Hike at 382 Upper Bukit Timah Road (☎67638382) rent out mountain bikes at $6 an hour. The dirt tracks that crisscross Pulau Ubin, off Changi Point at the eastern tip of the island, are ideal for cycling – a day's rental at one of the cluster of shops near the jetty again costs $4–8, though the price doubles during the school holidays (June, Nov & Dec). Finally, there's a range of bikes – including tandems – available for rent next to the ferry terminal on Sentosa Island ($2–5 an hour), which provide by far the best way to see the island.

Organized tours

If you're pushed for time, there are several reputable companies in Singapore offering **sightseeing tours**. The main operators are listed on p.197, or ask at your hotel or the tourist office. Tours vary according to the operator, but four-hour city tours typically take in Orchard Road, Chinatown, and Little India, and cost around $30. Specialist tours are also available – on such subjects as Singapore by night, World War II sights, Chinese opera, Asian cuisines, even feng shui – costing $30–80 per person. For more details, contact the STB. Members of the Registered Tourist Guides Association (☎63392114) charge $25–50 an hour (minimum 4hr) for a personalized tour – as can the guides of Geraldene's Tours (☎67375250).

Trishaws – three-wheeled bicycles with a carriage on the back – were once a common form of transport in Singapore, though they're a bit of an anachronism these days. You'll still see a few trishaws providing a genuine service around Little India and Chinatown, but most drivers now congregate on the open land opposite the *Summer View Hotel* on Bencoolen Street, from where they'll give you a 45-minute sightseeing ride for $50.

Boat cruises

Fleets of **cruise boats** ply Singapore's southern waters day and night. Singapore River Cruise boats (9am–11pm; ☎63366111, ⓦwww.rivercruise.com.sg) cast off from Clark Quay for a $12 cruise (children $6) on a traditional bumboat, passing the old **godowns** where traders once stored their merchandise. A slightly longer cruise that begins at Robertson Quay costs $15 (children $8).

In addition, several cruise companies operate out of Clifford Pier, offering everything from luxury catamaran trips around Singapore's southern isles to dinner on a Chinese sailing boat. A straightforward cruise will set you back around $20, and a dinner special $35–50. Cruise companies include Eastwind (☎63333432), Singapore Riverboat (☎63389205), Singapore River Cruises (☎63366111) and Watertours (☎65339811). If you don't relish the idea of an organized cruise, you can haggle with a **bumboat** man on Clifford Pier: if you're lucky, he'll take a group up and down the river for $50 an hour.

Opening hours, holidays and festivals

Shopping centres are open daily 10am–9.30pm, while offices generally work Monday to Friday 8.30am–5pm and sometimes on Saturday mornings (see p.32 for banking hours). In general, Chinese temples open daily from 7am to around 6pm, Hindu temples 6am–noon and 5–9pm, and mosques 8.30am–noon and 2.30–4pm; specific opening hours for all temples and museums are given in the text.

As there are so many ethnic groups and religions in Singapore, your visit could easily coincide with a **festival**. Bear in mind that the major festival periods will make traffic on the island heavier and crossing into Malaysia much slower. Over Ramadan in particular, transport networks and hotel capacity are stretched to their limits, as countless Muslims engage in *balik kampung* – the return to one's home village. Chinese New Year causes similar problems. Some, but by no means all, festivals are also public holidays (when everything closes); check the list opposite for those. For full details on Singapore's festivals see p.177 and Festive Singapore colour insert.

Most of the festivals have **no fixed dates**, but change annually according to the lunar calendar; the Islamic calendar shifts forward relative to the Gregorian calendar by about ten days each year, so that, for example, a Muslim festival, which happens in mid-April one year, will be nearer the beginning of April the following year. We've listed rough timings, but for specific dates each year it's a good idea to check with the local tourist office.

Public holidays

January 1 New Year's Day
January/February Chinese New Year (2 days)
January/February Hari Raya Haji
March/April Good Friday
May 1 Labour Day
May Vesak Day
August 9 National Day
November Deepavali
October/November Hari Raya Puasa
December 25 Christmas Day

Communications

The communications network in high-tech Singapore is fast and efficient and you can bank on easy access to the Internet. You can send mail to Singapore care of the poste restante section of the General Post Office (see below); when picking up mail, be sure to have the staff check under first names as well as family names – misfiling is common.

Postal services

In Singapore, the GPO (Mon–Fri 8am–6pm, Sat 8am–2pm), housing the **Poste Restante**, is beside Paya Lebar MRT station.

There are more than sixty other post offices across the state, with usual opening hours of Monday to Friday 8.30am–5pm and Saturday 8.30am–1pm. In addition, postal services are available until 9pm at the Comcentre on Killiney Road. Call ☏1605 to find your nearest post office.

Singapore's **postal system** is predictably efficient, with letters and cards often reaching their destination within three days. Stamps are available at post offices (some have vending machines operating out of hours) and some stationers and hotels. Airmail letters to Europe and the USA rise from $1, aerogrammes to all destinations cost 50c and postcards cost 50c to send. You'll find **fax and telex** facilities at all major post offices, too.

Telephones

Local calls from private phones in Singapore cost next to nothing; calls from public phones cost 10c for three minutes, with the exception of the free courtesy phones at Changi airport.

Singapore has no area codes. The only time you'll punch more than eight digits for a local number is if you are dialling a toll-free number (☏1800-) or a pager. Bear in mind that Singapore recently added a prefix of 6- to all seven-digit landline numbers; if you are trying a number and having no luck, adding an extra 6 might do the trick.

Payphones accept 10c, 20c and 50c coins. That said, **cardphones** are taking over from payphones in Singapore. It's possible to make **IDD calls** from all public phone-card and **credit-card** phones. Cards are available from post offices, stationery shops, bookshops, 7-Elevens and money-changers, and come in $3–50 denominations. International cards come in $10–50 denominations. You can also use the **booths** at the 24-hour Comcentre, on Killiney Road.

IDD calls made from hotel rooms in Singapore carry no surcharge.

The country code to **call Singapore from abroad** is 65.

Calling home from abroad

One of the most convenient ways of phoning home from abroad is via a **telephone charge card** from your phone company back home. Using a PIN number, you can

---

Dialling codes

To call home **from Singapore**, dial ☏00 plus the country code. Note that the initial zero is omitted from the area code when dialling the UK, Ireland, Australia and New Zealand from abroad.

UK international access code + 44 + city code.
Republic of Ireland international access code + 353 + city code.
USA and Canada international access code + 1 + area code.
Australia international access code + 61 + city code.
New Zealand international access code + 64 + city code.

make calls from most hotels, public and private phones that will be charged to your account. Since most major charge cards are free to obtain, it's certainly worth getting one at least for emergencies; enquire first though whether your destination is covered, and bear in mind that rates aren't necessarily cheaper than calling from a public phone.

In **the UK and Ireland**, British Telecom (℡0800/345 144, ⊛www.chargecard .bt.com) will issue free to all BT customers the BT Charge Card, which can be used in 116 countries; AT&T (dial ℡0800/890 011, then 888/641-6123 when you hear the AT&T prompt to be transferred to the Florida Call Centre; free 24 hours) has the Global Calling Card; while NTL (℡0500/100 505) issues its own Global Calling Card, which can be used in more than sixty countries abroad, though the fees cannot be charged to a normal phone bill.

In the **US and Canada**, AT&T, MCI, Sprint, Canada Direct and other North American long-distance companies all enable their customers to make credit-card calls while overseas, billed to your home number. Call your company's customer service line to find out if they provide service from Singapore, and if so, what the toll-free access code is.

To call **Australia and New Zealand** from overseas, telephone charge cards such as Telstra Telecard or Optus Calling Card in Australia, and Telecom NZ's Calling Card can be used to make calls abroad, which are charged back to a domestic account or credit card. Apply to Telstra (℡1800/038 000), Optus (℡1300/300 937), or Telecom NZ (℡04/801 9000).

Mobile phones

If you want to use your **mobile phone** abroad, you'll need to check with your phone provider if it will work abroad, and what the call charges are. **In the UK**, for all but the top-of-the-range packages, you'll have to inform your phone provider before going abroad to get international access switched on. You may get charged extra for this depending on your existing package and where you are travelling. You are also likely to be charged extra for incoming calls when abroad, as the people calling you will be paying the usual rate. If you want to retrieve messages while you're away, you'll have to ask your provider for a new access code, as your home one is unlikely to work abroad. Most UK mobiles use GSM too, which gives access to most places worldwide, except the US. For further information about using your phone abroad, check out ⊛www .telecomsadvice.org.uk/features/using_ your_mobile_abroad.htm.

Unless you have a tri-band phone, it is unlikely that a mobile bought for use outside the US will work inside the States and vice versa. For details of which mobiles will work outside the US, contact your mobile service provider. Most mobiles in Australia and New Zealand use GSM, which works well in Southeast Asia – again, check with your provider.

Email, the Internet and VoIP

One of the best ways to keep in touch while travelling is to sign up for a free Internet email address that can be accessed from anywhere, for example YahooMail or Hotmail – accessible through ⊛www.yahoo.com and ⊛www.hotmail.com. Once you've set up an account, you can use these sites to pick up and send mail from any Internet café, or hotel with Internet access.

You can get online at numerous cafés in Singapore; some of the more central ones are listed on p.165. Internet cafes are increasingly offering the services of Skype or other Voice over Internet Protocol (VoIP) technology to let customers make long distance calls for a fraction of what a normal long-distance call would cost.

In addition, hotels increasingly offer in-room modems, or Web access through the TV.

For details of how to plug your laptop in when abroad, plus information on country codes around the world, and electrical systems in different countries, check out the useful website, ⊛www.kropla.com.

The media

As well as dailies in Chinese, Malay and Tamil, Singapore has two English-language newspapers, the Straits Times, a decent broadsheet, with good coverage of international events, and the Business Times, dealing mainly with commercial and financial news. In addition, an amusingly tame tabloid, the New Paper, hits the streets every afternoon, though there's little of real interest in it for non-Singaporeans. All three are owned by Singapore Press Holdings, which is careful to steer well clear of any criticism of the government.

International publications include the ubiquitous Time and Newsweek, as well as a widening range of glossy consumer magazines. Those titles that do reach the stands are effectively sold on remand – one word of criticism and they are pulled, as FHM and the now defunct Far Eastern Economic Review discovered to their cost in recent years.

The Media Corporation of Singapore screens TV programmes in English, Chinese, Malay and Tamil. Channel 5, NewsAsia and Channel i feature the most English-language programmes, while Channel 8 specializes in Chinese soap operas. Most Singaporean TV sets also receive a handful of Malaysian channels.

MediaCorp broadcasts four English-language radio shows daily: Gold (90.5FM), an information and classic hits channel; Symphony (92.4FM) featuring classical music; NewsRadion (93.8FM); Class (95FM) playing middle-of-the-road hits; and Perfect (98.7FM), playing contemporary hits. Another channel that's good for current chart-toppers is SAFRA Radio's Power 98FM. There's also a decent pirate radio station operating from Indonesia's Batam Island. For locals, there are daily shows in Chinese (95.8FM), Malay (94.2FM) and Tamil (96.8FM). For listings, check in the daily newspapers, or in 8 Days magazine.

You can also pick up the BBC World Service (⊛www.bbc.co.uk/worldservice), Radio Canada (⊛www.rcinet.ca) and Voice of America (⊛www.voa.gov). Most stations post an up-to-date schedule on their websites.

Trouble and the police

If you lose something in Singapore, you're more likely to have someone running after you with it than running away. Nevertheless, you shouldn't become complacent – muggings have been known to occur and theft from dormitories by other tourists is a common complaint. Guesthouses and hotels will often have a safety deposit box. Always keep a separate record of the numbers of your travellers' cheques, together with a note of which ones you've cashed. It's a good idea to take a photocopy of the relevant pages of your passport, too, in case it's lost or stolen.

It's very unwise to have anything to do with **drugs** of any description in Singapore. The penalties for trafficking drugs in or out of the country are severe in the extreme – foreigners have been executed in the past – and if you are arrested for drugs offences you can expect no mercy and little help from your consular representatives.

Emergencies

In an emergency, dial the following numbers:
Police ☏999
Fire brigade/Ambulance ☏995.

Singapore's **police**, who wear dark blue, keep a fairly low profile, but are polite and helpful when approached. For details of the main police station, and other emergency information, check "Directory", pp.196–197.

Singapore is known locally as **fine city**. There's a fine of $500 for smoking in public places such as cinemas, trains, lifts, air-conditioned restaurants and shopping malls, and a one-off $50 fine for "jaywalking" – crossing a main road within 50m of a pedestrian crossing or bridge. Littering carries a $1000 fine, with offenders now issued Corrective Work Orders and forced to do litter-picking duty; eating and drinking on the MRT could cost you $500.

Other fines include those for urinating in lifts (legend has it that some lifts are fitted with urine detectors), not flushing a public toilet and chewing gum (which is outlawed in Singapore).

For Singapore's legal position on **homosexuality**, see p.170.

Travellers with disabilities

Singapore is an accessible city for travellers with disabilities, as hefty tax incentives are provided for developers who include access features for the disabled in new buildings. However, life is made a lot easier if you can afford to pay for more upmarket hotels and to shell out for taxis. Similarly, the more expensive international airlines tend to be better equipped to get you there in the first place: MAS, British Airways, KLM and Qantas all carry aisle wheelchairs and have at least one toilet adapted for disabled passengers. However, few, if any, tour operators offering holidays in the region accommodate the needs of those with disabilities.

The best resource for pre-trip advice is the **Disabled People's Association of Singapore**, #02-00 Day Care Centre, 150a Pandan Gardens (☏68991220; ⊛www.dpa.org.sg). Their informative website links to *Access Singapore*, a Singapore Council of Social Service publication, which, while in need of updating, is still a thorough and informative brochure detailing amenities for the disabled in Singapore's hotels, hospitals, shopping centres, cinemas and banks. You'll find Access Singapore at ⊛www.dpa.org.sg/DPA/access/contents.htm.

Access is improving all the time, and most **hotels** now make some provision for disabled guests, though often there will be only one specially designed bedroom in an establishment – always call first for information, and book in plenty of time. **Getting around** the city is less straightforward: buses are not accessible to wheelchairs and there are no elevators in the MRT system. However, SMRT (☏65558888) has a fleet of wheelchair accessible taxis, and two private taxi companies, Comfort Cab (☏65521111) and CityCab (☏65520220), have drivers that will assist a wheelchair-bound passenger in embarking and disembarking from their cabs. There are acoustic signals at most street crossings.

Contacts for travellers with disabilities

In the UK and Ireland

Holiday Care 2nd floor, Imperial Building, Victoria Rd, Horley, Surrey RH6 7PZ ☎0845/124 9971, minicom ☎0845/124 9976, ⓦwww .holidaycare.org.uk. Provides free lists of accessible accommodation abroad – European, American and long-haul destinations – plus a list of accessible attractions in the UK. Information on financial help for holidays available.

Irish Wheelchair Association Blackheath Drive, Clontarf, Dublin 3 ☎01/818 6400, ⓦwww.iwa.ie. Useful information provided about travelling abroad with a wheelchair.

Tripscope Alexandra House, Albany Rd, Brentford, Middlesex TW8 0NE ☎0845/7585 641, ⓦwww .tripscope.org.uk. This registered charity provides a national telephone information service offering free advice on UK and international transport for those with a mobility problem.

In the US and Canada

Access-Able ⓦwww.access-able.com. Online resource for travellers with disabilities.

Directions Unlimited (Accessible Tours) 720 N. Bedford Rd, Bedford Hills, NY 10507 ☎1-800/533-5343 or 914/241-1700. Travel agency specializing in bookings for people with disabilities.

Mobility International USA 451 Broadway, Eugene, OR 97401 ☎541/343-1284, ⓦwww .miusa.org. Information and referral services, access guides, tours and exchange programmes.

Society for the Advancement of Travelers with Handicaps (SATH) 347 5th Ave, New York, NY 10016 ☎212/447-7284, ⓦwww.sath.org. Non-profit educational organization that has actively represented travellers with disabilities since 1976.

Wheels Up! ☎1-888/38-WHEELS, ⓦwww .wheelsup.com. Provides discounted airfare, tour and cruise prices for disabled travellers, also publishes a free monthly newsletter and has a comprehensive website.

In Australia and New Zealand

ACROD (Australian Council for Rehabilitation of the Disabled) PO Box 60, Curtin ACT 2605; Suite 103, 1st floor, 1–5 Commercial Rd, Kings Grove 2208; ☎02/6282 4333, TTY ☎02/6282 4333, ⓦwww.acrod.org.au. Provides lists of travel agencies and tour operators for people with disabilities.

Disabled Persons Assembly 4/173–175 Victoria St, Wellington, New Zealand ☎04/801 9100 (also TTY), ⓦwww.dpa.org.nz. Resource centre with lists of travel agencies and tour operators for people with disabilities.

The City

The City

The Colonial District

T he British left Singapore an impressive legacy in the stately nineteenth-century piles of the **COLONIAL DISTRICT**. From the Bencoolen Street/Beach Road area, it's an easy jaunt on foot to survey the fruits of grandiose empire building; if you're coming from further afield, you'll need to take the MRT to either Raffles Place, Clarke Quay or City Hall MRT stations.

As the colony's trade grew in the nineteenth century, the Singapore River became its main artery, clogged with the traditional cargo boats known as bumboats, with painted eyes, as though they could see where they were going. The boats ferried coffee, sugar and rice to the riverbank warehouses (godowns), where coolies loaded and unloaded sacks. These days, with the bumboats all but gone, the river is quieter, cleaner and inevitably less fascinating, though both banks are undergoing a profound commercial revitalization, as new restaurants and bars move into formerly abandoned buildings.

The heart of the Colonial District is the immaculately groomed grass of the **Padang** ("field" in Malay), which stretches out below **St Andrew's Cathedral** towards the river. To the south of the Padang are the **Empress Place Building** (now home to the Asian Civilizations Museum), **Old Parliament House** and the **Singapore Cricket Club** – the epitome of the colonizers' stubborn refusal to adapt to their surroundings. To the north is grand old **Raffles Hotel**, beyond which a string of nineteenth- and twentieth-century churches leads to Singapore's once famous entertainment centre, **Bugis Village**. Also in the north of the district are the **Singapore Art Museum**, **National History Museum**, and the shops and restaurants of the **CHIJMES** complex. Heading west from the Padang, you pass **City Hall**, the **former Supreme Court** and its new, Norman Foster-architected replacement, before climbing the slopes of **Fort Canning Hill**, ten minutes' walk from the Padang, and one of the few hills in Singapore not lost to land reclamation. Dominating the newly reclaimed land to the east of the Padang, the bug's-eye beauty of the **Theatres on the Bay** project hauls the Colonial District into the twenty-first century.

Along the north riverbank

From Raffles Place MRT it's just a couple of minutes' walk, past Singapore's former GPO (now the splendid *Fullerton Hotel)*, to the elegant suspension struts of **Cavenagh Bridge** – a good place to start a tour of the colonial centre. Named after Major General Orfeur Cavenagh, governor of the Straits Settlements from 1859 to 1867, the bridge was constructed in 1869 by Indian convict labourers using imported Glasgow steel. Times change, but not necessarily here, where a police sign maintains: "The use of this bridge

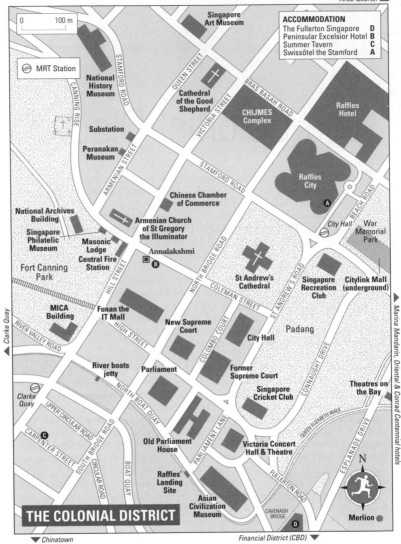

THE COLONIAL DISTRICT

is prohibited to any vehicle of which the laden weight exceeds 3cwt and to all cattle and horses."

Stepping off the bridge, you're confronted by **Empress Place Building**, a robust Neoclassical structure named after Queen Victoria and completed in 1865. It served for ten years as a courthouse before the Registry of Births and Deaths and the Immigration Department moved in. Today it houses the **Asian Civilization Museum** (Mon 1–7pm, Tues–Thurs, Sat & Sun 9am–7pm, Fri 9am–9pm; $5/2.50 including free guided tour Mon–Fri 2pm, Tues–Fri 11am & 2pm, Sat & Sun 11am, 2pm & 3.30pm; ☎63327798,

@www.nhb.gov.sg/acm). The ACM traces the origins and growth of Asia's many and varied cultures. Its ten themed galleries hold approaching 2000 artefacts bringing to life the religions, history and cultures of every corner of Asia, from South to Southeast Asia, and from Islamic West Asia to China. Temporary exhibitions in the Special Exhibitions Gallery allow the visitor to drill down further into specific facets of Asian life and culture. There is also an engaging Singapore River Interpretive Gallery, featuring oral history accounts of the river delivered by individuals from generations that lived beside and worked it all their lives.

The time capsule in the grounds in front of the building was sealed in 1990 as part of Singapore's silver jubilee celebrations. It contains "significant items" from Singapore's first 25 years of independence: the clever money says that when opened it will yield a speech or two from Singapore's patriarch Lee Yuan Yew (see p.205). The southern flank of the Empress Place Building has been appropriated by the all-conquering *Indochine* bar and restaurant chain. Its string of Khmer-influenced outlets afford peerless views of the Singapore River (see "Eating", p.165).

Next to the Empress Place Building stand two fine examples of colonial architecture, the **Victoria Concert Hall** and adjoining **Victoria Theatre**, still the venues for some of Singapore's most prestigious cultural events. The theatre was completed in 1862 as Singapore's town hall, while the concert hall was added in 1905 as a memorial to the monarch's reign. During the Japanese occupation, the clock tower was altered to Tokyo time, while the statue of Raffles that once stood in front of the tower narrowly escaped being melted down. The newly installed Japanese curator of the National Museum (where the statue was sent) hid the statue and reported it destroyed. A copy can be seen by the river at **Raffles' landing site**, where, in January 1819, the great man apparently took his first steps on Singaporean soil. Sir Stamford now stares contemplatively across the river towards the business district. Singapore River cruise boats (see p.43) depart from a tiny jetty, a few steps along from Raffles' statue.

North of the statue, up Parliament Lane, the dignified white Victorian building ringed by fencing is the **Old Parliament House**, built as a private dwelling for a rich merchant by Singapore's pre-eminent colonial architect, the Irishman George Drumgould Coleman. Relived of its legislative duties, the building now goes under the name of the **Arts House** and is home to cafés, shops, galleries and a film/theatre space. The bronze elephant in front of Old Parliament House was a gift to Singapore from King Rama V of Thailand (whose father was the king upon whom *The King and I* was based) after his trip to the island in 1871 – the first foreign visit ever made by a Thai monarch. It is sometimes possible to watch Singapore's parliament in session in the **New Parliament House**, across Parliament Lane from its predecessor; call ☎63326666 for details, or check out @www.parliament.gov.sg.

The Padang

The **Padang** is the very essence of colonial Singapore. Earmarked by Raffles as a recreation ground shortly after his arrival, such is its symbolic significance that its borders have never been encroached upon by speculators and it remains much as it was in 1907, when G.M. Reith wrote in his *Handbook to Singapore*: "Cricket, tennis, hockey, football and bowls are played on the plain . . . beyond the carriage drive on the other side, is a strip of green along the sea wall, with a footpath, which affords a cool and pleasant walk in the early morning and afternoon." Once the last over of the day had been bowled, the Padang assumed a more social role: the image of Singapore's European community hastening

Sir Stamford Raffles

Let it still be the boast of Britain
to write her name in characters of light;
let her not be remembered as the tempest
whose course was desolation,
but as the gale of spring reviving
the slumbering seeds of mind and
calling them to life
from the winter of ignorance and oppression.
If the time shall come
when her empire shall have passed away,
these monuments will endure when her triumphs
shall have become an empty name.

This verse, written by Sir Stamford Raffles himself, speaks volumes about the man whom history remembers as the founder of modern Singapore. Despite living and working in a period of imperial arrogance and self-motivated land-grabbing, Raffles maintained an unfailing concern for the welfare of the people under his governorship, and a conviction that British colonial expansion was for the general good. He believed Britain to be, as Jan Morris says in her introduction to Maurice Collis's biography of Raffles, "the chief agent of human progress . . . the example of fair Government".

Fittingly for a man who was to spend his life roaming the globe, Thomas Stamford Raffles was born at sea on July 6, 1781 on the *Ann*, whose master was his father Captain Benjamin Raffles. By his fourteenth birthday, the young Raffles was working as a clerk for the **East India Company** in London, his schooling curtailed because of his father's debts. Even at this early age, Raffles' ambition and self-motivation was evident as, faced with a lifetime as a clerk, he resolved to educate himself, staying up through the night to study and developing a hunger for knowledge which would later spur him to learn Malay, amass a vast treasure-trove of natural history artefacts and write his two-volume *History of Java*.

Abdullah bin Kadir, Raffles' clerk while in Southeast Asia, describes him in his autobiography, the *Hikayat Abdullah*: "He was broad of brow, a sign of his care and thoroughness; round-headed with a projecting forehead, showing his intelligence. He had light brown hair, indicative of bravery; large ears, the mark of a ready listener . . . He was solicitous of the feelings of others, and open-handed with the poor. He spoke in smiles. He took the most active interest in historical research. Whatever he found to do he adopted no half-measures, but saw it through to the finish."

Raffles' diligence and hard work showed through in 1805, when he was chosen to join a team going out to Penang, then being developed as a British entrepôt; overnight, his annual salary leapt from £70 to £1500. Once in Southeast Asia, Raffles' rise was meteoric. By 1807 he was named **chief secretary to the governor in Penang** and soon Lord Minto, the governor-general of the East India Company in India, was alerted to his Oriental expertise. Meeting Minto on a trip to Calcutta in 1810, Raffles was appointed **secretary to the governor-general in Malaya**, a promotion quickly

to the corner once known as Scandal Point to catch up on the latest gossip is pure Somerset Maugham. Today the Padang is kept as pristine as ever by a bevy of gardeners mounted on state-of-the-art lawnmowers. As an April Fool's Day joke, the *Straits Times* reported in 1982 that the Padang was to be sold off for development; the ensuing public outcry jammed the newspaper's switchboard.

The brown-tiled roof, whitewashed walls and dark-green blinds of the **Singapore Cricket Club**, at the southwestern end of the Padang, have a nostalgic followed by the **governorship of Java** in 1811. Raffles' rule of Java was wise, liber-tarian and compassionate, his economic, judicial and social reforms transforming an island bowed by Dutch rule.

Post-Waterloo European rebuilding saw the East Indies returned to the Dutch in 1816 – to the chagrin of Raffles, who foresaw problems for British trade should the Dutch regain their hold on the area. From Java, Raffles transferred to the **gover-norship of Bencoolen**, on the southern coast of Sumatra, but not before he had returned home for a break, stopping at St Helena en route to meet Napoleon ("a monster"). While in England he met his second wife, Sophia Hull (his first, Olivia, had died in 1814), and was knighted.

Raffles and Sophia sailed to Bencoolen in early 1818, Sophia reporting that her husband spent the four-month journey deep in study. Once in Sumatra, Raffles found the time to study the region's flora and fauna as tirelessly as ever, discovering the **rafflesia arnoldii** – "perhaps the largest and most magnificent flower in the world" – on a jungle field trip. By now, Raffles felt strongly that Britain should establish a base in the Straits of Melaka. Meeting Hastings (Minto's successor) in late 1818, he was given leave to pursue this possibility and in 1819 duly sailed to the southern tip of the Malay Peninsula, where his securing of **Singapore** early that year was a daring masterstroke of diplomacy.

For a man whose name is inextricably linked with Singapore, Raffles spent a remarkably short time on the island. His first stay was for one week, and the second for three weeks, during which time he helped delineate the new settlement (see p.201): "Looking a century or two ahead so as to provide for what Singapore may one day become," as Raffles himself later put it. Subsequent sojourns in Bencoolen ended tragically with the loss of four of his five children to tropical illnesses, while his own health also began to deteriorate. Raffles visited Singapore one last time in late 1822; his final public duty there was to lay the foundation stone of the Singapore Institution (later the **Raffles Institution**), an establishment created to educate local Malays, albeit upper-class ones. From Singapore, Raffles and Sophia travelled back to Bencoolen to pick up their personal effects, and from there journeyed home to Europe. The *Fame*, on which they set sail on February 2, 1824, caught fire 80km out to sea, claiming no lives but destroying Raffles' vast collection of natural history specimens and notes.

By August 1824, Raffles was back in England. Awaiting news of a possible pension award from the East India Company, he spent his free time founding the London Zoo and setting up a farm in Hendon. But the new life Raffles had planned for Sophia and himself never materialized. Days after hearing that a Calcutta bank holding £16,000 of his capital had folded, his pension application was refused; worse still, the Company was demanding £22,000 for overpayment. Three months later, the brain tumour that had caused Raffles headaches for several years took his life on July 4, 1826. Buried at Hendon, he was honoured by no memorial stone – the vicar had investments in slave plantations in the West Indies and was unimpressed by his friendship with William Wilberforce. Only in 1832 was Raffles commemorated, with a statue in Westminster Abbey.

charm. Founded in the 1850s, the club was the hub of colonial British society and still operates a "members only" rule, though there's nothing to stop you watching the action from outside on the Padang itself. The Singapore Rugby Sevens are played here, as well as a plethora of other big sporting events and parades; a timetable of forthcoming events is available at the club's recep-tion. Eurasians, who were formerly ineligible for membership of the Cricket Club, founded their own establishment in 1883, the **Singapore Recreation**

△ Sir Stamford Raffles statue

Club, which lies across on the north side of the Padang. The current grandiose, colonnaded clubhouse dates back to a $65-million overhaul completed in 1997.

Just to the west of the Cricket Club, Singapore's erstwhile **Supreme Court** (formerly the site of the exclusive *Hotel de L'Europe*, whose drawing rooms allegedly provided Somerset Maugham with inspiration for many of his Southeast Asia short stories) was built in Neoclassical style between 1937 and 1939, and sports a domed roof of green lead and a splendid, wood-panelled entrance hall. Since its replacement opened a block back, on Northbridge Road, early in the new Millennium, the building has sat idle, awaiting a fresh purpose. The Sir Norman Forster-designed **New Supreme Court** is also worthy of note, though more for its impressive, flying saucer-shaped upper tier than for its lumpen marble-and-glass main body.

Next door to the former Supreme Court is the older **City Hall**, whose uniform rows of grandiose Corinthian columns lend it the austere air of a mausoleum. Wartime photographs show Lord Louis Mountbatten (then Supreme Allied Commander in Southeast Asia) on the steps announcing Japan's surrender to the British in 1945. Fourteen years later, Lee Kuan Yew chose the same spot from which to address his electorate at a victory rally celebrating self-government for Singapore. Nowadays, rather less dramatic photographs are taken on the steps as newlyweds line up to have their big day captured in front of one of Singapore's most imposing buildings. Like the old Supreme Court, City Hall currently lies empty, though it can't be long before it is reinvented as a gallery, museum or arts space.

The final building of note on the west side of the Padang, **St Andrew's Cathedral**, on Coleman Street, gleams even brighter than the rest. The third church to be built on this site, the cathedral was constructed in high-vaulted, Neo-Gothic style, using Indian convict labour, and was consecrated by Bishop Cotton of Calcutta on January 25, 1862. Its exterior walls were plastered using Madras *chunam* – an unlikely composite of eggs, lime, sugar and shredded coconut husks which shines brightly when smoothed – while the small cross behind the pulpit was crafted from two fourteenth-century nails salvaged from the ruins of Coventry Cathedral in England, which was destroyed during World War II.

During the Japanese invasion of Singapore, the cathedral became a makeshift hospital; the vestry was an operating theatre and the nave a ward. Closed-circuit

The Sepoy Mutiny

Plaques on the west wall of St Andrew's Cathedral commemorate the victims of one of Singapore's bloodiest episodes, the **Sepoy Mutiny** of 1915. The mutiny began when a German warship, *Emden*, was sunk by an Australian ship off the Cocos Islands: its survivors were brought to Singapore and imprisoned at Tanglin Barracks, at the western end of Orchard Road. With almost all of Singapore's troop contingent away in Europe fighting the Kaiser, the Muslim Punjabi soldiers of the **Fifth Light Infantry**, known as sepoys, were sent to guard the prisoners. Unfortunately, these men's allegiance to the British had recently been strained by the news that Turkey had come out against the Allies in Europe. A rumour that they were soon to be sent to Turkey to fight fellow Muslims upset them still further, and the German prisoners were able to incite the sepoys to mutiny. In the ensuing rampage through the city on February 15, 1915, the sepoys killed forty other soldiers and civilians before they were finally rounded up by some remaining European sailors and a band of men led by the Sultan of Johor. All were court-martialled and the resultant executions saw 36 sepoys shot before huge crowds. As for the Germans, they took the opportunity to effect an escape. Nine of them finally got back to Germany via Jakarta and one, Julius Lauterbach, received an Iron Cross in recognition of his daring and rather convoluted flight home through China and North America.

TVs have been installed, which allow the whole congregation to view proceedings up at the altar – a reflection of the Chinese fascination with all things high tech, since the cathedral's size hardly requires it.

Esplanade – Theatres on the Bay

Singapore's skyline seems to change almost by the day, but rarely has a building caused such ripples as the $600-million **Esplanade – Theatres on the Bay** project (@www.esplanade.com), which occupies six hectares of waterfront land to the east of the Padang. Esplanade boasts a concert hall, theatre, recital studio, theatre studio, gallery space and outdoor theatre. Esplanade Mall threads round these various auditoria, offering shopping, eating and drinking and making the complex as much a social hub as a cultural landmark. From the waterfront restaurants and bars on the south side of the complex, there are unbeatable views across the bay. On the third floor is library@esplanade, a performing arts library with a wide range of arts-related resources.

Opinion is split over whether the two huge, spiked shells that roof the complex are peerless modernistic architecture or plain indulgent kitsch. They have variously been compared to hedgehogs, kitchen sieves, golf balls, huge microphones, even mating aardvarks; locals have taken to calling them "the durians" after the spikey and pungent fruit, though they are perhaps best described as resembling two giant insects' eyes.

The idea for an integrated national arts centre was first mooted in the 1970s. The project's radical architecture was unveiled to the Singaporean public in 1994, and work began officially in 1996. The gala opening night, in October 2002, saw thousands of Singaporeans turn out for a spectacular fireworks display. In giving this ambitious project a green light, the government has upped the ante in its attempts to nurture a unified Singaporean culture. The authorities are viewing Esplanade as an iconic statement of Singapore's developing nationhood.

Should you decide to investigate Esplanade's monthly schedule, you'll find a varied programme of **events** spanning jazz, Asian dance, pipe-organ recitals, classical ballet, musicals such as *Singin' in the Rain* and contemporary drama.

Real theatre buffs might enjoy the 45-minute **guided tours** (Mon–Fri 11am & 2pm, Sat & Sun 11am; $8/5; ☏68288377) of the area that start from the Concourse Information Counter.

Raffles City and Raffles Hotel

Northwest of the Theatres on the Bay is **Raffles City**, a huge development that sits beside the intersection of Bras Basah and North Bridge roads and comprises two enormous hotels – one of which is the 73-storey **Swissôtel** – a multi-level shopping centre and floor upon floor of offices and hotel rooms. Completed in 1985, the complex was designed by Chinese-American architect I.M. Pei (the man behind the Louvre's glass pyramid) and required the highly contentious demolition of the venerable Raffles Institution, established by Raffles himself and built in 1835 by George Drumgould Coleman. The *Swissôtel* holds an annual vertical marathon, in which hardy athletes attempt to run up to the top floor in as short a time as possible: the current record stands at under seven minutes. Lifts transport lesser mortals to admire the view from the sumptuous bars and restaurants on the top floors. The imposing **Singapore War Memorial** stands on the open land east of Raffles City; comprising four seventy-metre-high white columns, it's known locally as the "chopsticks".

If the *Swissôtel* was once the tallest hotel in the world, across the way is perhaps the most famous. The lofty halls, restaurants, bars, and peaceful gardens of the legendary **Raffles Hotel**, almost a byword for colonialism, prompted Somerset Maugham to remark that it "stood for all the fables of the exotic East". Oddly, though, this most inherently British of hotels started life as a modest seafront bungalow belonging to an Arab trader, Mohamed Alsagoff. After a spell as a tiffin house, the property was bought in 1886 by the enterprising Armenian Sarkies brothers, who eventually controlled a triumvirate of quintessentially colonial lodgings: the *Raffles*, the (still extant) *Eastern and Oriental* in Penang, and the *Strand* in Rangoon.

Raffles Hotel opened for business on December 1, 1887 and quickly attracted some impressive guests. It is thought that Joseph Conrad stayed in the late 1880s; certainly Rudyard Kipling visited soon after this, though the hotel was far from sumptuous. "Let the traveller take note," wrote Kipling, "feed at Raffles and stay at the *Hotel de l'Europe*". The hotel enjoyed its real heyday during the first three decades of the new century, when it established its reputation for luxury and elegance – it was the first building in Singapore with electric lights and fans.

In 1902, a little piece of Singaporean history was made at the hotel, according to a (probably apocryphal) tale, when the last tiger to be killed on the island was shot inside the building. Thirteen years later another *Raffles* legend, the Singapore Sling cocktail, was created by bartender Ngiam Tong Boon.

The rich, famous and influential have always patronized the hotel, but it is its literary connections of which the hotel is proudest. Herman Hesse, Somerset Maugham, Noël Coward and Günter Grass all stayed at *Raffles* at some time – Maugham is said to have written many of his Asian tales under a frangipani tree in the garden.

During World War II, when the Japanese swept through the island, the hotel became the invading officers' quarters. After the Japanese surrender in 1945, *Raffles* was a transit camp for liberated Allied prisoners. Postwar deterioration earned it the affectionate but melancholy soubriquet "grand old lady of the East" and the hotel was little more than a shabby tourist diversion when the government finally declared it a national monument in 1987. A $160-million facelift followed and the hotel reopened on September 16, 1991.

The new-look *Raffles* gets a very mixed reception. Though it retains much of its colonial grace, the shopping arcade that now curves around the back of the hotel lacks finesse, selling *Raffles*-related souvenirs, exclusive garments, leatherware and perfume. Still, if you're in Singapore, there's no missing *Raffles* and, if you can't afford to stay here, there are other ways to soak up the atmosphere. A free **museum** (daily 10am–9pm), located upstairs, at the back of the hotel complex, is crammed with memorabilia, much of which was recovered in a nationwide heritage search that encouraged Singaporeans to turn in souvenirs that had found their way up sleeves and into handbags over the years. Otherwise, a Singapore Sling in *The Bar and Billiards Room* – one of thirteen food and beverage outlets in the hotel – will cost you around $20.

Along Bras Basah Road

Bras Basah Road cuts west from *Raffles*, crossing North Bridge Road and then passing one of Singapore's most aesthetically pleasing eating venues, the **CHIJMES** complex. Based around the Neo-Gothic husk of the former Convent of the Holy Infant Jesus (from whose name the complex's acronymic title is derived), CHIJMES is a rustic version of London's Covent Garden, whose lawns, courtyards, waterfalls, fountains and sunken forecourt give a sense of spatial dynamics that is rare indeed in Singapore. A relic from CHIJMES' convent days survives on its Victoria Street flank, where local families left unwanted babies at the **Gate of Hope**, to be taken in by the convent. Many were "Tiger girls", so called because they were born in the year of the tiger and were therefore thought to bring bad luck to their families. CHIJMES' shops and boutiques open from 9am to 10pm, the restaurants and bars from 11am to 1am.

Beyond CHIJMES, Bras Basah crosses Victoria and Queen streets, where elderly trishaw drivers in yellow T-shirts tout for custom, before arriving at the

△ Singapore Art Museum

Singapore Art Museum at 71 Bras Basah Road (daily 10am–7pm, Fri till 9pm; $3 including free tour, Mon 2pm, Tues–Thurs 11am & 2pm, Fri 11am, 2pm & 7pm, Sat & Sun 11am, 2pm & 3.30pm; ☎63323222, ⊛www.singart .com). A long-overdue replacement for the tired art wing of the National History Museum when it opened in 1996, the art museum has a peerless location in the venerable St Joseph's Institution, Singapore's first Catholic school, whose silvery dome rang to the sounds of school bells and rote learning until 1987. Though extensions have been necessary, many of the original rooms survive, among them the school chapel (now an auditorium), whose Stations of the Cross and mosaic floor remain intact. The school quad, the former gymnasium, periodically displays statues and sculptures such as the glassworks of American designer Dale Chihuly.

The Art Museum's rolling schedule of visiting collections brings work by such acclaimed artists as Marc Chagall and the sculptor Carl Milles to Singapore. But greater emphasis is placed on contemporary local and Southeast Asian artists and artwork. Indeed, the museum's real strength lies in its permanent collection's mapping of the Asian experience. Only a selection from the collection is displayed at any one time, but works you may be lucky enough to catch are Bui Xian Phai's *Coalmine*, an unremittingly desolate memory of his labour in a Vietnamese re-education camp, and Srihadi Sudarsono's *Horizon Dan Prahu*, in which traditional Indonesian fishing boats ply a Mark Rothko-esque canvas. Look out, too, for local artist, Liu Kang's sketches and paintings of postwar kampung life in Singapore.

Outside the museum, the souvenir shop stocks prints and postcards, and there's a classy branch of *Dôme*, where you can have a coffee under the watchful gaze of a statue of the seventeenth-century saint, John Baptist de la Salle, which stands over the museum's porch.

Waterloo Street to Bugis Village

Semi-pedestrianized **Waterloo Street** is at its best on Sundays, springing to life as worshippers throng to its temples and churches. Thanks to an expansion and modernization project back in 1982, **Kuan Yim Temple**, named after the Buddhist goddess of mercy, may not have the cluttered altars, dusty old rafters and elaborate roofs of Chinatown's temples, but it remains one of Singapore's most popular. Thousands of devotees flock to the temple every day, and all along the pavement outside, old ladies in floppy, wide-brimmed hats sell them fresh flowers from baskets. Religious artefact shops in the surrounding buildings opposite are well placed to catch worshippers on their way out – one shop specializes in small **shrines** for the house: the de luxe model boasts flashing lights and an extractor fan to expel unwanted incense smoke. **Fortune-tellers** and street traders operate along this stretch of the road, too, and look out for the cage containing turtles and a sleepy old snake: make a donation, touch one of the creatures inside, and it's said that good luck will come your way. **Sri Krishnan Temple**, next door, began life in 1870, when it amounted to nothing more than a thatched hut containing a statue of Lord Krishna under a banyan tree. Nearing a century and a half later, it is a popular venue for Hindu weddings. Now called Sculpture Square, the unassuming church across Middle Road from the temple was erected in the 1870s as the Christian Institute, where residents could debate and read about their faith. After a short stint as the focal point of Singapore's Methodist missionaries, the building became a girls' school in 1894, before transforming into a Malay Church. Today, its grounds and interior gallery space feature modernist works by local artists. The courtyard café out back makes a peaceful place to break up a day's sightseeing.

One block east of Waterloo Street's shops and temples, at the junction of Rochor Road and Victoria Street, sits **Bugis Village**, a rather tame manifestation of infamous Bugis Street. Until it was demolished in the 1990s to make way for an MRT station, Bugis Street embodied old Singapore: after dark it was a chaotic place, crawling with rowdy sailors, preening transvestites and prostitutes – and as such it was anathema to the Singapore government, keen to clean up the country's reputation. Singaporean public opinion demanded a replacement, though when Bugis Village opened in 1991 it was revealed as a shadow of its former self, its beer gardens, restaurants and stalls drawing a largely negative local reaction and only a modest stream of tourists. Today, Bugis Village is reduced to little more than a dull crossroads of market stalls and snack sellers. The transvestites that used to be so much a part of the area are noticeable only by their absence, and even the weak cabaret shows of the *Boom Boom Room* nightclub have gone.

Along Hill Street to Fort Canning Park

From Stamford Road, Hill Street heads south to the river, flanking the eastern side of Fort Canning Park. The **Singapore Chinese Chamber of Commerce**, at 47 Hill Street, a brash, Chinese-style building from 1964 featuring a striking pagoda roof, lies 30m down on the left. Along its facade are two large panels, depicting nine intricately crafted porcelain dragons. By way of contrast, the tiny **Armenian Church** of St Gregory the Illuminator, across the road and next to the former American Embassy, was designed by George Drumgould Coleman in 1835 (which makes it one of the oldest buildings in Singapore). Inside is a single, circular chamber, fronted by a marble altar and a painting of the Last Supper. Among the white gravestones and statues in the church's frangipani-scented gardens is the tombstone of Agnes Joaquim, a nineteenth-century Armenian resident of Singapore, after whom the national flower, the delicate, purple Vanda Miss Joaquim Orchid, is named; she discovered the orchid in her garden and had it registered at the Botanic Gardens.

The **Central Fire Station**, a stone's throw from the Armenian Church, across Coleman Street at 62 Hill Street, is a splendid red-and-white striped edifice. When it was first built in 1908, the watchtower was the tallest building in the region, making it easy for firemen to scan the downtown area for fires. Though the station remains operational, part of it is now taken up by the **Civil Defence Heritage Galleries** (Tues–Sun 10am–5pm; free), which traces the history of fire fighting in Singapore from the formation of the first Voluntary Fire Brigade in 1869. The galleries display old helmets, extinguishers, hand-drawn escape ladders and steam fire engines, all beautifully restored and buffed up; and upstairs there are explanations of current equipment and practices. Of most interest, though, are the accounts of the island's two most destructive fires. The first of these was the Bukit Ho Swee fire of 1961, which claimed four lives and 16,000 homes when it ripped through a district of atap thatched huts and timber yards, and which led directly to a public housing scheme that spawned today's network of new towns and HDB blocks. The second was the blaze in Robinson's department store in Raffles Place, in 1972, when a short circuit in old wires led to the deaths of nine people.

Directly behind the Central Fire Station on Coleman Street, Singapore's **Masonic Lodge** with its colonial facade of moulded garlands and protractors, sits beside the cream walls of the **Singapore Philatelic Museum** (Mon 1–7pm, Tues–Sun 9am–7pm; $3/2; ☎63373888; ⊛www.spm.org.sg). The museum occupies Singapore's former Methodist book rooms, which date back to 1906. Although clearly a niche destination, it manages to use its stamp collection imaginatively to highlight facets of the multi-cultural history and heritage of Singapore. The **National Archives Building** (Mon–Fri 9am–5.30pm, Sat 9am–1.30pm, free; ☎63327973; ⊛www.nhb.gov.sg/NAS), next door at 1 Fort Canning Rise, houses enough records, documents, maps and photographs to keep the most committed amateur historian busy for weeks. Much of the NAS collection of over 3,000 audio-visual history accounts is available to the public, allowing access to fascinating interviews on such subjects as vanishing Singaporean trades, the Japanese occupation and traditional performing arts.

Given its past, it seems appropriate that the spectacular colonial-era mansion, fronted by two black eagles, around the corner on Armenian Street, should house a museum. Dating from 1910, the building was once home to the Tao Nan School, the first school in Singapore to cater for new arrivals from the Hokkien region of China. The old school gates are displayed upstairs. When it reopens in 2008, the museum's galleries will provide a cultural and historical context to Singapore's Peranakan community.

Adjacent to the museum, the **Substation**, a disused power station, has been converted into a multimedia arts centre. Even if you don't have the time to check out its classes, discussions and performances (see p.176 for more details), the coffee shop is a pleasant place to hang out for a while. A market takes place in the courtyard every Sunday afternoon, with stalls selling anything from local crafts to second-hand Russian watches.

National History Museum

Turning left at the end of Armenian Street, you'll see the eye-catching dome of stained glass that tops the entrance to the **National History Museum** on Stamford Road (☎63323659, ⊛www.nhb.gov.sg), which is due to reopen in late 2006 after a top-to-bottom renovation. The museum's forerunner, the Raffles Museum and Library, was opened in 1887 and soon acquired a reputation for the excellence of its natural history collection. In 1969, the place was renamed the National Museum in recognition of Singapore's independence, and subsequently altered its bias towards local history and culture. Out front, a stack of silver triangles marks the site of the "Singapore at the turn of the millennium" capsule, to be opened in January 2050; near it stands a chunky slate statue of t'ai chi boxers by Taiwanese sculptor, Ju Ming.

Fort Canning Park and around

When Raffles first caught sight of Singapore, **Fort Canning Park** was known locally as Bukit Larangan (Forbidden Hill). Malay annals tell of the five ancient kings of Singapura, said to have ruled the island from this point six hundred years ago – and archeological digs have unearthed artefacts which prove it was inhabited as early as the fourteenth century. The last of the kings, Sultan Iskandar Shah, reputedly lies here, and a *keramat*, or auspicious place, on the eastern slope of the hill marks the supposed site of his grave. It was out of respect for and fear of his spirit that the Malays decreed the hill forbidden, and these days the *keramat* still attracts a trickle of Singaporean Muslims, as well as childless couples who offer prayers here for fertility.

However, when the British arrived, Singapore's first British resident, William Farquhar, displayed typical colonial tact by promptly having the hill cleared and building a bungalow on the summit; named Government House, it stood on what was then called Government Hill. The bungalow was replaced in 1859 by a fort named after Viscount George Canning, governor-general of India, but of this only a gateway, guardhouse and adjoining wall remain. An early European **cemetery** survives, however, upon whose stones are engraved intriguing epitaphs to nineteenth-century sailors, traders and residents, among them the pioneering colonial architect, George Coleman. In colonial times, the report of a 68-pound artillery gun fired at Fort Canning Hill marked the hours of 5am, noon and 7pm.

History apart, Fort Canning Park is spacious and breezy, and offers respite from, as well as fine views of, Singapore's crowded streets. There's a "back entrance" to the park that involves climbing the exhausting flight of steps that runs from beside the MICA Building on Hill Street. Once you reach Raffles Terrace at the top, there's a brilliant view along High Street towards the mouth of the river.

The hill, which houses two theatres, cannons, the colonial flagstaff and a lighthouse, is ringed by two walks, signs along which illuminate aspects of the park's fourteenth- and nineteenth-century history. If you circumnavigate the park, look out for some truly magnificent **old trees** on the western (River Valley) side. There's also a nod to more recent wartime history.

The Battle Box

On the northwest flank of Fort Canning Hill lies the **Battle Box** (Tues–Sun 10am–6pm; adults $8, children $5), the underground operations complex from which the Allied war effort in Singapore was masterminded. The complex uses audio and video effects and animatronics to bring to life the events leading up to the decision by British officers to surrender Singapore to Japanese occupation, on February 15, 1942. Authentic, if a little clunky, it provides an engaging enough context to Singapore's darkest hour.

Conceived as a gas- and bombproof operations chamber, the Battle Box was completed in October 1939, after which it became a part of the Malaya Command World War II Headquarters. So well protected was it against gas attack, that its residents were forced to hack the tops off internal doors in order to increase circulation and combat the stifling heat. Following faithful restoration of its 26 rooms, the complex now conveys a palpable sense of the claustrophobia and tension suffered by the British as the Japanese bore down upon Singapore.

The experience gets off to a low-key start, with a history lesson on a small TV set whose muddy sound is barely audible over the buzzing air-con unit. Thankfully, things look up once you proceed to the chambers themselves. First stop is the switchboard and exchange room, where an animatronic signalman is hard at work patching through messages from bases at Changi, Pulau Bukum and Pulau Blakang Mati (modern-day Sentosa). Next door, in the cipher rooms, the air crackles with the rat-tat-tat of Morse sets and the furious tapping of typewriters, cipher machines and coding machines. Meanwhile, soldiers shift Jap fighter planes around a huge map of Malaya in the operations room, like croupiers raking up chips in a casino.

The Battle Box reaches a theatrical climax in the conference room, where more life-sized figures act out the debate that convinced Lieutenant-General Arthur Percival that surrender was the only option open to him.

River Valley Road

Fort Canning Park's southern boundary is defined by **River Valley Road**, which skirts below the park from Hill Street. At its eastern end is the **MICA**

Building – formerly the Hill Street Police Station, but now home to the Ministry of Information, Communications and the Arts. The MICA Building's rows of shuttered windows are painted a rainbow of colours, making it a vibrant addition to the riverfront area; its central atrium houses several galleries majoring in Asian artworks. Further west, **River Valley** sweeps past **Clarke Quay**, a chain of nineteenth-century godowns, or warehouses, renovated into a shopping and eating complex. Unless a mooted makeover is successful, nearby Boat Quay (see p.85) will remain the better bet for evening drinks and fine dining. Clarke Quay's problem is that it touts itself as a riverside dining experience, yet its geography means that most of its outlets have no sightline of the water. The mushroomy rain canopies that have recently sprouted, and the gaudy banquette-style seating that have been laid out along the riverside, have done nothing to help the ambience. The arrival of *Hooters* bar and the topless shows at *Crazy Horse* nightclub hint at a more adult-oriented future for Clarke Quay. **GMAX**, Singapore's first ever bungee jump (Mon–Fri 3pm–12am, Sat & Sun noon–12am, $50 per ride; ☎63381146; ⊛www.gmax.com.sg) is probably best sampled before, rather than after, you settle into one of Clarke Quay's many bars and restaurants. River taxis for Clarke Quay (daily 11am–11pm; $3–8) depart every five minutes from several quays further down the river (see p.43).

Robertson Quay, further inland from Clarke Quay, is extending the gentrifications of the Singapore River. Already, restaurants, bars and hotels are amassing beside its banks – though one or two pleasingly tumble-down godowns still survive, inland of Pulau Saigon Bridge.

The **Chettiar Hindu Temple** (daily 8am–noon & 5.30–8.30pm), to the west of Fort Canning Park, is the goal of every participant in Singapore's annual Thaipusam Festival (see p.178 and Festive Singapore colour insert). This large temple is dedicated to Lord Subramaniam and boasts a wonderful *gopuram*, or bank of sculpted gods and goddesses. Erected in 1984, it replaced a nineteenth-century temple built by Indian *chettiars* (moneylenders); inside, 48 glass panels etched with Hindu deities line the roof.

Orchard Road

t would be hard to conjure an image more opposed to the reality of modern-day **ORCHARD ROAD** than C.M. Turnbull's description of it during early colonial times as "a country lane lined with bamboo hedges and shrubbery, with trees meeting overhead for its whole length". One hundred years ago, a stroll down Orchard Road would have passed row upon row of nutmeg trees and would have been enjoyed in the company of strolling merchants taking their daily constitutionals, followed at a discreet distance by their trusty manservants. Today, Orchard Road is synonymous with **shopping** – indeed, tourist brochures refer to it as the "Fifth Avenue, the Regent Street, the Champs Elysées, the Via Veneto and the Ginza of Singapore". Huge malls selling everything you can imagine line the road, but don't expect shopping to be relaxing as hordes of dawdling Singaporeans and tourists from the numerous hotels along the road make browsing difficult. The road runs northwest from Fort Canning Hill and is served by three MRT stations: Orchard, Somerset and Dhoby Ghaut, of which Orchard is the most convenient for shopping expeditions.

The coming years will see Orchard Road morph into a more **tourist-oriented district** than it is now. Mindful that several of its older shopping centres are looking a little on the shabby side, the Singapore Tourism Board recently unveiled grand, $1.6bn plans to revamp the area into what it calls "a giant events stage … a dynamic, vibrant and vital urban centre for overseas visitors and locals".

Orchard Road does have one or two other diversions if you get tired of staring at CDs, watches and clothes. Near its eastern extent, the president of Singapore's abode – the **Istana Negara Singapura** – is open to the public a few times a year, and rows of houses that hark back to old Singapore flank Cuppage Road and Emerald Hill Road. And, way up beyond the westernmost point of the road, the **Singapore Botanic Gardens** make for a relaxing stroll in beautiful surroundings. On the whole, though, people really only come to Orchard Road in the daytime to shop and at night for a whole host of clubs and bars (see p.169 & p.170 for details).

Dhoby Ghaut to Emerald Hill

In the **Dhoby Ghaut** area, at the eastern tip of Orchard Road, Indian *dhobies*, or laundrymen, used to wash clothes in the Stamford Canal, which once ran along Orchard and Stamford roads. Those days are long gone, and today the area is ringed by shopping centres, though there is a remnant of old Singapore in the **Hotel Rendezvous**, on the corner of Selegie and Bras Basah roads, where the venerable *Rendezvous Restaurant* is once again cooking up its famous

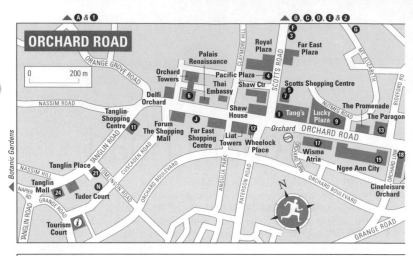

ACCOMMODATION

The Elizabeth	**G**	Metropolitan Y	**C**	YMCA International	
Garden Hotel	**B**	New Sandy's Place	**D**	House	**M**
Goodwood Park Hotel	**F**	The Regent Singapore	**N**	YWCA Fort Canning	
Hilton Singapore	**J**	Shangri-La Hotel	**A**	Lodge	**O**
Holiday Inn Park View	**H**	Singapore Marriott Hotel	**I**		
Lloyd's Inn	**P**	Sloane Court Hotel	**E**		
Meritus Mandarin Hotel	**L**	Hotel Supreme	**K**		

RESTAURANTS

Akashi	**11**
Bengawan Solo	**16**
Blu	**1**
Bombay Woodlands	**11**
Café Espresso	**3**
Crystal Jade	**5 & 19**
Cuppage Thai	**8**

curries (see p.160). Three minutes' walk west along Orchard Road from Dhoby Ghaut MRT takes you past Plaza Singapura, beyond which stern-looking soldiers guard the gate of the **Istana Negara Singapura**. Built in 1869, the istana, with its ornate cornices, elegant louvred shutters and high mansard roof, was originally the official residence of Singapore's British governors, though on independence it became the residence of the president of Singapore – currently S.R. Nathan, whose portrait you'll see in banks, post offices and shops across the state. The shuttered palace is only open to visitors on public holidays (free for locals but foreigners pay $1); the president goes walkabout at some point during every open day as thousands of Singaporeans flock to picnic on the well-landscaped lawns, and local brass bands belt out jaunty tunes. The changing of the guard ceremony at the istana takes place at 5.45pm on the first Sunday of the month (ⓦwww.istana.gov.sg/guard.html).

The **Tan Yeok Nee Mansion**, across Orchard Road from the Istana Negara Singapura at 207 Clemenceau Avenue, is now home to the Chicago Graduate School of Business. Built in traditional South Chinese style for a wealthy Teochew pepper and gambier (a resin used in tanning) merchant, and featuring ornate roofs and massive granite pillars, the mid-1880s mansion served as headquarters to the Singapore Salvation Army from 1940 until 1991.

Further west, in the **Emerald Hill** area of Orchard Road, most of Cuppage Road has been pedestrianized, making it a great place to sit out and have a beer or a meal. **Cuppage Terrace**, halfway along Cuppage Road on the left, is an unusually (for Orchard Road) old row of shophouses, where a burgeoning restaurant and bar scene has developed. A number of even more architecturally notable houses have also survived the developers' bulldozers in Emerald Hill Road, parallel to Cuppage Road. Emerald Hill was granted to Englishman William Cuppage in 1845 and for some years afterwards was the site of a large

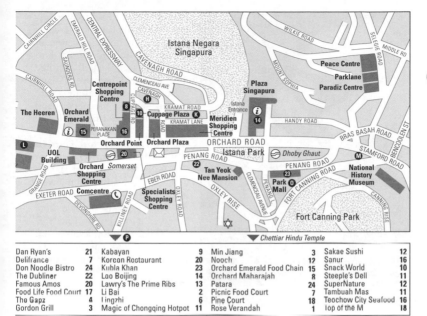

Dan Ryan's	21	Kabayan	9	Min Jiang	3	Sakae Sushi	12
Delifrance	7	Korean Restaurant	20	Nooch	12	Sanur	16
Don Noodle Bistro	24	Kublai Khan	23	Orchard Emerald Food Chain	15	Snack World	10
The Dubliner	22	Lao Beijing	14	Orchard Maharajah	8	Steeple's Deli	11
Famous Amos	20	Lawry's The Prime Ribs	13	Patara	24	SuperNature	12
Food Life Food Court	17	Li Bai	2	Picnic Food Court	7	Tambuah Mas	11
The Gapz	4	Lingzhi	6	Pine Court	18	Teochow City Seafood	16
Gordon Grill	3	Magic of Chongqing Hotpot	11	Rose Verandah	1	Top of the M	18

nutmeg plantation. After Cuppage's death in 1872, the land was subdivided and sold off, much of it bought by members of the **Peranakan** community, which evolved in Malaya as a result of the intermarriage between early Chinese settlers and Malay women. A walk up Emerald Hill Road takes you past a number of exquisitely crafted houses dating from this period, built in a decorative architectural style known as Chinese Baroque, typified by highly coloured ceramic tiles, carved swing doors, shuttered windows and pastel-shaded walls with fine plaster mouldings.

West to the Botanic Gardens

West of Emerald Hill Road, the shopping centres of Orchard Road come thick and fast. A couple of minutes north of Orchard Road along Scotts Road, the impressive **Goodwood Park Hotel** started life in 1900 as the *Teutonia Club* for German expats. With the start of war across Europe in 1914, the club was commandeered by the British Custodian of Enemy Property, and it didn't open again until 1918, after which it served for several years as a function hall. In 1929, it became a hotel, though by 1942 the *Goodwood* – like *Raffles* – was lodging Japanese officers. It was fitting that after the war, the hotel was chosen as one of the venues for a war crimes court.

After a few hours' shopping you'll be glad of the open space afforded by the **Singapore Botanic Gardens** (daily 5am–midnight), a ten-minute walk beyond the western end of Orchard Road on Cluny Road. Founded in 1859, it was here, in 1877, that the Brazilian seeds from which grew the great **rubber plantations** of Malaysia were first nurtured. No one had taken much notice of them by the time Henry Ridley was named director of the Botanic Gardens the following year, but he recognized their financial potential and spent the next

△ Sculpture in the Botanic Gardens

twenty years of his life persuading Malayan plantation-owners to convert to this new crop, an occupation which earned him the nickname "Mad" Ridley. The fifty-odd hectares of land feature a mini-jungle rose garden, topiary, fernery, palm valley and lakes that are home to turtles and swans. There's also the **National Orchid Garden** (daily 8.30am–7pm; $5, children $1) with one thousand species and 2,000 hybrids; orchid jewellery, made by plating real flowers with gold, is on sale here – pieces start from around $35. At dawn and dusk, joggers and students of t'ai chi haunt the lawns and paths of the gardens, while at the weekend, newly-weds bundle down from church for their photos to be taken – a ritual recalled in Lee Tzu Pheng's poem *Bridal Party at the Botanics*, whose bride's "two hundred dollar face/is melting in the sun", while beside her is her groom, "black-stuffed, oil-slicked, fainting/in his finery, by the shrubbery". You can pick up a free **map** of the grounds at the ranger's office, a little to the right of the main gate.

Chinatown and the Central Business District

T he two square kilometres of **Chinatown** once constituted the focal point of Chinese life and culture in Singapore. Nowadays, the area is on its last traditional legs, scarred by demolition and dwarfed by the skyscrapers of the financial **Central Business District**, where the island's city slickers oversee the machinations of one of Asia's most dynamic money markets. Even so, a wander through the surviving nineteenth-century streets still unearths musty and atmospheric temples, traditional craft shops, clan associations and old style coffee shops and restaurants. Provision stores crammed with birds' nests, dried cuttlefish, ginger, chillies, mushrooms and salted fish do a brisk trade, and you might hear the rattle of a game of mahjong being played. Chinatown is bounded by New Bridge Road to the west, Neil and Maxwell roads to the south and Cecil Street to the east, while to the north, the Singapore River snakes west and inland passing the last few surviving godowns from Singapore's original trade boom.

Chinatown

The area now known as **CHINATOWN** was earmarked for settlement by the Chinese community by Sir Stamford Raffles himself, who decided in June 1819 that the ethnic communities should live separately. As increasing numbers of **immigrants** poured into Singapore, Chinatown became just that – a Chinese town, where new arrivals from the mainland, mostly from the Canton and Fujian provinces, would have been pleased to find temples, shops and, most importantly, clan associations (*kongsi*), which helped them to find food, lodgings and work, mainly as small traders and coolies. The prevalent architectural form was the **shophouse**, a shuttered building with a moulded facade fronting living rooms upstairs and a shop on the ground floor. The three-day Verandah Riots of

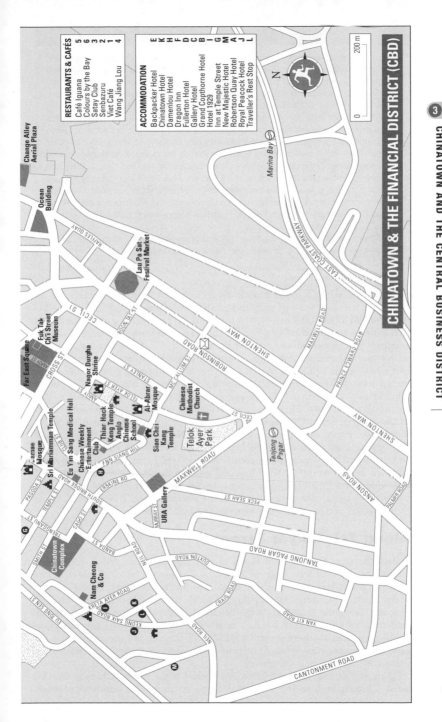

CHINATOWN & THE FINANCIAL DISTRICT (CBD)

RESTAURANTS & CAFÉS

Café Iguana	5
Colours by the Bay	6
Satay Club	3
Senbazuru	2
Viet Café	1
Wang Jiang Lou	4

ACCOMMODATION

Backpacker Hotel	E
Chinatown Hotel	K
Damenlou Hotel	H
Dragon Inn	F
Fullerton Hotel	D
Gallery Hotel	C
Grand Copthorne Hotel	B
Hotel 1929	I
Inn at Temple Street	G
New Majestic Hotel	M
Robertson Quay Hotel	A
Royal Peacock Hotel	J
Traveller's Rest Stop	L

Songbirds

One of the most enduringly popular of Singaporean hobbies is the keeping and training of **songbirds**. Every Sunday morning scores of enthusiasts and their birds congregate at an unnamed nondescript coffee shop on the corner of Tiong Bahru and Seng Poh roads, just west of Chinatown. Songbird competitions are commonplace in Singapore, but this gathering is an informal affair with bird owners coming to show off their pets and admire those of fellow collectors. The **exquisite cages** that house the birds are hung on a metal frame that fronts the coffee shop. Birds are grouped according to their breed, lest they pick up the distinctive songs of other breeds. The various breeds of bird you'll see include the delicate green mata puteh, or "white eye bird", the jambul, with its showy black crest and red eye patches, and the sharma, with beautiful long tail feathers. You can have toast and coffee at the café while watching and listening to the proceedings, which start around 6am – a good early morning start to a tour around nearby Chinatown. Bus #851 travels along North Bridge Road and past Outram Park MRT station before which passing along Tiong Bahru Road; otherwise, hop in a cab.

Another central Sunday songbird venue is Sturdee Road, off Petain Road, which lies between Serangoon Road and Jalan Besar in Little India.

1888 erupted when colonial administrators ordered Chinatown's merchants to clear their five-foot ways of stalls and produce to enable pedestrians to pass by.

By the mid-twentieth century, the area southwest of the Singapore River was rich with the imported cultural heritage of China, but with independence came ambition. The government regarded the tumbledown slums of Chinatown as an eyesore and embarked upon a catastrophic **redevelopment** campaign that saw whole roads bulldozed to make way for new shopping centres, and street traders relocated into organized complexes. Only in the last decade has public opinion finally convinced the Singaporean authorities to restore rather than redevelop Chinatown. There are some renovated buildings that remain faithful to the original designs, though there's a tendency to render once characterful shophouses improbably perfect. The latest problem to threaten the fabric of Chinatown is spiralling rents, which have driven out all but a last few families, and traditional businesses like medicine shops, bakers, *popiah* skin makers (*popiah* skins are the soft wrappings used to make spring rolls), leaving the area open for full exploitation by bistros, advertising agencies and souvenir shops. Ironically, if you want to get a taste of the old ways of Chinatown, you'll need to spurn its central streets and head into the surrounding housing blocks.

Along Telok Ayer Street

Follow the signs for Maxwell Road out of Tanjong Pagar MRT and you'll surface on the southern edge of Chinatown. Cross Maxwell Road and cut through Telok Ayer Park and you'll quickly hit **Telok Ayer Street**, whose Malay name – meaning "Watery Bay" – recalls a time when the street would have run along the shoreline of the Straits of Singapore. Nowadays, thanks to land reclamation, it's no closer to a beach than is Beach Road, but alongside the shops and stores there are still a number of temples and mosques that have survived from the time when immigrants and sailors stepping ashore wanted to thank the gods for their safe passage.

Facing you as you approach Telok Ayer Street is the square **Chinese Methodist Church**, built in 1889, whose design – portholes and windows adorned

CHINATOWN RESTAURANTS

0   200 m

RESTAURANTS

Ann Siang 5	21
Ban Seng	1
Bee Heong	23
Belachan	16
Beng Thin Hoon Kee	3
Beng Hiang	12
Beppu Menkan	6
China Square Food Centre	10
Chinese Opera Teahouse	19
Da Paolo Il Ristorante	17
Gorkha Grill	18
Happy Realm	20
Hillman	24
Indochine	15
Jing	2
Mouth	4
Old Shanghai	8
Soup	14
Spinelli	9
Spizza	13
Starbucks	3
Swee Kee	22
Tan Hock Seng Cake Shop	11
Ya Kun Kaya Toast	5
Yum Cha	7

N

with white crosses and capped by a Chinese pagoda-style roof – is a pleasing blend of East and West. The Muslim faith holds sway a short walk up the street and beyond McCallum Street, where the simple lines of the sky-blue **Al-Abrar Mosque** mark the spot where Chulia worshippers from the coast of southern India first set up a thatched *kuchu palli* (in Tamil, "small mosque"), in 1827.

Thian Hock Keng Temple

Further up, the enormous **Thian Hock Keng Temple** (Temple of Heavenly Happiness) is a hugely impressive Hokkien building and sprucer than ever after a recent makeover. Built on the site of a small joss house where immigrants made offerings to Ma Chu Por (or Tian Hou), the queen of heaven, the temple was started in 1839 using materials imported from China. By the time the temple was finished in 1842 a statue of the goddess had been shipped in from southern China, and this still stands in the centre of the temple's main hall, flanked by the god of war on the right and the protector of life on the left. From the street, the temple looks spectacular: dragons stalk its broad roofs, while the entrance to the temple compound bristles with ceramic flowers, foliage and figures. Two stone lions stand guard at the entrance, and door gods, painted on the front doors, prevent evil spirits from entering. Look out for the huge ovens, always lit, in which offerings to gods and ancestors are burnt.

It's a testament to Singapore's multicultural nature that Thian Hock Keng's next-door neighbour should be the **Nagore Durgha shrine**, built in the 1820s by Chulias from southern India as a shrine to the ascetic, Shahul Hamid of Nagore. The shrine's tiered minarets, onion domes and Islamic facades have long been in a state of disrepair, but ongoing renovation works are rectifying this slowly. **Telok Ayer Green**, a tranquil, paved garden dotted with life-sized metal statues depicting the area's earliest settlers, separates temple and shrine.

Amoy Street

A block west of Telok Ayer Street is **Amoy Street**, which – together with China and Telok Ayer streets – was designated as a Hokkien enclave in the colony's

△ Worshipper at the Thian Hock Keng Temple

early days. Long terraces of shophouses flank the street, all featuring characteristic **five-foot ways**, or covered verandahs, so called simply because they jut five feet out from the house. A few of the shophouses are in a ramshackle state, but most have been marvellously renovated and bought up by companies in need of some fancy office space. It's worth walking down to mustard-coloured **Sian Chai Kang Temple**, at 66 Amoy Street. Below the fiery dragons on its roof, it's a musty, open-fronted place dominated by huge urns, full to the brim with ash from untold numbers of burned incense sticks. Guarding the temple are two carved stone lions whose fancy red neck ribbons are said to attract good fortune and prosperity.

The shophouse just beyond the temple and across the path up to Ann Siang Hill Park, at no.70, was the first home of the Singapore's **Anglo-Chinese School**, which opened in 1886 when Reverend William Oldham, Singapore's first missionary, began teaching thirteen sons of Chinese businessmen.

Far East Square and around

North of Cross Street, Amoy Street strikes into the heart of **Far East Square**, a shopping-cum-dining centre which taps Chinatown's heritage for its inspiration, and which boasts the **Fuk Tak Ch'i Street Museum** (daily 10am–10pm; free) as its party piece. It's the surest sign yet of the gentrification of Chinatown that one of its oldest temples has had to suffer the ignominy of being turned into a tourist attraction – and a fairly dull one at that. The **Fuk Tak Ch'i Temple** was established by Singapore's Hakka and Cantonese communities in 1824. The temple has scrubbed up nicely – too nicely, in fact: none of the musty ambience that once made it such an interesting and atmospheric place has survived its $200,000 renovation. A model junk of the kind that would have brought across Singapore's earliest Chinese settlers sits on what used to be the temple's main altar. Elsewhere, you'll see odds and sods – opium pillows and pipes, Peranakan jewellery, an instrument once used by food hawkers to drum up trade from old Singapore, though the most arresting exhibit is a diorama depicting how Telok Ayer would have appeared when it was still a waterfront street in the nineteenth century. The recent addition of tables and chairs means you can now take Chinese tea in the temple, but you'd be better advised to head for nearby **Ya Kun** (see p.145) for a cup of strong, sweet coffee and a plate of melt-in-the-mouth kaya toast.

Wak Hai Cheng Bio Temple

Just north of Far East Square, an ugly concrete courtyard, crisscrossed by a web of ropes supporting numerous spiralled incense sticks, fronts the **Wak Hai Cheng Bio Temple** on Philip Street. Its name means "Temple of the Calm Sea", which made it a logical choice for early worshippers who had arrived safely in Singapore; an effigy of Tian Hou, the queen of heaven and protector of seafarers, is housed in the temple's right-hand chamber. This temple, too, has an incredibly ornate roof, crammed with tiny models of Chinese village scenes. The temple cat meanders across here sometimes, dwarfing the tableaux like a creature from a Godzilla movie.

China Street and Club Street

Far East Square has subsumed **China Street** and its offshoots, meaning another slice of residential Chinatown has been lost forever. To get a flavour of the old ways that survived in these streets until the turn of the millennium you'll have to push on across South Bridge Road into the **Hong Lim Complex**, a modern housing estate where old men in white T-shirts and striped pyjama trousers sit chewing the cud in walkways lined with medical halls, chop makers, and stores selling birds' nests, pork floss, dried mushrooms and gold jewellery.

At the southern end of China Street is steep **Club Street**, once noted for its temple-carving shops, though these too have now fallen to the demolition ball and been replaced by swish apartment blocks and swanky bars and restaurants. An impromptu **flea market** still takes place on the far side of the car park opposite, where traders squat on their haunches surrounded by catalogues, old coins, sleeveless records and phone cards.

Even the **clan associations** and **guilds** that gave Club Street its name are fast disappearing, though there are still a few to be seen, higher up the hill. These are easy to spot; black-and-white photos of old members cover the walls, and behind the screens that almost invariably span the doorway, old men sit and chat. From upstairs, the clacking sound of mahjong tiles reaches the street. Most notable of all, is the **Chinese Weekly Entertainment Club**, at no.76 - flanked by roaring lion heads, it's an imposing, 1891-built mansion that was established by a Peranakan millionaire.

Along South Bridge Road

South Bridge Road, stretching all the way from the Elgin Bridge to Tanjong Pagar, is Chinatown's backbone. During the Japanese occupation roadblocks were set up at the point where South Bridge meets Cross Street, and Singaporeans were vetted at an interrogation post for signs of anti-Japanese feeling in the infamous Sook Ching campaign (see p.203). Those whose answers failed to satisfy the guards and their hooded local informants either ended up as POWs or were never seen again. Today, South Bridge Road is fast becoming antiques-central, as more and more of the numerous dingy shops that line it are spruced up and turned into Asian arts curiosity shops.

Eu Yan Sang Medical Hall

The beautifully renovated **Eu Yan Sang Medical Hall** (Mon–Sat 8.30am–6pm), at 267–271 South Bridge Road, offers a great introduction to traditional Chinese medicines. First opened in 1910, the shop is partially geared to the tourist trade – some of the staff speak good English. It smells a little like a compost heap on a hot day and there is a weird assortment of ingredients on the shelves, which to the uninitiated look more likely to kill than cure. Besides the usual herbs and roots favoured by the Chinese are various dubious remedies derived from exotic and endangered species. Blood circulation problems and external injuries are eased with centipedes and insects crushed into a "rubbing liquor", the ground-up gall bladders of snakes or bears apparently work wonders on pimples, monkey's gallstones aid asthmatics, and deer penis is supposed to provide a lift to any sexual problem. Antlers, sea horses, scorpions and turtle shells also feature regularly in Chinese prescriptions, though the greatest cure-all of Oriental medicine is said to be **ginseng**, a clever little root that will combat anything from weakness of the heart to acne and jet lag. If you need a pick-me-up, or are just curious, the shop administers free cups of ginseng tea.

Above the hall is the small but engaging **Birds Nest Gallery** (Mon–Sat 10am–5.30pm; $5), which casts light on the history, harvesting and processing of this most famous of Chinese delicacies, which can command prices to its weight in gold. Birds' nests emerged as a prized supplement among China's royal and noble classes during the Ming Dynasty, and today they are still valued

∧ Medical Hall, Chinatown

for their high glycoprotein, calcium, iron and vitamin B1 content, and for their efficacy in boosting the immune system and curing bronchial ailments. Produced by swiftlets in the limestone and coastal caves of Southeast Asia, birds' nests are a mixture of saliva, moss and grass. It's the painstaking process of picking out this moss and grass by hand that makes the product so expensive – that, and the slow and precarious business of initial harvesting. A screen presentation in English shows nest harvesters or "spidermen" scaling bamboo poles as long as 25 metres in the caves of Borneo, with only the torches attached to the poles to guide them. To visit the gallery, ask a member of staff in Eu Yan Sang.

The egg tarts, walnut cookies, buns and other Chinese cakes at the Tong Heng Chinese pastry shop just up the road at 285 South Bridge Road offer a great way to top up your blood-sugar level before pressing on to further sights.

Sri Mariamman Hindu Temple and the Jamae Mosque

Opposite the Eu Yan Sang Medical Hall on South Bridge Road, the compound of the **Sri Mariamman Hindu Temple** bursts with primary-coloured, wild-looking statues of deities and animals. There's always some ritual or other being attended to by one of the temple's priests, drafted in from the subcontinent and dressed in simple loincloths. A wood-and-atap hut was erected on this site in 1827, on land belonging to Naraina Pillay – a government clerk who arrived in Singapore on the same ship as Stamford Raffles. The present temple was completed in 1843 and boasts a superb *gopuram* over the front entrance. Once inside the temple, look up at the roof and you'll see splendidly vivid friezes depicting a host of Hindu deities, including the three manifestations of the supreme being: Brahma the Creator (with three of his four heads showing), Vishnu the Preserver, and Shiva the Destroyer (holding one of his sons). The main sanctum, facing you as you walk inside, is devoted to Goddess Mariamman, who's worshipped for her power to cure diseases. Smaller sanctums dotted about the open walkway which runs round the temple honour a host of other deities. In the one dedicated to Goddess Periachi Amman, a sculpture portrays her with a queen lying on her lap, whose evil child she has ripped from her womb. Odd, then, that the Periachi Amman should be the protector of children, to whom one-month-old babies are brought. Sri Aravan, with his bushy moustache and big ears, is far less intimidating. His sanctum is at the back on the right-hand side of the complex.

To the left of the main sanctum there's a patch of sand which, once a year during the festival of **Thimithi** (see p.179), is covered in red-hot coals, across which male Hindus run to prove the strength of their faith. The participants, who line up all the way along South Bridge Road waiting their turn, are supposedly protected from the heat of the coals by the power of prayer, though the ambulance parked round the back of the temple suggests that some aren't praying quite hard enough.

Hanging a left out of the temple quickly brings you to the twin octagonal minarets of the **Jamae Mosque**, at 218 Southbridge Road. Established by southern Indian Muslims in 1826, the mosque has barely changed since it was completed four years later.

The URA Gallery

A skip around the **URA Gallery** (Mon–Fri 9am–4.30pm, Sat 9am–12.30pm, free; ☎63218321, ⊚www.ura.gov.sg) at the URA Centre, set back from South Bridge Road at 45 Maxwell Road, offers a fascinating insight into the grand designs of Singapore's Urban Redevelopment Authority. Town planning may not sound the most inspiring premise for a gallery; but, then again, no other nation plans with such extravagant ambition as Singapore, whose land architects continue to remould their island like a ball of putty, erasing roads here and reclaiming land there. You need only consider the distance between downtown Beach Road and the shoreline it used to abut, to appreciate the extent of change that Singapore has undergone up to now. At the URA Gallery, you can view the blueprint for the island's future.

Interactive exhibits, touch-screen terminals and scale models trace Singapore's progress from sleepy backwater to modern metropolis and chart ongoing efforts to reshape and redefine specific regions of the island. The URA has rightly been criticized in the past for its disregard for Singapore's architectural heritage, so it is heartening to see displays making such reassuring noises about the future of the venerable shophouses and colonial villas that remain in such districts as Balestier Road, Tanjong Katong and Joo Chiat. But the gallery's emphasis is more upon the future than the past. A vast model of the downtown area of Singapore – which highlights districts currently under development and offers new arrivals to the island the chance to get their bearings – is best scrutinized through one of the telescopes set up on the floor above. Elsewhere on the upper floor, there is the chance to control a sky cam high above the city, try your hand at a little municipal planning and learn more about Singapore's state-of-the-art MRT system.

Tanjong Pagar

The district of **Tanjong Pagar** at the southern tip of South Bridge Road, between Neil and Keong Saik roads, has changed beyond recognition in recent years. Once a veritable sewer of brothels and opium dens, it was earmarked as a conservation area, following which over two hundred shophouses were painstakingly restored, painted in sickly pastel hues and converted into bars, restaurants and shops. The emergence of other entertainment hubs such as Boat Quay and CHIJMES has seen the area's star wane in the new

Taking Chinese tea

If you're in need of a quick, thirst-quenching drink, avoid **Chinese teahouses**: the art of tea-making is heavily bound up with **ritual**, and unhurried preparation time is crucial to the production of a pleasing brew. What's more, when you do get a cup, it's barely more than a mouthful and then the whole process kicks off again.

Tea-drinking in China traces its origins back thousands of years. Legend has it that the first cuppa was drunk by Emperor Shen Nong, who was pleasantly surprised by the aroma produced by some dried tea leaves falling into the water he was boiling. He was even more pleased when he tasted the brew. By the eighth century, the art form was so complex that Chinese scholar Lu Yu produced a three-volume tome on the processes involved.

Teashops normally have conventional tables and chairs but the authentic experience involves kneeling at a much lower traditional table. The basic procedure is as follows: the server places a towel in front of himself and his guest, with the folded edge facing the guest, and stuffs leaves into the pot with a bamboo scoop. Water, boiled over a flame, has to reach an optimum temperature, depending on which type of tea is being made; experts can tell its heat by the size of the bubbles rising, which are described, rather confusingly, as "sand eyes", "prawn eyes" and "fish eyes". Once the pot has been warmed inside and out, the first pot of tea is made, transferred into the pouring jar and then, frustratingly, poured back *over* the pot – the thinking being that over a period of time, the porous clay of the pot becomes infused with the fragrance of the tea. Once a second pot is ready, a draught is poured into the **sniffing cup**, from which the aroma of the brew is savoured. Only now is it time actually to drink the tea and, if you want a second cup, the whole procedure has to start again.

Millennium, though there are plans – as the URA Gallery will attest – to reinvent it and bring back the revellers. Curiously, Tanjong Pagar Road is now the site of many bridal shops.

While touring Tanjong Pagar, it's worth making time for a stop at one of the traditional **teahouses** along Neil Road. At *Tea Chapter* at no. 9a–11a (daily 11am–11pm), you can have tea in the very chair in which Queen Elizabeth sat when she visited in 1989; the shop is plastered with photographs of the occasion. The Chinese take tea drinking very seriously. Buy a bag of tea here and one of the staff will teach you all the attached rituals (see box above); 100g bags cost from $5 to over $65 and tea sets are also on sale, though they don't come cheap.

Sago Street to Mosque Street

Today, the tight knot of streets west of South Bridge Road between Sago Street and Mosque Street is tour-bus Chinatown, heaving with gangs of holidaymakers plundering souvenir shops. But in days gone by these streets formed Chinatown's nucleus, their shophouses harbouring opium dens and brothels, their streets teeming with trishaw drivers, peddlers and food hawkers. From the upper windows of tumbledown shophouses, wizened old men in white T-shirts and striped pyjama trousers would stare out from behind wooden gates, flanked by songbird cages and laundry poles hung with washing.

Until as recently as the 1950s, **Sago Street** was home to several death houses – rudimentary hospices where skeletal citizens saw out their final hours on rattan camp beds. These houses were finally deemed indecent and have all now gone, to be replaced by restaurants, bakeries, medicine halls and shops stacked to the rafters with Chinese vases, teapots and jade. Sago, Smith, Temple and Pagoda

△ Paper cars for the next life

streets only really recapture their youth around the time of Chinese New Year, when they're crammed to bursting with stalls selling festive branches of blossom, oranges, sausages and waxed chickens – which look as if they have melted to reveal a handful of bones inside.

Sago Street skirts to the right of the Chinatown Complex, and its name changes to Trengganu Street. Despite the hordes of tourists, and the shops selling Singapore Airlines uniforms, presentation chopstick sets and silk hats with false pigtails, there are occasional glimpses of Chinatown's **old trades** and industries, such as Nam's Supplies at 22 Smith Street, which offers shirts, Rolex watches, Nokia mobile phones, money, laptops and passports – all made out of paper – which the Chinese burn to ensure their ancestors don't want for creature comforts in the next life. They even have "Otherworld Bank" credit cards, "Hell Airlines" air tickets and "Hell City" cigarettes. Nam Cheong and Co, off nearby Kreta Ayer Street, takes this industry to its logical conclusion, producing huge paper houses and near life-sized paper safes, servants and Mercedes for the self-respecting ghost about town; the shop is at 01-04 Block, 334 Keong Saik Road, between Chinatown Complex and New Bridge Road.

The Chinatown Complex

The hideous concrete exterior of the **Chinatown Complex**, at the end of Sago Street, belies the charm of the teeming market it houses. Walk up the front steps, past the garlic, fruit and nut hawkers, and once you're inside, the market's many twists and turns reveal stalls selling silk, kimonos, rattan, leather, jade, tea, Buddhist paraphernalia and clothes. There are no fixed prices, so you'll need to haggle. Deep in the market's belly is shop 01-K3, selling Buddhist amulets; while the Capitol Plastics stall (01-16) specializes in **mahjong sets**. There's a food centre on the second floor, and the wet market within the complex gets pretty packed early in the morning, when locals come to buy fresh fish or meat. Here, abacuses are still used to tally bills and sugar canes lean like spears against the wall.

The Chinatown Heritage Centre

Many of Chinatown's links with its cultural and mercantile history have been erased, but at least the excellent **Chinatown Heritage Centre** (daily 10am–7pm; adults $8, children $4.80), at 48 Pagoda Street, offers a window on the district's past. If you go to just one museum in Singapore, this should be it. Housed in three superbly restored shophouses, the centre is an invaluable social document, where the history, culture, pastimes and employments of Singapore's Chinese settlers spring vividly to life. The museum is crammed to bursting with displays, artefacts and information boards; but its masterstroke is to give voice to former local residents, whose first-hand accounts of Chinatown life, projected onto walls at every turn, form a unique oral history of the Chinese in Singapore.

A model junk, like those on which early immigrants ("singkehs") came in search of work, sets the scene at the start of the tour. Accounts on the wall tell the story of their perilous journeys across the South China Sea. Once ashore at Bullock Cart Water (the name they gave the area that would become Chinatown), settlers quickly formed clan associations, or less savoury secret societies, and looked for employment. As you move through the centre's narrow shophouse corridors, these associations and societies, and every other facet of Chinatown life, work and leisure, are made flesh. All the while, you progress to a soundtrack of crashing gongs and cymbals, age-old songs of mourning and Fifties' crooners on scratchy 78s.

The genius of the centre lies in its detail, from the mock-up of the shabby flourishes of a prostitute's boudoir, and the marble table of a traditional coffee shop, to the pictures and footage of thin and haunted addicts seeking escape from the pain of their backbreaking work through opium, their "devastating master". Among the many artefacts, look out for an example of an original hawker stall – a charcoal burner and a collection of ingredients yoked over the shoulders and carried from street to street, and a million miles away from the air-con luxury of today's incarnations. Look out, too, for the section focus-ing upon the death houses of Sago Street, where the sick and old went to die. Trishaw riders collecting the dead would, one Chinatown veteran recounts, "put a hat on the corpse, put it onto the trishaw, and cycle all the way back to the coffin shop".

The tour climaxes with a superb re-creation of the unbearable living quarters that settlers endured in the shophouses of Chinatown. Landlords were known to shoe-horn as many as forty tenants into a single floor; their cramped cubicles, cooking and bath-ing facilities are reproduced in all their grisly squalor. (Plumbing was non-existent in these times. One former resident tells of an occasion when a tenant knocked a full bucket of human waste down a staircase, and was forced to burn incense for ages afterwards, to

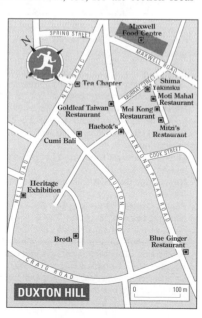

mask the stench.) The absence of the cooling effect of any air-con goes some way towards conveying the stifling heat that residents daily suffered.

Back on the ground floor is a tailor's shop, the mercantile element of the shophouse. Beside that, a traditional *kopi tiam*, featuring old metal signs advertising Horlicks, Brylcreem, and huge biscuit boxes on the counter, is a good place to grab a coffee and reflect on what you've seen. There are sometimes walking tours of Chinatown based out of the centre; call ☏63252878 for more details.

New Bridge Road and Eu Tong Sen Street

Chinatown's main shopping drag comprises southbound **New Bridge Road** and northbound **Eu Tong Sen Street**, along which are found a handful of large malls (see box below). Try to pop into one of the *bak kwa* barbecue pork vendors around the intersection of Pagoda Street and New Bridge Road – the squares of red, fatty, delicious meat that they cook on wire meshes over fires produce an odour that is pure Chinatown. As you eat your *bak kwa*, check out two striking buildings across the road. Nearest is the flat-fronted **Majestic Opera house**, which no longer hosts performances but still boasts five images of Chinese opera stars over its doors. Just beside it, the Yue Hwa Chinese Products Emporium occupies the former **Great Southern Hotel**, which was built in 1927 by Eu Tong Sen, the son of Eu Yan Sang. In its fifth floor nightclub, *Southern Cabaret*, wealthy locals would drink liquor, smoke opium and pay to dance with so-called local "taxi girls".

The **Thong Chai Medical Institute** has been sited at the top of Eu Tong Sen Street since 1892, when it first opened its doors with the avowed intention of dispensing free medical help regardless of race, colour or creed. Listed as a national monument, this beautiful southern Chinese-style building has recently been transformed into a bar-restaurant complex (see p.156) whose decor is thankfully sympathetic to the wonderful serpentine gables and wooden inscribed pillars.

Shopping in Chinatown

As well as the markets and stores covered in the text, look out for the following, all either on or near to New Bridge Road and Eu Tong Sen Street. Opening hours are generally 10am–9.30pm.

Chinatown Point 133 New Bridge Rd. One of its two buildings houses bright, fashionable, Orchard Road-style shop units; the other is a handicraft centre, with scores of tourist-oriented businesses.

Hong Lim Complex 531–531a Upper Cross St. Several Chinese provisions stores, fronted by sackfuls of dried mushrooms, cuttlefish, chillies, garlic cloves, onions, fritters and crackers. Other shops sell products ranging from acupuncture accessories to birds' nests.

Lucky Chinatown Complex 11 New Bridge Rd. Fairly upmarket place with lots of jewellery shops.

New Bridge Centre 336 Smith St. The Da You Department Store (second floor) sells Chinese religious artefacts, tea sets and crockery.

Pearl's Centre 100 Eu Tong Sen St. A centre for Chinese medicine. Sinchong Traditional Medicine at 03-19 and TCM Chinese Medicines at 02-20 both have a Chinese clinic, where a consultation will cost you $5.

People's Park Centre 101 Upper Cross St. Stall-like shop units selling Chinese handicrafts, CDs, electronics, jade and gold.

People's Park Complex 1 Park Rd. The Overseas Emporium is at 02-70 and sells Chinese instruments, calligraphy pens, lacquer work and jade. Cobblers set up stall in the courtyard beside the complex, behind which is a market and food centre.

The Central Business District

Until an early exercise in land reclamation in the mid-1820s rendered the zone fit for building, the patch of land south of the river where Raffles Place now stands was a swampland. However, within just a few years, Commercial Square (later renamed Raffles Place) was the colony's busiest business address, boasting the banks, ship's chandlers and warehouses of a burgeoning trading port. The square now forms the nucleus of the **CENTRAL BUSINESS DISTRICT** the commercial heart of the state, home to many of its banks and financial institutions. Cutting through the district is **Battery Road**, whose name recalls the days when Fort Fullerton (named after Robert Fullerton, first governor of the Straits Settlements) and its attendant battery of guns used to stand on the site of the Fullerton Building.

Raffles Place and the south riverbank

Raffles Place was Singapore's central shopping area until Orchard Road superseded it in the late 1960s. Two department stores, Robinsons and John Little, dominated the area then, but subsequent development turned it into the centre of Singapore's financial epicentre, ringed by buildings so tall that pedestrians crossing the square feel like ants in a canyon. The most striking way to experience the giddy heights of the Central Business District is by surfacing from Raffles Place MRT, following the signs for Raffles Place itself out of the station,

The Barings Bank scandal

Singapore hit the international headlines early in 1995, when the City of London's oldest merchant bank, **Barings**, collapsed as a result of what the London *Evening Standard* called "massive unauthorized dealings" in derivatives on the Japanese stock market. The supposed culprit – "the man who broke the bank", as the press dubbed him – was named as Nick Leeson, an Englishman dealing out of the bank's offices in the Central Business District of Singapore. Leeson, it was alleged, had gambled huge funds in the hope of recouping losses made through ill-judged trading, only calling it a day when the bank's losses were approaching one billion pounds. One of his colleagues claimed that Leeson made "other fraudsters look like Walt Disney", although many have questioned the quality of Barings' management and financial controls, which allowed such a catastrophe to happen.

By the time the scandal broke, Leeson was missing, and a pan-Southeast Asian search was in full swing when he finally turned up and was promptly arrested – six days later in Frankfurt. News of his capture was greeted with cheers from dealers in the Singapore Stock Exchange when it flashed across their screens. In the weeks that followed, Dutch bank ING bought out Barings for one pound sterling, while Nick Leeson languished in a Frankfurt jail. In time, Singapore's application for extradition was duly granted, and less than two weeks after being passed into Singaporean custody, on December 2, 1995, the rogue trader pleaded guilty to two charges of deceit, and received a six-and-a-half-year sentence, three and a half years of which he served out in Tamah Merah Prison. While inside, Leeson was divorced from his wife, and diagnosed with cancer of the colon. In 1999, the movie *Rogue Trader* was released with Ewan McGregor playing the part of Leeson.

The new millennium has been kinder to Leeson than the last one. Since returning to the UK, he has fully recovered from cancer, gained a psychology degree, remarried and forged a fresh career on the after-dinner speaking circuit.

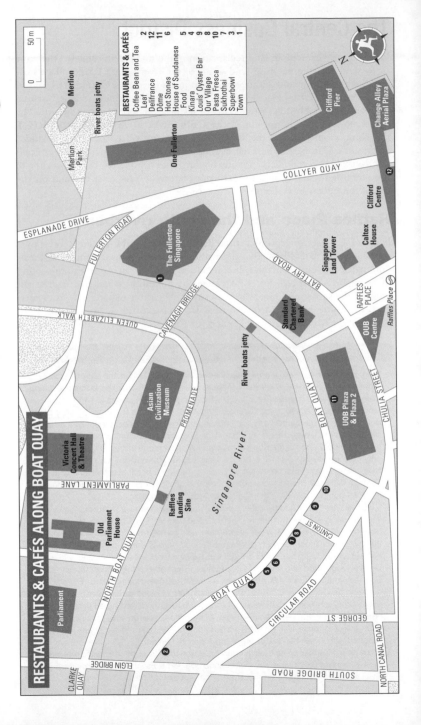

RESTAURANTS & CAFÉS ALONG BOAT QUAY

RESTAURANTS & CAFÉS

Coffee Bean and Tea Leaf	2
Delifrance	12
Dôme	11
Hot Stones	6
House of Sundanese Food	5
Kinara	4
Louis' Oyster Bar	9
Our Village	8
Pasta Fresca	10
Sukhothai	7
Superbowl	3
Town	1

Parliament

Old Parliament House

Victoria Concert Hall & Theatre

Asian Civilization Museum

Raffles Landing Site

Singapore River

The Fullerton Singapore

One Fullerton

Merlion Park

Merlion

River boats jetty

River boats jetty

Standard Chartered Bank

Clifford Pier

Change Alley Aerial Plaza

Clifford Centre

Caltex House

Singapore Land Tower

OUB Centre

Raffles Place

UOB Plaza & Plaza 2

CLARKE QUAY

ELGIN BRIDGE

NORTH BOAT QUAY

PARLIAMENT LANE

QUEEN ELIZABETH WALK

CAVENAGH BRIDGE

ESPLANADE DRIVE

FULLERTON ROAD

COLLYER QUAY

BATTERY ROAD

PROMENADE

BOAT QUAY

CIRCULAR ROAD

SOUTH BRIDGE ROAD

NORTH CANAL ROAD

GEORGE ST

CANTON ST

CHULA STREET

BOAT QUAY

RAFFLES PLACE

0   50 m

and looking up to gleaming towers, blue skies and racing clouds. To your left is the soaring metallic triangle of the **OUB Centre** (Overseas Union Bank), and to its right, the rocket-shaped **UOB Plaza 2** (United Overseas Bank); in front of you are the rich brown walls of the **Standard Chartered Bank**, and to your right rise sturdy **Singapore Land Tower** and the almost Art Deco **Caltex House**. A smallish statue, entitled *Progress and Advancement*, stands at the northern end of Raffles Place. Erected in 1988, it's a miniature version of what was then the skyline of central Singapore. Inevitably, the very progress and advancement it celebrates has already rendered it out of date – not featured, for instance, is the **UOB Plaza**, a vast monolith of a building only recently built beside its twin, the UOB Plaza 2. The three roads that run southwest from Raffles Place – Cecil Street, Robinson Road and Shenton Way – are all chock-a-block with more high-rise banks and financial houses; to the west is Chinatown.

Boat Quay

Just north of Raffles Place, and beneath the "elephant's trunk" curve of the Singapore River, the pedestrianized row of shophouses known as **Boat Quay** has enjoyed an upturn in fortunes. Derelict until the early 1990s, it's currently one of Singapore's most fashionable hangouts, sporting a huge collection of thriving restaurants and bars, and is an excellent spot for an alfresco meal or drink. There are those around the Singapore restaurant scene who think that the authorities aren't vetting tenants of Boat Quay's units rigorously enough, and that the area's charm is becoming diluted as a result. Certainly, some stretches of the quay are noisier than others, so it's worth taking a stroll before you pick a spot for dinner.

Around Raffles Place

Branching off the second floor of the Clifford Centre, on the eastern side of Raffles Place, is **Change Alley Aerial Plaza**. The original Change Alley was a cheap, bustling, street-level bazaar, which redevelopment wiped off the face of Singapore; all that remains is a sanitized, modern-day version, housed on a covered footbridge across Collyer Quay. The tailors here have a persuasive line in patter – you'll have to be very determined not to waste half an hour being convinced that you need a new suit. But if you want to have a suit made, there are better places to make for (see p.186).

Walking through Change Alley Aerial Plaza deposits you at **Clifford Pier**, long the departure point for trips on the Singapore River and to the southern islands (see p.43). There are still a few bumboats tied up here, though these days they're rented out as cruise boats rather than earning a living as cargo boats. Just north of Clifford Pier, **One Fullerton** is a new entertainments venue that has been constructed on land reclaimed from Marina Bay. Its bars, restaurants and nightclub share peerless views out over the bay. Just above One Fullerton a statue of Singapore's national symbol, the **Merlion**, guards the mouth of the Singapore River. Half-lion, half-fish, and wholly ugly, the creature reflects Singapore's name (*Singapura* means "Lion City" in Sanskrit) and its historical links with the sea.

Across the road stands the elegant **Fullerton Building**, fronted by sturdy pillars. Built in 1928 as the headquarters for the General Post Office – a role it fulfilled until the mid-1990s – remarkably, this was once one of Singapore's tallest buildings. Old photographs of Singapore depict Japanese soldiers marching past the building after the surrender of the Allied forces during World War II. These days, the building is a luxury hotel (see p.136) and the lighthouse that used to flash up on the roof is a swanky restaurant.

Back at Clifford Pier, it's a short walk south along Raffles Quay to Telok Ayer Market, now called **Lau Pa Sat Festival Market**. Built in 1884 on land reclaimed from the sea, its octagonal cast-iron frame has been turned into Singapore's most tasteful food centre (daily 24hr), which offers a range of Southeast Asian cuisine, as well as laying on free entertainment such as local bands and Chinese opera. After 7pm, the portion of Boon Tat Street between Robinson Road and Shenton Way is closed to traffic, and traditional satay stalls and other hawker stalls take over the street.

Marina South and the Port of Singapore

One of Singapore's most ambitious land reclamation projects, **Marina South**, is plainly visible from Raffles Quay and Shenton Way to the south of the Central Business District. For years, the project has shown all the makings of a splendid folly – the entertainment and recreation park that was built on it during the 1980s has gone bankrupt, and the large patch of land now seems to serve no other purpose than to carry the East Coast Parkway on its journey west. For now, Marina South is a ghost town, its only real asset an imaginative children's playground within a pleasant park. But plans are afoot to extend Singapore's downtown area into this space. Construction starts soon on an integrated **resort** with casino, entertainment and shops due to open on its northern tip, from where city planners aim to run a helix-shaped, glass-and-steel bridge to the waterfront east of the Theatres on the Bay complex (see p.57).

Below Marina South, Singapore's **port** begins its sprawl westwards. Singapore is the world's busiest container port (the second busiest port overall after Rotterdam) and hundreds of ships are at anchor south of the island at any one time, waiting for permission from the Port of Singapore Authority to enter one of the state's seven terminals.

Little India and the Arab Quarter

aces, temples and sights suddenly change from Oriental to Indian when you head north of the Colonial District to Serangoon Road and **Little India**. Little India MRT station deposits you a minute's walk from all the action. The **Arab Quarter**, the focal point of Singapore's Muslim population, is no more than a ten-minute stroll from Little India across the Rochor Canal – take Syed Alwi Road if you're at the top of Serangoon; it's more convenient to loop around Rochor Canal Road if you're down by Tekka Market. From elsewhere, hop on the MRT and alight at Bugis station.

Little India

A tour around Singapore's answer to Delhi amounts to an all-out assault on the senses. Indian pop music blares from gargantuan speakers outside cassette shops, the air is perfumed with incense, spices and jasmine garlands, Hindu women promenade in bright sarees, and a wealth of "hole-in-the-wall" restaurants serve up superior curries.

Indians did not always dominate this convenient central niche of Singapore; its original occupants were Europeans and Eurasians who established country houses here, and for whom a racecourse was built (on the site of modern-day Farrer Park) in the 1840s. Many of the roads in Little India started out as private tracks leading to these houses, and their names – Dunlop, Cuff, Desker, Norris – recall these early colonial settlers.

Only when Indian-run **brick kilns** began to operate here did a pronouncedly Indian community start to evolve. The enclave grew when a number of **cattle** and **buffalo yards** opened in the area in the latter half of the nineteenth century, and more Hindus were drawn in, in search of work. Street names hark back to this trade: side by side off the western reach of Serangoon Road are Buffalo Road and Kerbau ("buffalo" in Malay, confusingly) Road, along both of which cattle were kept in slaughter pens. Singapore's largest maternity hospital, nearby on Bukit Timah Road, is called Kandang Kerbau (Buffalo Pen) Hospital. Indians featured prominently in the development of Singapore, though not always out of choice: from 1825 onwards, convicts

LITTLE INDIA & THE ARAB QUARTER

RESTAURANTS & CAFÉS

Al-Tazzag	7
Bay View Café	21
Billy Bombers	12
Blu Jazz Café	8
Bobby Rubino's	29
Bumbu	5
Cherry Garden	28
Crystal Jade	16
Doc Cheng's	3
El Sheikh	13
Food Junction	1
Fut Sai Kai	27
Hai Tien Lo	19
Imperial Herbal	31
Inagiku	2
Islamic	25
Kopitiam	10
Kwan Yim	29
Lei Garden	14
Madam Saigon	12
Mooi Chin Palace	6
Mr Bean's Café	17
Noorul Ameen	15
Ocho Tapas	29
Pacific Coffee Company	31
Paulaner Bräuhaus	22
Ponderosa	31
Rendezvous	24
Rumah Makan Minang	4
Seah Street Deli	20
Seoul Garden	30
Sim Lim Square Food Court	9
Singapura Seafood	11
Starbucks	31
Tatsu Sushi	29
Tiffin Room	26
Victoria Street Food Court	23
Viet Lang	29
Warung M Nasir	14
Yet Con	18

ACCOMMODATION

Ali's Nest	B
Boon Wah Hotel	H
Broadway Hotel	C
Dickson Court	G
Fortuna Hotel	A
Haising Hotel	I
InnCrowd Hostel I	K
InnCrowd Hostel II	J
Kerbau Hotel	E
Little India Guest House	D
Perak Lodge	L
Sleepy Sam's	F

Map: Little India & the Arab Quarter, showing streets including Serangoon Road, Jalan Besar, Syed Alwi Road, North Bridge Road, Victoria St, Arab St, Nicoll Highway. Landmarks include Sri Srinivasa Perumal Temple, Sakaya Muni Buddha Gaya Temple, Sri Veeramakaliamman Temple, Chinese Mansion, Tekka Market, Little India Arcade, Serangoon Plaza, Mustafa Centre, Sim Lim Tower, Abdul Gaffoor Mosque, Malabar Mosque, Sultan Mosque, Malay Heritage Centre, Alsagoff Arab School, Hajjah Fatimah Mosque, Golden Mile Complex, Ban San Bus Terminal, Lavender St Bus Terminal, Farrer Park. Scale 0–200 m.

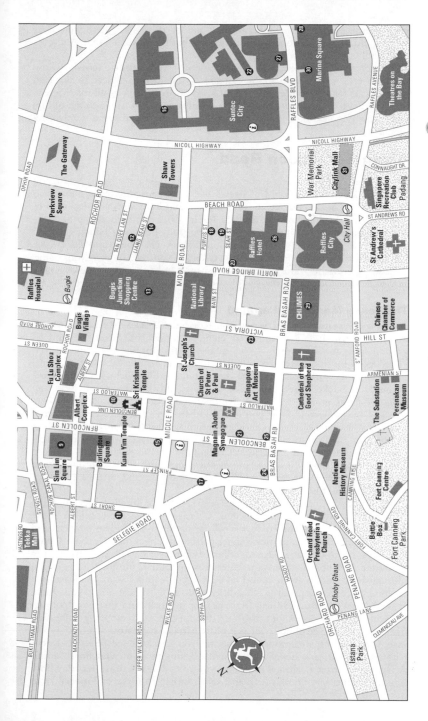

89

were transported from the subcontinent and by the 1840s there were over a thousand Indian prisoners labouring on buildings such as St Andrew's Cathedral and the istana.

The district's backbone is the north–south **Serangoon Road**, whose southern end is alive with shops, restaurants and fortune-tellers; to the east, stretching as far as Jalan Besar, is a tight knot of roads that's good for exploration. Parallel to Serangoon Road, **Race Course Road** boasts a clutch of fine restaurants (for details of Indian restaurants, see p.158) and some noteworthy temples.

Along Serangoon Road

Dating from 1822 and hence one of the island's oldest roadways, Serangoon Road is a kaleidoscopic whirl of Indian life, its shops selling everything from nose studs and ankle bracelets to incense sticks and kum kum powder (used to make the red dot Hindus wear on their foreheads). Little stalls, set up in doorways and under "five-foot ways", sell garlands, gaudy posters of Hindu gods and gurus, movie soundtracks and newspapers such as *The Hindu* and *India Today*. Look out for parrot-wielding **fortune-tellers** – you tell the man your name, he passes your name onto his feathered partner, and the bird then picks out a card with your fortune on it.

The Tekka Market and around

At the southwestern end of Serangoon Road, the **Tekka Market** combines many of Little India's commercial elements under one roof. Beyond its ground-floor food centre is a wet market that's not for the faint-hearted – traders push around trolleys piled high with goats' heads, while the halal butchers go to work in full view of the customers. Elsewhere, live crabs shuffle busily in buckets, their claws tied together, and there's a mouth-watering range of fruits on sale, including mangoes and whole branches of bananas. Upstairs, on the second floor, you'll find Indian fabrics, leatherware, footwear, watches and cheap electronic goods. On Sunday, the forecourt of the centre becomes an ad hoc social club for immigrant labourers working in Singapore, most of whom are Bangladeshi. Along the northern side of the market, **Buffalo Road** has a cluster of provisions stores with Ayurvedic medicines, incense sticks, sacks of spices and fresh coconut, ground using a primitive machine out on the road.

Little India's remaining shophouses are fast being touched up from the same pastel paintbox that has "restored" Chinatown to its present doll's house tweeness. Fortunately, the colours work far better in an Indian context, and the results are really quite pleasing. In particular, check out **Kerbau Road**, one block north of Buffalo Road, where shophouses have been meticulously renovated and now harbour a proliferation of Indian produce stores and a pleasant beer garden. If the mood takes you, you can get your hands painted with intricate henna patterns at Traditional Body Charm at no. 9; while Ansa, at no. 27, is a traditional Indian framer's shop, packed with images of colourful Hindu deities. Look out, too, for the curving staircase, dragon-headed banisters and carved shutters of the old **Chinese mansion** at no.37 – pop into TM Silks on the ground floor, and you can still see Chinese scenes painted high up on the walls and oriental beams finished with floral motifs. A right turn from Kerbau Road takes you onto Race Course Road, whose fine restaurants serve both north and south Indian food; several specialize in fish-head curry.

Little India Arcade and around

Bounded by Serangoon Road to the west, Campbell Lane to the north, and Hastings Road to the south, the lovingly restored block of shophouses comprising **Little India Arcade** was opened a few years back as a sort of Little India in microcosm: behind its lime walls and green shutters you can purchase textiles and tapestries, bangles, religious statuary, Indian sweets, tapes and CDs, and even traditional Ayurvedic medicines. At the time of Deepavali, the arcade's narrow ways are choked with locals hastening to buy decorations, garlands, traditional confectionery and fine clothes.

The roads nearby are also worth exploring. Exiting Little India Arcade onto Campbell Lane leaves you opposite the riot of colours of **Jothi flower shop** where staff thread jasmine, roses and marigolds into garlands, or *jothi*, for prayer offerings. Campbell Lane is a good place for buying Indian sandals, while walking along Clive Street towards Upper Dickson Road you'll find on your right a batch of junk dealers patiently tinkering with ancient cookers, air-con units and TVs. Left along Upper Dickson Road – past an old barber's shop where a short back and sides is followed by a crunching head yank to "relieve tension" – are the *Madras New Woodlands Restaurant*, at no. 12–14 and, around the corner, *Komala Vilas*, 76 Serangoon Road, two of Little India's best southern Indian restaurants (see p.159 for full details). Chances are that they make their delicious curries with spices bought nearby at Cuff Road, where **traditional spice grinders** still ply their trade at no.2.

Dunlop Street has become something of a backpacker enclave in the past few years, but it remains defined by beautiful **Abdul Gaffoor Mosque** (at no. 41; daily 8.30am–noon & 2.30–4pm), whose green dome and bristling minarets have enjoyed a comprehensive and sympathetic renovation in the last few years. Set amid gardens of palms and bougainvillea and within cream walls decorated with stars and crescent moons, the mosque features an unusual sundial whose face is ringed by elaborate Arabic script denoting the names of 25 Islamic prophets. Staff will give you a sarong or headdress to enable you to enter the prayer

△ Abdul Gaffoor Mosque

Deepavali

Never dull, Little India springs even more gloriously to life over the colourful Hindu festival of Deepavali (sometimes written as Diwali), which falls annually within either October or November. Local Hindus mark the festival by stringing Serangoon Road and its offshoots with fairy lights, and by lighting oil lamps (*diyas*) or candles in their homes. And no wonder – this is, after all, the Festival of Lights.

The festival of Deepavali marks Lord Krishna's slaying of the demon Narakasura. According to Hindu legend, Narakasura ruled the kingdom of Pradyoshapuram with a reign of terror, torturing his subjects, and kidnapping the women and imprisoning them in his palace. Witnessing these depravities, Lord Krishna destroyed the demon, and Hindus across the world have given praise ever since.

More universally, the festival celebrates the triumph of light over darkness, and of good over evil. For Hindus, Deepavali is a period of great excitement, a time to dress up in colourful new clothes, deck their houses out in colourful decorations, prepare sweet and savoury festive delicacies, exchange cards and gifts, pay respects to their elders and visit the local temple.

On the morning of the festival, worshippers bathe themselves in oil, then proceed to the temple to thank the gods for the happiness, knowledge, peace and prosperity they have enjoyed in the year past, and to pray for more of the same in the coming year.

hall and see the mihrab, or arched niche, where the Imam sits; and the mimbar, or raised pulpit, from where he preaches. Traditionally, the Imam always preaches from the second step of the mimbar as the top step is symbolically reserved for the prophet Mohammed. Renovated shophouses to the left of the mosque as you enter the grounds, have been converted into a madrasah, or Islamic school.

From the Abdul Gaffoor mosque, it's just a short walk to 13 Upper Dickson Road, where you can buy a cooling *kulfi* (Indian ice cream).

The Sri Veeramakaliamman Temple and Pink Street

In the heart of Little India on Serangoon Road, opposite the turning to Veerasamy Road, the **Sri Veeramakaliamman Temple** (6am–noon & 4–9pm) – dedicated to the ferocious Hindu goddess, Kali – features a fanciful *gopuram* that's flanked by majestic lions on the temple walls. Worshippers ring the bells hanging on the temple doors as they enter, so that their prayers are answered. Inside, the *mandapam*, or worship hall, holds a jet-black image of Kali, the goddess of power and incarnation of Lord Shiva's wife, depicted with a club in hand. Flanking here are her sons, Ganesh and Murugan. Each year during Deepavali (see box above), a pulsating market takes place on the open land above the temple.

North from the temple, and off to the right, lies **Pink Street**, one of the most incongruous and sordid spots in the whole of clean, shiny Singapore – but

△ Sri Veeramakaliamman Temple sculpture

you won't find it on any city map. The entire length of the "street" (in fact it's merely an alley between the backs of Rowell and Desker roads) is punctuated by open doorways, inside which gaggles of bored-looking prostitutes sit knitting or watching TV, oblivious to the gawping local men who accumulate outside. Stalls along the alley sell distinctly un-Singaporean merchandise such as sex toys, blue videos and potency pills, while con men work the "three cups and a ball" routine on unwary passers-by.

North of Desker Road

Beyond Desker Road, a five-minute walk north takes you to the edge of Little India, a diversion worth making to see two very different temples. Each year, on the day of the Thaipusam festival (see p.178), the courtyard of the **Sri Srinivasa Perumal Temple** (daily 6am–noon & 4–9pm), at 397 Serangoon Road, witnesses a gruesome melee of activity, as Hindu devotees don huge metal frames (*kavadis*) topped with peacock feathers, which are fastened to their flesh with hooks and prongs. The devotees then leave the temple, stopping only while a coconut is smashed at their feet for good luck, and parade all the way to the Chettiar Temple on Tank Road, off Orchard Road. Even if you miss the festival, it's worth a trip to see the five-tiered *gopuram* with its sculptures of the various manifestations of Lord Vishnu, the Preserver. On the wall to the right of the front gate is a sculpted elephant, its

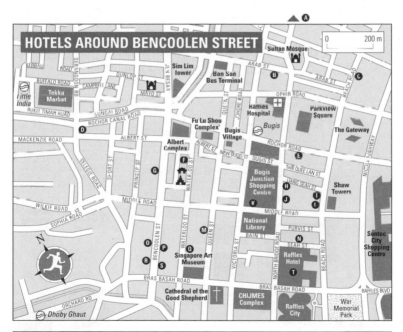

HOTELS AROUND BENCOOLEN STREET

ACCOMMODATION							
Ah Chew	H	City Bayview	S	Lee Home Stay	J	Plaza Park Royal	C
Albert Court Hotel	D	Golden Landmark Hotel	B	Lee Traveller's Club	L	Raffles	T
Aliwal Park Hotel	A	Hawaii Hostel	G	Metropole	N	South East Asia Hotel	F
Beach Hotel	I	Intercontinental	K	New 7th Storey	E	Strand Hotel	R
Bencoolen Hotel	O	Lee Boarding House	P	Oxford Hotel	M	Waterloo Hostel	Q

leg caught in a crocodile's mouth. The temple is dedicated to Lord Perumal, the Preserver of the Universe and god of mercy.

The Sakaya Muni Buddha Gaya Temple

Just beyond the Sri Srinivasa temple complex, a small path leads northwest to Race Course Road, where the **Sakaya Muni Buddha Gaya Temple** (or Temple of the Thousand Lights; daily 7am–6pm) is on the right at no. 366. It's a slightly kitsch building that betrays a strong Thai influence – not surprising, since it was built entirely by a Thai monk, Vutthisasala. On the left of the temple as you enter is a huge replica of the Buddha's footprint, inlaid with mother-of-pearl, and beyond is a 300-ton, 15-metre-high Buddha ringed by the thousand electric lights from which the temple takes its alternative name. Twenty-five scenes from the Buddha's life decorate the pedestal on which he sits. It is possible to walk inside the statue, through a door in its back; inside is a smaller representation of the Buddha, this time reclining. The left wall of the temple features a sort of wheel of fortune – spin it (for 30c) and take the numbered sheet of paper that corresponds to the number at which the wheel stops, to discover your fortune. Further along the left wall, a small donation entitles you to a shake of a tin full of numbered sticks, after which, again, you get a corresponding sheet of forecasts.

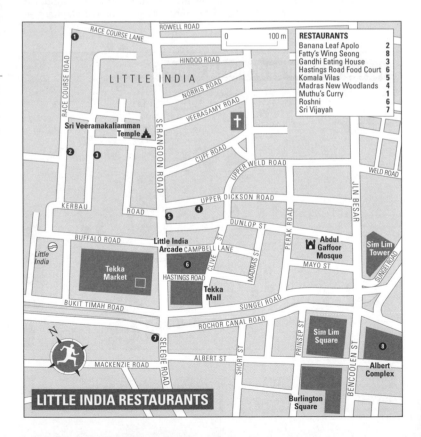

Double back onto Serangoon Road and a five-minute walk southeast along Petain Road leads to Jalan Besar, a route that takes in some immaculate examples of **Peranakan** (Straits Chinese) shophouses, their facades covered with elegant ceramic tiles reminiscent of Portuguese *azulejos*. There's more Peranakan architecture on display on Jalan Besar itself – turn right at the end of Petain Road – and along Sam Leong Road, where the shophouse facades are decorated with depictions of stags, lotuses and egrets. Further south a daily **flea market** takes place around Pitt Street, Weld Road, Kelantan Lane and Pasar Lane – secondhand tools, odd shoes and foreign currency are all laid out for sale on plastic sheets at the side of the road by citizens whom Singapore's economic miracle has passed by.

The Arab Quarter

Before the arrival of Raffles, the area of Singapore west of the Rochor River housed a Malay village known as Kampong Glam, after the *gelam* trees that used to proliferate in this area. After signing a dubious treaty with the newly installed "Sultan" Hussein Mohammed Shah, Raffles allotted the area to the sultan and designated the land around it as a Muslim settlement. Soon the zone was attracting Malays, Sumatrans and Javanese, as well as Hadhrami Arab traders from the region of southern Arabia that is now Yemen, as the road names in today's **ARAB QUARTER** – Baghdad Street, Muscat Street and Haji Lane – suggest. Until it was redeveloped as a heritage centre a few years ago, descendants of Sultan Hussein lived in the grounds of the Istana Kampong Glam, a palace right in the centre of the district, bounded by Arab Street, Beach Road, Jalan Sultan and Rochor Canal Road. Just outside the quarter, **Beach Road** still maintains shops which betray its former proximity to the sea – ships' chandlers and fishing tackle specialists – and you should also take the time to walk southeast from Arab Street to see the two logic-defying office buildings that together comprise **The Gateway**. Designed by I.M. Pei (who also designed the *Swissôtel* complex, see p.58), they rise magnificently into the air like vast razor blades and appear two-dimensional when viewed from certain angles. When **Parkview Square**, the huge, Gotham-esque building across Beach Road was built, much care was taken to site it dead between the Gateway's sharp points, so as to ward off bad feng shui. To be on the safe side its developers placed four giant figures carrying good-luck pearls along the top of the tower.

Arab Street

While Little India is memorable for its fragrances, it's the vibrant colours of the shops of **Arab Street** and its environs that stick in the memory. The street boasts the highest concentration of shops in the Arab Quarter; its pavements are an obstacle course of carpets, cloths, baskets and bags. Most of the shops have been renovated, though one or two (such as Bamadhaj Brothers at no. 97 and Aik Bee at no. 73) still retain their original dark-wood and glass cabinets, and wide wooden benches where the shopkeepers sit. Textile stores are most prominent, their walls, ceilings and doorways draped with cloths and batiks. Elsewhere you'll see leather, basketware, gold, gemstones and jewellery for sale, while the most impressive range of basketware and rattan work – fans, hats and walking sticks – is found at Rishi Handicrafts, at no. 58. It's easy to spend a couple of hours weaving in and out of the stores, but don't expect a quiet window-shopping session – the traders here are masters of the forced sale, and will have you loaded with sarongs, baskets and leather bags before you know it.

Around North Bridge Road

The Arab Quarter's most evocative patch is the stretch of **North Bridge Road** between Arab Street and Jalan Sultan. Here, the men sport long sarongs and Abe Lincoln beards, the women fantastically colourful shawls and robes, while the shops and restaurants are geared more towards locals than tourists: Kazura Aromatics, at 705 North Bridge Road, for instance, sells alcohol-free perfumes, while neighbouring shops stock rosaries, prayer mats and the *songkok* hats worn by Muslim males in mosques, and *miswak* sticks – twigs the width of a finger used by some locals to clean their teeth. A gaggle of superb Muslim Indian restaurants operates along this stretch of North Bridge Road: see p.158 for details.

Several roads run off the western side of North Bridge Road, including Jalan Pisang (Banana Street), on which a street barber works under a tarpaulin. A walk up Jalan Kubor (Grave Street) and across Victoria Street takes you to an unkempt Muslim **cemetery** where, it is said, Malay royalty are buried. On Sundays, Victoria Street throngs with children in full Muslim garb on their way to study scripture at the Arabic school, **Madrasah Al Junied Al-Islamiah**.

Istana Kampong Glam

Squatting between Kandahar and Aliwal streets, the **Istana Kampong Glam** was built as the royal palace of Sultan Ali Iskandar Shah, son of Sultan Hussein who negotiated with Raffles to hand over Singapore to the British; the sultan's descendants lived here until just a few years ago. Today, this modest, colonial building houses the **Malay Heritage Centre** (Mon 1–6pm, Tues–Sun 10am– 6pm, $3, children $2; cultural show Wed 3.30pm & Sun 11.30am, $10/5), a mixed bag of history and culture spanning maps, model boats, cannons, ceremonial drums and daggers from around the Malay archipelago. The most engaging exhibits are upstairs, where touch screens cast light on Malay community life in the pre-war years of the Twentieth Century, and where a mocked-up kampong house allows you to peek inside a traditional Malay dwelling. The twice-weekly **cultural show** offers a passable blend of Malay music, dance and costumes.

The Sultan Mosque and around

Looking down palm tree-lined, pedestrianized Bussorah Street from Baghdad Street, you get the best initial views of the golden domes of the **Sultan Mosque** or Masjid Sultan (Fri 9–11.30am and 2.30–4pm, Sat–Thurs 9am–1pm & 2–4pm), the beating heart of the Muslim faith in Singapore. An earlier mosque stood on this site, finished in 1825 and constructed with the help of a $3000 donation from the East India Company. The present building was completed a century later, according to a design by colonial architects Swan and MacLaren: if you look carefully at the glistening necks of the domes, you can see that the effect is created by the bases of thousands of ordinary glass bottles, an incongruity which sets the tone for the rest of the building. Steps at the top of Bussorah Street lead past papaya and palm trees into a wide lobby, where a digital display lists current prayer times. Beyond, and out of bounds to non-Muslims, is the main prayer hall, a large, bare chamber that's fronted by two more digital clocks.

△ Sultan Mosque

An exhaustive set of rules applies to visitors wishing to enter the lobby: shoes must be taken off and shoulders and legs covered, no video cameras are allowed inside the mosque, and entry is not permitted during the Friday mass congregation (11.30am–2.30pm). The best time to come is in the Muslim fasting month of Ramadan – the faithful can eat only after dusk, and Kandahar Street is awash with stalls selling *biriyani*, barbecued chicken and cakes.

   Bussorah Street itself has undergone quite a transformation in recent years, and efforts to morph it into the heart of a busier, buzzier Arab quarter have brought in cafés, Islamic book-, music- and aromatics shops, and even, at no. 61, a Balinese spa into its restored shophouses. A renewed interest in the Arabic roots of this district has resulted in a handful of middle-eastern restaurants and cafés that make pleasing venues for a drink, a snack or a *shisha*.

Hajjah Fatimah Mosque and around

From the Sultan Mosque, it's only a five-minute walk on to the **Hajjah Fatimah Mosque** (daily 8.30am–noon & 2.30–4pm) on Beach Road, where a collection of photographs in the entrance porch show the mosque through the years following its construction in 1846 – first surrounded by shophouses, then by open land, and finally by huge housing projects. The mosque is named after a wealthy Malaccan businesswoman who amassed a fortune through her mercantile vessels, and whose family home formerly stood here. After two break-ins and an arson attack on her home, Hajjah Fatimah decided to move elsewhere, then underwrote the construction of a mosque on the site. The minaret looks strangely like a church steeple (perhaps because its architect was a European) and is beautifully illuminated at night. Its 6-degree tilt – locals call the mosque Singapore's Leaning Tower of Pisa – is barely noticeable.

Across from the mosque, the Golden Mile Complex at 5001 Beach Road attracts so many Thai nationals that locals refer to it as "**Thai Village**". Numerous bus firms selling tickets to Thailand operate out of here, while inside, the shops vend Thai foodstuffs, cafés sell Singha beer and Mekong whisky, and authentic restaurants serve up old favourites. On Sundays, Thais come down here in hordes to meet up with their compatriots, listen to Thai pop music and have a few drinks.

5

Northern Singapore

W hile land reclamation has radically altered the east coast and industrialization the west, the **northern** expanses of the island up to the Straits of Johor still retain pockets of the **rainforest** and mangrove swamp which blanketed Singapore until the British arrival in 1819. These are interspersed today with sprawling, maze-like **new towns** such as Toa Payoh, Bishan and Ang Mo Kio, built in the 1970s. The name of the last, meaning "red-haired devil's bridge", refers to the nineteenth-century British surveyor, John Turnbull Thomson, under whose supervision the transport network of Singapore began to penetrate the interior of the island. Man-eating tigers roamed these parts well into the twentieth century, and it was here that Allied forces confronted the invading Japanese army in 1942, a period of Singaporean history movingly recalled by the **Kranji War Memorial** on Woodlands Road and the new **Memories at Old Ford Factory** gallery in Bukit Timah. Still visible at the far northern sweep of the island are the remnants of Singapore's agricultural past: you'll see prawn and poultry farms, orchards and vegetable gardens when travelling in these parts.

Dominating the central northern region are two nature reserves, divided by the main road route to Malaysia, the Bukit Timah Expressway. West of the expressway is **Bukit Timah Nature Reserve**, an accessible slice of primary rainforest, while to the east, the four reservoirs of the Central Catchment Area are one of Singapore's main sources of water. North of here, the principal tourist attractions are the excellent **Singapore Zoological Gardens** and the adjacent **Night Safari**, sited on a finger of land pointing into the Seletar Reservoir. To the east are two of Singapore's most eye-catching Buddhist temples – **Lian Shan Shuang Lin Temple** and the **Kong Meng San Phor Kark See** complex – as well as tiny Tai Gin Road, where the sometime residence of Chinese nationalist leader Dr **Sun Yat Sen** and Singapore's **Burmese Temple** are found.

Travel between the attractions in northern Singapore is decidedly tricky unless you are driving, or in a cab, so don't expect to take in everything in a day. However, Lian Shan Shuang Lin Temple, Sun Yat Sen Villa and the Burmese Temple all nestle around the outskirts of Toa Payoh new town and could be incorporated into a single expedition; as could the zoo, Mandai Orchid Gardens and the Kranji War cemetery and memorial. The Kong Meng San Phor Kark See temple complex really requires a separate journey.

Bukit Timah Nature Reserve and around

Bukit Timah Road runs northwest from the junction of Selegie and Serangoon roads, to the faceless town of **Bukit Timah**, 8km further on. Bukit

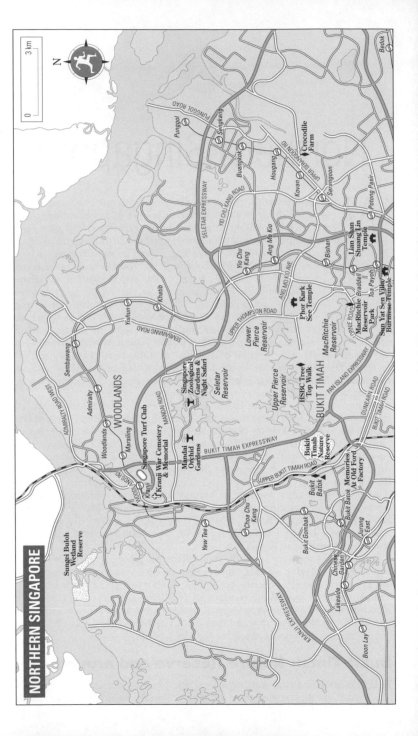

NORTHERN SINGAPORE

N

0   3 km

Sungei Buloh Wetland Reserve

WOODLANDS

Woodlands
Marsiling
Admiralty
Sembawang
Yishun
Khatib

ADMIRALTY ROAD WEST
ADMIRALTY ROAD EAST

Kranji
Singapore Turf Club
Kranji War Cemetery & Memorial

Mandai Orchid Gardens

Singapore Zoological Gardens & Night Safari

MANDAI ROAD

Seletar Reservoir

SEMBAWANG ROAD

Yew Tee
Choa Chu Kang

BUKIT TIMAH EXPRESSWAY

Bukit Gombak

UPPER BUKIT TIMAH ROAD

Bukit Batok
Bukit Batok Memorial

Memories At Old Ford Factory

Bukit Timah Nature Reserve

BUKIT TIMAH

HSBC Tree Top Walk

Upper Pierce Reservoir

Lower Pierce Reservoir

UPPER THOMPSON ROAD

Phor Kark See Temple

ANG MO KIO AVE

MacRitchie Reservoir

MacRitchie Reservoir

BRADDELL ROAD

Sun Yat Sen Villa
Burmese Temple

Toa Payoh

Lian Shan Shuang Lin Temple

Bishan

Ang Mo Kio

Yio Chu Kang

YIO CHU KANG ROAD

SELETAR EXPRESSWAY

Buangkok

Hougang

Kovan

Serangoon

Potong Pasir

UPPER SERANGOON ROAD

Crocodile Farm

Sengkang
Punggol

PUNGGOL ROAD

Bedok

PAN ISLAND EXPRESSWAY

DUNEARN ROAD

BUKIT TIMAH ROAD

KRANJI EXPRESSWAY

Lakeside
Chinese Garden
Boon Lay
Jurong East

Timah boasts Singapore's last remaining pocket of primary rainforest, which now comprises **Bukit Timah Nature Reserve** (daily 6.30am–7.30pm; free; ☎1800-4685736, ⊛www.nparks.gov.sg). Visiting this area of Singapore in the mid-eighteenth century, natural historian Alfred Russel Wallace found Bukit Timah's vegetation "most luxuriant … in about two months I obtained no less than 700 species of beetles … in all my subsequent travels in the East I rarely if ever met with so productive a spot". Wallace reported "tiger pits, carefully covered with sticks and leaves and so well concealed, that in several cases I had a narrow escape from falling into them . . . Formerly a sharp stake was stuck erect in the bottom," he continued, "but after an unfortunate traveller had been killed by falling into one, its use was forbidden." Today the reserve, established in 1883 by Nathaniel Cantley, who was superintendent of the Botanic Gardens, yields no such hazards and is a refuge for the dwindling numbers of species still extant in Singapore – only 25 types of mammal now inhabit the island. Creatures you're most likely to see in Bukit Timah are long-tailed macaques, butterflies and other insects, and birds like the dark-necked tailorbird, which builds its nest by sewing together leaves. Scorpions, snakes, flying lemurs and pangolins (anteaters, whose name is derived from the Malay word *peng-goling*, meaning "roller", a reference to the animal's habit of rolling into a ball when threatened) still roam here too.

You'd be well advised to begin your trip at the informative **visitor centre** (daily 8.30am–6pm), full of displays, specimens and photos relating to the reserve's flora and fauna. Several paths from the centre twist and turn through the forest around and to the top of **Bukit Timah Hill**, which, at a paltry 163m, is actually Singapore's highest hill. These paths are all well signposted, colour-coded and dotted with rest points, and they're clearly mapped on the free leaflet handed out to all visitors. Bike tracks have also been added (see p.42 for bike rental details).

Bus #171 passes along Somerset and Scotts roads en route to Bukit Timah Reserve; a second option is to take bus #170 from the Ban San Terminal on Queen Street. Both buses drop you beside a row of shops on Upper Bukit Timah Road, where you can pick up light snacks and bottled water to take into the reserve. You'd do best to visit in the cool of early morning and midweek, when there are fewer visitors.

Memories at Old Ford Factory and Bukit Batok

Across Upper Bukit Timah Road from the reserve, another forested hill, **Bukit Batok**, is where British and Australian POWs were forced to erect a fifteen-metre-high wooden shrine, the Syonan Tyureito, for their Japanese captors in 1945. Only the steps at its base now remain, and the hill is now topped by a communications transmitter. Legend has it that termites, which the prisoners secretly introduced to the structure, destroyed the shrine itself. Gone, too, is the wooden cross erected by the POWs to honour their dead. The hill is located at the end of Lorong Sesuai, a left turn opposite Bukit Timah fire station, 500m further up the road from the entrance to Bukit Timah reserve. Lorong Sesuai was laid by the same prisoners who built the shrine. The surrender that consigned them to such labours took place 400m further up Upper Bukit Timah Road, at the Art Deco old Ford car factory; a new gallery, **Memories at Old Ford Factory** (Mon–Fri 9am–5.30pm, Sat 9am–1.30pm; free), tells the story of that surrender, and of the dark years of Japanese occupation from 1942 to 1945. The exhibition uses period newspapers, first-hand audio accounts and relics such as Morse coders, anti-tank guns, signal lamps and grenades to fascinating effect. Details of life as a POW are kept to a minimum (this facet of

△ Bukit Timah Nature Reserve

Singaporean history is well covered at Changi Prison Museum); instead, it's the civilian experience of Japanese occupation that comes to life. When the factory opened in October 1941, it was the first car assembly plant in Southeast Asia. During the Malayan campaign, its assembly equipment was used by the RAF to assemble fighter planes. But by February 1942, Japanese forces had advanced into Singapore, and on February 15, Lt Gen Percival, head of the Allied forces in Singapore, surrendered to Japan's General Yamashita in the Ford Motor Company Board Room. While Percival was taken to Changi prison as a POW (he would fly to Tokyo Bay three years later to witness the Japanese surrender), the Japanese commanders gathered for a ritual ceremony of thanks, ate their Emperor's gifts of dried cuttlefish and chestnuts and drank a silent *sake* toast.

Then it was down to business. Stung by overseas Chinese efforts to raise funds for China's defence against Japan, Japanese troops launched *Sook Ching*, a brutal purge of anti-Japanese Chinese in Singapore. *Kempaitei* (military police) officers established screening centres, to which Chinese men had to report. Even the most tenuous of evidence – tattoos, a Chinese education, wearing glasses or having the soft hands of the educated – could result in individuals being loaded onto lorries and taken to massacre grounds around the island. The Japanese estimated the number of dead around 5000; Singapore's Chinese Chamber of Commerce thought it was eight times that many.

Concurrently, the occupying army began a mass "Japanisation" process. Locals were urged to learn Japanese and celebrate imperial birthdays; the press was controlled by the Japanese Propaganda Department; and Japanese cultural shows were held at Victoria Theatre and memorial hall. The new currency introduced by the Japanese came to be known as "banana money", as the $10 note featured a banana plant. The gallery ends with images of General Seishiro, commander in chief of Jap 7th area army, surrendering to Admiral Lord Louis Mountbatten, Supreme Allied Commander of Southeast Asia, on September 12, 1945. At the ceremony, Allied troops raised the same Union Jack that had been handed over at the Ford Factory three years earlier. Oil palm, tapioca, sweet potato, papaya and other food crops grown during the occupation have been planted in the **wartime garden** outside the factory, but the garden's location amongst the air-con units behind the building is puzzling.

The MacRitchie Trails

East of Bukit Timah, the shoreline and environs of MacRitchie Reservoir play host to the **MacRitchie Trails** (daily 6.30am–7.30pm; free), a network of six colour-coded tracks and boardwalks that allow you to experience Singapore's lowland tropical dipterocarp forest. Bisecting lush vegetation and skirting the reservoir's glassy waters, the trails offer the chance to see macaques, monitor lizards, terrapins, squirrels, eagles and kingfishers in the wild. If you happen to be in town on the second Sunday of the month, you can join the free nature appreciation walk that starts from the head of the Prunus Trail at 9.30am (☎65545127 to pre-book). One of the longer trails, MacRitchie Nature Trail, leads to the **HSBC TreeTop Walk** (Tues–Fri 9am–5pm, Sat & Sun 8.30am–5pm; free), a free-standing, 25-metre-high, 250-metre-long suspension bridge that gives you a monkey's-eye view of the forest canopy. As long as there are no noisy school parties bustling across, you've got a pretty good chance of spotting some colourful fauna and birdlife. The MacRitchie Trails all start at MacRitchie Reservoir Park, where there are restrooms, a café and information boards. To reach the park, take bus #132, #166 or #167 from downtown, and alight at

Thomson Road. If you don't fancy the 4km hike to the TreeTop Walk, stay on any of the buses listed previously at the turning to the Singapore Island Country Club, on Upper Thomson Road.

Tai Gin Road: Sun Yat Sen Villa and the Burmese Temple

Between Jalan Toa Payoh to the north, and Balestier Road to the south, is **Sun Yat Sen Villa** (Tues–Fri & Sun 9am–5pm, Sat 10am–10pm; $3; ☎62567377, ⊛wanqingyuan.com.sg) on tiny Tai Gin Road, reached by bus #139 from outside Dhoby Ghaut MRT station. Built to house the mistress of a wealthy Chinese businessman, this attractive Palladian-style bungalow changed hands in 1905, when one Teo Eng Hock bought it for his mother. Chinese nationalist leader Dr Sun Yat Sen paid the first of several visits to Singapore the following year, and was invited by Teo to stay at Tai Gin Road, where he quickly established a Singapore branch of the Tong Meng Hui – a society dedicated to replacing the Manchu dynasty in China with a modern republic. After serving as a communications camp for the Japanese during World War II, the villa fell into disrepair until 1966, when it was done up and opened to the public. A recent renovation has added an extra wing to the building, allowing space for six **galleries**, whose displays, artefacts and visuals variously focus upon the villa's history, the life of Dr Sun, and the historical context to the Chinese revolution in which he played such a substantial part. There's also a gallery celebrating the role of Southeast Asia's overseas Chinese in supporting the revolution – a huge painting of Dr Sun rallying support from the tin miners and rubber tappers in Malaya dominates it. There's enough to engage the mind for a while, but, realistically, this is best left to visitors with an active interest in Chinese history. Around the villa's attractive gardens, stretches the 58-metre-long "Common Memories" **mural**, which portrays the multi-racial, multi-cultural existence of the Singaporeans from the early nineteenth century to World War II.

Next door to the Sun Yat Sen Villa is the **Sasanaramsi Burmese Buddhist Temple** (daily 6am–10pm; ☎62511717, ⊛www.bbt.org.sg) reconstructed in just two years after being forced to move from its previous site at Kinta Road because of redevelopment. Craftsmen from Burma decorated the temple, and its ground floor is dominated by a large, white marble statue of the Buddha brought over from Burma in the 1920s – a series of **murals** on the top floor depict the statue's journey by ship, train, barge, truck, elephant and fork-lift from Sagyin Hill in Burma to Singapore. Upstairs on the first floor is another Buddha statue, this time standing, and ringed by blue skies painted on the wall behind.

The Lian Shan Shuang Lin and Phor Kark See temples

Two of Singapore's largest Chinese temples are situated in the island's central region, east of the Central Catchment Area. Both are rather isolated, but buzz with activity at festival times and have plenty to interest temple enthusiasts.

The name of the **Lian Shan Shuang Lin Temple** (daily 7am–5pm), at 184e Jalan Toa Payoh, means "Twin Groves of the Lotus Mountain" – a reference to the Buddha's birth in a grove of trees and his death under a Bodhi tree. The Chinese abbot Sek Hean Wei established the temple at the turn of the last century when, passing through Singapore on his way home after a pilgrimage to Sri Lanka, he was waylaid by wealthy Hokkien merchant and philanthropist Low Kim Pong, who supplied both land and finances for the venture. Several renovations have failed to rob the temple of its grandeur: set behind a half-moon pool, it is accessed by the **Hall of Celestial Kings**, where statues of the Four Kings of Heaven stand guard to repel evil, symbolized by the demons under their feet. The kings flank Maitreya Bodhisattva, the **Laughing Buddha**, believed to grant good luck if you rub his stomach. Beyond, a courtyard dotted with bonsai plants and lilies in dragon jars leads, to the main Mahavira Hall, where a sakyamuni Buddha in lotus position takes centre stage. To his right is the medicine Buddha, the great healing teacher, and to his left, the Amitabha. Elsewhere in the compound is a grand hall with a 100-armed Kuan Yin, goddess of mercy, flanked by chandeliers; and the seven tiered **Dragon Light Pagoda**. To **get here**, take the MRT to Toa Payoh station, from where the temple is a ten-minute walk.

The largest temple complex in Singapore – and one of the largest in Southeast Asia – lies north of MacRitchie Reservoir, right in the middle of the island. **Phor Kark See Temple** (known in full as the Kong Meng San Phor Kark See Temple Complex; daily 7am–5pm), at 88 Bright Hill Drive, spreads over nineteen acres and combines temples, pagodas, pavilions, a Buddhist library and a vast crematorium. So impressive is the site, that it has been used several times as a backdrop to Chinese kung fu movies. More modern than Lian Shan Shuang Lin, Phor Kark See boasts none of the faded charm of Singapore's older temples, but relies instead on sheer magnitude and exuberant decor for effect. Multi-tiered roofs bristle with ceramic dragons, phoenixes, birds and human figures, while around the complex are statues of various deities including a nine-metre-high marble statue of Kuan Yin, goddess of mercy, and a soaring pagoda capped by a golden *chedi* (reliquary tower). The inauguration, in early 2006, of a prayer hall housing a vast seated Buddha reputed to be the biggest in Southeast Asia rendered the complex even more striking. Even the **crematorium**, handily placed for the nearby Bright Hill Evergreen Home for the elderly – doesn't do things by half. Housed below a Thai-style facade of elaborately carved gilt wood, it can cope with five ceremonies at a time.

Below the crematorium is a pair of ponds, where thousands of turtles sunbathe precariously on wooden planks that slant into the waters. A nearby sign prohibits worshippers from putting new turtles into the ponds, a practice supposed to bring good luck. Old ladies beside the viewing gallery sell bunches of vegetables for "one dolla, one dolla", which purchasers then throw to the lucky turtles.

To **reach the complex** take bus #130 up Victoria Street, alighting at the far end of Sin Ming Drive.

Singapore Zoological Gardens and Night Safari

The **Singapore Zoological Gardens** (daily 8.30am–6pm; $15, kids $7.50, $28/14 incl. Night Safari, $35/17.50 incl. Night Safari and Bird Park; ⓦwww .zoo.com.sg) on Mandai Lake Road are spread over a promontory jutting into peaceful Seletar Reservoir. The gardens attract 1.2 million visitors a year – a fact perhaps explained by their status as one of the world's few open zoos, where moats are preferred to cages. Spacious exhibits manage to approximate the natural habitats of the animals, and though leopards, pumas and jaguars still have to be kept behind bars, this is a thoughtful, humane environment, described as "one of the really beautiful zoos" by no less an authority than conservationist Sir Peter Scott.

There are some 3200 animals here, representing more than 330 species, so it's best to allow a whole day for your visit. A **tram** ($5/2.50 for three stops) circles the grounds on a one-way circuit, but be prepared for a lot of footwork. Highlights include orang utans, Komodo dragons, polar bears, which you view underwater from a gallery, and the primate kingdom. Also worth checking out is the **special loan enclosure** that has played host to a giant panda, an Indian white tiger and a golden monkey. No exhibit lets you get any closer to the resident animals than the **Fragile Forest** biodome, a magical zone where you can walk amid ring-tailed lemurs, tree kangeroos, sloths and fruit bats. Various **animal** and **feeding shows** run throughout the day from 10am until 5pm, featuring sea lions, elephants, polar bears and other exotic creatures. There are also elephant ($6/3) and pony ($4) rides and, in the **Children's World**, there's the chance to hold young chicks and watch a milking demonstration. At 9am daily, you can even share breakfast with a selection of the zoo's residents, including orang utans and snakes.

Upon **arrival**, pick up the leaflet with details of riding and feeding times and the helpful map, which suggests itineraries taking in all the major shows and attractions. At the other end of your trip, you might care to drop by the **gift shop** next to the exit, which stocks the usual cuddly toys, key rings and pencil cases. Several food and drink kiosks are dotted around the zoo, or you can head for *Jungle Flavours*, bang in the centre of the grounds, and offering a range of local dishes.

The opening of the **Night Safari** (daily 7.30pm–midnight; $20, kids $10, $28/14 incl. zoo, $35/17.50 incl. zoo and Bird Park; ⓦwww.zoo.com.sg) a few years back substantially increased the grounds of the zoo. Here, a thousand animals representing well over a hundred species – elephants, rhinos, giraffes and leopards, hyenas and otters – play out their nocturnal routines under a forest of standard lamps. Three **walking trails**, geared around forest giants, leopards, and the incredibly cute fishing cats, respectively, wind through the safari. However, only five of the safari's eight zones are walkable – to see the rest you'll need to take a 45-minute *Jurassic Park*-style tram ride ($8/4), and tolerate the intrusive chattering of its taped guide. A meal at one of the restaurants outside the entrance will pass the time between the zoo's closing and the safari's opening.

To **get to** the zoo and the Night Safari, take bus #171 to Mandai Road, then #927, or go to Ang Mo Kio MRT and then take bus #138.

Mandai Orchid Gardens

It's only a ten-minute walk from the Singapore Zoological Gardens down Mandai Lake Road to the **Mandai Orchid Gardens** (daily 8.30am–5.30pm; $3; ☏62691036, ⓦwww.singaporeorchids.com.sg) or you can take the #138 bus from the zoo, which stops right outside. Orchids are big business in tropical Singapore. Here, the flowers are cultivated on a gentle slope, tended by old ladies in wide-brimmed hats. Unless you are a keen horticulturist, the place will be of limited interest, as little effort has been taken to make it instructive. Still, if you've been to the zoo, the gardens make a colourful detour on the way home, and the price of a gift box of orchids (starting from $20) compares favourably with more central flower shops.

Woodlands: Kranji War Cemetery and around

Five kilometres north of the zoo is the bustling town of **Woodlands**, from where a **causeway** spanning the Straits of Johor links Singapore to Johor Bahru in Malaysia – for the moment, at least. The causeway has become a bone of contention between the governments of Singapore and Malaysia in recent years, with Malaysia pressing hard for its demolition and replacement with a new, "scenic" bridge. It cites an untenable increase in traffic volume and dangerous levels of pollution in the Strait of Johor as its reasons. By March, 2006, several rounds of talks had still not resolved the issue, and Malaysia had commenced construction of a bridge to replace just its half of the causeway. At peak hours (6.30–9.30am & 5.50–7.30pm) and at weekends, the roads leading to the causeway seethe with cars and trucks – all full of petrol, after a law passed in the early 1990s banned Singaporeans from driving out of the country on an empty tank. Previously, people crossed into Malaysia, filled up with cut-price fuel and then headed home; now, signs line the roads approaching the causeway requesting that "Singapore cars please top up to_tank" – or risk a $500 fine.

Bus #170 from Ban San Terminal on Queen Street heads towards Woodlands on its way to Johor Bahru, passing the **Kranji War Cemetery and Memorial** (daily 7am–6pm) on Woodlands Road, where only the sound of birds and insects breaks the silence in the immaculately kept grounds. (You can also get here by alighting at Kranji MRT station, from where it's a five hundred metre walk.) The cemetery is the resting place of the many Allied troops who died in the defence of Singapore. As you enter, row upon row of graves slope up the landscaped hill in front of you, some identified only as "known unto God". The graves are bare: flowers are banned, as still water encourages mosquitoes to breed. A simple stone cross stands over the cemetery and above is the **memorial**, around which are recorded all the names of more than twenty thousand soldiers (from Britain, Canada, Sri Lanka, India, Malaysia, the Netherlands, New Zealand and Singapore) who died in this region during World War II. Two unassuming **tombs** stand on the wide lawns below the cemetery, belonging to Yusof Bin Ishak and Dr Benjamin Henry Sheares, independent Singapore's first two presidents.

Singapore Turf Club

Singapore's only racecourse is at the **Singapore Turf Club**, adjacent to Kranji MRT station and also reachable by bus #170. As legal gambling outside the course is restricted, the annual racing calendar here is very popular. The course typically holds twenty or so race meets annually, spaced throughout the year. The most prestigious events include the Lion City Cup, the Singapore Gold Cup and the Singapore Derby. Race dates change from year to year, so it's worth calling the information hotline or checking the website (☎68791000, ⓦwww.turfclub.com.sg) if you want to time your visit to coincide with a big race day. When there's no racing in Singapore, a giant video screen links the racecourse to various courses across the causeway in Malaysia. There's a fairly strict dress code – strapless sandals, jeans, shorts and T-shirts are out – and foreign visitors have to take their passports with them. Friday cards begin at 6.30pm, Saturday's and Sunday's after lunch, and tickets cost from $3 to $20. A day's racing viewed from the grandstand's posher upper tiers can be booked in advance, but you'd do far better just to turn up, eat at the lower grandstand's decent food court and soak up the atmosphere in the stands.

Sungei Buloh Wetland Reserve

The 130-hectare swathe of **Sungei Buloh Wetland Reserve** (Mon–Sat 7.30am–7pm, Sun 7am–7pm; $1, children 50c, free Sat & Sun; ☎67941401, ⓦwww.sbwr.org.sg), 4km northwest of Kranji cemetery on the north coast of Singapore, is the island's only protected wetland nature park. Beyond its visitor centre, café and video theatre (shows Mon–Sat 9am, 11am, 1pm, 3pm & 5pm, Sun hourly 9am–5pm), walking routes thread through an expanse of mangrove, mud flats, orchards and grassland, home to kingfishers, herons, sandpipers, kites and sea eagles and, in the waters, mudskippers, needlefish and archerfish – which squirt water into the air to knock insects out of the air and into devouring range. The reserve's five hundred-metre-long mangrove boardwalk offers an easy means of getting a sense of the shoreline environment. You'll take your stroll to the accompaniment of cicadas and birdsong. En route, you'll spot tortoises, crabs and mudskippers among the reaching fingers of the mangrove swamp. From here you can graduate to walks ranging from three to seven kilometres into the guts of the reserve. Visit between September and March and you're likely to catch sight of migratory birds from around Asia roosting and feeding. Come on a Saturday and you can join a free guided tour (9am, 10am, 3pm & 4pm); at other times you'll need to pre-book a tour ($50 per group).

To **get to** Sungei Buloh, take the MRT to Kranji MRT station, then transfer to bus #925, which stops at Kranji Reservoir car park from Monday to Saturday, and at the reserve's entrance on Sundays.

6

Eastern Singapore

hirty years ago, **eastern Singapore** was largely rural, dotted with Malay kampung villages that perched on stilts over the shoreline, harbouring the odd weekend retreat owned by Europeans or monied locals. Massive **land reclamation** and development programmes have altered the region beyond recognition, wiping out all traces of the kampungs and throwing up huge housing projects in their place. Today, former seafront suburbs like Bedok are separated from the Straits of Singapore by a broad crescent of man-made land, much of which constitutes the **East Coast Park**, a five-kilometre strip with leisure and watersports facilities, imported sand beaches and seafood restaurants. Despite the massive upheavals that have ruptured the communities of the east coast, parts of it, including the suburbs of **Geylang** and **Katong**, have managed to retain a strong Malay identity.

Dominating the eastern tip of the island is Changi airport, and beyond that **Changi Village**, where the Japanese interned Allied troops and civilians during World War II – a period of history commemorated at the thought provoking **Changi Museum**. From Changi Point, it's possible to take a boat to **Pulau Ubin**, a small island that has echoes of pre-development Singapore.

Geylang and Katong

Malay culture has held sway in and around the adjoining suburbs of **Geylang** and **Katong** since the mid-nineteenth century, when Malays and Indonesians first arrived to work in the local *copra* (coconut husk) processing factory and later on its *serai* (lemon grass) farms. Many of its shophouses, restaurants and food centres are Malay-influenced, less so the thriving trade in prostitution that carries on here, unchecked by the local authorities. **Geylang Road** itself runs east from the Kallang River; off the road are 42 lorongs, or lanes, down which clusters of brothels are easily recognised being decked out with fairy lights. At its far eastern end, Geylang Road meets **Joo Chiat Road**, which – after the restrictions of downtown Singapore – has a refreshingly laid-back and shambolic air.

The Malay Village

Before striking off down Joo Chiat Road, cross Changi Road, to the north, where, east of a side street called Geylang Serai, a hawker centre and wet market of the same name provide more Malay atmosphere, from the clove cigarettes to the line of sarong sellers beyond the food stalls. Geylang Serai market is due

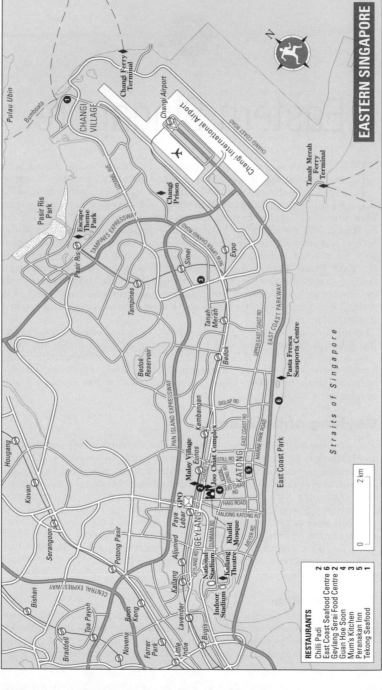

EASTERN SINGAPORE

Pulau Ubin

Bumboats

CHANGI VILLAGE

Changi Ferry Terminal

Changi International Airport

Changi Airport

CHANGI COAST ROAD

Tanah Merah Ferry Terminal

Boats to Malaysia

Boats to Indonesia

Changi Prison

Pasir Ris Park

Pasir Ris

Escape Theme Park

LOYANG AVE

TAMPINES EXPRESSWAY

Simei

Expo

Tampines

OLD UPPER CHANGI ROAD

Tanah Merah

Bedok Reservoir

UPPER EAST COAST RD

Bedok

Pasta Fresca Seasports Centre

EAST COAST PARKWAY

PAN ISLAND EXPRESSWAY

Kembangan

SIGLAP RD

Straits of Singapore

Hougang

Malay Village

Eunos

Joo Chiat Complex

STILL RD

EAST COAST RD

MARINE PARK ROAD

East Coast Park

Kovan

KATONG

JOO CHIAT RD

Serangoon

Paya Lebar

GPO

HAIG ROAD

TANJONG KATONG RD

Potong Pasir

GEYLANG RD

GEYLANG

DUNMAN RD

Khalid Mosque

MEYER RD

Central Expressway

Bishan

Kallang

Aljunied

National Stadium

Indoor Stadium

Kallang Theatre

Toa Payoh

Braddell

Novena

Boon Keng

Farrer Park

Lavender

Little India

Bugis

RESTAURANTS
Chilli Padi   2
East Coast Seafood Centre   6
Geylang Serai Food Centre   2
Guan Hoe Soon   4
Mum's Kitchen   3
Peranakan Inn   5
Tekong Seafood   1

0   2 km

N

to be demolished and then rebuilt on the same site in mid-2006. The chances are that when it is complete, the new market will still be a more authentic slice of life than the **Malay Village** (daily 10am–9pm; $5, kids $3 for attractions, otherwise free) on the other side of Geylang Serai, and a short walk from Paya Lebar MRT. Opened in 1990, and conceived as a celebration of the cuisine, music, dance, arts and crafts of the Malays, the village has conspicuously failed either to woo tourists or to rent out its replica wooden kampung-style shops to locals, and seems to be dying a slow but certain death. Its tourist lures pack very little punch: the **Kampung Museum** features a humdrum array of household instruments, cloths, kites and *kris*, and a mock-up of a Malay wedding scene; the dismal **Kampung Days** exhibition reproduces a traditional Malay kampung homestead, complete with fishing and rice-pounding scenes, a *wayang kulit* stage, an open-air cinema, and another (seemingly obligatory) wedding scene; and the **Cultural Demonstration Corner** hosts half-hearted exhibitions of Malay games and crafts. If you give these attractions a miss, you're left with the village's **shops**, selling batik, kites, spinning tops, bird cages and textiles, and the evening **food court** with free cultural performances on Saturday and Sunday nights.

Joo Chiat Road and East Coast Road

As you walk south down Joo Chiat Road from Geylang Road, you'll have to negotiate the piles of merchandise that spill out of shophouses and onto the pavement – but before you do, be sure to visit the **Joo Chiat Complex** at the northern end of the road, where textile merchants drape their wares on any available floor and wall space, transforming the drab interior. More market than shopping centre, it's a prime destination for anyone interested in buying silk, batik, rugs, muslin or the traditional *baju kurung* worn by Malay women. Stalls around the perimeter of the complex sell dates, honey, Malay CDs and *jamu* (Malay medicine).

With its ochre tiled roof and green walls, low key **Khalid Mosque**, a stone's throw from Joo Chiat Complex, belies the eye-catching architecture on view elsewhere on or around Joo Chiat Road. Joo Chiat itself has some beautifully restored shophouses – like Chiang Pow Joss Paper Trading at no. 252, where funerary paraphernalia is made beneath elaborate facades of flowers and dragons – but none as magnificent as the immaculate **Peranakan shophouses** on Koon Seng Road (on the left about halfway down Joo Chiat Road), where painstaking work has restored multicoloured facades, French windows, eaves and mouldings.

Back on Joo Chiat, several shops are worthy of a detour. Kway Guan Huat at no. 95 makes *popiah* skin; while mackerel *otah* is produced at

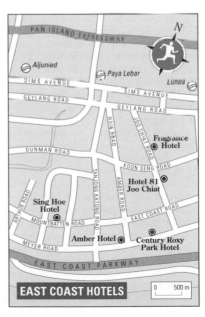

EAST COAST HOTELS

no. 267. There are non-alcoholic perfumes and Arab CDs at Haruman Makkah at no. 142; and Malay medicines next door at Fatimah Trading.

Hang a right when Joo Chiat hits East Coast Road and at no. 113 you'll find **Rumah Bebe**, a delightful Peranakan shop that sells beaded shoes and handbags, costume jewellery, porcelain tiffin carriers and the traditional garb – *kebaya* and *sarong* – of Nonya women. From Rumah Bebe, it's just a couple of minutes' walk east to the **Katong Antiques House** at 208 East Coast Road where owner Peter Wee has amassed a treasure trove of Peranakan artefacts, from wedding costumes to furniture. You'll need to call ahead (☏63458544) to book an appointment. Head west from Rumah Bebe, to the junction with Ceylon Road, and you'll find a clutch of venerable food stalls selling peerless Katong *laksa*.

Changi Prison

Infamous **Changi Prison** was the site of a World War II POW camp in which Japanese jailers subjected Allied prisoners to the harshest of treatment. The prison itself is still in use (drug offenders are periodically executed here), and its terrible past is marked in the hugely moving **Changi Museum** (daily 9.30am–4pm; free; ☏62142451, ⊛www.changimuseum.com), just up the road.

A recent appeal for artefacts by the Singapore Tourist Board to Australian veterans' associations mustered a Samurai sword, a prisoner's chipped enamel mug, ration cards, a Nippon-Go primer and assorted other relics. In truth, though, the museum's power lies more in the many cruelties it portrays, than in the miscellanies it has amassed. Sketches, photographs and information boards plot the Japanese occupation of Singapore and the fate of the soldiers and civilians subsequently incarcerated in camps around the Changi area. Most movingly of all, though, is the board of remembrance, where children, wives and compatriots have pinned messages for the dead.

Novelist James Clavell was a young British artillery officer in Singapore at the time of the Japanese invasion; later he drew on his own experience of the "obscene forbidding prison" at Changi in writing *King Rat*, never forgetting that in the cells of the prison camp, " … the stench was nauseating. Stench from rotten bodies. Stench from a generation of confined human bodies." You can get the merest sense of what Clavell means by entering the Changi Cell, a dark, stuffy alleyway that approximates the cramped confinement suffered by POWs, and in which the voices of former POWs recall enduring the "howling, crying, shouting" of fellow inmates being tortured in the middle of the night.

Clavell's recollections are borne out by the selection of photos by **George Aspinall**, in a cabinet at the entrance to the museum. Aspinall, then a young Australian trooper, recorded the appalling living conditions and illnesses suffered by POWs in Malaya and Thailand during the occupation using a folding Kodak 2 camera, later developing his shots with a stock of processing materials which he found while working on a labour gang in Singapore's docks.

The museum's **gallery** section showcases the work of various prison artists, among them W.R.M. Haxworth, who produced over 400 paintings and sketches during his internment. Haxworth's tongue-in-cheek sketches of daily Changi life reveal the dry sense of humour and stiff upper lips that sustained internees in the face of adversity. One, entitled "Changi Comforts", depicts a variety of rickety stools, some fruit and a battered biscuit tin. Another sketch, in which a character holds up two shirts, one white and one black, is entitled "White and Changi white". Elsewhere, there are full-scale reproductions of the

Singapore food

Singaporeans live to *makan* ("eat", in Malay) – so much so that "Have you eaten?" often replaces "How are you?" as a social greeting – yet the country has no indigenous cuisine to boast of. The island's ethnic diversity is reflected in its culinary offerings which range from hearty noodle dishes, cleansing soups and melt-in-the-mouth fried and steamed fish from China; the breads and meats of the tandoor oven, and the vegetable daals and curries from the Indian sub-continent; and rich, coconut-based dishes, fiery with chilli, from the Malay kitchen.

Unofficial national dishes

You could stay in Singapore for a year and never eat the same meal twice. That said, some dishes have attained iconic status, and locals return to them time and again.

Chicken satay sticks

- ❑ **Chilli crab** Crabs wok-fried with garlic, chilli and tomato paste.
- ❑ **Chicken rice** Poached chicken on rice cooked in chicken stock.
- ❑ **Char Kway Teow** Rice noodles fried with Chinese sausage, prawns and fishcake and mixed in soy sauce.
- ❑ **Murtabak** Indian bread parcel stuffed with minced meat, onion and egg.
- ❑ **Laksa** Noodles, prawns and fishcake steeped in a hot chilli-coconut soup.
- ❑ **Satay** Meat skewers roasted over coals and dipped in a sweet peanut sauce.
- ❑ **Fish head curry** A fiery, hot-sour sauce with a whole fish head – eyes and all.

Breakfast

No meal demonstrates the multicultural nature of the Singaporean dining experience better than breakfast. Chinese residents often favour a bowl of congee, a thin rice gruel served with spring onion, shredded chicken or other extras. **Dim sum** – dumplings, buns and assorted titbits steamed in bamboo baskets – is another classic Chinese breakfast, and best washed down with cleansing jasmine tea. Malay mornings typically begin with **nasi lemak** (rich rice) which comprises coconut rice with **ikan bilis** (dried anchovies), sliced omelette and cucumber, and is traditionally served in a banana leaf. Strange as it may sound, **roti prata**, a layered and griddle-fried south Indian bread dipped in curry sauce, is a hugely popular breakfast choice among Singaporeans. For something a little more familiar to western taste buds, try **kaya toast**, a local jam made from coconut, sugar and egg, that's slathered between buttered slices of bread toasted over charcoal.

Steaming dim sum – breakfast Chinese style

Hawker food tradition

A diner at a hawker centre

Food-loving Singaporeans have little time for the airs and graces of fine dining. For the most authentic eating experience in Singapore you'll need to visit a hawker centre, where avenues of common seating are served by scores of tiny stalls allowing punters to mix and match from a huge range of snacks, meals, desserts, fruits and drinks. Hawker centres emerged in the 1950s and 1960s to address the problem of unhygienic food preparation by unlicensed street vendors and in recent years many have been replaced by more modern food courts. However, with their air-con units and contemporary design, these modern counterparts lack the earthy character of the remaining hawker centres where smoke, steam and aromas mingle, and the air rings to the clatter of spatula on wok and the cries of coffee sellers calling out orders.

Nonya cuisine

The closest Singapore comes to an indigenous cuisine is the food of the Straits Chinese, or Peranakans – descendants of early Chinese settlers in Penang, Malacca and Singapore who married local Malay women. The resulting cuisine (known as Nonya after the local word for Peranakan women) blends Chinese and Malay ingredients, cooking techniques and dishes to mouthwatering effect. Most Nonya menus are framed around the same handful of classic dishes. Otak otak, or fish mashed with coconut milk and chilli and then steamed in banana leaf, makes a piquant starter. Next, you could try ikan assam pedas (sour and spicy fish), itek tim (duck and salted vegetable soup) or babi ponteh (pork cooked in soy sauce). But for the quintessential taste of Nonya food, order up bitter ayam buah keluak, chicken cooked in black nuts. The traditional Nonya dessert of bubur cha-cha – yam, sweet potato, tapioca flour and coconut milk – rounds a meal off in style.

A selection of south Indian curries, served on a banana leaf.

Fruits

Western supermarkets may have you believe that no fruit is ever unavailable, but Singaporeans have more respect for the seasons. Listed below are a few of the fruits to look out for, with their approximate seasons.

- ❑ **Rambutan** Bright red and hairy fruit yielding white segments similar to lychee (June–September)
- ❑ **Mangosteen** Within a crimson rind is a fruit whose sweetness bears an acidic tang (May–September)
- ❑ **Durian** Spiky rugby ball of a fruit whose pungent, custard-y flesh reveals notes of garlic, onion, almond and caramel (April–July)
- ❑ **Jackfruit** Huge, sack-like fruit with sweet segments (March–September)
- ❑ **Star fruit** Apple-y in taste, star-shaped in appearance (March–July)

Singapore Food Festival

Gourmands planning a trip to Singapore will want to time their visit to coincide with July's **Food Festival** (ⓦwww.singaporefoodfestival.com), when shopping centres, stalls and restaurants across the island offer a month of tastings, cooking demonstrations and culinary workshops. Scores of events take place, focusing on everything from Asian haute cuisine to the local street food heritage, and from kids' dining to Chinese tea appreciation. Even the island's main tourist destinations get in on the act. The Zoo, National Museum and Mandai Orchid Gardens are just some of the attractions that have offered food-themed events during the festival in previous years, and in 2005 the Night Safari's Gourmet Safari Express offered the chance to dine onboard a tram as it toured the park.

Liquid pleasures

It's not only the food of Singapore that excites the taste buds. The island also boasts some memorable beverages. Nothing kick starts the day better than a hot mug of **kopi C** – strong, black coffee sweetened with a huge dollop of evaporated milk. Tea lovers may prefer a cup of **teh halia**, a rich, sweet tea infused with fresh ginger; but for pure theatre, nothing beats a cup of milky **teh tarik** (in Malay, "pulled tea"), which is poured from a height from one beaker to another to create a frothy tea milkshake. The juice released by running sugar canes through a mangle is one of a hawker centre's sweetest coolest treats.

A **Singapore Sling** is de rigueur while in the country – it's a heady blend of gin, cherry brandy, pineapple and lime juices and cointreau – but for the quintessential Singapore experience, order up an ice-cold bottle of **Tiger beer** and drink it from a mug fresh from the chiller cabinet.

Sugar-cane juice

murals of Stanley Warren, who used camouflage paint, crushed snooker chalk and aircraft paints smuggled in by fellow POWs to paint Bible scenes on a Changi chapel wall.

Outside in a courtyard is a replica of a simple wooden chapel, typical of those erected in Singapore's wartime camps; the brass cross on its altar was crafted from spent ammunition casings, while its walls carry more poignant messages of remembrance penned by visiting former POWs and relatives.

Journey's end is at the **museum shop**, where a video screen plays footage of the Japanese attack and the living conditions in Changi. On a lighter note, among the war-related books stocked in the shop is *The Happiness Box*, the first copy of which was written, illustrated and bound by POWs in Changi in 1942 as a Christmas present for children in the prison. The Japanese became suspicious of the POWs' motives when they noticed one of the book's central characters was called Winston, but it was buried in the prison grounds before it could be confiscated, and only recovered after the war had ended.

To **get to** the museum, take bus #2 from Chinatown or Victoria Street; alternatively, you could take the MRT to Tanah Merah station, and pick up the #2 there.

Changi Village

There's little to bring you out to sleepy **CHANGI VILLAGE**, ten minutes further on from the prison on bus #2, save to catch a boat from **Changi Point**, behind the bus terminal, for Pulau Ubin (see below) or for the coast of Johor in Malaysia (see "Departure", p.38). The left-hand jetty is for Ubin, the right-hand one for bumboats to Johor.

A stroll over the footbridge to the right of the two jetties takes you to **Changi Beach**, the execution site of many thousands of Singaporean civilians by Japanese soldiers during World War II. As a beach it wins few prizes – apart from its casuarinas and palms. Its most pleasant aspect is its view: to your left as you look out to sea is Pulau Ubin, while slightly to the right is the island of Tekong (a military zone), behind which you can see a hill on mainland Malaysia. In the water you'll find boats galore, from bumboats to supertankers. Changi Village Road, the village's main drag, has a growing number of decent restaurants and a few bars, or try the hawker centre near the bus terminal.

Pulau Ubin

PULAU UBIN, 2km offshore, gives visitors a pretty good idea of what Singapore would have been like fifty years ago. A lazy backwater tucked into the Straits of Johor, it's a great place to come if you're tired of shops, high-rises and traffic. It's almost worth coming for the ten-minute boat trip alone, made in an old, oil-stained bumboat ($2 each way) that chugs noisily across Serangoon Harbour, belching fumes all the way. Boats depart from Changi Point throughout the day from 6am onwards, leaving whenever they are full. The last boat back to Changi leaves as late as 10pm, if there's a demand, but plan to be at the jetty by 8.30pm at the latest, just in case.

Boats dock at the pier in **Ubin Village**, where palm trees slope and Malay stilt houses teeter over a sludgy mangrove beach that's stippled with the remains of collapsed, rotting jetties. Bear left from the jetty, and you'll soon hit the village square – but before that, swing by the **information kiosk** (daily 8.30am–5pm; ☎65424108, ⊛www.nparks.gov.sg) to the right of the jetty for an island map. A

△ East-coast beach

short, circular **sensory trail** created by the Singapore Society for the Visually Handicapped, starts and finishes at the kiosk, taking in herbs, spices and orchids en route.

The main road into the village is lined with scores of battered old mopeds, locals sit around, watching the day take its course, roosters run free in the dirt and dogs bask under the hot sun. The best, and most enjoyable, way to explore the dirt tracks of Ubin is by mountain bike. A cluster of **bike rental shops** operates along the jetty road, charging $2–15 for a day's rental, depending upon the bike and the season (it's most expensive during school holidays). A labyrinthine network of tracks veins Ubin, but it's only a small island (just 7km by 2km) and all roads are well signposted, so you won't get lost. As you go, look out for the monitor lizards, long-tailed macaques, lizards, butterflies, kites and eagles that inhabit Ubin, and listen for the distinctive rattle-buzz of cicadas.

The **hall** on the left flank of the square is used periodically for Chinese opera, ceremonial occasions and other Ubin functions. Opposite it is a tiny, fiery-red Chinese temple. Bear left past the hall until you come to a basketball court, where a left turn takes you to the west of the island and a right turn to the east.

Taking the left turn west, after about five minutes you'll come to an impressively deep **quarry**, from which granite was taken to build the causeway linking Singapore to Johor Bahru – Ubin is the Malay word for granite. Don't swim in this or any other Ubin quarry, however tempting it might be: the government has erected signs warning of hefty fines for doing so. A right turn after the first bridge you cross brings you to a peaceful lean-to **Chinese temple** fronted by wind chimes, a shrine holding three colourful figurines of tigers and a pool of carp, and shielded from the surrounding mangrove by a pretty lily-pad pond.

Further north along the track, over a second bridge and down a right turn marked Jalan Wat Siam, is a rather incongruous **Thai Buddhist Temple** fronted by two big, polished wooden elephants, complete with portraits of the king and queen of Thailand, and a bookcase full of Thai books. Pictures telling the story of the life of Buddha ring the inner walls of the temple, along with images of various Buddhists hells – the most disturbing of which depicts demons pouring boiling liquid down the mouths of "those who always drink liquor". Boonrai, the temple's head monk, holds free **meditation classes** every Saturday and Sunday; call ☎65423468 to book yourself into a class.

Biking **east** from the basketball court takes you past the prawn and fish farms, rubber trees and raised kampung houses of the centre and eastern side of Ubin. **Noordin Beach**, at the top of the island, offers an unprepossessing but smart enough patch of sand, though its views across the Johor Straits to southern Malaysia have been spoilt by the ugly metal fence recently erected in the water to keep out illegal immigrants. Further east, towards **Kampong Melayu**, are some beautifully maintained and brightly painted examples of kampung-style stilt houses. Beyond the village, **Tanjong Chek Jawa**, the far eastern tip of the island, constitutes Ubin's most pristine patch of mangrove; call the information kiosk on ☎65424108 to pre-arrange a free guided tour of the mudskippers, crabs, seabirds and other wildlife here.

You'll happen upon the odd drinks stop as you bike around Ubin. For **food**, there's a restaurant (daily 8am–10pm) at *Ubin Lagoon Resort*. Otherwise, of the several eating options in the village, the best bets are the *Sin Lam Huat* for its chilli crab and kampung chicken dishes, or the Malay coffee shop beside the jetty, which knocks out curries, noodles and *rendangs*.

Escape Theme Park

With kids in tow, you'll be glad of the **Escape Theme Park** (Mon & Wed–Fri 4–10pm, Sat & Sun 10am–10pm; adults $16, kids $8 incl. all rides and one go-kart ride; ☎65819112, ⊕www.escapethemepark.com.sg) west of Changi Village at 1 Pasir Ris Close. Singapore's largest theme park, it boasts fifteen fairground-style rides, among them the Cadbury Inverter, the Daytona Multi tier Go Kart and Asia's highest flume ride, Wet & Wild. Clowns wander the park's byways, offering light relief while you queue for rides; and in the central pavilion there are oodles of games, galleries and food outlets. From Pasir Ris, you'll need to hop on bus #354.

7

Western Singapore

S ince the government's industrialization programme began in the late 1960s, far **western Singapore** has become the manufacturing heart of the state, and today thousands of companies occupy units within the towns of Jurong and Tuas. Manufacturing is the backbone of Singapore's economic success – the state currently produces more than half the world's hard disk drives, for example. Despite this saturation, much of the western region – developed from former swampland and wasteland – remains remarkably verdant. Surprisingly, given the industrial surroundings, several major tourist attractions are located here; the pick of them all is the fascinating **Jurong Birdpark**. Slightly further east, the **Singapore Science Centre** is packed with imaginative and informative exhibitions, and is not to be missed if you've got kids to entertain, while further west – and not to be missed if you've got adults to entertain – is the **Tiger Brewery**. Just west of Chinatown is the district of **Telok Blangah**, once the seat of Singapore's *temenggong* or chieftain, and still dominated by Mount Faber, as well as the **Harbourfront** complex from where cable cars, boats and buses make for Sentosa (see p.124). **Haw Par Villa**, as garish a theme park as you'll ever set eyes on, is just a short hop west of Mount Faber, as are the reminders of World War II at **Labrador Secret Tunnels** and **Reflections at Bukit Chandu**. All of these places are easily reached from the city centre, using either buses or the MRT.

HarbourFront and Mount Faber

A twenty-minute walk west of Chinatown is the district of **Telok Blangah**, home to **HarbourFront**, a shopping centre-cum-marine terminal from where boats depart for Indonesia's Riau Archipelago, and from which cable cars rock across the skyline, on their way to and from **Mount Faber** and across to Sentosa Island (see p.124).

Mount Faber (hillock would be a better word), 600m north of Harbourfront commands fine views of Keppel Harbour and central Singapore to the north-east, which are even more impressive at night when the city is lit up. Originally called Telok Blangah, the mount was renamed in 1845 after government engineer Captain Charles Edward Faber. In the early days of colonial rule, Temenggong Abdul Rahman played prime minister to Sultan Hussein Shah's president, and his signature graced the treaty authorizing the East India Company to operate out of Singapore. All that's left of his settlement on the southern slopes of Mount Faber is its pillared mosque – the **State of Johor Mosque** – and, behind that, a small Malay cemetery and a portion of the brickwork that once housed the Temenggong's baths.

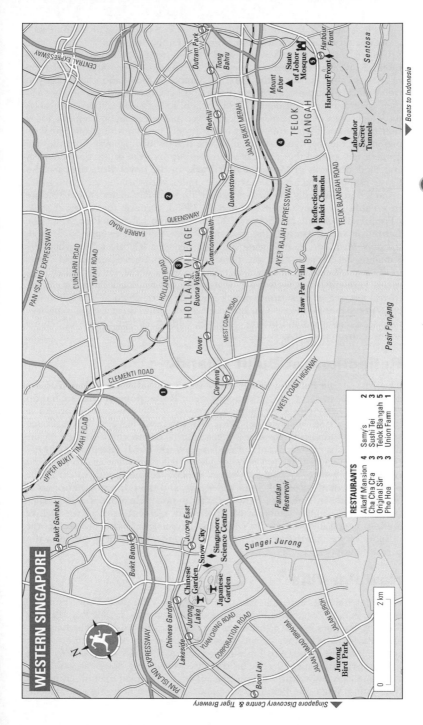

RESTAURANTS

Alkaff Mansion	4
Cha Cha Cha	3
Original Sin	3
Pho Hoa	3
Samy's	2
Sushi Tei	3
Telok Blangah	5
Union Farm	1

N

0   2 km

▶ Boats to Indonesia

▲ Singapore Discovery Centre & Tiger Brewery

WESTERN SINGAPORE | Harbourfront and Mount Faber

7

117

It's a long, steep walk from Telok Blangah Road up to the top of Mount Faber, and it's better to take the **cable car** from the Harbourfront (daily 8.30am–9pm; $10.90 return, children $5.50 for up to 4 stations; $15, children $8 for glass cabin). As well as Harbourfront, the cable car has two more stations, at the top of Mount Faber and across the water on Sentosa. A four-station ticket lets you ride from Harbourfront to Mount Faber and back down, over to Sentosa and then back again. An accident in 1983, when a ship's mast clipped the cables on which the cars are suspended, cost seven passengers their lives, but today laser eyes ensure that history won't repeat itself. There's a strong souvenir shop presence at the top, though you can escape this by moving away from the area immediately around the cable car station and up into the palms, bougainvilleas and rhododendrons of **Mount Faber Park**. In the **Jewel Box**, the park also boasts a sophisticated bar and restaurant complex with thrilling views out to sea – though undoubtedly the area's most thrilling culinary experience is to **dine in a cable car** (daily 6.30–8.30pm; ☏63779633; set meals for two from $88).

From Harbourfront, it's 1500m as the crow flies to Labrador Park, where the **Labrador Secret Tunnels** (hourly guided tours daily 10am–6pm; $8/5) recall the days when Fort Pasir Panjang stood on this spot. It's hard to see where the $5million development cost was spent: the two dark tunnels feature old copies of the Straits Times, dummies in wartime costume and the detritus – shell fragments, kerosene lamps, mess tins – of army life, but realistically if you are going to visit just one set of wartime tunnels, you'd do better to go to Fort Siloso (see p.127) or Battle Box (see p.63). Elsewhere in the park, there are gun emplacements, six-inch guns and bronze statues of soldiers; and fine views of Sentosa and the surrounding bay.

Reflections at Bukit Chandu

The 1st and 2nd Battalion of the Malay Regiment's defence of Pasir Panjang against the Japanese, in 1942, is remembered at **Reflections at Bukit Chandu** (Tues–Sun 9am–5pm; $2, children $1; ☏63327978; ⊛www.1942.org.sg), a low-key attraction 3km west of Telok Blangah, at 31K Pepys Road. Facing some 13,000 advancing Japanese soldiers, the battalions chose to fight to the death rather than retreat. Wordily billed as a "World War II interpretive centre", Reflections uses exhibits and photographs to tell their story, and to track the unsuccessful defence of Malaya. Visitors experience the sounds of battle, the cold weight of a cast-iron helmet and a rifle, and the fear and claustrophobia of watch duty in a pillbox. However, this is no celebration of war. Rather, the emphasis is upon sombre meditation, with elements such as the Well of Reflection and the Windows of Memories encouraging visitors to ponder the purpose of war and to muse over the terrible loss of life that occurred in this part of Singapore.

Haw Par Villa

As an entertaining exercise in bad taste, **Haw Par Villa** (daily 9am–7pm; free) has few equals. Located 7km from the downtown area at 262 Pasir Panjang Road, it describes itself as a "historical theme park founded on Chinese legends and values", for which read a gaudy, gory parade of over a thousand grotesque statues. Previously known as Tiger Balm Gardens, the park now takes its name from its original owners, the Aw brothers, Boon Haw and Boon Par, who made a fortune early last century selling Tiger Balm – a cure-all unction created by their father. When the British government introduced licensing requirements for the possession of large animals, the private zoo that the brothers maintained on their estate here was closed down and replaced by statues.

The rides, theatre shows and multimedia attractions that were added a few years back to broaden the appeal of the place actually did no such thing. All have now been closed, leaving only the statues for which the park is famous. These statues feature characters and creatures from Chinese legend and religion, Fu Lu Shou, Confucius and the Laughing Buddha among them, as well as a fantastical menagerie of snakes, dragons, elephants, kissing locusts, monkeys and crabs with women's heads.

The best – and most gruesome – series of statues lies in the **Ten Courts of Hell** exhibit (daily 9am–5pm, $2), whose explanation of the Buddhist belief in punishment for sins and reincarnation is not for the faint-hearted. Accessed through the open mouth of a huge "walk-in" dragon, the statues depict sinners undergoing a ghastly range of tortures meted out by hideous, leering demons, before being wiped of all memory in the Pavilion of Forgetfulness and sent back to earth to have another stab at Godliness. Prostitutes are shown drowned in pools of blood, drug addicts tied to a red-hot copper pillar, thieves and gamblers frozen into blocks of ice and moneylenders who charge exorbitant interest rates thrown onto a hill of knives. If you are thinking of cracking the spine on this guidebook, bear in mind that being sawn in two is the penalty for the misuse of books. Before you enter the courts of hell, check out the replica of Aw Boon Haw's **tiger car** at the ticket desk, which had a huge tiger's head across the radiator to advertise the family wares.

Elsewhere, another series of statues retells the classic Chinese legend of the monk Xuanzang's **Journey into the West** in search of Buddhist scriptures. The trials and tribulations that beset the monk and his disciples, featuring such characters as the Spider Women, the Monkey God and the Scarlet Child, are all colourfully depicted.

A new attraction, the **Hua Song Museum** (Tues–Sun noon–7pm, $8.40/5.25), has taken up residence on the western flank of the compound. Roughly translated, its name means "in praise of the Chinese", making it an appropriate addition to a park so dedicated to Oriental faith and legend. The Hua Song Museum traces the struggles of early Chinese immigrants as they settled, assimilated and flourished around the world, and the global impact upon the world of the Chinese diaspora.

"Robust like bamboo, able to thrive in rich soil and stay alive in poor soil", reads one sign in the museum, "the early Chinese immigrant had to bend and blend in to survive." Successive **galleries** describe how this survival was affected. Visitors follow the Chinese migrants' long road from village to dockside and from dockside to far-flung corners of the world. In the Floating Hell gallery, displays and exhibits convey the hardships they endured on board the junks that transported them to their new lives and the struggles they had to stay alive when they came ashore. From there, the museum tells of how they assimilated into their adopted lands while still, with the support of their clan associations, preserving their ancestral identities. The lion's share of the museum's focus falls on China's male migrants but one gallery highlights the peculiar challenges that confronted female migrants – the young girl sold into slavery at auction, the samsui woman working on Singapore building sites. Food, one of the cornerstones of Chinese culture, merits its own gallery, where visitors become acquainted with the **cooking** implements and ingredients of its cuisine.

To **get to** HawPar Villa, take bus #200 from Buona Vista MRT, bus #143 from HarbourFront or #51 from Chinatown.

Holland Village

Holland Village was previously home to some of the British soldiers based in Singapore and has now developed into an expat stronghold, with a whole row of Western restaurants and shops. The **Holland Road Shopping Centre** at 211 Holland Avenue is the place to head for if you want to purchase Asian art, crafts or textiles: there are shops on two levels where you can buy anything from an Indian pram to a Chinese opium pipe, while newsagents, cobblers and key-cutters ply their trade outside. The small road alongside the shopping centre is called Lorong Liput, and off it is Lorong Mambong, home to a thriving restaurant scene and to **craft shops** that specialize in ceramic elephants, dragon pots, porcelain, rattan and bamboo products. **Pasar Holland**, opposite the shops, is a small, tumbledown market selling fruit, flowers, fish and meat, as well as housing a handful of hawker stalls. Details of arts and crafts outlets are given on pp.182–184. The nearest **MRT station** to Holland Village is Buona Vista, just a short walk away; bus #7 from Orchard Boulevard also stops here.

Jurong Lake and around

Several tourist destinations are dotted around the environs of tranquil **Jurong Lake**, about 4km northwest of the new town of Clementi. You're far likelier to want to come out this way if you've got children in tow.

Singapore Science Centre

At the **Singapore Science Centre** (Tues–Sun 10am–6pm; $6, children $3; ☎64252500, ⊛www.science.edu.sg), situated southwest of tranquil Jurong Lake, a broad range of exhibition galleries hold approaching a thousand hands-on exhibits designed to inject interest into even the most impenetrable scientific principles. The majority of the centre's visitors are local schoolchildren, who sweep around the galleries in vast, deafening waves, frantically trying out each interactive display. Exhibitions focusing on aviation, genetics, space science, marine ecology, IT, biotechnology and other disciplines allow you to experience sight through an insect's eyes, write in Braille, make smoke rings, speak with a frog's voice and see a thermal heat reflection of yourself. The **Omni-Theatre** (various times; $10, kids $5; call ☎64252500 for details of current movie), within the centre's grounds, features heart-stopping movies about science, space, history and adventure sports shown, planetarium-style, on a huge dome screen. Recently, it has also started showing blockbusters like *Harry Potter* and *Lord of the Rings*; check the local press for details of current showings. To **get out here** take the MRT to Jurong East station, then transfer to bus #335, or brave the ten-minute walk.

Snow City

High-tech machines at **Snow City** (Tues–Sun 9am–8.30pm, $12, including loan of jackets and boots; ☎65602306, ⊛www.snowcity.com.sg) let it snow twelve months a year in one corner of equatorial Singapore. Don't come expecting an Alpine piste though: the slope at this indoor centre, one stop north of the Science Centre on bus #335, on 21 Jurong Town Hall Road, is just 60m long and less than three storeys high, meaning that there's no scope for meaningful skiing or snowboarding, only for tobogganing on rubber rings. Nevertheless, the complex offers an invigorating alternative to the hot sun, its constant temperature of minus 5 degrees centigrade setting it on a par with most Singaporean cinemas. Snow City is an offshoot of the Singapore Science

Centre, and as such has an educational, as well as a recreational slant, in the shape of a very worthy cold-temperature science exhibition. However, faced with the chance to explore an igloo, make snowmen, engage in snow-gun combat and even come face to face with the Abominable Snowman, kids are likely to eschew extracurricular studies.

The Chinese and Japanese gardens

The **Chinese and Japanese gardens** (daily 6am–11pm; free), by Jurong Lake, just a hop and a skip from Chinese Garden MRT, defy categorization – too far out to visit for just a sit down in the park and too dull to be a fully fledged tourist attraction. In the **Chinese Garden**, pagodas, pavilions, bridges, arches and weeping willows attempt to capture the style of Beijing's Summer Palace – and fail. That said, if you're out this way, the **Bonzai Garden** (daily 9am–5pm; free), with its hundreds of miniature trees on raised plinths, is worth a look. The same cannot be said for the **Live Turtle and Tortoise Museum** (daily 9am–6pm; $5), a faintly depressing collection of creatures, whose prize exhibit, a two-headed turtle, is straight out of a freak show. Come to the Chinese Garden at the weekend and be prepared to be confronted by hordes of newlyweds scouring the garden for a decent photo opportunity. The Chinese Garden is best explored on the day of the annual **Moon Cake Festival** (see p.179), when it stays open late so that children can parade with their lanterns after dark.

Walking across the impressive, 65-metre Bridge of Double Beauty takes you to the **Japanese Garden** (or Seiwaen, meaning "Garden of Tranquillity"), whose wooden bridges, carp ponds, pebble footpaths and stone lanterns do much to help you forget the awful Formica chairs and tables in the central pavilion.

△ The Chinese Garden

Jurong BirdPark

The **Jurong BirdPark** (daily 9am–6pm; $14, children $7; ☎62650022, ⊛www
.birdpark.com.sg) on Jalan Ahmad Ibrahim contains nine thousand birds from
over six hundred species, ranging from Antarctic penguins to New Zealand
kiwis, making it one of the world's largest bird collections, and the biggest in
Southeast Asia. A ride on the **Panorail** (9am–5pm; $4, children $2) is a good
way to get your bearings; the bullet-shaped monorail skims over, past or through
all the main exhibits, with a running commentary pointing out the attractions.

Be sure at least to catch the **Waterfall Aviary**, which allows visitors to
walk amongst 1500 free-flying birds in a specially created tropical rainforest,
dominated by a thirty-metre-high waterfall. Other exhibits to seek out are
the Australian **Lory Loft**, the colourful **Southeast Asian Birds** (a tropical thunderstorm is simulated daily at noon), featuring the Luzon Bleeding
Heart Pigeon, which looks like it's just walked off the set of *Reservoir Dogs*;
the **Penguin Parade** (feeding times 10.30am & 3.30pm); and the **World
of Darkness**, a fascinating exhibit which swaps day for night with the aid
of a system of reversed lighting, in order that its cute collection of nocturnal
residents doesn't snooze throughout the park's opening hours. There are **bird
shows** throughout the day, the best of which is undoubtedly the "Kings of the
Skies" show (4pm) – a *tour de force* of speed flying by trained eagles, hawks and
falcons. Entrance to this, and to the similar "World of Hawks" show (10am) and
"All Star Bird Show" (11am & 3pm) is free. Back at the entrance complex you'll
find snacks and drinks for sale. **Getting to** the park involves MRT-ing to Boon
Lay station, then transferring to bus #194 or #251.

The Singapore Discovery Centre and Tiger Brewery

The hands-on **Singapore Discovery Centre** (Tues–Fri 9am–7pm; $9,
children $5; ☎67926188, ⊛www.sdc.com.sg), at 510 Upper Jurong Road, is
mainly geared towards local school parties. The emphasis is on Singapore's
history, technological achievements and national defences, but there are
exhibits with broader appeal, such as **motion simulator** rides that let you
experience flying a jet or driving a tank, and a clutch of virtual reality games.
In the grounds outside the centre are a cluster of military vehicles of varying vintages, and an imaginative playground complete with its own maze. To
reach the Singapore Discovery Centre, travel to Boon Lay MRT station and
then transfer to bus #193.

Three kilometres due west of the Discovery Centre, on the approach road
that links with Malaysia, is the home of one of Singapore's best-liked exports.
Tiger Beer, now the flagship brew of the Asia Pacific Breweries Limited, has
been brewed in Singapore since 1931, though back then its home was the
Malayan Breweries on Alexandra Road, where it was developed with help
from Heineken. A few years later, the establishment of Archipelago Brewery
by German giants Beck's seemed to set the scene for a Singaporean **beer war**,
especially when Tiger's new rival, Anchor Beer, was priced slightly lower. But
in 1941, Archipelago was bought out by Malayan Breweries, since when the
organization has gone from strength to strength, moving in May 1990 into new
holdings in Tuas, and changing its name to reflect "the new international role
the company has assumed", although it's still commonly known as the Tiger
Brewery.

Today, the tiger beneath a palm tree that adorns the label on every bottle of
Tiger Beer can be seen in ads across the state. Anthony Burgess borrowed *Time
for a Tiger*, the original slogan for the beer, for the title of his debut novel. As the

embattled, debt-ridden police-lieutenant, Nabby Adams, gulps down another beer, " . . . fresh blood flowed through his arteries, the electric light seemed brighter, what were a few bills anyway?"

A **tour** of the brewery (Mon–Fri 9.30am, 11am, 2.30pm & 5.30pm, free; ☎68603007, ⊚www.tigerbeer.com) is made up of three component parts, arranged in rising order of appeal: first comes a film show which fills visitors in on the history of the setup; next a walk through the space-age brewing, bottling and canning halls; and finally an hour or two's free drinking in the company's own bar – Nabby would have approved. You need at least ten people in the party, though all is not lost if you are travelling alone – phone up, and if there's a tour already arranged, ask to tag along. To get to the brewery get off at Boon Lay MRT, then take bus #192.

8

Sentosa and the southern isles

Many little **islands** stud the waters immediately south of Singapore. Some, like Pulau Bukom, are owned by petrochemical companies and are off-limits to tourists. Others, like **Sentosa**, **St John's** and **Kusu**, are served by ferries and can be visited without difficulty, though their accessibility has geared them very much to tourism. If you crave a more secluded spot, you'll have to charter a bumboat to one of the **more remote islands** from the Sentosa Ferry Terminal or Clifford Pier (see p.85 for details) or head for Pulau Ubin, off Singapore's east coast (see p.113).

Sentosa

Given the rampant development that over the past two decades has transformed **Sentosa** (tourist information line: ☎67368672, ⊛www.sentosa.com.sg) into the most developed of Singapore's southern islands, it's ironic that its name means "tranquillity" in Malay. Sentosa has come a long way since World War II, when it was a British military base known as Pulau Blakang Mati, or the "Island of Death Behind". Today, promoted for its beaches, sports facilities, hotels and attractions, it's a contrived but enjoyable recreational experience. The island is linked to the mainland by a five-hundred-metre causeway and a necklace of cable cars. Big changes are afoot for Sentosa. An $8-billion revamping program is underway which will spawn a casino, several new hotels and attractions and the Sentosa Express – a light railway linking the island to Harbourfront. Another development, an oceanfront residential project with marina facilities called **Sentosa Cove**, is at an advanced stage of development at the far eastern end of the island. Even before all these initiatives reach fruition, Sentosa is big business: five million visitors descend upon this tiny island, measuring just 3km by 1km, every year. Nevertheless you'll hear mixed reports of the place around Singapore. Ultimately it's as enjoyable as you make it; there's certainly plenty to do (though few of the attractions would make the grade at Disneyland), so much so that it's a good idea to arrive early, with a clear plan of action.

    Admission to several attractions is included in the Sentosa entry ticket (see "Practicalities" on p.128), though for the more popular attractions a

SENTOSA

Singapore River

N

Fulau Brani

Sentosa
Cove

Harbour
Front MRT   Vivo City

Harbour
Front

Ferry Terminal

Sentosa
Food Centre   Visitor
Cable Car   *i* Arrival Centre
Plaza   Musical   Cinemania
          Fountain   Sijori   Sentosa Orchid
Sijori   Wonder Golf   Gardens
          Sky Tower Carlsberg
Sentosa   Sijori Resort
4D Magix Images of   Merlion Sentosa
Sentosa   Singapore
Luge

Underwater World   *Siloso Beach*   The Beaufort
                                                   Hotel
Butterfly Park
& Insect Kingdom   Nature Walk   Dolphin Lagoon
Flying Trapeze   Dragon Trail   *Tanjong Beach*
                         Palawan Beach
Fort
Siloso

Shangri-la's
Rasa Sentosa
Beach Resort

Singapore River

0 ───── 500 m

further charge is levied. It's wise to avoid coming at the weekend, or on public holidays.

Sentosa's main attractions

Three attractions outshine all others on Sentosa. At the **Underwater World** (daily 9am–9pm; $19.50, kids $12.50), a moving walkway carries you the length of a hundred-metre acrylic tunnel that snakes through two large tanks: sharks lurk menacingly on all sides, huge stingrays drape themselves languidly above you, and immense shoals of gaily coloured fish dart to and fro. This may not sound all that exciting, but the sensation of being engulfed by sea life – there are more than 2500 fishes here – is a breathtaking one, and the nearest you'll get to the ocean floor without a wet suit. Of particular interest is the Deadly Corridor, which is home to electric eels, piranha and stonefish. If that isn't enough to get the adrenaline pumping, there's even the chance to dive with the sharks by pre-arrangement ($95 per person); call ☎62750030 for more details. A **touchpool** beside the entrance allows you to pick up starfish and sea cucumbers – the latter rather like socks filled with wet sand – while beyond that is the **Marine Theatre** which screens educational films throughout the day.

The **Dolphin Lagoon** (daily 10.30am–6pm) is free with the Underwater World ticket, though located away on Sentosa's Palawan Beach; the marine acrobatics of its resident school of Indo-Pacific humpback dolphins are best viewed during one of the daily "Meet the Dolphins" sessions (Mon–Fri 11am, 1.30pm, 3.30pm & 5.30pm).

Another major-league attraction is **Images of Singapore** (daily 9am–9pm; $10, children $7). Here, life-sized dioramas present the history and heritage of Singapore from its early days as a fourteenth-century trading post through to the surrender of the Japanese in 1945. Though the scene-setting AV presentation is contrived and flaky, and some of the wax dummies look as if they've

△ Fort Siloso

been pinched from clothes shop windows, the effect is nonetheless fascinating. Iconic images from Singapore's past – Raffles forging a treaty with the island's Malay rulers, rubber tappers at the Botanical Gardens, coolies working the Singapore River, the street barber, satay man and dhoby washer at work – spring to life, and there are actors dressed as coolies and kampung dwellers on hand to provide further insight. There are more wax dummies in the Singapore Celebrates gallery, this time dolled up in festive costumes to represent Singapore's various ethnic celebrations.

A trip up to **Fort Siloso** (daily 10am–6pm; $8, children $5) at the far western tip of the island, forms Sentosa's third real highlight. The fort – actually a cluster of buildings and gun emplacements above a series of tunnels bored into the island – guarded Singapore's western approaches from the 1880s until 1956, but was rendered obsolete in 1942, when the Japanese moved down into Singapore from Malaysia. Today, the recorded voice of Battery Sergeant Major (BSM) Cooper talks you through a mock-up of a nineteenth-century barracks, complete with living quarters, guard room, laundry and assault course. Be sure to check out the Surrender Chambers, recently moved from Images of Singapore, where life-sized figures re-enact the British and Japanese surrenders of 1942 and 1945, respectively. After that you can explore the complex's hefty gun emplacements and tunnels, and sit in on the Battle for Singapore, when British soldiers were forced to surrender to the Japanese.

Other attractions on Sentosa

The rest of Sentosa has lots of less interesting options. You might consider one of Sentosa's newer attractions: **Sentosa Luge** (Mon–Thurs 10am–6pm, Fri–Sun 10am–7pm; one ride $8), an enjoyable go-carting track; **Sentosa 4D Magix** (daily 10am–9pm; $16, children $9.50), where state-of-the-art audiovisual systems, environmental effects and synchronized-motion seats combine to breath-taking effect to bring movies to life; or the **Flying Trapeze** (Mon–Fri 4–6pm, Sat & Sun 4–7pm; $12 for three swings), where safety harnesses allow you to discover your inner Cirque du Soleil.

Scale the 110-metre-high **Carlsberg Sky Tower** (daily 9am–9pm; $10, children $6), and you'll enjoy panoramic views across Singapore to Malaysia and Indonesia; while back at ground level, **Sijori WonderGolf** (daily 9am–7pm; $8, children $4) has 54 crazy holes to challenge you.

Otherwise you could do worse than strolling in the elegant, scented grounds of the **Sentosa Orchid Gardens** (Mon–Fri 11am–7.30pm, Sat & Sun 11am–10pm; free). For something slightly more exciting head for the **Butterfly Park and Insect Kingdom Museum** (daily 9am–6.30pm; $10, children $6), is stuffed with all sorts of creepy-crawlies.

Musical Fountain

By the early evening, many of Sentosa's attractions are closed, but not so the **Musical Fountain** (shows at 5pm, 5.30pm, 7.40pm, 8.40pm), which is either cute or tacky, depending on your point of view. The fountain dances along to a throbbing soundtrack, with lights, lasers, CGI cartoon characters and pyrotechnics adding to the effect. Overlooking the display is the **Merlion**, a 37-metre-high statue of Singapore's tourism totem that takes centre-stage in the shows. It's possible to walk up to the viewing decks at the top of the Merlion (10am–8pm; $8, children $5) from where there are great views of Singapore's harbour, skyline and surrounding islands.

Beaches on Sentosa

Probably the best option on Sentosa, after a trip on the monorail and a visit to one or two attractions, is to head for the three beaches, **Siloso**, **Palawan** and **Tanjong** on the southwestern coast. Created with thousands of cubic metres of imported white sand and scores of coconut palms, they offer canoes, surfboards and aqua-bikes for rent, as well as plain old deckchairs. The water here is great for swimming and Singapore does not demand the same modesty on its beaches as Malaysia, although topless and nude bathing are out. From Palawan Beach, a suspended rope bridge connects Sentosa with a tiny islet that's the southern-most part of continental Asia. In recent years, Singapore's annual Dragon Boat Festival (see p.178) has been held off Siloso Beach. There are also beach raves, Singapore-style, from time to time, which are advertised in the local press way in advance.

Sentosa Practicalities

Admission to Sentosa costs $2 if you walk across from the mainland, and $3 if you take the bus from HarbourFront MRT station (Exit A signposted Telok Blangah Road then follow the signs to the island shuttle bus). This route will cease when the light railway currently under construction is completed. However, the most spectacular route is by the **cable cars** (daily 8.30am–9pm) that travel on a loop between mainland Mount Faber (see p.116) and Sentosa. For the round trip from Harbourfront up to Mount Faber, across to Sentosa and back to Harbourfront, you'll pay $10.90 (kids $5.50), including admission fee.

Sentosa's basic admission fee gives unlimited rides on the island's four **bus routes**. But the best way to get about is to **rent a bike** for the day ($5–10 an hour depending on the machine) from the kiosk beside the ferry terminal; tandems are also available.

The *Asian Food Lover's Place*, beside the ferry terminal, is one of the cheapest of Sentosa's many **eating** options; otherwise, try the nearby *Steword's Riverboat* for Tex-Mex and Cajun dishes, or the *SEA Village Restaurant*, near the visitor arrival centre, where there are reasonably priced Asian buffet lunches and dinners. Sentosa currently has three international-class **hotels**, cheaper chalets and limited camping possibilities (see p.141 for more details).

Kusu and St John's islands

Well kept and clean as they are, Sentosa's beaches do tend to get overcrowded and you may do better to head for either **St John's** or **Kusu** islands, which are 6km south of Singapore and connected to the mainland by a **ferry** from Sentosa Ferry Terminal. Great things are planned for these islands: $1-billion redevelopment plans are in place that will transform them by the addition of restaurants, spas, resorts and other entertainments concepts. Already, St John's has been linked by causeways to adjacent **Lazarus** and **Seringat** islands in preparation for these plans. Both St Johns and Kusu have decent sand beaches, though for the moment the more interesting of the two is Kusu, also known as **Turtle Island**. Singaporean legend tells of a Chinese and a Malay sailor who were saved from drowning by a turtle that transformed itself into an island; a pool of turtles is still kept on Kusu. Another legend describes how an epidemic afflicting a ship moored off Kusu was banished by the god Tua Pek Kong.

Whatever the truth in these tales, once a year during the ninth lunar month (usually in October or November), tens of thousands of Singaporean pilgrims descend upon the **Chinese temple** and **Malay shrine** a few minutes' walk from the jetty on Kusu, to pray for prosperity. The island is impossibly crowded during this time, but the rest of the year it offers a tranquil escape from the mainland. There is a modest cafeteria on St John's, but if you're going to Kusu it's wise to take a picnic.

Ferries (Mon–Sat 10am & 1.30pm, Sun 9am, 11am, 1, 3 & 5pm; $9, children $6) for Kusu and St John's depart from the Sentosa Ferry Terminal. Check the return times with the boatmen.

Other islands

Since no regular ferries run to any of Singapore's other southern islands, you'll have to **charter** a bumboat from Clifford Pier. Boats take up to twelve passengers, and cost at least $40 an hour. Unless you rent a boat for the whole day, you must arrange to be picked up. The attractive **Sister's Islands**, which lie in the same cluster of isles as St John's and Kusu, are a popular snorkelling and fishing haunt, as is **Pulau Hantu** ("Ghost Island" in Malay), 12km further west and under the shadow of Shell-owned Pulau Bukum. Most interesting of all, though, is **Pulau Seking**, 3 or 4km east of Hantu; here a handful of Malays continue to live in traditional stilt houses that teeter over the sea, their lifestyle almost untouched by the progress that has transformed the mainland. These islands are all very basic, so take a picnic and a day's supply of bottled water with you.

Listings

Listings

Accommodation

A ccommodation in Singapore needn't take too big a bite out of your holiday budget; good deals abound if your expectations aren't too lofty or – at the budget end of the scale – if you don't mind sharing. Singapore's status as one of the main gateways to Southeast Asia means that occupancy rates at all levels of accommodation are permanently high. Even so, you shouldn't encounter too many difficulties in finding a room, and advance booking isn't really necessary unless your visit coincides with Chinese New Year or Hari Raya (see "Festivals", p.180).

The **Singapore Hotel Association** (Ⓦwww.sha.org.sg) has a booking counter at each of Changi airport's two terminals (Terminal One Mon–Thurs, Sat & Sun 7am–6am, Fri 7am 11.30pm, Ⓣ65426966; Terminal Two Mon 7am–11.30pm, Tues–Sun 7am–3am, Ⓣ65459789) and will find you a room in the city for a $10 deposit that's deducted from your bill at the end of your stay, though they represent only Singapore's official hotels, all of which are listed in two free STB booklets, *Hotels Singapore* and *Budget Hotels Singapore*. Touts at the airport also hand out flyers advertising rooms in guesthouses and hostels. If you prefer to plan ahead, you might wish to book online through Ⓦwww .stayinsingapore.com or Ⓦwww.singaporehotelbooking.com.

The cheapest beds are in the communal **dormitories** of many of Singapore's resthouses, where you'll pay $10 or less a night. Have a good look before parting with your cash though, as most of these places are simply flats whose inner walls have been knocked down and every available space crammed with bunk beds. Bedbugs can be a problem and the lights are left burning all night. These crashpads serve as cheap accommodation for many of Singapore's guest workers, so if you want to practise your Thai or Tagalog, you'll have ample opportunity. The next best deals are at **guesthouses**, most of which are situated in the Beach Road and Little India areas, with some south of the river in Chinatown. A makeover of the Bencoolen area has seen most of its guesthouses closed down to make way for new hotels and commercial premises.

Guesthouses aren't nearly as cosy as their name suggests; at the $20–30 mark, rooms are tiny, bare, and divided by paper-thin partitions; toilets are shared and showers are cold. However, paying another $10–20 secures a bigger, air-con room, often including TV, laundry and cooking facilities, lockers and breakfast. Always check that everything works before you hand over any money. It's always worth asking for a discount, too, especially if you are staying a few days.

The appeal of Singapore's **Chinese-owned hotels**, similar in price to guesthouses, is their air of faded grandeur – some haven't changed in forty years. Sadly, faded grandeur is something the government frowns upon, with the result that there are precious few left. In more modern, **mid-range hotels**, a room for two with air-con, private bathroom and TV will set you back around

$60–90 a night. From there, prices rise steadily, and at the top end of the scale Singapore boasts some extraordinarily opulent hotels, ranging from the colonial splendour of *Raffles* to the awesome spectacle of the *Swissôtel The Stamford* (see p.137) – until recently the world's tallest hotel. Though you'll find the greatest concentration of **upmarket hotels** around Orchard Road, most of the new breed of **boutique hotels** – which use antique furniture and fittings to create an air of Oriental nostalgia – are based in Chinatown.

The majority of mid-range and upmarket hotels in Singapore make no charge for **children** under 12 if they are occupying existing spare beds in rooms. However, if you require an extra bed to be put in your room, ten to fifteen percent of the room rate is usually charged. Cots are provided free.

Bencoolen Street and around

Central **Bencoolen Street** has long been the mainstay of Singapore's backpacker industry. Times are changing, though, and many of the decrepit buildings that once housed the lion's share of Singapore's budget guesthouses have already fallen to the demolition ball and been replaced by posher hotels. Peony Mansion, the classic Singapore crash pad, has survived up to now, but its days are surely numbered and guesthouse owners are fast deserting its warren of seedy halls and stairways.

Despite the changing nature of the area, however, you'll still find dorm beds and rooms as cheap as any in Singapore – at least for the time being. Bencoolen Street is a five-minute walk from **Dhoby Ghaut MRT station**. All the hotels in this section are keyed on the **map** on p.93.

Albert Court Hotel 180 Albert St ☏ 63393939, ⓦ www.albertcourt.com.sg. This charmingly conceived boutique hotel, designed around the restaurants of lively Albert Court Mall, is just a short walk from both Bugis Village and Little India; rooms have all the standard embellishments. Singles start at $190.

Bencoolen Hotel 47 Bencoolen St ☏ 63360822, ⓦ www.hotelbencoolen.com. With business facilities, laundry service, air-ticketing facilities, a modest rooftop spa pool and smart rooms with all mod cons, the friendly *Bencoolen* represents great value. Singles start at $90.

City Bayview 30 Bencoolen St ☏ 63372882, ⓦ www.bayviewintl.com. A pleasing, recently renovated, mid-range hotel, with comfortable rooms, a compact rooftop swimming pool and a friendly, modern café. Doubles from $105.

Hawaii Hostel 2nd floor, 171b Bencoolen St ☏ 63384187. Small, tidy enough, air-con rooms with breakfast included, as well as dorm beds for $12.

Lee Boarding House 7th floor, Peony Mansion, 46–52 Bencoolen St ☏ 63383149. Peony Mansion's last remaining guesthouse, with bare but clean enough rooms, a breakfast area and laundry facilities. If you want a dorm you'll need to go to the *Hawaii Hostel* or one of the *Lee* branches on Beach Road (see opposite). Doubles with a/c from $60.

South East Asia Hotel 190 Waterloo St ☏ 3382394, ⓦ www.seahotel.com.sg. Behind a jolly, yellow-and-white 1950s facade, lie spotless doubles with air-con, TV and phone for those yearning for a few creature comforts. Downstairs is the *Kwan Im* vegetarian restaurant (see p.156) serving Western breakfasts, and right next door is Singapore's liveliest Buddhist temple. Noisy, though atmospheric singles start at $77.

Strand Hotel 25 Bencoolen St ☏ 63381866, ⓦ www.strandhotel.com.sg. Excellent-value hotel with clean, welcoming rooms, a café serving Western and local dishes, and a variety of services. Doubles from $95.

Waterloo Hostel 4th Floor, Catholic Centre Building, 55 Waterloo St ☏ 63366555, ⓦ www.waterloohostel.com.sg. Catholic-run hostel, centrally located, spick and span, and boasting rooms with air-con, TV and phone. Complimentary breakfast thrown in. The mixed and single-sex dorms ($15–20) are welcoming.

Beach Road to Victoria Street

A few blocks east of Bencoolen Street, **Beach Road** boasts a full range of accommodation options, from charismatic old Chinese hotels to swish, new, five-star affairs. What's more, you can brag about having stayed down the road from *Raffles Hotel* – or even in it – when you get home. All the hotels in this section are keyed on the **map** on p.93.

Ah Chew Hotel 496 North Bridge Rd ☎68370356. Simple but charismatic rooms with "Wild West" swing doors, crammed with period furniture, and run by T-shirted old men lounging on antique opium couches. There are also fan and air-con dorms ($8–12), and baggage storage and self-service laundry facilities. Try and get a room at the front of the building – despite its address, the *Ah Chew* is just around the corner from North Bridge Road, on buzzing Liang Seah Street. Rooms around $50.

Aliwal Park Hotel 77 Aliwal St ☎62939022, ✉aliwal@pacific.net.sg. One of the few hotels in the Arab Street district, the *Aliwal* has spruce doubles with TV, air-con and attached bathrooms, at competitive prices. From $50.

Beach Hotel 95 Beach Rd ☎63367712, ⊛www.beachhotel.com.sg. The Lee Empire's most salubrious address is professionally run and very tidy. The location in the CDB is not quite as atmospheric as a Chinatown or Colonial District address, but central nonetheless. Doubles start at $75.

Golden Landmark Hotel 390 Victoria St ☎62972828, ⊛www.goldenlandmark.com.sg. Very pleasant and well appointed, once you get past the dated shopping centre downstairs, and handy for Bugis MRT station and Arab Street. Doubles start at $105.

Intercontinental 80 Middle Rd ☎63387600, ⊛www.intercontinental.com. Great hotel within the thriving Bugis Junction development, convenient and sumptuously furnished, with business centre, swimming pool, health club and an array of excellent restaurants including *Pimai Thai* and *Olive Tree*. Doubles start at $105.

Lee Home Stay 3rd floor, 490a North Bridge Rd ☎63341608. Bare but adequate rooms and dorms ($10), whose rates include free flow of hot drinks – but no breakfast or hot showers. All rooms share common facilities. The rooftop terrace is a pleasant place to relax. To enter, walk to the back of the curry house below and up the stairs to your left. Rooms from $30.

Lee Traveller's Club 6th floor, Fu Yuen Building, 75 Beach Rd ☎63395490. A bright and breezy common room overlooking Middle Road sets this place a cut above the other Lee addresses in the area. All rooms have air-con, but private facilities cost an extra $10. Laundry service is available. Dorm beds are $12.

Metropole Hotel 41 Seah St ☎63363611, ⊛www.metrohotel.com. Friendly, great-value establishment, just across the road from *Raffles Hotel* and home to the recommended *Imperial Herbal Restaurant* (see p.155). Doubles start at $103.

New 7th Storey Hotel 229 Rochor Rd ☎63370251, ⊛www.nsshotel.com. Despite its rather old-fashioned exterior, this is a clean and characterful hotel with perfectly respectable rooms, all with TV. Rooms with bathrooms en suite are available, though the communal ones are fine. Booking online saves a few dollars; dorm beds are $17. Doubles from $70.

Oxford Hotel 218 Queen St ☎63322222, ⊛www.oxfordhotel.com.sg. Terrific, well-run 135-room hotel, centrally sited, well serviced, friendly and affordable; prices are inclusive of breakfast. Recommended. Singles start at $120.

Plaza Parkroyal 7500 Beach Rd ☎62980011, ⊛www.plaza.singapore.parkroyalhotels.com. Luxurious, eye-catching hotel whose amenities include restaurants, and a business centre. Slightly off the beaten track, though there is a free shuttle service into town. Doubles start at $250.

Raffles Hotel 1 Beach Rd ☎63371886, ⊛www.raffleshotel.com. The flagship of Singapore's

△ Terrace, Raffles Hotel

tourism industry, *Raffles* takes shameless advantage of its reputation: $25 buys you a Singapore Sling and a glass to take home, while the souvenir shop stocks *Raffles* golf balls, socks and cuddly tigers. Still, it's a beautiful place, dotted with frangipani trees and palms, and the suites (there are no rooms) are as tasteful as you would expect at these prices. See p.58 for more details. Rooms start at $750.

The Colonial District

There is a clutch of expensive hotels at the edges of the **Padang**, just north of the Singapore River. Several of them, including the *Marina Mandarin* and *Oriental*, stand on the reclaimed land that robbed Beach Road of its beach. All the hotels in this section are keyed on the map on p.52.

Conrad Centennial Singapore 2 Temasek Blvd ☎63348888, Ⓦ www.conradhotels.com. This relatively recent arrival has elbowed its way into the very top ranks of the island's hotels; all imaginable comfort can be found within its monolithic structure. Rooms start at $270.

Fullerton Hotel 1 Fullerton Sq ☎67338388, Ⓦ www.fullertonhotel.com. Chic, harmonious rooms that show an awareness of the *Fullerton*'s heritage. Luxury extras include in-room playstations, Bulgari smellies, and Internet access on the TVs. An expensive treat. Rooms start at $250.

Marina Mandarin Hotel 6 Raffles Blvd ☎63383388, Ⓦ www.marina-mandarin.com. sg. Top-flight hotel, architecturally interesting and affording great harbour views; the atrium is particularly impressive. Rooms start at $225.

Oriental Singapore 5 Raffles Ave ☎63380066, Ⓦ www.mandarinoriental.com. Housed, like the *Marina Mandarin*, in Marina Square (claimed to be Southeast Asia's largest shopping centre and hotel complex), the *Oriental* is one of Singapore's priciest hotels, but with very good reason. Rooms are exquisitely furnished, views out over Marina

△ The Fullerton Hotel

Bay and the Theatres Project are breathtaking, and all the luxuries you could want are on hand. Rooms from $260.

Peninsular Excelsior Hotel 5 Coleman St ☎63372200, ⊛www.ytchotels.com.sg/ **spytcexcel.** Really two hotels merged together – hence the name – this place is as handy for the Financial District as for Orchard Road's shopping centres. There are several food outlets (best is the excellent *Annalakshmi* Indian vegetarian restaurant), and a swimming pool whose glass walls abut the Lobby Lounge. Rooms start at $240.

Swissôtel The Stamford 2 Stamford Rd ☎63388585, ⊛www.singapore-stamford .swissotel.com. Upper-floor rooms aren't for those with vertigo, though the views are as splendid as you'd expect from the second-tallest hotel in the world. There are 1253 classy rooms here, oodles of restaurants and bars, and an MRT station downstairs. Rooms start at $240.

Summer Tavern 31 Carpenter St ☎65366601, ⊛www.summertavern.com. Popular hostel in a prime location near the quays. Kitchen and lock-up facilities are provided, and there's a beer-lounge, roof terrace and free Internet access. Guests can also use the gym and spa next door. Dorms are large (beds $22) and there's only one double room ($60). Prices include breakfast.

Orchard Road and around

Sumptuous hotels abound in and around **Orchard Road**; at all except a handful, you should be prepared to spend at least $80 a double. You can multiply that figure by five or six, if you decide to treat yourself. All the hotels in this section are keyed on the map on pp.66–67.

The Elizabeth 24 Mount Elizabeth ☎67381188, ⊛www.theelizabeth.com.sg. Within its toy-town exterior, this boutique hotel has delightful and well-appointed rooms. Rooms start at $145.

Garden Hotel 14 Balmoral Rd ☎62353344, ⊛garden@pacific.net.sg. Adequate hotel with attractive rooms, a ten-minute walk north of Orchard Road. Rooms start at $110.

Goodwood Park Hotel 22 Scotts Rd ☎67377411, ⊛www.goodwoodparkhotel .com.sg. This opulent hotel may remind you of *Raffles* – both were designed by the same architect. The building has a long history (see p.67), and it's still a study in elegance. Its arching facades fronting exquisitely appointed rooms. Doubles from $178.

Hilton Singapore 581 Orchard Rd ☎67372233, ⊛www.hilton.com. Situated in the middle of Orchard Road, a gargantuan slab of a hotel with every conceivable facility. Doubles start at $355.

Holiday Inn Park View 11 Cavenagh Rd ☎67338333, ⊛www.singapore.holiday-inn .com. Guests of this smart hotel with all the trimmings are next-door neighbours of Singapore's president for the duration of their stay – the palace is just across the road. Doubles start at $224.

Lloyd's Inn 2 Lloyd Rd ☎67377309, ⊛www .lloydinn.com. Motel-style building boasting attractive rooms and a fine location, just five minutes from Orchard Road. Doubles start at $80.

Meritus Mandarin Hotel 333 Orchard Rd ☎67374411, ⊛www.mandarin-singapore.com. Every luxury you could hope for; even if you don't stay, it's worth taking a trip up to the top-floor bar-restaurant for its magnificent view of central Singapore. Doubles from $280.

Metropolitan Y 60 Stevens Rd ☎67377755, ⊛www.mymca.org.sg. Not as central as the Y on Orchard Road, but perfectly adequate rooms with air con, bathroom, TV and minibar, and suitable for travellers in wheel-chairs. Rooms start at $130

New Sandy's Place 3c Sarkies Rd ☎67341431, ⊛www.geocities.com/sandysplacesingapore/ index/htm. Rooms are all very tidy in this friendly, laid-back place, set across a field from Newton MRT. Expect to pay $15 above the basic rate for air-con. Prices include a tropical fruit breakfast and free flow of hot drinks. It's best to phone ahead. Fan singles start at $25.

The Regent Singapore 1 Cuscaden Rd ☎67338888, ⊛www.regenthotels.com. At the western end of Orchard Road, the elegant rooms of this sumptuous hotel are a short stroll from the Botanic Gardens. Rooms from $330.

Shangri-La Hotel 22 Orange Grove Rd
☎67373644, ⊛www.shangri-la.com. Top-flight hotel whose 700-plus rooms are set in six hectares of landscaped greenery, only five minutes from Orchard Road. Choose from the business wing, or the more holiday-maker-oriented wing, which overlooks the free-form pool. Rooms start at $275.

Singapore Marriott Hotel 320 Orchard Rd
☎67355800, ⊛www.marriotthotels.com/SINDT. A superior hotel and a Singapore landmark, housed in a 33-storey building with a unique pagoda-style roof next door to C.K. Tangs Department Store. Rooms start at $300.

🏃 **Sloane Court Hotel 17 Balmoral Rd**
☎62353311, ⓔsloane@singnet.com.sg. As close to a Tudor house as you get in Singapore, the *Sloane Court* is tucked away in a prime residential area, near Newton MRT. Rooms are cosy and well appointed. Singles start at $88.

Hotel Supreme 15 Kramat Rd ☎67378333, ⓔsupremeh@starhub.net.sg. A great-value budget hotel well placed at the eastern end of Orchard Road, offering laundry and room service along with many other facilities. Rooms start at $185 with a/c.

YMCA International House 1 Orchard Rd
☎63366000, ⊛www.ymcaih.org.sg. Smack bang in the middle of town, the *Y* offers plush but overpriced rooms, excellent sports facilities (including rooftop pool) and free room service from the *McDonald's* downstairs. Dorm beds are $25. Bus #36 from the airport stops right outside. Rooms start at $85.

YWCA Fort Canning Lodge 6 Fort Canning Rd
☎63384222, ⊛www.ywcafclodge.org.sg. Not women-only, as you might imagine, but still a secure and friendly place with pool and tennis courts – and just a stone's throw from Dhoby Ghaut MRT station. Rooms start at $105.

Little India and the Arab Quarter

Little India, along with Chinatown, is fast becoming the budget hotel centre of Singapore. What's more, the arrival of Little India and Farrer Park MRT stations means this colourful enclave is more accessible than ever. All the hotels in this section are keyed on the map on pp.88–89.

Ali's Nest 23 Roberts Lane (no tel). Grubby, shambolic, but undeniably welcoming homestay, one minute from Farrer Park MRT, where rooms and dorm beds ($9) share common bathrooms. When they're full, new arrivals can sleep on the floor. Prices include breakfast and free flow of hot drinks.

Boon Wah Hotel 43a Jalan Besar ☎62991466, ⓕ62942176. This decent Chinese hotel offers clean, if slightly cramped, rooms with TV, air-con and shower. The entrance is around the corner, on Upper Dickson Road. Rooms start at $45.

Broadway Hotel 195 Serangoon Rd ☎62924661, ⓔbroadway@pacific.net.sg. Ugly-looking but affordable hotel on Little India's main drag, boasting pleasant enough rooms with air-con, bathroom and TV. Rooms from $70.

Dickson Court 3 Dickson Rd ☎62977811, ⊛www.dicksoncourthotel.com.sg. With smart, well-furnished rooms off light courtyard corridors, the peaceful *Dickson Court* is pretty good value; most corners of central

Singapore are accessible from the bus stop across the road on Jalan Besar. Doubles start at $89.

Fortuna Hotel 2 Owen Rd ☎62953577, ⓔfortunac@singnet.com.sg. Mid-range hotel offering brilliant value for money; facilities include a health centre and secretarial services. Rooms at $95.

Haising Hotel 37 Jalan Besar ☎62981223. Set between Dunlop and Dickson roads, the *Haising* offers plain but spotless rooms and air-con dorms ($20). The friendly staff organise a self-service laundry ($10). Rooms from $50.

🏃 **InnCrowd Hostel I 35 Campbell Lane**
☎62969169, ⊛www.the-inncrowd.com. Singapore's best guesthouse, thanks to scrupulous cleanliness, peerless facilities and the warm welcome from its owners. Guests have free use of the kitchen and free Internet access, and lockers are available for long-term rental. If the one double room is taken you'll have to make do with a dorm bed ($18).

InnCrowd Hostel II 73 Dunlop St ☎62969169, ⓦwww.the-inncrowd.com. Just around the corner from the original, this place is just as well run, with spotless common areas and comfortable dorm beds for $18.

Kerbau Hotel 54/62 Kerbau Rd ☎62976668, ⓔkerbauinn@pacific.net.sg. Friendly place, if rather dark, with clean and welcoming rooms; there are discounts for stays of three days or more. Rooms start at $50.

Little India Guest House 3 Veerasamy Rd ☎62942866, ⓦwww.singapore-guesthouse.com. A smart guesthouse with excellent, fresh-looking rooms and spotless communal toilets. Fan singles cost $25, air-con singles $40.

Perak Lodge 12 Perak Rd ☎62997733, ⓦwww.peraklodge.net. One of the new breed of upper-bracket guesthouses, set within an atmospheric blue-and-white shop-house in a back street behind the Little India arcade, and run by friendly staff. The rooms are secure (all have safes), well appointed and welcoming, and the price includes a continental breakfast. Downstairs there's an airy, residents-only living area. Singles start at $88.

Sleepy Sam's 55 Bussorah St ☎92774988, ⓦwww.sleepysams.com. Welcoming and surprisingly stylish hostel, located in a row of traditional houses round the corner from the Sultan Mosque. *Sam's* offers a kitchen for self-caterers and a decent café for anyone else; laundry service, free Internet access and safe deposit box facilities. Dorms (mixed and female only) from $25, and doubles from $65.

Chinatown and the waterfront

The range of budget and mid-range accommodation in **Chinatown** has grown in inverse proportion to that of Bencoolen Street's. Whatever your budget, you're sure to find an address to suit you in this most charismatic of enclaves, which boasts a mass of upmarket hotels that benefit from their proximity to the business district. All the hotels in this section are keyed on the map on pp.70–71.

Backpacker Hotel 11a Mosque St ☎62246859. Unremarkable rooms ($35–40) in an equally unremarkable place that nevertheless locates you bang in the middle of China town.

Chinatown Hotel 12–16 Teck Lim Rd, ☎62255166, ⓦwww.chinatownhotel.com. Intimate boutique hotel with smart rooms and a well stocked business centre. The remodelled facade gives a hint at what this original shophouse building looked like Inside, everything is clean and new. Rooms start at $108.

Damenlou Hotel 12 Ann Siang Rd ☎62211900, ⓦwww.damenlou.com. Given its lovingly restored 1925 facade, the twelve compact but well-appointed rooms in this friendly hotel are surprisingly modern. After a pre-dinner drink on the rooftop garden overlooking Chinatown head down to the excellent *Swee Kee* restaurant (see p.153). Rooms start at $70.

Dragon Inn 18 Mosque St ☎62227227, ⓕ62226116. Sizeable and comfortable enough double rooms in the middle of Chinatown, all with air-con, TV, fridge and bathroom, and set in attractive shophouses. Try to avoid rooms backing onto the central airshaft, which houses many noisy air-con units. Doubles from $80.

Gallery Hotel 76 Robertson Quay ☎68498686, ⓦwww.galleryhotel.com.sg. Extravagantly lit with neon stripes at night, and boasting some striking post-modern architecture, the *Gallery* is getting listed in those trendy "hip hotel" coffee-table books. The pool is to die for, some of Singapore's coolest nightspots are on-site, and all the urban-chic rooms offer free broadband access. Rooms start at $158 but check out the website for reduced Internet booking rates.

Grand Copthorne Waterfront 392 Havelock Rd ☎67330880, ⓦwww.millenniumhotels.com. Equidistant from the Orchard and China-town districts, and a short stroll along the river from the nightspots of Clarke Quay, the *Grand Copthorne* demands consideration. Its 500-plus rooms are piled up above a selection of riverfront restaurants, and *Zouk*, one of Singapore's best nightclubs, is next door. Rooms start at $228.

Hotel 1929 50 Keong Saik Rd ☎62223377, ⓦwww.hotel1929.com.

This old shophouse building looks very 1929 on the outside, but the interior has been renovated to look like a twenty-first century version of the early 1960s; it's very retro chic and all tastefully done with a hip, boutique feel about it. Rooms start at $120.

The Inn at Temple Street 36 Temple St ☏ 62215333, ⊛ www.theinn.com .sg. Glossy and grand inside, this boutique hotel has been sculpted out of a row of Chinatown shophouses. Its owners have filled it to bursting with furnishings and curios from old Singapore. Rooms start at $100.

New Majestic Hotel 31–37 Bukit Pasoh Rd ☏ 62223377, ⊛ www .newmajestichotel.com. This Chinatown classic has recently undergone major renovations, giving the interior a stylish, modern makeover that would not be out of place in New York or London. If you're looking for a hip boutique hotel, this is probably it. Rooms from $120.

Robertson Quay Hotel 15 Merbau Rd ☏ 67353333, ⊛ www.robertsonquayhotel .com.sg. Cylindrical riverside hotel, whose compact but inviting rooms off circular corridors yield great views of the river and city skyline. There's a cute circular pool with slide and waterfall on the third-floor terrace. Can't be faulted. Rooms start at $120.

Royal Peacock Hotel 55 Keong Saik Rd ☏ 62233522, ⊛ www.royalpeacockhotel.com. Keong Saik Road was once a notorious red-light district, and the silky, sassy elegance of the *Royal Peacock* recalls those days. Sculpted from ten shophouses, it's a superb boutique hotel, with great rooms, a bar, café and business services. Rooms from $75.

Traveller's Rest-Stop 5 Teck Lim St, ☏ 62254812, ℉ 62254813. In a wedge-shaped building with some palpable Chinatown atmosphere, this place has clean rooms, and brightly lit corridors, and benefits from nice touches like watercolours of Old Chinatown, TVs and fridges. Rooms start at $65.

The East Coast: Geylang and Katong

Geylang and **Katong**, along Singapore's southeastern coast, have traditionally both been Malay–dominated areas. If you can't face the noise and the bustle of central Singapore, this region might appeal – certainly its cool sea breezes and Malay markets are an advantage. MRT and buses connect you quickly with downtown Singapore. All the hotels in this section are keyed on the map on p.111.

Amber Hotel 42 Amber Rd ☏ 63442323, ℮ ambergoh@pacific.net.sg. Comfortable rooms with TV, air-con and bathroom just a short walk from the coast. Rooms start at $50.

Century Roxy Park Singapore 50 East Coast Rd ☏ 63448000, ℉ 63448010. One of the East Coast's more upmarket options, located midway between the city and Changi airport. The design theme is contemporary Asian, the rooms sophisticated, and the choice of restaurants varied. Rooms start at $90.

Fragrance Hotel 219 Joo Chiat Rd ☏ 63449888, ⊛ www.fragrancehotel.com. Behind its chocolate-box exterior, this is a bright and cheery place whose clean rooms boast fresh sheets, sparkling bathrooms, TV, air-con and fridge. Their website lists all other *Fragrance* branches in Singapore. Rooms start at $58.

Hotel 81 Joo Chiat 305 Joo Chiat Rd ☏ 63488181, ⊛ www.hotel81.com.sg. Housed in a beautifully restored cream-and-burgundy Peranakan building, *Hotel 81* offers rooms pleasant enough for any self-respecting business person, but at a fraction of the prices of the downtown heavyweights. Great place. Check out the *Hotel 81* website for details of the chain's many other addresses. Rooms from $49.

Sing Hoe Hotel 759 Mountbatten Rd ☏ 64400602, ℉ 63465996. Beautifully kept colonial house, with attractive reliefs on its external walls, but overpriced for its unmemorable, air-con rooms. Rooms start at $50.

Sentosa and Ubin islands

Three luxury hotels on the island of **Sentosa** allow you to bypass the bustle of downtown Singapore. If you aren't too keen to negotiate any of the more long-winded means of transport to the island, it's possible to get a taxi direct from the airport to Sentosa (though note that from 7am to 10pm a $3 surcharge is levied). All the Sentosa hotels are keyed on the map on p.125.

The Beaufort 2 Bukit Manis Rd ☎62750331, ⓦwww.beaufort.com.sg. A swanky hotel, fitted out in varnished wood, bounded by two 18-hole golf courses and a beach. The Spa Botanica makes it the perfect place for a pampering getaway. Rooms start at $290.
Shangri-La's Rasa Sentosa Beach Resort ☎62750100, ⓦwww.shangri-la.com. Opened in 1993, the *Rasa Sentosa* is the first hotel in Singapore to have its own beach front, and its situation on Sentosa makes it a good option if you've got kids to amuse.

Adults might prefer to check out the spa or sea sports centre. Prices take a $210 hike on Fri and Sat, and rooms with sea views cost extra. Rooms start at $220.
Sijori Resort Sentosa 23 Beach View ☎62712002, ⓦwww.sijoriresort.com.sg. Sentosa's latest accommodation option, the *Sijori* is slap-bang in the middle of the island, making it an ideal base for exploring. There's a lovely pool, should you tire of theme parks and adventure rides. Rooms from $180.

Camping

Changi Beach and East Coast Parkway
Camping at Changi and East Coast Parkway is free, but you'll need to be issued a permit on weekdays. Park rangers make the rounds and issue the permits to camp-

ers, checking up on things daily. This is done to keep people from squatting in the park. At weekends and on public holidays rangers don't bother to register campers.

Eating

A long with shopping, **eating** ranks as a national pastime for Singaporeans, and a mind-boggling number of food outlets cater for this obsession. However, eating out is not afforded the same reverence that it receives in the West: as often as not, you'll find yourself eating off plastic plates in bare, unpretentious restaurants that ring to the sound of agitated conversation (invariably about the food at table). In Singapore, it's the food, and not the surroundings, that's important. Singapore offers new arrivals in Asia the chance to sample the whole spectrum of the region's dishes. What's more, strict government regulations ensure that food outlets are consistently hygienic – you don't need to worry about food cooked at even the cheapest stall. Dining out in Southeast Asia is a family affair, so unless you're going really upmarket don't be shy of taking the kids with you. If they're not culinary adventurers, there are always burger bars or pizza joints near at hand. The mass of establishments serving **Chinese** cuisine reflects the fact that Chinese residents account for around three-quarters of the population. Singapore's development into a thriving seaport in the nineteenth century attracted labourers from many different regions of China and the cuisines they brought with them still dominate the restaurant scene. You're most likely to come across Cantonese, Beijing and Szechuan restaurants, though there's not a region of China whose specialities you can't sample. **North** and **south Indian** cuisines give a good account of themselves, too, as do restaurants serving **Malay**, **Indonesian**, **Korean**, **Japanese** and **Vietnamese** food. One thing you won't find, however, is a Singaporean restaurant: the closest Singapore comes to an indigenous cuisine is **Nonya**, a hybrid of Chinese and Malay food that developed following the intermarrying of nineteenth-century Chinese immigrants with Malay women. Of course, if you insist, you can eat **Western food** in Singapore – venture beyond the ubiquitous burger chains and pizza parlours, and you'll find a host of excellent restaurants cooking anything from haggis to jambalaya. These and other dishes may be enjoyed at places geared to the dishes of a particular nation, or at **international restaurants**, whose confused menus are a patchwork of Western cuisines. A more informal alternative is to opt for a plate of **British** food – fish and chips, say – at a pub or bar.

Several specialist Chinese restaurants and a number of Indian restaurants serve **vegetarian food**, but otherwise, tread very carefully: chicken and seafood will appear in a whole host of dishes unless you make it perfectly clear that you don't want them. **Halal food** is predictably easy to find, given the number of Muslims in Singapore; the Arab Street end of North Bridge Road and Serangoon Road's Zhu Jiao Centre both have proliferations of restaurants and stalls. There are no **kosher** restaurants, but you could try the food store at the Maghain Aboth Synagogue opposite the Church of St Peter and Paul on Waterloo Street.

Some guesthouses do have cooking facilities, and if you want to buy your own food or fancy a bag of fresh fruit, you're most likely to go to a **wet market** – so called because of the pools of water perpetually covering the floor. If you don't know a mango from a mangosteen, vendors are usually very helpful (see also Singapore food colour insert). In addition Singapore has plenty of **supermarkets**, most of which have a delicatessen counter and bakery – some offer familiar beers from back home, too.

Wet markets

Little India is served by the large wet market in the Tekka Market (Little India MRT; see p.90), at the southern end of Serangoon Road; the Chinatown Complex (Chinatown MRT; see p.80) market in **Chinatown** rewards a visit, too; and you'll find other wet markets out of the city centre, in Singapore's new towns.

Supermarkets

Carrefour 01-43 Suntec City Mall, 3 Temasek Blvd. French chain, and Singapore's first hypermarket.

Cold Storage branches at Centrepoint, Orchard Road (Somerset MRT); 293 Holland Rd (Buona Vista MRT or bus #7); 31 Amber Rd, Katong (Paya Lebar MRT, then bus #135). Local chain that stocks a wide range of Western products.

Good Gifts Emporium Golden Mile Complex, 5001 Beach Rd (bus #82 or #100 from *Raffles Hotel*). A smallish supermarket with a leaning towards Thai produce.

Isetan Wisma Atria, 435 Orchard Rd. Japanese department store and supermarket.

NTUC Fairprice Nearly thirty branches, including a branch in Terminal 1 of the airport, make this one of Singapore's most convenient supermarket chains.

Takashimaya Ngee Ann City, 391 Orchard Rd. One of the largest department stores; the supermarket has a Fortnum & Mason franchise.

By far the cheapest and most fun place to dine in Singapore is in a **hawker centre** or **food court**, where scores of stalls let you mix and match good Asian dishes at really low prices. For a few extra dollars you graduate into the realm of proper **restaurants**, ranging from no-frills, open-fronted eating houses and coffee shops to sumptuously decorated establishments – often, though not always, located in swanky hotels. Restaurant **opening hours**, on average, are 11.30am–2.30pm and 6–10.30pm daily; hawker-stall owners tend to operate to their own schedules, but are almost always open at peak eating times.

Breakfast

Guesthouses sometimes include coffee or tea and toast in the price of the room, but the chances are you'll want to head off elsewhere for breakfast. **Western breakfasts** are available, at a price, at all bigger hotels, most famously at the *Hilton* or *Raffles*; otherwise, there are a number of cafés serving continental breakfasts, while *McDonald's*, *KFC* and *Burger King* all rustle up breakfasts before reverting to chicken and burgers after 11am. For a really cheap **fry-up** you can't beat a Western food stall in a hawker centre: here, $8 will buy you enough steak, chops and sausage to challenge even the most starving carnivore. Many visitors to Singapore find the **local breakfasts** a little hard to stomach, but if you shelve your preconceptions there are some tasty possibilities. The classic Chinese breakfast is *congee*, a watery rice porridge augmented with chopped spring onion, crispy fried onion and strips of meat, though the titbits that comprise a *dim sum* breakfast (see "Chinese: Cantonese", p.153) tend to be more palatable to occidental tastebuds. An abiding favourite among Malays is *nasi lemak*, rice cooked in coconut milk and served with *sambal ikan bilis* (tiny crisp-fried anchovies in hot chilli paste), fried peanuts and slices of fried or hard-boiled egg. Otherwise, try investigating one of the scores of Indian establishments that serve up curry and bread breakfasts.

Ann Siang 5 5 Ann Siang Rd, Chinatown ☎63230061; see map on p.73. Civilized, cheery and airy café, just off trendy Club Street, serving scrambled eggs, Spanish omelettes and squidgy homemade cakes. Before you leave, check out the sumptuous Chinese-style dining rooms upstairs. Open Mon–Sat 9am–11.30pm.

Breakfast With An Orang Utan Singapore Zoo, 80 Mandai Lake Rd, ☎62693411; see map on p.100. A bumper buffet-style spread with seasonal tropical fruits, shared with whichever orang utan is on duty; $15.50. Daily 9–10am.

Coffee Bean & Tea Leaf 82 Boat Quay ☎65364355; see map on p.84. This is the most atmospheric branch of Singapore's most reliable coffee and tea chain. Open Sun–Thurs 10am–11pm, Fri & Sat 10am–2am.

Delifrance Branches at 01-K3, Scotts Shopping Centre, 6 Scotts Rd (see map on pp.66–67) and 02-19 Clifford Centre, 24 Raffles Place; see map on p.84. This chain of cafés is neither French nor a deli, but their filled croissants and pastries are not bad. Daily 7.30am–10pm.

Dôme Ground floor, UOB Plaza, Boat Quay; branch at Singapore Art Museum; see map on p.84. Slick café, part of a global chain, boasting an impressive range of coffees and teas and a superb view over the Singapore River. Muffins, toast and croissants are reasonable, and a selection of international papers is on hand for the full breakfast effect. Open 9am–8pm.

Famous Amos 01-05 Specialists' Shopping Centre, 277 Orchard Rd; see map on pp.66–67. Sublime handmade cookies to take away. Daily 10am–9pm.

Halia Singapore Botanic Gardens, 1 Cluny Rd ☎64766711; see map on pp.66–67. The weekend buffet breakfast ($18) in this peaceful and enchanting restaurant, serenaded by the sounds of insects, birds and whispering trees, has to be one of Singapore's most relaxing experiences. Open Sat & Sun 8–10.45am.

Mr Bean's Café 30 Selegie Rd; see map on pp.88–89. Based in the same wedge-shaped colonial building as the Selegie Arts Centre, *Mr Bean's* draws an interesting crowd, who breakfast on muffins, croissants, toast and coffee. American/ English and continental breakfasts are available (around $6) until 11am, after which the menu turns to pizzas, sandwiches and finger food. Open 24hr.

Noorul Ameen Restaurant 127 Bencoolen St; see map on pp.88–89. Does a roaring trade in *roti prata* (fried bread) and curry sauce each morning. Open 24hr.

Pacific Coffee Company B1-26 Citylink Mall, Raffles Link One ☎68210098; see map on pp.88–89. Free Internet access is laid on for partakers of the fine coffee on offer in this pleasing coffee shop, whose sassy red velvet sofas provide an ideal vantage point for people-watching. Open Mon–Fri 8am–11pm, Sat & Sun 9am–11pm.

Spinelli Coffee Company 01-02 Far East Square, 45 Pekin St, Chinatown; see map on p.73. Some say *Spinelli* brews the finest coffee in Singapore – you can make your own mind up at this tiny courtyard outlet. Daily 10am–10pm.

Starbucks Branches at 01-46 Raffles City Shopping Centre, 252 North Bridge Rd, 01-01 OCBC Centre East, 63 Chulia St; see map on p.73 & pp.88–89. Central branches of the American coffee chain that has spread like wildfire across the island. Open Mon–Fri 7.30am–10.30pm, Sat & Sun 8am–midnight.

Steeple's Deli 02-25 Tanglin Shopping Centre, 19 Tanglin Rd, off Orchard Rd ☎67370701; see map on pp.66–67. Singapore's original deli, *Steeple's* has been knocking out high-quality homemade sandwiches, soups, cakes and savouries for over two decades now. Open Mon–Sat 9am–9pm.

Tan Hock Seng Cake Shop 88 Telok Ayer St; see map on p.73. They've been baking cakes and biscuits on site for more than fifty years at this famous Hokkien shop, just next door to the Fuk Tak Chi Street Museum. Daily 10am–8pm.

Tiffin Room Raffles Hotel, 1 Beach Rd; see map on pp.88–89. Have your buffet breakfast here and you won't need to eat until dinner; $30 per person. Daily 7–10.30am.

Ya Kun Kaya Toast 01-01 Far East Square, 18 China St, Chinatown ☎64383638; see map on p.73. This Hainanese joint started out as a Chinatown stall in 1944, and still offers a stirring start to the day: piping-hot, strong coffee with *kayu* toast – a slab of butter and a splodge of egg and coconut spread oozing from folded toast. Open Mon–Fri 7.30am–7pm, Sat & Sun 9am–5pm.

Hawker centres and food courts

To eat inexpensively in Singapore, you go to the hawker stalls, traditionally simple wooden stalls on the roadside, with a few stools to sit at. Today, tighter regulations have swept the hawkers off the streets, and corralled them in custom-made **hawker centres**, where scores of permanent stalls line wide corridors, bristling with fixed stools and chairs. Though hygienic, hawker centres are often housed in functional buildings that tend to get extremely hot and, if you're sat next to a stall cooking fried rice or noodles, extremely smoky. As a result an increasing number of smaller, air-con **food courts** are popping up; brighter and more civilized than hawker centres, these suffer from a lack of atmosphere. In both hawker stalls and food courts, it's possible to pick up different dishes from a variety of stalls.

The standard of cooking is also very high at most stalls, and politicians and pop stars crowd in with the locals to eat at a cramped hawker's table.

Hawker stalls serve a range of cuisines reflecting Singapore's ethnic make-up. Indian and Malay noodle and rice dishes are widely available, but it's Chinese food that is prevalent. In certain venues, you'll also come across Western food like burgers, and steak and eggs, or Indonesian or Korean food.

Hawker stalls don't have menus, though most have signs in English detailing their specialities; otherwise point at anything you like the look of. When you order a dish, make it clear if you want a small, medium or large portion – or else you'll get the biggest and most expensive one. You don't have to sit close to the stall you're patronizing: find a free seat, and the vendor will track you down when your food is ready. Meals are paid for when they reach your table. A hearty meal – say, curry and rice, a fruit juice and a dessert – will cost you around $8, though if your budget doesn't run that far, you can eat well for half the price.

Hawker centres and food courts are open from lunchtime through to dinner and sometimes beyond, though individual stalls tend to open and shut as they please. Most close well before midnight, one notable exception being **Newton Circus**, where the **late-night** seafood is a constant tourist draw. There are always hot and cold drinks stalls on hand, and getting a bottle of beer is rarely difficult. If you avoid the peak lunching (12.30–1.30pm) and dining (6–7pm) periods, when hungry Singaporeans funnel into their nearest hawker centre, you should have no problems in finding a seat.

China Square Food Centre see map on p.73. Three floors of spick-and-span stalls – mainly Chinese but with Japanese, Korean and Western representation.

Chinatown Complex Smith St, at end of New Bridge Rd; see map on pp.70–71. A huge range of dishes with a predictably Chinese bias.

△ Hawker Centre

Food Junction B1, Seiyu Department Store, Bugis Junction, 200 Victoria St; see map on pp.88–89. Recently renovated, this basement food court is very popular. Culinary themes as diverse as Thai, Japanese, *nasi padang* and claypot are represented, and there's a choice of local desserts or Häagen Dazs ice creams.

Food Life Food Court Level 4 Wisma Atria, Orchard Rd; see map on pp.66–67. Not a great selection, but clean, welcoming and central.

Funan Centre IT Mall Food Court 109 North Bridge Rd; see map on p.52. Smart basement court whose stalls serve herbal soup, claypots, Hainanese chicken and local desserts.

Geylang Serai Food Centre Geylang Serai; see map on p.110. In the heart of Singapore's Malay quarter, with a corresponding range of Malay stalls. Turn left out of Paya Lebar MRT and left again onto Sims Avenue; the centre is five minutes' walk along, on your right. This is being rebuilt at the time of writing

Hastings Road Food Court Little India Arcade, Serangoon Rd; see map on pp.88–89. Diminutive food court whose handful of stalls are labelled by region – Keralan, Mughal, Sri Lankan and so on.

Kopitiam Plaza by the Park, 51 Bras Basah Rd; see map on pp.88–89. Bright and brash food court, popular among late-night revellers with the munchies. Open 24hr.

Lau Pa Sat Festival Market 18 Raffles Quay; see map on pp.70–71. Dating back to the nineteenth century, this is the oldest and most atmospheric selection of hawker stalls in Singapore – but it's also a mite pricier than the norm. At lunchtime the place is full to bursting with suits from the city; at night the clubbers take over. Open round the clock.

Maxwell Food Centre Junction of South Bridge Rd and Maxwell Rd; see map on p.81. Old-style hawker centre, a stone's throw from the centre of Chinatown. This is no-frills fast food at its cheapest and most basic.

New Bugis Street see map on pp.88–89. A handful of evening hawkers dish up Asian specialities such as satay, *laksa*, *kueh* and sushi. This place is very popular with tourists and hence many of the stalls use photograph-driven menus that provide a crash course on hawker cuisine.

Newton Circus Hawker Centre North end of Scotts Rd. Prices are a little higher than at other centres because it's on the mainstream tourist trail, but it has the advantage of staying open until late (as long as there are customers). Noted for its seafood stalls.

Orchard Emerald Food Chain Basement, Orchard Emerald, 218 Orchard Rd; see map on pp.66–67. Smart food court, halfway along Orchard Road, where the Indonesian buffet is great value.

Picnic Food Court Scotts Shopping Centre, 6 Scotts Rd; see map on pp.66–67. Slap-bang in the middle of the Orchard Road district, squeaky clean and with lots of choice.
Satay Club Clarke Quay. A Singapore institution, serving inexpensive chicken and mutton satay. Open eves only, from around 7pm.
Sim Lim Square Food Court (Tenco Food Court) 1 Rochor Canal Rd; see map on pp.88–89. Convenient if you are staying on Bencoolen Street; it's even got its own jukebox.
Smith Street Chinatown; see map on pp.70–71. At night, this narrow street is made still narrower by the two rows of food stalls that open up along it.
Tekka Market Corner of Bukit Timah and Serangoon roads; see map on pp.88–89. The bulk of its stalls, naturally enough, serve Indian food.
Telok Blangah Telok Blangah Rd; see map on p.117. Opposite the World Trade Centre, and good for a snack before or after a trip to Sentosa.
Victoria Street Food Court 83 Victoria St. Open-fronted food court with around ten stalls; good for evening seafood and handy for Beach Road and Raffles City.

Restaurants and coffee shops

Restaurants in Singapore range from simple coffee shops to the most sumptuous establishments you could imagine. **Coffee shops**, invariably Chinese- or Indian-run, and usually open throughout the day, serve basic noodle and rice dishes, and sometimes feature a selection of cakes and sweetmeats. The culinary standard is never spectacularly high, but you'll be hard pressed to spend more than $10 for a filling meal. Indian coffee shops tend to be a bit livelier, and are sometimes decidedly theatrical. Here you can watch the Muslim *mamak* men at work, whose job it is to make the frothy *teh tarik* (tea) by pouring liquid from a height from one vessel into another, and pound and mould the *roti* into an oily, bubble-filled shape; in some Indian coffee shops, you'll also be treated to the sight of plate-sized *murtabaks* being spun and griddle-fried.

On the whole, proper **restaurants** are places you go if you want a bit of comfort, or to savour particular delicacies found nowhere else, such as fish-head curry, Chinese specialities like shark's-fin dishes and bird's-nest soup, high-quality seafood and fine international cuisine. Singapore also has a tradition of **haute cuisine**, usually available in the top-notch hotels. Many of the best hotel-restaurants in Singapore boast reputable chefs, drawing in the punters with well-received French, Thai, Italian and Japanese food as well as more local delicacies. That said, in many restaurants, the food is not necessarily superior to that served at a good café or hawker stall – you're just paying the (often considerable) extra for air-conditioning and tablecloths. One reason to splash out, though, is to experience a **cultural show** of music and dance, found in several of the large Chinese seafood restaurants, all of which are detailed on p.154.

Unless you're in a Muslim restaurant, you'll be able to wash down your meal with a glass of cold **beer**; wine is less common, though smarter establishments will normally retain a modest choice. Few **desserts** feature on Southeast Asian restaurants' menus, but the region's bounty of tropical **fruit** more than compensates; the glossary on p.150 lists some of the less familiar fruits you may come across.

Tipping is not expected in Singaporean restaurants and bills arrive complete with service charge and government tax (presently fourteen percent). Making yourself understood is rarely a problem, nor is negotiating a menu, as nearly all are written in English.

Many menus in Singapore are written in English, but it's worth noting that trans-literated spellings are not standardized – you may well see some of the following dishes written in a variety of ways; we've used the most widely accepted spellings.

General terms

Assam	Sour	Istimewa	Special (as in "today's special") or extra
Garam	Salt		
Goreng	Fried	Kari	Curry
Gula	Sugar	Makan	Food
		Manis	Sweet

Meat, fish and basics

Ayam	Chicken	Sayur	Vegetable
Babi	Pork	Sotong	Squid
Daging	Beef	Sup	Soup
Ikan	Fish	Tahu	Bean curd
Kambing	Mutton	Telor	Egg
Kepiting	Crab	Udang	Prawn

Noodles (mee) and noodle dishes

Bee hoon	Thin rice noodles, like vermicelli; *mee fun* is similar.
Char kuey teow	Flat noodles with any combination of prawns, Chinese sausage, fishcake, egg, vegetables and chilli.
Foochow noodles	Steamed and served in soy and oyster sauce with spring onions and dried fish.
Hokkien fried mee	Yellow noodles fried with pieces of pork, prawn and vegetables.
Kuey teow	Flat noodles, comparable to Italian tagliatelle; *hor fun* is similar.
La mien	"Pulled noodles", made by spinning dough skipping-rope-style in the air.
Laksa	Noodles, beansprouts, fishcakes and prawns in a spicy coconut soup.
Mee	Standard round yellow noodles made from wheat flour that looks like spaghetti.
Mee goreng	Indian fried noodles.
Mee suah	Noodles served dry and crispy.
Sar hor fun	Flat rice noodles served in a chicken stock soup, to which prawns, fried shallots and beansprouts are added: a Malaysian speciality.
Wan ton mee	Roast pork, noodles and vegetables in a light soup containing dumplings.

Rice (nasi) dishes

Biriyani	Saffron-flavoured rice cooked with chicken, beef or fish; a north Indian speciality.
Claypot	Rice topped with meat (as diverse as chicken and turtle), cooked in an earthenware pot over a fire to create a smoky taste.
Daun pisang	Malay term for banana-leaf curry, a south Indian meal with chutneys and curries, served on a mound of rice, and presented on a banana leaf with *poppadoms*.

Hainan chicken rice	Singapore's unofficial national dish: steamed or boiled chicken slices on rice cooked in chicken stock, served with chicken broth and chilli and ginger sauce.
Kunyit	Rice cooked in tumeric; a side dish.
Nasi campur	Rice served with an array of meat, fish and vegetable dishes.
Nasi goreng	Fried rice with diced meat and vegetables.
Nasi lemak	A Malay classic: fried anchovies, cucumber, peanuts and fried or hard-boiled egg slices served on coconut rice.
Nasi puteh	Plain boiled rice.

Other specialities

Ayam goreng	Malay-style fried chicken.
Bak kut teh	Literally "pork bone tea", a Chinese dish of pork ribs in soy sauce, herbs and spices.
Char siew pow	Cantonese steamed bun stuffed with roast pork in a sweet sauce.
Chay tow kueh	Also known as "carrot cake", this is actually an omelette made with white radish and spring onions.
Congee	Rice porridge, cooked in lots of water and eaten with slices of meat and fish.
Dim sum	Chinese titbits – dumplings, rolls, chicken's feet – steamed or fried and served in bamboo baskets.
Dosai	South Indian pancake, made from ground rice and lentils, and served with *daal* (lentils) and spicy dips.
Fish-head curry	The head of a red snapper (usually), cooked in a spicy curry sauce with tomatoes and okra; one of Singapore's most famous dishes.
Gado gado	Malay/Indonesian salad of lightly cooked vegetables, boiled egg, slices of rice cake and a crunchy peanut sauce.
Ikan bilis	Deep-fried anchovies.
Kai pow	Similar to *char siew pow*, but contains chicken and boiled egg.
Kerupuk	Crackers.
Murtabak	Thick Indian pancake, stuffed with onion, egg and chicken or mutton.
Otak-otak	Fish mashed with coconut milk and chilli paste and steamed in a banana leaf; a Nonya dish.
Popiah	Chinese spring rolls, filled with peanuts, egg, beansprouts, vegetables and a sweet sauce; sometimes known as *lumpia*.
Rendang	Dry, highly spiced coconut curry with beef, chicken or mutton.
Rojak	Indian fritters dipped in chilli and peanut sauce; the Chinese version is a salad of greens, beansprouts, pineapple and cucumber in a peanut-and-prawn paste sauce, similar to *gado gado*.
Roti canai	Light, layered Indian pancake served with a thin curry sauce or *daal*; sometimes called *roti pratha*.

Roti john	Simple Indian dish of egg, onion and tomato sauce spread on bread and heated.
Satay	Marinated pieces of meat, skewered on small sticks and cooked over charcoal; served with peanut sauce, cucumber and *ketupat* (rice cake).
Sop kambing	Spicy Indian mutton soup.
Steamboat	Chinese equivalent of the Swiss fondue: raw vegetables, meat or fish dunked into a steaming broth until cooked.

Desserts

Bubor cha cha	Sweetened coconut milk with pieces of sweet potato, yam and tapioca balls.
Cendol	Coconut milk, palm sugar syrup and pea-flour noodles poured over shaved ice.
Es kachang	Shaved ice with red beans, cubes of jelly, sweetcorn, rose syrup and evaporated milk.
Pisang goreng	Fried banana fritters.

Tropical fruit

The more familiar fruits available in Singapore include coconut, watermelon, several types of banana, seven varieties of mango and three types of pineapple.

Ciku	Looks like an apple; varies from yellow to pinkish brown when ripe, with a soft, pulpy flesh.
Durian	Singapore's most popular fruit has a greeny-yellow, spiky exterior and grows to the size of a football. It has thick, yellow-white flesh and an incredibly pungent odour likened to a mixture of mature cheese and caramel.
Guava	A green, textured skin and flesh with five times the vitamin C content of oranges.
Jackfruit	This huge, oblong-shaped fruit grows up to 50cm long and has a spikey greeny-yellow exterior with yellow sweet flesh inside.
Langsat	Together with its sister fruit, the *duku*, this looks like a small, round potato, with juicy white flesh which can be anything from sweet to sour.

If possible, try to book ahead at more upmarket restaurants, particularly on Saturday nights and Sunday lunchtimes, when they are at their busiest; moreover, bear in mind that many restaurants close over Chinese New Year, and those that don't are often bursting at the seams.

Arabic

The Arabic connection with Singapore goes back a long way, but it has recently taken on a new lease of life with modern Singaporeans rediscovering their Arab routes and encouraging connections with the Middle East. Convivial restaurants are springing up in the Arab quarter, with generally cheap and tasty food.

Al Tazzag 24 Haji Lane ☎ 62955024; see map on pp.88–89. Unpretentious street-corner Egyptian diner in the heart of the Arab quarter, with great shish kebabs, baba ghanoush, hummus, and hookahs. Daily noon–2am.

Longgan	Similar to the lychee, this has juicy white flesh and brown seeds.
Mangosteen	Available from June to August and November to January, it has a sweet and tangy flavour. Its smooth rind deepens to a distinctive purple colour when ripe.
Markisa	Known in the West as passion fruit, this has purple-brown dimpled skin with a rich flavour; frequently an ingredient in drinks.
Papaya	The milky orange-coloured flesh is a rich source of vitamins A and C.
Pomelo	The pomelo, or *limau bali*, is the largest of all the citrus fruits and looks rather like a grapefruit, though it is slightly drier and has less flavour.
Rambutan	The bright red rambutan's soft, spiny exterior has given it its name – *rambut* means "hair" in Malay. Usually about the size of a golf ball, it has a white, opaque fruit of delicate flavour, similar to a lychee.
Salak	Teardrop shaped, the *salak* has a skin like a snake's and a bitter taste.
Star fruit	Waxy, pale-green star-shaped fruit said to be good for high blood pressure; the yellower the fruit, the sweeter its flesh.
Zirzat	Inside its bumpy, muddy green skin is smooth white flesh like blancmange, hence its other name, custard apple; also known as soursop.
Drinks	
Kopi	Coffee.
Kopi-o	Black coffee.
Kopi susu	Coffee with milk.
Lassi	Sweet or sour yoghurt drink of Indian origin.
Teh	Tea.
Teh-o	Black tea.
Teh susu	Tea with milk.
Teh tarik	Sweet, milky tea, poured between two cups to produce a frothy drink.

El Sheikh 18 Pahang St ☏62969116, ⓦwww .elsheikh.com.sg; see map on pp.88–89. Lebanese restaurant with a choice of indoor dining areas or terrace and garden. Starters include hummus or spinach pie from $4 and mains such as shawarma from $10 are served with rice or chips and delicious freshly baked breads; also good for veggies. Board games and flavoured hookahs are on offer too. Open Mon–Thurs and Sun 6.30pm–1am, Fri and Sat 6.30pm–2.30am.

Chinese

The majority of the **Chinese** restaurants in Singapore are **Cantonese**, that is, from the province of Canton (Guangdong) in southern China, though you'll also come across northern **Beijing** (or Peking) and western **Szechuan** cuisines, as well as the **Hokkien** specialities of the southeastern province of Fujian, and **Teochew** dishes from the area east of Canton.

Eating in Singaporean restaurants is quite different to dining out Western-style. Singaporeans – and particularly Singapore Chinese – tend to choose as many dishes as there are people at the table, and then order a couple more for good luck. When the food arrives, everyone dips in. English menus are available in most restaurants.

Depending on the cuisine you are eating, you have a choice of utensils at your command. **Chinese food** is traditionally eaten with **chopsticks**, which look nightmarishly difficult to use, but are actually quite easily mastered. One is laid between thumb and forefinger, and supported by your fourth and little fingers; the second chopstick is held between thumb, forefinger and second finger, and manipulated to form a pincer. To make your task slightly easier, eat, not from your plate, but from the bowl provided, holding it right up to your lips. Chinese eaters are able to feed rice from bowl to mouth with such speed that they seem to be sucking it up a tube; a china spoon is always provided in case you can't get the hang of chopsticks, but don't give up just because you're making a mess, as this isn't frowned upon in the least.

In upmarket **Indian restaurants** your placing will be set with spoon and fork, but in more basic establishments, food often arrives at table minus any utensils, and sometimes on a **banana leaf** instead of a plate. Traditionally, Indians eat by affecting a scooping action with their right hands, but if you don't fancy this, it's perfectly acceptable to ask for cutlery.

A Chinese meal is typically taken with plain steamed rice. In an Indian restaurant, you can either eat your main course with rice, or scoop and mop it up with hunks of Indian bread.

Whatever the region, it's undoubtedly the real thing – Chinese food as eaten by the Chinese – which means it won't always sound particularly appealing to foreigners: the Chinese eat all parts of an animal, from its lips to its entrails, and it's important to retain a sense of adventure when exploring menus. Fish and seafood are nearly always outstanding in Chinese cuisine, with prawns, crab, squid and a variety of fish on offer. Noodles, too, are ubiquitous, and come in wonderful variations (see p.148). For something a little more unusual, try a **steamboat**, a Chinese-style fondue filled with boiling stock in which you cook meat, fish, shellfish, eggs and vegetables; or a **claypot** – meat, fish or shellfish cooked over a fire in an earthenware pot.

The other thing to note is that in many Cantonese restaurants (and in other regional restaurants, too), lunch consists of **dim sum** – steamed and fried dumplings served in little bamboo baskets.

Beijing

Beijing was traditionally the seat of China's Imperial households, and the sumptuous presentation of its cuisine reflects its opulent past. Meat dominates, typically flavoured with garlic and spring onions, though the dish for which Beijing is most famous is roast duck, served in three courses: the skin is eaten in a pancake filled with spring onion and radish, and smeared with plum sauce; afterwards, the flesh is stir-fried with vegetables, and the carcass boiled to make a soup.

Lao Beijing 03-01 Plaza Singapura, 68 Orchard Rd ☎67387207; see map on pp.66–67. Charming teahouse-style restaurant. If the braised pork trotters don't appeal, try the more mainstream dishes like sweet-and-sour fish and *popiah*; the steamboat with lamb slices is exceptional. Daily 11.30am–3pm & 6–10pm.

Pine Court Restaurant 35th floor, Mandarin Hotel, 333 Orchard Rd ☎68316262; see map on pp.66–67. Three elegant pine trees dominate this beautiful restaurant, where the speciality is whole Peking duck – enough for three hungry people. Cheaper set meals are available, too. You'll need to reserve in advance. Daily noon–3pm & 6.30–11pm.

Cantonese

Cantonese cuisine is noted for its delicacy of flavour and memorable sauces. Cantonese dishes are stir-fried, steamed or roasted, and often taken with black bean, lemon, oyster or soy sauce. Fish and seafood weigh in heavily on a Cantonese menu, either fried or steamed, and other specialities include pigeon, roast meats and frogs' legs. **Dim sum** is also a classic Cantonese meal: literally translated as "to touch the heart", it's a blanket term for an array of dumplings, cakes and titbits steamed in bamboo baskets. Though you do occasionally see it on lunch menus, traditionally *dim sum* is eaten by the Chinese for breakfast, with one basket (of three or four pieces) costing as little as $3.

Bugis Village see map on pp.88–89. Touts at the several seafood restaurants here hassle you incessantly to take a seat and a menu. The furious competition ensures prices are reasonable, despite the high proportion of tourists; all restaurants have similar, mainstream menus. Daily 5pm–3am.

Fatty's Wing Seong Restaurant 01-33 Albert Complex, 60 Albert St ☎63381087; **see map on p.94.** A Singapore institution where every dish on the wide Cantonese menu is well cooked and speedily delivered. Around $20 a head. Daily noon–11pm.

Hai Tien Lo 37th floor, Pan Pacific Hotel, 7 Raffles Blvd, Marina Square ☎68268338; **see map on pp.88–89.** If you have money enough for just one blow-out, come here for exquisitely presented food and stunning views of downtown Singapore. Extravagant set meals are available, while Sunday lunchtimes (11.30am–2.30pm) are set aside for *dim sum*. Daily noon–2.30pm & 6.30–10pm.

Hillman Restaurant 01-159, Block 1, Cantonment Rd ☎62215073; **see map on p.73.** Extremely popular, thanks to its famous paper-wrapped chicken, and its rich-tasting earthen pot dishes of flavoursome stews featuring various meats and seafood in a rich sauce; small pots (around $10) fill two. Daily 11.30am–2.30pm & 5.30–10.30pm.

Lei Garden 01-24 CHIJMES, 30 Victoria St ☎63393822; **see map on pp.88–89.** Refreshingly understated, *Lei Garden* lets its classy Cantonese dishes do the talking. Stunning seafood, most of which starts the day swimming in the tanks in the dining room. Daily 11.30am–3pm & 6–11pm.

Li Bai Sheraton Towers Hotel, 39 Scotts Rd ☎7376888; **see map on pp.66–67.** Named after a poet of the Tang dynasty, a suitably sophisticated place in the bowels of the *Towers*, where your best bet is the five-course luncheon, weighing in at $50; alternatively, you can opt for lighter *dim sum*. Daily noon–2.30pm & 6.30–10.30pm.

Mitzi's 24–26 Murray Terr ☎62220929; **see map on p.81.** The cracking Cantonese food in this simple place, situated in a row of restaurants known as "Food Alley", draws crowds, so be prepared to queue. Two can eat for $30, drinks extra. Daily 11.30am 3pm & 5.30–10pm.

Mouth Restaurant 02-01 Chinatown Point, 133 New Bridge Rd ☎65344233; **see map on p.73.** Beside a popular *dim sum* menu, this jam-packed restaurant offers classy Hong Kong new-wave Cantonese food, at under $20 a head. Daily 11am–4am (*dim sum* 11.30am–5pm).

Sin Lam Huat Ubin Village, Ubin Island. Offers the best dining on Ubin; the specialities are chilli crab and tasty kampong chicken. Moderate. Daily noon–7pm.

Soup Restaurant 25 Smith St ☎62229923; **see map on p.73.** Traditional Cantonese double-boiled and simmered soups are the speciality at this steam-heat-dependent soup shop whose elegant tables and low-hung lights recall old Chinatown. The *samsui* ginger chicken comes recommended. Cheap. Daily 11.30am–10.30pm.

Swee Kee Damenlou Hotel, 12 Ann Siang Rd ☎62211900; **see map on p.73.** A Cantonese restaurant with real pedigree: Tang Swee Kee hawked the first bowl of his trademark *ka shou* fish-head noodles more than sixty years ago, and now his son sells this and other well-cooked dishes from the attractive coffee shop on the ground floor of this Chinatown hotel. Daily 11am–2.30pm & 5.30–11pm.

Tekong Seafood 01-2100 Blk 6, Changi Village Rd ☎65428923; **see map on p.110.** This Cantonese/Teochew seafood joint moved over to the mainland when Pulau Tekong was earmarked as an army shooting range; but the food is as good as ever – the

Teochew steamed fish with sour prunes is particularly fab. Moderate. Daily 11am–2.30pm & 5.30–11pm.

Union Farm Eating House 435a Clementi Rd. Bus #154 from Clementi MRT, alight at Maju army camp ℡64662776; see map on p.117. Until thirty years ago, this used to be a poultry farm, and palms and bamboos still surround the restaurant. The house special, *Chee Pow Kai* (marinated chicken wrapped in greaseproof paper and deep fried; $15 buys enough for two), is messy and wonderful. Daily 11.30am–8.30pm.

Wang Jiang Lou Blk A, Clarke Quay ℡63383001; see map on pp.70–71. Slick Cantonese-Teochew restaurant where the ingredients of a full seafood menu eye you suspiciously from tanks on the walls. Moderate. Daily 11.30am–3pm & 6–11pm.

Yum Cha 02-01, 20 Trengganu St ℡63721717; see map on p.73. Big, buzzing *dim sum* joint, above the bustle of Trengganu Street, with marble tables and pictures of dumplings and teapots on the walls. Great fun. Entry is via Temple Street. Cheap. Daily 8am–11pm.

Hainanese

Hainanese cuisine is synonymous in Singapore with chicken rice – the country's unofficial national dish. Chicken rice is a simple but tasty platter featuring, predictably enough, slices of chicken laid on rice that has been cooked in chicken stock. A chilli and ginger sauce is always served with the meal. Also sliced cucumbers are served as a garnish.

Mooi Chin Palace Restaurant Golden Landmark Hotel, ℡63921600; see map on p.52. Hainanese immigrants often worked as domestics to colonial families, resulting in crossover dishes such as Hainanese mutton soup and Hainanese pork chop – both cooked to perfection here, where whole *pomfret sambal* ($25) is a speciality, and set menus start from around $30 for two. Daily 11.30am–3pm & 6–10pm. Open for *dim sum* daily 7.30–9am.

Yet Con Chicken Rice Restaurant 25 Purvis St ℡63376819; see map on pp.88–89. Cheap and cheerful, old-time restaurant: try "crunchy, crispy" roast pork with pickled cabbage and radish, or chicken rice, washed down with barley water; $15 for two people. Daily 10.30am–9.30pm.

Hokkien

The **Hokkien** chef relies heavily upon sauces and broths to cook his meat and (primarily) seafood. Without doubt, Hokkien fried *mee* (noodles) is the most popular Hokkien dish in Singapore – you'll find it in nearly every hawker centre on the island.

Bee Heong Palace 4th floor, Pil Building, 140 Cecil St ℡62229075; see map on p.73. Customers are pumped through at a rate of knots in this lunchtime-only, cafeteria-style place; there's no menu, but the beggar chicken and dried chilli prawn come recommended, or ask the friendly staff for advice. Cheap. Daily 11am–2.30pm.

Beng Hiang Restaurant 112–115 Amoy St ℡62216684; see map on p.73. The lack of a menu makes ordering distinctly tricky, but persistence is rewarded by well-cooked food at good-value prices – you can eat heartily for under $15. Daily 11.30am–2.30pm & 6–9.30pm.

Beng Thin Hoon Kee Restaurant 05-02 OCBC Centre, 65 Chulia St ℡65332818; see map on p.73. Hidden inside the OCBC car park, this minty green restaurant is very popular at lunchtime with city slickers from the nearby business district. Big portions make it a good and filling introduction to Hokkien cuisine. Cheap. Daily 11.30am–3pm & 6–10pm.

Szechuan and Hunanese

Szechuan food is hot and spicy, with chilli, pepper, garlic and ginger conspiring to piquant effect in classic dishes such as camphor-and-tea-smoked duck and chicken with dried chilli. The food of neighbouring Hunan province is similarly fiery; popular dishes include Hunanese honey-glazed ham and minced pigeon steamed in a bamboo tube.

Cherry Garden Restaurant The Oriental, 5 Raffles Ave, Marina Square ℡68853538; see map on pp.88–89. Elegant restaurant, designed to resemble a Chinese courtyard, and serving tasty Szechuan and Hunanese dishes. Hunanese honey-glazed ham is delectable, as is the Szechuan house speciality, camphor-smoked duck and bean curd crust (both under $30); the set lunches cost $40–60 a head. Daily noon–3pm & 6–11pm.

Magic of Chongqing Hotpot 4th floor, Tanglin Shopping Ctr, 19 Tanglin Rd ℡67348135; see map on pp.66–67. Established in 1995, this homely DIY restaurant has got local pundits raving over its zesty Szechuan hotpots: choose a stock, drop in ingredients, and fish them out when cooked. Two can dine well for $70. Daily noon–3pm & 6–11pm.

Min Jiang Restaurant Goodwood Park Hotel, 22 Scotts Rd ☎67375337; see map on pp.66–67. This restaurant's reputation for fine Szechuan classics makes reservations a good idea. The decor's red tones match the fieriness of the food on offer. The hot and sour soup is really challenging; or try the simpler steamed fish in black bean sauce. A meal for two costs around $70. The location in this historic old hotel is a plus. Daily noon–2.30pm & 6.30–10.30pm.

Teochew

Steaming is the most commonly used form of cooking in the **Teochew** kitchen, producing light but flavourful dishes such as fish steamed with sour plums. Other Teochew classics are braised goose, steamed crayfish and *oh nee* – a dessert made from creamed yam. Teochew meals are traditionally washed down with strong Chinese tea.

Ban Seng Restaurant B1-44 The Riverwalk, 20 Upper Circular Rd ☎65331471; see map on p.73. The food is top-notch at this well-established place: try the steamed crayfish, braised goose or stuffed sea cucumber; all moderately priced. Daily noon–2pm & 6–10pm.

Teochew City Seafood Restaurant 05-16 Centrepoint, 176 Orchard Rd ☎67333338; see map on pp.66–67. Standard Teochew restaurant whose karaoke facilities are, mercifully, confined to two private rooms. Try the steamed and then chilled cold crabs as an appetizer. Moderate. Daily 11.30am–3pm & 6.30–10pm.

Other speciality Chinese restaurants

Chinese Opera Teahouse 5 Smith St ☎63234862; see map on p.73. The *Sights and Sounds of Chinese Opera Show* ($35), a set dinner serenaded by Chinese musicians, and followed by excerpts from Chinese operas, is a memorable cultural treat. The dinner begins at 7pm. If you don't want a dinner but want to catch the show while drinking tea and munching on

Chinese snacks, the cost is $25 and you'll be admitted at 7.50pm. Open Fri & Sat.

Crystal Jade La Mian Xiao Long Bao Ngee An City #04-27 ☎62381661; Scotts Shopping Centre #B1-05 ☎67340200; Suntec City Mall #B1-028 ☎63376678; and other locations. See map on pp.66–67 & pp.88–89. Very popular chain specializing in Shanghai and Beijing cuisine. The name is a bit of a mouthful, but encapsulates their signature dishes – *xiao long bao*, incredibly succulent pork dumplings, and *la mian*, literally "pulled noodles", the strands of dough being stretched and worked by hand (the version cooked with wood-ear fungus is particularly good). Not great for vegetarians, though veggie versions of a few dishes can be made to order.

Doc Cheng's Raffles Hotel, 328 North Bridge Rd ☎63311612; see map on pp.88–89. East meets West in the most recent addition to Raffles, an ice-cool joint themed around the global travels of imagined local *bon viveur* Doc Cheng. Though the menu betrays Thai, Indian, Japanese and Pacific Rim influences, Chinese culinary ideology provides the backbone to much of the food; the decor presents a similarly eclectic blend of Oriental, Art Deco and modernist influences. Two pay around $60. Open Mon–Fri noon–2pm, daily 7–10pm.

Goldleaf Taiwan Restaurant 24–24a Tanjong Pagar Rd ☎62256001; see map on p.81. Long-established but dowdy joint that's fine if you've got a taste for congee: Taiwan porridge is the speciality, augmented by such fillings as century egg, oysters and abalone. Daily 11am–3pm & 6pm–4am.

Imperial Herbal Restaurant 3rd floor, Metropole Hotel, 41 Seah St ☎63370491; see map on pp.88–89. The place to go if you are concerned about your Yin and Yang balance: after checking your pulse and tongue, a resident Chinese physician recommends either a cooling or a "heating" dish from the menu. For migraine sufferers, scorpions pickled in some foul-tasting liquor are, by all accounts, a must; rheumatics should opt for crispy black ants. It's a good old-fashioned gross-out of the type that used to be what travel to the Orient was all about. The downside is the cost – be prepared to pay through the nose. Daily 11.30am–2.30pm & 6.30–10.30pm.

🏃 **Jing 50 Eu Tong Sen St** ⊤65326006; see map on p.73. An ecstasy of raw silk, cushions, transparent silk drapes, elegant lighting, gilt woodwork, and conducive planting has transformed the former Thong Chai Medical Institution into a sensational dining venue. The cuisine – listed as "signature Chinese" – offers a contemporary spin on traditional Middle Kingdom fare. Moderate. Daily noon–3pm & 6–10.30pm.

Kublai Khan Mongolian BBQ 04-01 Park Mall, 9 Penang Rd ⊤63344888; see map on pp.66–67. Choose from an array of meats, vegetables and sauces, which are then cooked for you on a hot griddle in the open kitchen. Then, if you are still hungry, you can go back again, and again. Two pay around $50 for unlimited visits to the food bar, including starters and desserts. Daily 6–10.30pm.

Moi Kong Hakka Restaurant 22 Murray St ⊤62217758; see map on p.81. The food of the semi-nomadic Hakka tribe relies heavily on salted and preserved ingredients, and dishes here, in the best Hakka food outlet in Singapore, encompass red wine prawns and stewed pork belly with preserved vegetables. Cheap. Daily 11.30am–2.30pm & 6–9.30pm.

Old Shanghai 55 Temple St ⊤63271218; see map on p.73. Drunken chicken, marinated ham hock, sauteed eel with chive shoots and many other Shanghainese favourites, served in unfussy surroundings. Daily 11.30am–3pm & 5.30–9.30pm.

Singapura Seafood Restaurant 01-31 Selegie House, Blk 9, Selegie Rd ⊤63363255; see map on pp.88–89. Sure the seafood is great, but it's hard to see beyond such fabulous Foochow classics as steamed white cabbage, fishball soup and fried noodles. Daily 11am–2.30pm & 6–10.30pm.

Snack World 01-12/13 Cuppage Plaza, 5 Koek Rd; see map on pp.66–67. Hectic terrace restaurant where the Chinese menu is enlivened by hotplate crocodile meat and emu. Daily 10am–midnight.

Superbowl 80 Boat Quay ⊤65386066; see map on p.84. An affordable range of 47 congees, served at marble-topped tables recalling a 1950s coffee shop. Daily 11am–11pm.

Vegetarian Chinese

Though their menus often feature "mock" meat dishes, the following selection of Chinese restaurants are all strictly **vegetarian** and use ingredi-

ents like yam, bean curd, mushrooms, water chestnuts and nuts to such imaginative effect that they'll appeal even to confirmed meat eaters.

Fut Sai Kai Restaurant 147 Kitchener Rd ⊤62980336; see map on pp.88–89. Behind the prayer beads and incense sticks in the window is an old-fashioned Cantonese restaurant with a strongly Oriental atmosphere and fiery red decor; $20 is sufficient for two. Bean curd forms the backbone of Chinese vegetarian cooking, though, oddly, it reaches your table shaped to resemble meat or fish. Tues–Sun 10am–9pm.

Happy Realm Vegetarian Food Centre 03-16 Pearl's Ctr, 100 Eu Tong Sen St ⊤62226141; see map on p.73. "The way to good health and a sound mind", boasts the restaurant's card; tasty and reasonably priced vegetarian dishes. Daily 11am–8.30pm.

Kwan Im Vegetarian Restaurant 190 Waterloo St ⊤63382394; see map on pp.88–89. A huge display of sweet and savoury *pow* is the highlight of this unfussy establishment, in the *South East Asia Hotel* sited close to Bencoolen Street. Cheap. Daily 8am–8.30pm.

Lingzhi Restaurant B1-17/18 Orchard Towers, 400 Orchard Rd ⊤67343788; see map on pp.66–67. A real treat, where skewers of vegetables served with satay sauce are the highlight of an imaginative menu; there's also a takeaway counter. Daily 11am–10pm.

American, North and South

Billy Bombers 02-52 Bugis Jtn, 200 Victoria St ⊤63378018; see map on pp.88–89. Shades of Arnold's diner in *Happy Days*: reasonably priced burgers and bowls of chilli eaten in speakeasy booths upholstered in red leather. Daily 11am–11pm.

Bobby Rubino's B1-03 Fountain Court, CHIJMES, 30 Victoria St ⊤63375477; see map on pp.88–89. Ribs are the speciality, but steaks, burgers and other big-boy platters are available; eschew the "wine-rack" partitions and rough-hewn, red-brick interior and make for the terrace, superbly located below CHIJMES' looming convent. There's also a popular bar with pool table. Daily 11am–midnight.

Café Iguana 01-03 Riverside Point, 30 Merchant Rd ⊤62361275; see map on pp.70–71. Riverfront Mexican restaurant and bar, in colourful surroundings. Tortillas, chilli, quesadillas and all the other favourites feature on the menu, plus a huge selection of tequilas. Daily 6pm–3am.

Cha Cha Cha 32 Lorong Mambong, Holland Village ☏64621650; see map on p.117. Classic Mexican dishes ($10–22) are served in this vibrantly coloured restaurant; outside are a few open-air patio tables, ideal for posing with a bottle of Dos Equis beer, but book ahead for these. Daily 11.30am–11pm.

Dan Ryan's Chicago Grill B1-01 Tanglin Place, 91 Tanglin Rd ☏67382800; see map on pp.66–67. Chug back a Budweiser and get stuck into "American portions" of ribs, burgers and chicken in a dining room that's crammed with Americana; main courses cost around $15. Daily 11.30am–midnight.

Lawry's The Prime Ribs 02-30 Paragon, 290 Orchard Rd ☏68363333; see map on pp.66–67. Superior ribs, served with Yorkshire pudding, mashed potato and whipped cream horseradish, in a room with a view onto frenetic Orchard Road. Plan on $50 a head, with wine. Daily 11am–3pm & 5–10pm.

Ponderosa 02-20 Raffles City Shopping Centre, 252 North Bridge Rd ☏63344926; see map on pp.88–89. The perfect cure for vitamin deficiency – chicken, steak and fish dishes come with baked potato and pineapple, if you can make it past the all-you-can-eat salad bar. Daily noon–10.00pm.

Seah Street Deli Raffles Hotel, 1 Beach Rd ☏63371886; see map on pp.88–89. New York-style deli boasting mountainous sandwiches, at around $10 each. The soda and root beer signs and outsized Americana on the walls make this the most un-colonial establishment in *Raffles Hotel*. Open Sun–Thurs 11am–10pm, Fri & Sat 11am–11pm.

European

🏃 **Broth** 21 Duxton Hill ☏63233353; see map on p.81. Superb fusion cuisine in an old shophouse on a delightfully quiet, tree-shaded Chinatown back street. A charming oasis – recommended. Moderate. Open Mon–Fri noon–2.30pm, Mon–Sat 6–10.30pm.

Gordon Grill Goodwood Park Hotel, 22 Scotts Rd ☏67301744; see map on pp.66–67. Upmarket restaurant lent a Scottish feel by the tartan décor and the haggis with tatties: excellent food – but at a price. Set lunch is your best bet. Daily noon–2.30pm & 7–11pm.

Ocho Tapas 01-12/13/14 CHIJMES, 30 Victoria St ☏68831508; see map on pp.88–89. Top tapas; sit inside, amid the rugs, terracotta tiles and Moorish panels, or venture out onto the terrace, where musicians play Gypsy Kings-style hits. The wine list impresses. Open Sun–Thurs 11am–1am, Fri & Sat 11am–3am.

High tea and tiffin

Many of Singapore's swisher hotels advertise that most colonial of traditions, **high tea**, in the local press; below are a few of the more permanent choices. Typically, a Singapore high tea comprises local and Western snacks, both sweet and savoury. If you really want to play the part of a Victorian settler, Singapore's most splendid food outlet at the *Raffles* still serves **tiffin** – the colonial term for a light curry meal (derived from the Hindi word for luncheon).

Alkhaff Mansion 10 Telok Blangah Green; Redhill MRT, then bus #145; or bus #124 ☏64154888. The *Verandah Bar* hosts an English afternoon tea ($15) on Saturday and Sunday only (3–5.30pm).

Café l'Espresso *Goodwood Park Hotel*, 22 Scotts Rd ☏67301743. A legendary array of English cakes, pastries and speciality coffees. Daily 2–5pm.

Halia Singapore Botanic Gardens, 1 Cluny Rd ☏64766711. High tea (daily 3–5.30pm) offers cake and coffee or tea for $7.50.

Rose Verandah *Shangri-La Hotel*, 22 Orange Grove Rd ☏67373644. Rated the best high tea in Singapore by the American Women's Association of Singapore, no less.

Tiffin Room *Raffles Hotel*, 1 Beach Rd ☏63371886. Tiffin lunch (noon–2pm) and dinner (7–10pm) both cost over $40 per person, though the spread of edibles and the charming colonial surroundings make them worth considering. Between tiffin sittings, high tea ($37) is served (3.30–5.30pm).

🏃 **Original Sin 01-62 Blk 43, Jln Merah Saga** ☎64755605; see map on p.117. The bank of awards over the bar bears testimony to the quality of the vegetarian Mediterranean fare on offer in this rust-and-aquamarine-painted dining room. The mezze plate makes an engaging appetizer; after that, you could do worse than a pizza Ibizi topped with roasted pumpkin, avocado, Spanish onion, asparagus and cheese. The most extensive wine list in Singapore. Expensive. Open Tues–Sun noon–3pm & 6–10.30pm.

Da Paolo II Ristorante 80 Club St ☎62247081; see map on p.73. Great homemade pasta or splash out on authentic Sicilian meat and fish dishes washed down with one of a range of Italian wines. Open Mon–Fri 11.30am–2.30pm, Sat 6.30–11.30pm.

Pasta Fresca 30 Boat Quay ☎65326283; see map on p.84. Match up fresh pasta (made at the owner's own factory) and a sauce from the menu, and sit out on the riverside terrace. Around $30 a head, drinks extra. Daily 11am–10pm.

Pasta Fresca Seasports Centre Seasports Ctr, 1210 East Coast Parkway ☎64418140; see map on p.110. There are peerless views out to sea from this atap hut located just above the beach, within a sailing club; the pizzas, pastas, meat and fish dishes are not at all bad, either. At night the lights of the tankers docked south of Singapore look like fairy lights strung along the horizon. Moderate. Daily 11.30am–midnight.

Paulaner Bräuhaus 01-01 Millennia Walk, 9 Raffles Blvd ☎68832572; see map on pp.88–89. German-theme-restaurant-cum-brewery, serving generous platters of *wurst*, *kartoffeln* and *sauerkraut*. Most people come here for the beer however – this is one of the few micro-breweries in Southeast Asia. Moderate. Bar open Mon–Thurs 11.30am–1am, Fri–Sat 11.30am–2am.

Spizza 29 Club St ☎62242525; see map on p.73. Homely, rustic and affordable pizzeria, whose menu boasts a tempting A–Z of thick-crust pizzas, cooked in a traditional wood oven. Moderate. Daily noon–3pm & 6.30–11pm.

Indian and Nepali

In the same way as the Chinese, immigrants from north and south India brought their own cuisines with them. Though they vary in emphasis and ingredients, all utilize *daal* (lentils), chutneys, yoghurts and sweet and sour *lassis* (yoghurt drinks); neither north nor south Indians eat beef. **North Indian** food tends to rely more on meat, especially mutton and chicken, and uses breads – *naan*, *chapatis*, *parathas* and *rotis* – rather than rice. The most famous style of north Indian cooking is *tandoori* – named after the clay oven in which the food is cooked – and you'll commonly come across *tandoori* chicken – marinated in yoghurt and spices and then baked.

South Indian (and **Sri Lankan**) food tends to be spicier and more reliant on vegetables. Its staple is the *dosai* (pancake), often served at breakfast time as a *masala dosai*, stuffed with onions, vegetables and chutney, and washed down with *teh tarik*. Indian Muslims serve the similar *murtabak*, a grilled *roti* pancake with egg, onion and minced meat. Many south Indian cafés turn to serving *daun pisang* at lunchtime, usually a vegetarian meal where rice is served on banana leaves and small, replenishable heaps of various vegetable curries are placed alongside; in some places, meat and fish are on offer, too.

Though Indian food outlets span the island, you'll find the highest concentration of really good ones in **Little India**. South Indian Muslim restaurants also tend to cluster on **North Bridge Road** in the Arab Quarter, where you'll find tasty *biriyanis* and *murtabaks*.

Annalakshmi Restaurant Peninsular, Excelsior Hotel & Shopping Ctr, 5 Coleman St ☎63399993; see map on p.52. Terrific north and south Indian vegetarian snacks, meals and set meals in sumptuous surroundings, with all profits going to Kala Mandhir, an Indian cultural association next door. Many of the staff are volunteers from the Hindu community, so your waiter might just be a doctor or a lawyer. All staff work on the adage that "the guest is god". From $10 a dish. Open Mon–Sat 11.30am–3pm & 6–9.30pm.

Banana Leaf Apolo 56–58 Race Course Rd ☎62938682; see map on p.94.
Recently refurbished and resplendent in marble (though eating with your hands is still the order of the day), this is a pioneering fish-head curry restaurant ($30 for two people) where a delicious selection of spicy south Indian dishes are all served on banana leaves. Make sure to fold over your banana leaf to show that you are full and finished eating, or you'll be given another dollop of rice and curry from the roving waiters. All you can eat and cheap too.

Bombay Woodlands Restaurant B1-01 Tanglin Shopping Ctr, 19 Tanglin Rd ☎62352712; see map on pp.66–67. The set lunch (from $15) offers a perfect introduction to the breads and vegetarian curries of south India. Daily 9.30am–10pm.

Gandhi Eating House 29 Chander Rd ☎62995343; see map on p.94. Many locals reckon this open fronted place at the back of the Race Course Road restaurants knocks out the best chicken curries in Little India; meals come on banana leaves, water in metal jugs. Daily 11am–11pm.

Gorkha Grill 21 Smith St ☎62270806; see map on p.73. There are fish, mutton and chicken dishes galore at this enchanting Nepali place, but be sure to start with *momo* (minced chicken dumplings) and end with *kheer*, or Nepali rice pudding, a tasty blend of cream, rice and cardamom. The set lunch ($9) is good value. If the murals of mountains and votive flags leave you wanting to see Nepal, speak to owner Dan, who leads treks from Kathmandu, and can book ahead for you. Daily 11.30am–11.30pm.

Islamic Restaurant 791–797 North Bridge Rd ☎62987563; see map on pp.88–89. Aged Muslim restaurant manned by a gang of old men who plod solemnly up and down between the tables. It boasts the best chicken *biriyani* in Singapore, cooked in the traditional way – heated from above and below with charcoal. $15 for two. Daily except Fri 9.30am–9.30pm.

Kinara 57 Boat Quay ☎65330412; see map on p.84. Exquisite restaurant boasting antique fittings imported from the subcontinent; a marvellous view of the river from upstairs, and elegantly presented Punjabi dishes. Around $60 for two. Daily noon–2.30pm & 6.30–10.30pm.

Komala Vilas 76–78 Serangoon Rd ☎62936980; see map on p.94. A cramped, popular vegetarian establishment specializing in fifteen varieties of *dosai*. The "South Indian Meal", served upstairs on a banana leaf, is great value at $12. Daily 7am–10pm.

Madras New Woodlands Restaurant 12–14 Upper Dickson Rd ☎62971594; see map on p.94. Functional, canteen-style place serving up decent vegetarian food at bargain prices. House specialities are the *thali* set meals; samosas, bhajis and other snacks are available after 3pm, and there's a big selection of sweets, too. Recommended. Daily 7.30am–11.30pm.

Moti Mahal Restaurant 18 Murray St ☎62214338; see map on p.81. Not cheap, but one of Singapore's very best Indian restaurants, serving tasty tandoori dishes in pleasant surroundings. The special is *murg massalam*, a whole chicken stuffed with rice (order in advance). Open Mon–Fri 11am–3pm, daily 6–10.30pm.

Muthu's Curry Restaurant 76–78 Race Course Rd ☎62932389; see map on p.94. Recent renovations have greatly spruced up this south Indian restaurant with no menu, but famous for its fish-head curry ($16–25). Daily 10am–10pm.

Orchard Maharajah 25 Cuppage Terr, Cuppage Rd ☎67326331; see map on pp.66–67. Set in a wonderful old Peranakan house, this splendid north Indian restaurant has a large terrace and a tempting menu that includes the sublime fish *mumtaz* – fillet of fish stuffed with minced mutton, almonds, eggs, cashews and raisins – worth the extra few dollars. Daily 11am–3pm & 6–11pm.

Our Village 5th floor, 46 Boat Quay ☎65383092; see map on p.84. A hidden gem, with fine north Indian and Sri Lankan food, and peachy views of the river, city and colonial district from its charming, lamplit roof terrace. Try the rich *murgh makhanwala* or the *malai kofta*, and finish with a palate-cleansing masala tea. Cheap. Open Mon–Fri 11.30am–1.45pm & 6–10.30pm, Sat & Sun dinner only.

Roshni 02-01 Little India Arcade, 48 Serangoon Rd ☎62924808; see map on p.94. It's best to come at night: tuck into tasty pakoras followed by spicy chicken pepper *chettinad*, then enjoy the Indian disco or (Wed–Sat) live band. Great fun. Daily 11.30am–3.30pm & 6–11pm.

Samy's Singapore Civil Service Club, Blk 25 Dempsey Rd ☎64745618. Bus #7 from Orchard MTR; alight when you see Pierce

Rd to the left; see map on p.117. Once you've sunk a few Tigers at the Civil Service Club next door, you'll be ready for a Samy's curry, served on a banana leaf, and best enjoyed overlooking the trees at a table on the fairy-lit verandah. Two pay around $15; beers can be ordered from the club. Daily 11am–3pm & 6–10pm.

Sri Vijayah 229 Selegie Rd ☎63361748; **see map on p.94.** Hole-in-the-wall vegetarian joint offering unbeatable value for money: $7 buys a replenishable mountain of rice and vegetable curries, and there's a mouthwatering display of sweetmeats at the front door. Daily 6am–10pm.

Indonesian

Similar to Malay cuisine (see p.163), **Indonesian** cookery is characterized by its use of fragrant, aromatic spices and sweet, peanut-based sauces. Specialities to look out for are *nasi padang* – a hot, dry style of cooking that hails from Sumatra – and *rijstaffel*, a Dutch-influenced concept that works along the same lines as a buffet, except that in this case the buffet comes to your table in the form of countless bowls of delicacies. You take a bit from each bowl until the rice on your plate is no longer visible, then you mix it all up into a mass and gobble it down. It doesn't taste as bad as it sounds, but one can imagine the horror this must have caused Indonesian onlookers.

Alkaff Mansion 10 Telok Blangah Grn ☎64154888. Redhill MRT, then bus #145; or bus #124; see map on p.117. Built in the 1920s as a weekend retreat for the Alkaff family, this splendidly restored mansion offers a superb *rijstaffel*: ten dishes served by a line of ten women in traditional *kebayas*. Or just have a beer in the bar, worth the exorbitant price for an hour or two of colonial grandeur. Daily noon–10.30pm.

🏃 **Bumbu 44 Kandahar St** ☎63928628; see map on pp.88–89. Crammed with Singaporean antiques amassed by owner, Robert Tan, *Bumbu* is as much a social history museum as a restaurant. Happily, the furnishings don't outshine the fine Indonesian/Thai cuisine on offer. The signature dish, crispy fish pillow – fish meat mixed with spices and deep-fried – is

worth the journey alone. Daily 11am–2pm & 6–10pm.

Cumi Bali 20 Duxton Rd ☎90050260; **see map on p.81.** Slender and jolly *nasi padang* joint whose walls are strung with Indonesian fishing nets, puppets, instruments and batiks. The beef *rendang* and *ikan bakar* (BBQ fish) both hit the spot; or try one of the generous set lunches. Cheap. Daily noon–9pm.

House of Sundanese Food 55 Boat Quay ☎65343775; **see map on p.84.** Spicy salads and barbecued seafood characterize the cuisine of Sunda (West Java), served here in simple yet tasteful surroundings. Try the tasty *ikan sunda* (grilled Javanese fish) – one fish feeds two to three people. Cheap. Open Mon–Fri noon–2.30pm & 5–10pm, Sat & Sun 5–10pm.

Rendezvous Restaurant 02-02 Hotel Rendezvous, 9 Bras Basah Rd ☎63397508; **see map on pp.88–89.** Revered *nasi padang* joint that still turns out lip-smacking curries, *rendangs* and *sambals*; the weighing machine in the corner is an unusual touch. Daily 11am–9pm.

Rumah Makan Minang 18a Kandahar St; see map on pp.88–89. Fiery *nasi padang* – highly spiced Sumatran cuisine – in the heart of the Arab Quarter; $4 ensures a good feed. Daily noon–2.30pm & 6–10.30pm.

Sanur Restaurant 04-17/18 Centrepoint, 176 Orchard Rd ☎67342192; **see map on pp.66–67.** Hearty, reasonably priced food served by waitresses in traditional batik dress; the beef *rendang* is terrific. It's best to book ahead. Daily 11.30am–2.45pm & 5.45–10pm.

Tambuah Mas Indonesian Restaurant 04-10, Tanglin Shopping Ctr, 19 Tanglin Rd ☎67333333; **see map on pp.66–67.** Friendly restaurant, approached through a Minang-kabau-style entrance, which offers *padang* food and a smattering of Chinese dishes. Daily 11am–10pm.

Warung M Nasir 01-05/06 1 Liang Seah St ☎63395935; **see map on pp.88–89.** This charming, open-fronted *nasi padang* café is a welcome addition to the Liang Seah's burgeoning dining scene. *Rendangs* and curries are taken, either at streetside tables or in the kopitiam-style dining room. Cheap. Open Mon–Sat 10am–10pm.

International

🏃 **Blu Shangri-La Hotel, Orange Grove Rd** ☎67302598; **see map on pp.66–67.** One of Singapore's most exquisite dining experiences: California fusion cuisine of the highest quality, overlooking downtown Singapore from the *Shangri-La*'s 24th floor. Daily 7–11pm.

Blu Jaz Café 11 Bali Lane ☎6292 3800; see map on pp.88–89. Chilled-out café-restaurant, tucked away on the edge of the Arab quarter. They do reliable Japanese and Western food – everything from beef teriyaki to fish-and-chips – and a range of local fare too, including satay and mee goreng. Not expensive either; a steak will set you back around $13. Live jazz Fri & Sat eves. Mon–Fri 11am–midnight; Sat till 1am.

Colours by the Bay Esplanade Mall, 8 Raffles Ave; see map on pp.70–71. Restaurant collective, offering a number of global cuisines – Japanese, Thai, Chinese, Italian, etc – overlooking the bay beside Singapore's main theatre. With luck, your meal will coincide with an alfresco cultural performance.

Don Noodle Bistro 01-16 Tanglin Mall, 163 Tanglin Rd ☎67383188; see map on pp.66–67. Minimalist yet chic, *Don* is something of a paradox – a Western-style take on the noodle bar, imported back to the East. The menu is not country-specific, meaning that you can enjoy Indonesian *kway teow goreng* while your dining companion tucks into Japanese *ramen* noodles. Daily 11.30am–10.30pm.

The Gapz 03-09/10 Pacific Plaza, 9 Scotts Rd ☎67379336; see map on pp.66–67. Self-styled "young and trendy Asian *dim sum* and noodles bar", where the *dim sum* appear on a conveyor belt, not a trolley, and there's MTV on a huge screen. If grazing on dumplings does not appeal, you could opt for a bento set – or try designing your own noodle dish from a palette of ingredients. Mon–Sat 11.30am–10pm, Sun 7am–7pm.

Halia Singapore Botanic Gardens, 1 Cluny Rd ☎64766711. Moonlit and candlelit after dusk, *Halia*'s magical garden-verandah setting whisks you a world away from downtown Singapore. The East-meets-West lunch menu spans sandwiches, pasta and laksa, plus set lunches; at night, there are more substantial dishes such as rack of lamb and seafood stew. The high-tea deal (daily 3–5.30pm) offers cake and coffee or tea for – or take along the papers and tuck into the weekend buffet breakfast. Moderate. Daily 11am–11pm, also Sat & Sun 8–10.30am for breakfast.

Hot Stones 53 Boat Quay ☎65345188; see map on p.84. A healthy and novel twist on dining: steaks, chicken and seafood grilled at table on non-porous Alpine rock heated to 200° – no oil or fat, but bags of flavour. Similar to a Korean BBQ, this DIY cookfest is not for the lazy. Daily noon–2.30pm & 6–10.30pm.

Louis' Oyster Bar 36 Boat Quay ☎65330534; see map on p.84. The Louis in question is Louis Armstrong, who beams down from all the walls. Oysters cost around $18 per half-dozen, but the "High Society Platter" (crayfish, crab, mussels, oysters and prawns on ice) is hard to resist. Open Mon–Fri 11–1am, Sat & Sun 5pm–3am.

Nooch 02-16 Wheelock Pl, 501 Orchard Rd ☎62350880; see map on pp.66–67. The blurb on its menu calls this cool and popular, crescent-shaped joint overlooking Orchard Boulevard a "nondestinational" restaurant – meaning that the idea is to order and scarf down your MSG-free Thai or Japanese noodles on the double, and be on your way. The Thai *tub tim krob*, or water chestnuts in coconut milk, is a good way to douse the fires after a *tom yam kung* soup. Moderate. Open Mon–Fri noon–3pm & 6–10.30pm, Sat & Sun noon–11pm.

SuperNature 01-21 Park House, 501 Orchard Rd ☎67354338; see map on pp.66–67. The very place to come when the toxins need flushing: salads, soy, lentil and falafel burgers, and a range of global rice and noodle dishes washed down with organic wines and lagers. Moderate. Open Mon–Sat 11am–10pm, Sun 10am–8pm.

Top of the M 39th floor, Mandarin Hotel, 333 Orchard Rd ☎68316258; see map on pp.66–67. Singapore's highest revolving restaurant, and a great place to pop that question, over pan-fried goose liver and grilled rock lobster; at night, the lights of the city below are pure *Blade Runner*. Book ahead at the weekend. Expensive. Daily noon–3pm & 6.30–10.30pm.

Town Restaurant The Fullerton Singapore, 1 Fullerton Sq ☎67338388; see map on p.84. Despite the eclectic range of Asian and Western cuisines on the menu, your best bet is to head out onto the terrace overlooking the Singapore River, and munch away on one of the BBQ set meals. There's also an Asian buffet on Saturday (noon–3pm). Moderate. Open Sun–Thurs 6.30am–midnight, Fri & Sat 6.30am–1am.

Japanese

Elegantly presented and subtly flavoured, **Japanese** cuisine is dominated by fish, which crops up in classic dishes such as sushi (raw fish wrapped in rice and seaweed) and *sashimi* (sliced or cubed raw fish). Other dishes that merit a try include *teriyaki* (chicken in a sweet sauce) and *teppanyaki* (grilled slices of meat or seafood), but bear in mind that Japanese food doesn't come cheap.

Akashi Japanese Restaurant B1-9, Tanglin Shopping Ctr, 19 Tanglin Rd ☎67324438; **branch at B1-23 City Link Mall, 1 Raffles Link** ☎62387767; **see map on pp.66–67.** Chain of understated, classical Japanese restaurants, where the sake *teriyaki* and the tempura are both good and there's a fine range of sakes with names as long as your arm. Daily noon–3pm & 6.30–10pm.

Beppu Menkan 01-01 Far East Sq, 134 Amoy St ☎64380328; **see map on p.73.** Choose from grilled eel, ramen noodle soup, *gyoza* dumplings and other Japanese favourites, taken amid Japanese lanterns and cartoons of avid noodle-slurpers. Should the mains leave you hungry, you could call in at the Japanese dessert stall next door. Open Mon–Fri 11am–2.30pm & 6–10pm, Sat noon–10.30pm, Sun 12.30–9pm.

Inagiku 3rd floor, Westin Plaza Hotel, 2 Stamford Rd ☎64316156; **see map on pp.88–89.** More of a maze than a restaurant, with four sections serving expensive, quality tempura, *teppanyaki*, sushi, and an à la carte menu – the latter the cheapest alternative. Daily noon–3pm & 6.30–11pm.

Japanese stalls Food Jctn, B1, Seiyu Department Store, Bugis Jctn, 200 Victoria St; see map on pp.88–89. *Sumo* has *sashimi*, tempura and *teriyaki* sets around $10, while nearby *Express-Teppanyaki*'s "big value meal" offers a choice of meats and vegetables flash-fried on the U-shaped hot bar. Daily 10am–9pm.

Sakae Sushi 02-13 Wheelock Pl, 501 Orchard Rd ☎67376281; **see map on pp.66–67.** One of a popular chain, this sushi and *sashimi* bar, bang in the centre of Orchard Road, has set lunches that start from $15. Diners choose to sit up at the conveyor-belt bar, or at diner-style booths around the restaurant's outer walls. Daily noon–10pm.

Senbazuru Hotel New Otani, 177a River Valley Rd ☎64338693; **see map on pp.70–71.** If the extensive menu proves too mind-boggling, choose from the selection of *kaiseki*, or traditional set dinners, which can run to ten courses, and will leave a sizeable hole in your pocket. Daily 11.30am–2.30pm & 6.30–10.30pm.

Shima Yakiniku 2 Murray Terr, Murray St ☎62235159; **see map on p.81.** A DIY delight: all the meat, salmon, prawns, frogs' legs you can eat, cooked on a hot stone at your table. Daily noon–2.30pm & 6.30–9.30pm.

Sushi Tei 20 Lorong Mambong, Holland Village ☎64632310; **see map on p.117.** Another popular chain, this is a cross-fertilization of Tokyo sushi bar and airport baggage reclaim: diners snatch sushi ($2–8) from the conveyor belt looping the bar. Daily 11.30am–10pm.

Tatsu Sushi 01-16, CHIJMES, 30 Victoria St ☎63325868; **see map on pp.88–89.** *Tatsu* is a veteran of the notoriously fluid CHIJMES restaurant scene. Owner Ronny Chia's culinary expertise, and the high quality of ingredients used (all fish is flown in from Japan), have resulted in a clientele that's around 75 percent Japanese. Open Mon–Sat noon–3pm & 6.30–10.30pm.

Korean

Newcomers to **Korean** food will find it both robust and exciting – perhaps this has something to do with the amount of ginseng in every dish. Meat features prominently on a Korean menu, and is often cooked by diners themselves on a table barbecue, or *bulgogi*. Another speciality is *kim chi,* or spicy pickled cabbage. For liquid refreshment, try the OB beer.

Haebok's Korean Restaurant 44–46 Tanjong Pagar Rd ☎62239003; **see map on p.81.** If you aren't acquainted with Korean food, plastic models of the meals available displayed in the front window lend a few pointers. The *fish jun* is recommended as is the *kalbi beef*. Daily 11.30am–3pm & 5.30–10.30pm.

Korean Restaurant Pte Ltd 05-35 Specialists' Ctr, 277 Orchard Rd ☎62350018; **see map on pp.66–67.** Singapore's first Korean restaurant, beautifully furnished and serving up a wide range of dependably good dishes at around $20 each. Daily noon–11pm.

Seoul Garden Korean Restaurant 03-119 Marina Sq, 6 Raffles Blvd ☎63391339; **see map on**

pp.88–89. Entertaining, busy restaurant where the best value is the all-you-can-eat Korean barbecue – a buffet of twenty seasoned meats, seafoods and vegetables cooked by customers at their tables. Open Mon–Fri 11am–3pm & 5.30–10.30pm, Sat & Sun 11am–10.30pm.

Malay and Nonya

Malay cuisine is based on rice, often enriched with coconut milk, which is served with a dizzying variety of curries and *sambal*, a condiment comprising pounded chillies blended with *belacan* (shrimp paste), onions and garlic. Other spices which characterize Malay cuisine include ginger and *galangal* (a root similar to ginger), coriander, lemon grass and lime leaves. Malaysia's most famous dish is satay, but the classic way to sample Malay food is to eat *nasi campur*, a buffet of steamed rice served with an array of accompanying dishes; other popular dishes include *nasi goreng* (mixed fried rice with meat, seafood and vegetables); and *rendang* (slow-cooked beef, chicken or mutton in lemon grass and coconut).

Pork, of course, is taboo to all Muslims, but it has been married with Malay cooking in **Nonya** cuisine, which evolved as a result of the intermarriage of early Chinese immigrants and local Malays. Typical Nonya dishes incorporate elements and ingredients from Chinese, Malay and Thai cooking, the end product tending to be spicier than Chinese food. Chicken, fish and seafood forms

the backbone of the cuisine, along with pork. Noodles (*mee*) flavoured with chillies, and rich curries made from rice flour and coconut cream, are common. A popular dish is *laksa*, noodles in spicy coconut soup served with seafood and chopped beansprouts. Other popular dishes include *ayam buah keluak*, chicken cooked with "black" nuts; and *otak-otak*, fish mashed with coconut milk and chilli paste and steamed in a banana leaf.

Bayview Café City Bayview Hotel, 30 Bencoolen St ☎63372882; see map on pp.88–89. This faceless hotel café's "Asian Hi Tea" offers a good, affordable introduction to Nonya cuisine. Sat & Sun noon–4pm.

Belachan 10 Smith St ☎62219810; see map on p.73. Friendly, refined *Bolachan* (the name is Malay for shrimp paste) offers sanctuary from Smith Street's throng. The *itek manis*, duck stewed in ginger and black beans, is sensational, though the set lunch (main course, veg, rice and *achar*) offers best value. Open Tues–Sun 11.30am–3pm & 6.30–10.30pm, Mon lunch only.

Bengawan Solo Centrepoint, 176 Orchard Rd; ☎67346641 also at Clifford Ctr, 24 Raffles Pl; see map on pp.66–67. Superior Asian cake shops, specializing in Malay *kueh* (cakes). Daily 10.30am–9.30pm

Blue Ginger 97 Tanjong Pagar Rd ☎62223928; see map on p.81. Housed in a renovated shophouse, this trendy Peranakan restaurant is a yuppy favourite, thanks to dishes such as *ikan masal assam gulai* (mackerel simmered in a tamarind and lemon-grass gravy), and that benchmark of Nonya cuisine, *ayam buah keluak* – braised chicken

EATING | Restaurants and coffee shops

Cookery schools

Should the fine dining that Singapore offers leave you wanting to replicate some of it back home, you could give yourself a head start by attending a cookery school. Classes tend to last from two to four hours and cost $65–100.

Academy at Sunrice Fort Canning Ctr, Fort Canning Pk ☎63363307. Hosts (expensive) week-long culinary adventure holidays.

Coriander Leaf Cookery School 02-01 The *Gallery Hotel*, 76 Robertson Quay ☎67323354. Southeast Asian, European and Middle Eastern courses.

Raffles Culinary Academy 02-17 *Raffles Hotel* Arcade, 328 North Bridge Rd ☎64121256. Classes include making traditional Indian pickles and chutneys, French Cambodian fare and Nonya cuisine.

with Indonesian black nuts. Moderate. Daily 11.30am–3pm & 6.30–11pm.

Chilli Padi 11 Joo Chiat Pl ☏62751002; see map on p.110. Red batik ceiling drapes and table-cloths bring homely warmth to this family-run restaurant, whose Nonya dishes, like spicy chilli fish and *popiah*, have justly won it plaudits galore. The jars of kaya and curry pastes on sale make unusual gifts to take home. Moderate. Daily 11.30am–2.30pm & 5.30–10pm.

Guan Hoe Soon 214 Joo Chiat Rd ☏63442761; see map on p.110. Fifty years old, and still turning out fine Nonya cuisine; try the *chen dool* (coconut milk, red beans, sugar, green jelly and ice), a refreshing end to a meal. Around $40 for two, with beer. Mon & Wed–Sun 1am–3pm & 6–9.30pm.

Mum's Kitchen 02-06, 3015 Bedok North St 5 ☏63460969; see map on p.110. The emphasis here, as you'd imagine, is on home-cooked food, Nonya-based, though with other Asian incursions. House speciality Mum's Curry is wonderful, and best chased down by homemade barley water; special business lunches (Mon–Fri) offer three courses at $18 for two. Daily 11am–10pm.

Peranakan Inn 210 East Coast Rd ☏64406195; see map on p.110. While officially touted, Nonya cuisine often gets panned by Singaporeans as bland and boring. Fortunately this restaurant proves them all wrong. As much effort goes into the food as went into the renovation of this immaculate, bright-green shophouse restau-rant, which offers authentic Nonya favourites at reasonable prices; around $10 a dish. Try the *babi chin* (stewed pork flavoured with miso). Daily 11am–3pm & 6–10.30pm.

Thai and Indochinese

You'll be thankful for a cooling bottle of Singha beer after you've done battle with a fiery Thai meal. Popular dishes include tom yam kung (a challengingly spicy prawn soup), green curry, fishcakes, chicken feet salad, and pineapple fried rice – which isn't fried rice with pineapple in it, but whole pineapple with fried rice inside. Vietnamese cuisine betrays Chinese, Thai, and French influences. Soups, chao tom (prawn paste barbecued on sugar cane) and spring rolls are perennial favourites, and are best washed down with Saigon's own "33" beer.

Cuppage Thai Food Restaurant 49 Cuppage Terr ☏67341116; see map on pp.66–67. Nonde-script inside, but boasting a great outdoor terrace, this cheap and cheerful restaurant offers quality Thai dishes for around $8. Daily 11am–3pm & 6–11pm.

Golden Mile Complex 5001 Beach Rd; see map on pp.88–89. Known locally as "Thai Village", the *Golden Mile* is always full of Thais waiting to catch buses home. Drop by any one of its countless Thai cafés and you're sure of authentic, affordable Thai cuisine, amid an atmosphere that's pure Bangkok.

△ Indochine

Internet cafés

As you'd expect of a nation so enamoured with cutting-edge technology, Singapore boasts numerous cafés offering email and Internet access. The emphasis is on the Internet, rather than the café side of the business, so don't expect to be spoilt for choice on the eating and drinking front. Most have nothing more than a fridge-full of soft drinks and a modest selection of pastries on display. Web access typically costs around $5 per hour, or $3 per half-hour. For more details, see p.45.

Chills Café 01-07 Stamford House, 39 Stamford Rd ☎68831016. Sedate place, focusing on email checkers, rather than gamers. Daily 9am–midnight.

i-surf 02-14 Far East Plaza, 14 Scotts Rd ☎67343225. Slap-bang in the middle of Orchard Road, and handy for checking prices online in mid-shopping spree. Open daily 9am–9pm.

Netzspiel 01-01, 44a Prinsep St. Central cybercafé where surfing sets you back $4 an hour. Mon–Sat 11am–11.30pm, Sun noon–11.30pm.

Travel Café 02-01, 44 Prinsep St. Backpacker-oriented café, with snacks, finger-food and soft and alcoholic drinks. Sun–Thurs 11am–11pm, Fri & Sat 11am–2am.

⑩

EATING | Restaurants and coffee shops

Indochine 49 Club St ☎63230503; see map on p.73. *Indochine* is one of Singapore's most elegant restaurants, its beautiful fixtures complemented by a truly great menu embracing Vietnamese, Lao and Cambodian cuisine. Try the Laotian *Larb Kai* (spicy chicken salad) or *Nha Trang* roast duck and mango salad. The Vietnamese *chao tom* (minced prawn wrapped round sugarcane) is also mouthwatering. Pricey but worth it. Mon–Sat noon–2.30pm & 6–11pm. Equally classy and in a prime location is the *Indochine Waterfront* restaurant at 1 Empress Pl ☎63391720, where you can dine on Cambodian chilli and basil chicken or sesame lamb with lemon grass and melt-in-your-mouth banana fritters.

Kabayan Filipino Restaurant 03-25 Lucky Plaza, 304 Orchard Rd ☎67380921; see map on pp.66–67. Big, dark chamber crammed with tables to cater for the Sunday melee of Filipino maids; dishes are laid out buffet-style, and best washed down with San Miguel beer. Cheap. Daily 10am–9pm.

Madam Saigon 30 Liang Seah St ☎63339798. Affordable, if unremarkably appointed, restaurant whose Vietnamese chef knocks out tasty *pho* and *com tam* (broken rice with chicken), both around the $12 mark. Daily 11.30am–2.30pm & 6–10.30pm.

Patara 03-14 Tanglin Mall, Orchard Rd ☎67370818; see map on pp.66–67. Refined dining room, where the tasting menus (around $40) are a good way of acquainting yourself with Thai flavours. Daily noon–3pm & 6–10pm.

Pho Hoa 18 Lorong Mambong ☎64662737; see map on p.117. Part of a global noodle franchise, *Pho Hoa* knocks out decent *pho*, or Vietnamese rice noodle soup, and *com suon* (grilled pork chop, rice and salad). The menu explains the fundamentals of *pho*, allowing you to sample a beginner's *pho*, create your own, or try the Adventurer's choice, with steak, meatballs, tripe and brisket. Cheap. Daily 11am–10pm.

Sukhothai 47 Boat Quay ☎65382422; see map on p.84. Chef's recommendations include fried cotton fish topped with sliced green mangoes, but you can't go far wrong whatever you plump for; the dining room is rather understated, so take advantage of the riverside tables. Daily 6.30–10.30pm, also Mon–Fri noon–3pm.

Viet Cafe 01-57 UE Sq, Unity St ☎63336453; see map on pp.70–71. The heady aromas of Vietnamese *pho* (soup) – mint, basil and citrus – hang heavy in the air at the sleek *Viet Cafe*. Follow the pebble path which leads up to the balcony or, better still, sit out on the forecourt and enjoy the night air. Handy for a late-night snack after a beer along Mohamed Sultan Road. Daily noon–3am.

Viet Lang Blk A, 01-26/27 CHIJMES, 30 Victoria St ☎63373379; see map on pp.88–89. The main dining room is dominated by a vast painting of Vietnamese ladies borne on a sea of flowers, and there's a similar textured lushness to the food. Start with a zingy pomelo salad, and then move on to the grilled pork chop with lemon grass, washed down with a 333 beer. Moderate. Daily 11am–10pm.

Nightlife

Singapore's nightlife has gone from strength to strength over the past decade. The island's well-developed bar and pub scene means there is now a vast range of drinking holes to choose from, with the Colonial District, riverside and Orchard Road areas offering particularly good pub-crawl potential. With competition so hot, more and more bars are turning to live music to woo patrons.

Clubs also do increasingly brisk business. Glitzy and vibrant, they feature the latest imported pop, rock and **dance music**, and are also more and more frequently booking the trendiest DJs from London, New York and Sydney.

Bars and pubs

With the **bars** and **pubs** of Singapore ranging from slick cocktail joints, through elegant colonial chambers to boozy dives, you're bound to find a place that suits you. Establishments open either in the late morning (to catch the lunchtime dining trade) or in the early evening, closing anywhere between midnight and 3am. On Friday and Saturday, opening hours almost invariably extend by an hour or two. Most serve snacks throughout the day, and many offer more substantial dishes. It's possible to buy a small glass of beer in most places for around $10, but **prices** can be double that amount in swankier joints. A glass of wine usually costs much the same as a beer, and spirits a dollar or two more. One way of cutting costs is to arrive in time for **happy hour** in the early evening, when bars offer local beers and house wine either at half price, or "one for one" – you get two of whatever you order, but one is held back for later. The happy hours mentioned in the listings are daily unless otherwise stated.

Singaporeans adore **rock music**, and a plethora of bars pander to this, presenting nightly performances by local or Filipino cover bands. These are listed below, but for more details, see p.171. Also hugely popular is **karaoke**, which almost reaches an art form in some Singapore bars.

The Colonial District

Balaclava 01-01b Suntec City Convention Ctr, 1 Raffles Blvd ☎63391600. A homage to G-Plan or a nod to 1960s James Bond movies? Both could be said of this retro jazz bar, whose leather chairs, sassy red lamps and dark-wood veneers may make the ambience too oppressive for some tastes.

There's live jazz from 8.30pm, and happy hour is 3–9pm. Mon–Thurs 3pm–1am, Fri & Sat 3pm–2am.

Bar and Billiards Room Raffles Hotel, 1 Beach Rd ☎63371886. A Singapore Sling in the colonial elegance of the hotel where the drink was invented by Ngiam Tong Boon in 1915, is a must on a visit to Singapore. Snacks are available through the afternoon, and playing billiards costs by the hour. Daily 11.30am–midnight.

Bar Opiume Asian Civilizations Museum, 1 Empress Place ☎63392876. Cool-as-ice cocktail bar, ideal for a pre-dinner sharpener at adjacent *Indochine Waterfront*, where the barmen mix a mean Singapore Sling. Outside, are drop-dead gorgeous views of the waterfront; inside is a bar of mature sophistication, graced by huge crystal chandeliers, modish, square-cut leather furniture and a lordly standing Buddha statue. Mon–Thurs 5pm–2am, Fri & Sat 5pm–3am.

City Space 70th floor, Swissôtel The Stamford, 2 Stamford Rd ☎68373875. Exquisitely appointed lounge bar – but decor be hanged: you come to *City Space* to drink in the peerless, seventy-storey views across Singapore to southern Malaysia. The cocktails aren't cheap, but the warmed chilli cashews that come with your drink are to die for. Sun–Thurs 5pm–1am, Fri & Sat 5pm–2am.

Divine Society Parkview Sq, 600 North Bridge Rd ☎63964466. All the decadence and excess of 1920s café society comes outrageously to life at *Divine*, a big, bonkers bar whose adoption of a wine angel (a waitress, kitted out in wings and harness, who is winched up and down the 40ft wine rack) might just be the most politically incorrect thing you'll ever see. Elsewhere, Art Deco murals of prancing deer line the walls, vast brass lamps hang from the lofty ceiling, and there are life-sized mannequins of Duke Ellington, Billie Holliday and Louis Armstrong. This is supposed to be a member's only establishment, but dress sharp and you'll have no trouble getting in. Mon–Sat noon–midnight.

Fat Frog Café The Substation, 45 Armenian St ☎63386201. Relaxed courtyard café, sited within the Substation arts centre, where Singapore's culture vultures come to sip coffees and cold drinks and deconstruct the latest arts sensation under the shade of the whispering trees. Sun–Thurs 11.20am–11.30pm, Fri & Sat 11.30am–2am.

Liberte 01-19/20 CHIJMES, 30 Victoria St ☎63388481. *Liberte* holds centre stage on CHIJMES' main square – and rightly so. Its artsy wall hangings, flickering tea lights, mellow, Middle Eastern influenced sounds and excellent cocktails make it one of the few CHIJMES addresses where you actually want to stay inside, rather than head out onto the terrace. Better still, there are free drinks for ladies from 9pm to midnight on Thurs. Mon–Wed 5pm–2am, Thurs–Sat 5pm–3am, Sun 4pm–1am.

Lot, Stock and Barrel Pub 29 Seah St. Frequented by an early office crowd and a late backpacker crowd (the guesthouses of Beach and North Bridge roads are just around the corner), who come for the rock classics on the jukebox; happy hour 4–8pm. Daily 4pm–midnight.

Paulaner Bräuhaus 01-01 Millennia Walk, 9 Raffles Blvd. Wurst and sauerkraut might be a priority upstairs, but down amidst the copper brewing vats in the bar of this themed microbrewery, lager is very much in the forefront of the punters' minds; predictably busy around Oktoberfest-time. Sun–Thurs 11.30am–1am, Fri & Sat 11.30am–2am.

The Quays

DQ Bar 39 Boat Quay ☎66360722. Arguably Boat Quay's coolest venue, thanks to its chilled dance music, comfy sofas and friendly staff. The second level affords memorable views of the river. Tues–Sat 11am–1am, Sun & Mon 11am–midnight.

Crazy Elephant 01-07 Trader's Market, Clarke Quay ☎63371990. The only bar with any real clout along Clarke Quay, playing decent rock music on the turntable between live sessions by the house blues band; decor comprises wood panelling and graffiti, but regulars prefer the tables out by the water's edge. Happy hour is daily 5–9pm. Mon–Thurs & Sun 5pm–1am, Fri & Sat 5pm–2am.

Harry's Quayside 28 Boat Quay ☎65383029. There's live jazz and R&B Tues to Sat in this upmarket place, and a blues jam every Sun evening. Light lunches are served and prices are lower in the early evening. Daily 11am–1am.

Home Beach Bar 15 Merbau Rd ☎68352413. Deckchairs, lanterns, reggae sounds – close your eyes and you'll swear there's sand, and not concrete, underfoot at this mellow riverfront venue, where happy hour lasts from 5pm to 8pm. Daily 3pm–1am.

Jazz @ Southbridge 82b Boat Quay ☎63274671. The crowd here can be rather self-consciously jazzy, but there's no faulting the quality of the nightly live music sessions. Sun–Thurs 11am–1am, Fri & Sat 11am–2am.

Milk Bar 01-09 The Gallery Hotel, Robertson Quay ☎668364431. Singapore's hippest hotel is also home to one of its coolest bars. *Milk*'s split-levels allow punters to chill out downstairs and get down, upstairs.

Molly Malone's 42 Circular Rd ☎65362029. With Kilkenny and Guinness ($12 a pint) on tap, sounds courtesy of Van Morrison and the Pogues, and a menu offering Connemara oysters and Irish stew, hardly your quintessential Singaporean boozer, but a good crack nonetheless, when full. Happy hour (11am–8pm) knocks a couple of bucks off a pint. Sun–Thurs 11am–1am, Fri & Sat 11am–2am.

Little India and around

Leisure Pub B1-01 Selegie Ctr, 189 Selegie Rd. Tame but endearing darts-oriented establishment that's ideal for a quiet chat and handy for Bencoolen Street; happy hour 4–9pm. Daily 5pm–midnight.

Roshni 02-01 Little India Shopping Arcade, 48 Serangoon Rd. Once the plates and cutlery have been cleared away, there's swinging Hindi and Tamil dance music into the night. Daily 11.30am–midnight.

Orchard Road

Alley Bar 2 Emerald Hill Rd ☎67388818. Stand up at the bar counter and you'll swear you are imbibing under the stars, such is the ingenuity of the decor in this slightly pricey joint, off Orchard Road. The candlelit, seated area behind the bar is cosier. Sun–Thurs 5pm–2am, Fri & Sat 5pm–3am.

Anywhere 04-08/09 Tanglin Shopping Ctr, 19 Tanglin Rd ☎67348233. Tania, Singapore's most famous covers band, plays nightly to a boozy roomful of expats that's at its rowdiest on Fri nights; happy hour Mon–Fri 6–8pm. Mon–Sat 6pm–2am.

Dubliner Windsland House, 165 Penang Rd ☎67352220. Set up in a colonial-era mansion, this is not your typical pre-fab Irish pub. The grub is a notch above as well, and there are sometimes live bands on offer. However enjoying a beer while parked out on the veranda may be the best seat in the house. Sun–Thurs 11.30am–1am, Fri & Sat 11.30am–2am.

Excalibur Pub B1-06 Tanglin Shopping Ctr, 19 Tanglin Rd ☎67388682. Cluttered and

cramped British-style pub, full of weather-beaten expats; the Whitesnake, Def Leppard and Scorpions posters on the walls give a true indication of the music that hogs the turntable. Sun–Thurs 4pm–midnight, Sat & Sun 4pm–1am.

Ice Cold Beer 9 Emerald Hill Rd ☎67359929. Noisy, hectic and happening place where the beers are kept on ice under the glass-topped bar; there are regular promotions, and there's a pool table upstairs. Happy hour is 5–9pm and 1–3am.

No. 5 Emerald Hill 5 Emerald Hill Rd ☎67320818. Quite a pleasant Peranakan-style bar-restaurant, if you can stomach the constant crunch of peanut shells under foot. There's nightly live jazz in the upstairs bar. Happy hours noon–9pm & 1–2am. Daily noon–2am.

Observation Lounge 38th floor, Mandarin Hotel, 333 Orchard Rd. Swanky cocktail bar offering awesome views over downtown Singapore. Mon–Thurs & Sun 11am–1am, Fri & Sat 11am–2am.

Snackworld Cuppage Terr, Cuppage Rd. Buy a bottle of Tiger from *Snackworld* and watch the world drifting by – a great place to hang out. Daily 11am–midnight.

The Sportsman 02-01 Far East Shopping Ctr. One for homesick British footie fans, this: the walls are plastered with pictures of the likes of Gazza and Beckham, big matches are screened live, and Tiger beer is $5 a mug. Daily 11am–midnight.

Swing 43a/45a Cuppage Terr, Cuppage Rd ☎67347669. Late-night drinking is the main draw of this otherwise unremarkable bar, just off Orchard Road. Daily 5pm–4am.

Vintage Rock Café 5 Koek Rd, Cuppage Plaza ☎62355736. Friendly staff and locals, great rock and R&B music on the speakers and cheapish beer make this joint. Posters of 1960s psychedelic gigs at the Fillmore and Winterland plaster the joint. Happy hour is 4–8pm. Daily 4–11pm.

Why? Pub 04-06 Far East Plaza, 14 Scotts Rd ☎67344914. The budget prices in this tiny, lively pub – in a corner of Far East Plaza dominated by tattoo parlours – attract big drinkers. Daily 2pm–midnight.

River Valley Road and around

Next Page Pub 17–18 Mohamed Sultan Rd. Cool, popular pub that's the elder states-man of Mohamed Sultan Road. Decor is a mixture of Chinese wooden screens, lanterns and rough brick wall, and there's a pool table out back. The adjacent *Front Page* annexe, with its comfy leather armchairs, is quieter and more chilled out. Daily 3pm–1am.

Siam Supper Club 01-53/55 UE Square, River Valley Rd ☎67350938. Semicircular red leather booths, a circular bar and lustrous red oval lamps lend the *Supper Club* a soothing fluidity; Buddha effigies in wall niches add an Asian twist. Cocktails are $12; bar snacks range from chicken wings to sashimi. Happy hour is 5–9pm. Mon–Sat 3pm–3am.

The Yard 294 River Valley Rd. This busy English pub was attracting a loyal crowd way back when Mohamed Sultan Road was nothing more than a row of dilapidated shophouses, and is still a great place for a beer. Bar snacks are available, and happy hour is 3–8pm. Mon–Thurs 3pm–1am, Fri & Sat 3pm–2am, Sun 5pm–1am.

Chinatown and around

Bar Savanh 49 Club St ☎63230145. You know a bar means business when it counts a six-metre waterfall and a Koi carp pond among its fixtures and fittings. Candle-lit, and crammed with Buddha effigies, scatter cushions and plants, the *Savanh* (the name means "Heaven" in Lao) is a chilled-out bar if ever there was one. The cool acid-jazz sounds round things off nicely. Happy hour 5–8pm. Upstairs is sister establishment, the *Indochine* restaurant (p.165). Mon–Thurs 5pm–2am, Fri & Sat 5pm–3am, Sun 5pm–1am.

Embargo 01-06 One Fullerton, 1 Fullerton Rd ☎62206556. Pre-clubbing cocktails with views over the bay are the order of the day at *Embargo*, so don't come along in jeans and pumps and expect to blend in with the

beautiful people that frequent the place. Daily 5pm–2am.

Jing 50 Eu Tong Sen St ☎65326006. Sumptuous Chinoiserie defines this extraordinary drinking and dining (see p.156) experience, sculpted from the shell of a traditional Chinese building.

Post Bar The Fullerton Singapore, 1 Fullerton Sq ☎68778135. The "refrigeration shelf" running around the island bar in this slick hotel boozer ensures icy booze from first swig to last. The Merlion cocktail, with passion fruit liquor and vodka, hits the spot. Mon–Fri noon–2am, Sat & Sun 5pm–2am.

Around Singapore

Diana Bar Civil Service Club, Blk 25 Dempsey Rd ☎64722080. There's something of the Officers' Mess about this quaint bar, located in an ex-army barracks on the road to Holland Village. High ceilings, clapboard walls and bamboo chairs make it a welcome change from the Buddhas, neon and black leather that define most Singaporean bars. Should the hunger pangs strike, there's a Chinese menu on hand – and *Samy's Indian Restaurant* (see p.159) is just next door. Daily 10.30am–10.30pm.

Full Moon Beach Bar & Grill 01-01 Costa Sands Resort, 1110 East Coast Parkway ☎64444644. The South China Sea is just a stone's skim away from this breezy, open-fronted beach front bar. Sun–Thurs noon–2am, Fri & Sat noon–3am.

Wala Wala Café & Bar 31 Lorong Mambong, Holland Village ☎64624288. Rocking Holland Village joint, now into its second decade, serving Boddington's, Stella and Hoegaarden and featuring a generous happy hour (4–9pm). A live band plays upstairs in the *Bar Above*. Sun–Thurs 4pm–1am, Fri & Sat 4pm–2am.

Discos and nightclubs

Singapore's **nightclub** scene has transformed itself over the last few years. Clubs are far more self-aware, and the dance music they feature is far more cutting-edge than previously, and the cult of the celebrity DJ has taken a firm hold. Happily, Singaporean clubbers themselves remain, on the whole, more intent on having fun than on posing. European and American dance music dominates (though some play Cantonese pop songs, too), and many feature live bands playing cover versions of current hits and pop classics.

Clubs tend to open around 9pm, though some start earlier in the evening with a happy hour. Indeed, the difference between bars and discos has recently begun to blur, and some now include bars or restaurants that kick off at lunchtime. Most have a **cover charge**, at least on busy Friday and Saturday nights, which fluctuates between $15 and $30, depending on what day it is and what sex you are (women are generally allowed in for less – especially on "ladies' nights") it almost invariably entitles you to a drink or two. It's worth checking the local press to see which venues are currently in favour; a scan through *8 Days*, *I-S* or *Juice* magazines will bring you up to date. Singapore also has a plethora of extremely seedy **hostess clubs**, in which Chinese hostesses working on commission try to hassle you into buying them an extortionately expensive drink. Fortunately, they are easy to spot: even if you get beyond the heavy wooden front door flanked by brandy adverts, the pitch darkness inside gives the game away.

Bar None Marriott Hotel 320 Orchard Rd ☎**68314656.** Popular *Bar None*'s house band Energy are a Singapore institution; when they aren't playing their polished rock covers sets, the DJs veer from Latino to alternative, and from R&B to top 40 hits; happy hour 7–9pm. Daily 6pm–3am.

Brix 10–12 Scotts Rd ☎**67307107.** Located in the *Grand Hyatt Singapore*, this large basement bar has shed its pick-up joint reputation, roughed up its decor a bit, and moved up into the premier league of Singapore clubs. On Mon, the usual R&B and jazz-funk sounds give way to salsa lessons. A cover charge of $20 applies Thurs–Sat. Sun–Tues 7pm–2am, Wed–Sat 7pm–3am.

China Black 12th floor Pacific Plaza, 9 Scotts Rd ☎**67347677.** *China Black*'s emphasis upon chart hits and R&B makes it a safe haven for occasional clubbers who don't know their trance from their handbag house. Fri 5pm–3am, Sat 7pm–3am, Sun 9pm–3am.

DBL-O 01-24 Robertson Walk, 11 Unity St ☎**67352008.** With its massive dance floor and three separate bar areas, roomy *DBL-O* really can pack in the punters. House, garage and R&B are the favoured musical styles. Wed night is free for ladies; on other nights, cover charges range from $15 to $25. Wed–Sat 8pm–3am.

Liquid Room 01/05 The Gallery Hotel, 76 Robertson Quay ☎**63338117.** Bring your dancing shoes – *Liquid Room* is a dark, cramped, pumping place majoring on trance and

techno, and the dance floor is a sea of bodies. Daily 7pm–3am.

Madam Wong's 28/29 Jalan Mohamed Sultan ☎**68340107.** Vast warren of a pub-cum-disco in a former rice warehouse, where scruffy red walls, weathered Chinese signage, opium beds and scatter cushions evoke an enticing retro-Asian chic. Early-evening acid jazz gives way to higher-octane dance music later on. Daily 5pm–3am.

Phuture 17 Jiak Kim St ☎**67382988.** Dark, smoky joint, with harder hip-hop, break beat and drum and bass sounds than the other *Zouk* venues and therefore a more youthful crowd. Cover charge is $18 for women, but men have to fork out $25. Tues–Sat 9pm–3am.

Velvet Underground 17 Jiak Kim St ☎**67382988.** Less thumping than *Phuture* and *Zouk*, and therefore favoured by a slightly older, more chilled-out crowd. Lava lamps create a suitably dreamy and chilled ambience. The cover charge ($25 for ladies, $35 for men) affords access to *Zouk* and *Phuture*. Tues–Sat 9pm–3am.

Zouk 17 Jiak Kim St ☎**67382988.** Singapore's trendiest club, fitted out with palm trees and Moorish tiles to create a Mediterranean feel. As well as *Zouk* itself, the warehouse it occupies also hosts *Phuture* and *Velvet Underground* (above). Famous DJs like Paul Oakenfold guest regularly. Cover charge is $15 before 9pm, then $25. Wed–Sat 7pm–3am.

Gay and lesbian nightlife

Singapore's **gay and lesbian scene**, recently underwent an unprecedented positive reversal in official attitudes towards the local gay nightlife scene. Sadly, the tolerance did not last and while Singapore has not completely reverted to its prudish past, recent developments, such as an official denial for permission to organize a local gay pride festival that had been annually held since 2001, make the future seem far from certain. Discretion is still advisable in Singapore, as practising homosexuality is officially illegal here. Enforcement of such laws seems lax however, perhaps even cyclical.

At night, the Singapore scene centres on Chinatown and Tanjong Pagar, where there are a fair number of **bars**.

The best way to keep abreast of the current hotspots is to go **online**. A portal for gay men in Singapore, Ⓦ www.sgboy.com, details all the best bars and clubs of the moment, as well as cruising hotspots, including MRT stations, shopping centres and swimming pools. The website Ⓦ www.fridae.com is a pan-Asian portal targeting lesbians as well as gays.

Actor's Bar 13–15 South Bridge Rd
☏65332436. Lesbian-friendly bar, just around the corner from Boat Quay, where the emphasis is on chilling out on big sofas. Daily 5pm–2am.

Backstage Bar 13a Trengganu St ☏62271712. Gay-friendly bar plastered with posters of *The Sound of Music* and other musicals, and with a small balcony over the hustle and bustle of Chinatown. Daily 7pm–2am.

Gold Dust 400 Orchard Rd ☏62357170. Drag queen Kumar, formerly of the infamous Bugis Street *Boom Boom Room*, hosts a nightly show of cabaret and gay-oriented stand up comedy.

Sugar 13 Jalan Mohamed Sultan ☏68351693. The darling of the art house crowd, *Sugar* seems to undergo a total makeover every few months. The decor never gets stale and the patrons are just as fresh. Daily 8pm–2am.

Taboo 21 Tanjong Pagar Rd ☏62256256. Currently Singapore's steamiest, most flirtatious gay bar – so much so that it received a warning about its crowd control policy a while back. Expect a full-on dance attack. Daily 5pm–2am.

Why Not? 56 Tras St ☏63233010. Pumping gay club, especially on Fri and Sat, when the dance floor and podiums are awash with young revellers. Daily 9pm–2am.

Xpose Café 49 Cuppage Terrace. Gay bar just off Orchard Road, serving decent Thai food, but best avoided on Wed, Fri and Sat unless you are prepared to take the karaoke mike. Daily 4pm–midnight.

Zouk/Velvet Undergound (see opposite). A mixed-crowd scene that is still popular with both the gay and lesbian communities of Singapore.

Live music

Singapore was once too far off the European and North American tour trail to attract many big-name **Western performers**, but that has changed, and thank God! How many more Michael Learns to Rock concerts and the like could Southeast Asia endure?

Nowadays, more and more big-name acts are performing in Singapore before heading on to Kuala Lumpur and Bangkok. Concerts of this calibre are usually staged at the Singapore Indoor Stadium, and exhaustively covered by the local press for weeks beforehand. **Local bands** do exist and some aren't at all bad, but these are more likely to perform in community centres, rather than decent venues. Rivalling Western music in terms of popularity in Singapore is **Canto-pop**, a bland hybrid of Cantonese lyrics and Western disco beats whose origins lie in the soundtracks of 1950s Cantonese movie musicals; Hong Kong Canto-pop superstars visit periodically, and the rapturous welcome they receive make their shows quite an experience, even for the non-connoisseur.

No matter who else is in town, you can always catch a set of cover versions at one of Singapore's bars and clubs; the main venues are picked out below. If you like **cover bands** music, you'll be in your element, as scores of local and Filipino bands nightly belt out Bryan Adams and Eagles hits. **Jazz** and **blues** ensembles are also popular. For more low-key musical accompaniment, go to any of the swankier hotels in town, and you're bound to find a resident pianist crooning Sinatra standards.

The most exhaustive lists of what's on are to be found in the weekly magazine, *8 Days*, the fortnightly *I-S* and monthly *Where Singapore,* though the "Life!" section of the *Straits Times* is also worth a scan.

Anywhere See p.168. Good-time rock music by local favourites Tania.

Balaclava See p.166. Live torch song and jazz sets nightly.

Crazy Elephant See p.167. Live blues and rock throughout the week.

Harry's Quayside See p.167. Live jazz Wed–Sat, and a blues jam Sun eve.

Jazz @ Southbridge See p.167. Mellow jazz played live.

Molly Malone's See p.168. Two guitar'n'fiddle sets nightly.

No. 5 Emerald Hill See p.168. Live jazz upstairs nightly.

Singapore Indoor Stadium Stadium Rd ⊤63442660. The usual venue for big-name bands in town; tickets are available through Sistic or Ticketcharge (see p.174).

Theatres on the Bay 1 Esplanade Drive ⊤68288222. Western and Asian stars take the stage, between musicals.

World Trade Centre 1 Maritime Sq ⊤63212187. Hosts international acts from time to time, as well as presenting free local gigs in its amphitheatre (check press for details).

Entertainment and the arts

The opening of Singapore's iconic integrated national arts centre, the Esplanade – Theatres on the Bay centre, in October 2002, has transformed Singapore's performing arts scene, and given the island a cultural focal point. But there is a plethora of venues away from the Esplanade that also serve up notable performances. Of all the performing arts, drama gets the best showing in Singapore, with the island's theatres staging productions that range from English farces to contemporary productions by local writers. Classical music also gets a good airing, thanks to the busy schedule of the Singapore Symphony Orchestra. Western and Asian dance events crop up periodically; you are sure to see some if you time your trip to coincide with the annual Singapore Festival of the Arts in June. Asian culture is showcased in Singapore's major venues from time to time, but tends to appear more often on the street than in the auditorium, particularly around the time of the bigger festivals. Cinema is big business in Singapore, with up-to-the-minute Asian and Western movies all drawing big crowds, especially at the annual Singapore International Film Festival in April.

Information, listings and tickets

For **information** on cultural events and performances, pick up a copy of either the *Singapore Straits Times* (whose daily "Life!" supplement has a good "what's on" section), *8 Days* magazine, the fortnightly – and free – *I-S* magazine, or *Where Singapore*, which is monthly and also free. Alternatively, phone the venue's box office – all the relevant numbers are given overleaf. **Sistic** and **Calendar-ONE TicketCharge** are Singapore's central ticketing agencies; see box overleaf for details. The cost of a ticket to a cultural performance in Singapore usually starts at around $10, though international acts command substantially higher prices.

Classical music

At the epicentre of the **Western** classical music scene in Singapore is the **Singapore Symphony Orchestra**. Performances by the national orchestra

Singapore has two ticketing agencies, Sistic and CalendarONE TicketCharge. Their booking lines and outlets are open Mon–Sat 10am–8pm, Sun noon–6pm.

Sistic

Booking hotline ☎63485555,
ⓦwww.sistic.com.sg.
Bhaskar's Arts Academy,
 19 Kerbau Rd.
Chinese Opera Teahouse,
 5 Smith St.
Far East Square, 43 Pekin St.
Parco Bugis Junction,
 200 Victoria St.
Raffles City Shopping Centre.
Scotts Shopping Centre,
 6 Scotts Rd.
Specialists' Shopping Centre,
 277 Orchard Rd.

Victoria Concert Hall,
 Parliament Lane.
Wisma Atria, 435 Orchard Rd.

CalendarONE TicketCharge

Booking hotline ☎62962929,
ⓦwww.ticketcharge.com.sg.
Centrepoint, 176 Orchard Rd.
Forum the Shopping Mall,
 583 Orchard Rd.
Funan the IT Mall, 109 North
 Bridge Rd.
Substation, 45 Armenian St.
Tanglin Mall, 163 Tanglin Rd.

take place at Esplanade – Theatres on the Bay and often feature guest soloists, conductors and choirs from around the world; occasional **Chinese** classical music shows are included in the programme. From time to time, ensembles from the orchestra also give **lunchtime concerts**. In addition, the Singapore Symphony Orchestra gives occasional free performances in Singapore's parks, while Sentosa island also hosts regular Sunday concerts – the shows are free, but the usual Sentosa entry fee applies.

Chinese Opera Teahouse 5 Smith St
☎63234862. $35 buys you Chinese dinner and an opera performance. See p.155 for more details.
Nanyang Academy of Fine Arts Chinese Orchestra 111 Middle Rd ☎63376636. Chinese classical and folk music.
Singapore Chinese Orchestra Singapore

Conference Hall, 7 Shenton Way ☎64403839, ⓦwww.sco.com.sg. Performances of traditional Chinese music throughout the year, plus occasional free concerts.
Singapore Symphony Orchestra Esplanade – Theatres on the Bay ☎63381230, ⓦwww.sso.org.sg. Performances throughout the year.

Film

With over fifty **cinemas** on the island, you should have no trouble finding a movie that appeals to you, and at a price ($5–8) that compares favourably with Europe and America. As well as Hollywood's latest blockbusters, a wide range of **Chinese**, **Malay** and **Indian movies**, all with English subtitles, are screened. Chinese productions tend to be a raucous blend of slapstick and martial arts, while Malay and Indian movies are characterized by exuberant song-and-dance routines. Cinema-going is a popular pastime so, if you plan to catch a newly released film, turn up early – and take a jacket along, as air-con units are perpetually on full blast. Be prepared, also, for a lot of noise during shows: Singaporeans tend to talk all the way through subtitled movies, and the rustling of a bag of popcorn pales next to the sound of melon seeds being cracked and crunched. The most central cinemas are listed opposite, but check the local press for a full rundown of any special events or one-offs that might be taking place.

For **Western films** in their original language, the Alliance Française, 1 Sarkies Rd (T 67378422), screens French films every Tuesday at 9pm and holds an annual film festival in November. There are also regular presentations at the British Council (see "Directory" on p.196 for address) and the Goethe Institute, 05-01 Winsland House II, 163 Penang Rd (T 67354555).

The **Singapore International Film Festival** (W www.filmfest.org.sg) takes place in April. Now an annual event, it screens over 150 films and shorts – mostly by Asian directors – over two weeks. Smaller festivals are mounted throughout the year by the Singapore Film Society (W www.sfs.org.sg).

Golden Village GV Grand 03-29 Great World City, 1 Kim Seng Promenade T 67358484. Singapore's poshest cinema, with state-of-the-art digital sound, fully reclinable seats. Pricey at $25 a ticket.

Lido Level 5, Shaw House, 350 Orchard Rd T 67380555. Five screens, including the luxurious Lido Classic.

Omni-Theatre Singapore Science Centre, 15 Science Centre Rd T 64252500. 3D movies; see p.120 for details.

Orchard Cineplex 8 Grange Rd T 62351155. Central and recently renovated cinema, with a swish new shopping centre constructed around it.

Suntec Cineplex 03-51 Suntec City Mall, 3 Temasek Blvd T 68369074. Latest releases and Asian blockbusters.

UA Beach Road 4th floor, Shaw Leisure Gallery, 100 Beach Rd T 63912550. Screens slightly more cerebral movies than most.

UA Bugis Junction Level 4, Parco Bugis Junction, 200 Victoria St T 63912550. Shows Western and Chinese blockbusters.

Yangtse Pearl's Centre, 100 Eu Tong Sen Rd T 62237529. Located in the heart of Chinatown, this place shows Western and Oriental films.

Theatre and the performing arts

Singapore boasts a thriving **drama** and performance scene, encompassing lavish musicals like *Singin' in the Rain* and the tiniest of repertory companies. Prices of tickets range from around $15 upwards. Foreign companies visit regularly, and usually perform at Esplanade – Theatres by the Bay or the Victoria or Kallang theatres. Performances of **dance** are also common – notably by the Singapore Dance Theatre (T 63380611, W www.singaporedancetheatre.com), which performs contemporary and classical works at various venues, and sometimes by moonlight, at Fort Canning Park.

Singapore's annual **Festival of the Arts** attracts class acts from all over the world. A schedule of events is published in May, a month before the festival

If you walk around Singapore's streets for long enough, you're likely to come across some sort of streetside **cultural event**, most commonly a **wayang**, or Chinese opera, played out on tumbledown outdoor stages that spring up overnight next to temples and markets, or just at the side of the road. Wayangs are highly dramatic and stylized affairs, in which garishly made-up and costumed characters enact popular Chinese legends to the accompaniment of the crashes of cymbals and gongs. Wayangs take place throughout the year, but the best time to catch one is during the Festival of the Hungry Ghosts, when they are held to entertain passing spooks, or during the Festival of the Nine Emperor Gods (see p.179). The STB may also be able to help you track down a wayang, and as usual the local press is worth checking.

Another fascinating traditional performance, **lion dancing**, takes to the streets during Chinese New Year, and **puppet theatres** appear around then, too.

begins so, unless you are in Singapore for quite a while, you'll probably have trouble getting tickets for the more popular events. However, an accompanying **fringe festival** takes place concurrently, and its programme always includes free street and park performances. In addition, Singapore hosts a biennial Festival of Asian Performing Arts in odd years, which showcases the cultures of neighbouring nations.

Action Theatre 42 Waterloo St ☏ **68370842.** Performances of contemporary works by Singaporean playwrights.

Drama Centre Canning Rise, Fort Canning Park ☏ **63360005.** Drama by local companies.

Esplanade – Theatres on the Bay 1 Esplanade Drive ☏ **68288222.** Sucks up all the biggest events to hit Singapore's shores.

Jubilee Hall Raffles Hotel, 1 Beach Rd ☏ **63371886.** Occasionally stages old-fashioned plays.

Kala Mandhir Cultural Association Peninsula, Excelsior Hotel, 5 Coleman St ☏ **63390492.** Dedicated to perpetuating traditional Indian art, music and dance.

Kallang Theatre 1 Stadium Walk ☏ **63458488.** Has played host to visiting companies such as the Bolshoi Ballet, and touring musicals like *Chicago*.

Singapore Repertory Theatre DBS Drama centre, 20 Merbau Rd, Robertson Quay ☏ **67338166.** Engligh-language theatre, showcasing Western plays with Asian actors.

Substation 45 Armenian St ☏ **63377800.** Self-styled "home for the arts" with a multipurpose hall that presents drama and dance, as well as art, sculpture and photography exhibitions.

Victoria Concert Hall and Theatre 11 Empress Place ☏ **63396120.** Visiting performers and successful local performances that graduate here from lesser venues.

Festive Singapore

There's something reassuring in the fact that ancient celebrations and traditions still survive on an island that has embraced all the trappings of the modern world, and, with so many ethnic groups and religions present in Singapore, you'll be unlucky if your trip doesn't coincide with at least one of its many religious and secular festivals, whether it's an exuberant, family-oriented pageant or a blood-curdlingly gory display of devotion.

Hindu festivals ▶

Would you walk over a bed of hot coals to prove the strength of your faith? According to Hindu legend, that's exactly what the Goddess Draupadi did to prove her innocence and fidelity to her husband. In Chinatown's Sri Mariamman temple, hundreds of Hindu devotees honour the goddess' efforts each October by fire walking at the festival of **Thimithi**. An even more gruesome display of faith takes place in the spring when the **Thaipusam Festival** sees penitents process from Serangoon Road to Tank Road carrying portable shrines (*kavadis*) that are attached to their bodies by assorted hooks and barbs. Other penitents opt to skewer their tongues and cheeks with metal spikes while along the route, supporters sing and dance in encouragement. The most important date in the Hindu calendar though, is **Deepavali**, the

Hindu festival of lights, when devotees mark the victory of light over darkness by lighting small, earthenware oil lanterns and by offering prayers at temple. There's no better time to experience Little India's colourful Serangoon Road, which is decked with fairy lights during the Deepavali Light-Up, and hosts cultural performances.

Dragon Boat Festival ◀

Singapore's **Dragon Boat Festival** recalls the legend of a Chinese scholar who cast himself into the sea to protest against corrupt politicians. The subsequent flotilla of boats that set out to save him is remembered in June or July each year when scores of long, dragon-headed rowing boats race one another on Bedok Reservoir. The scholar's would-be rescuers threw rice dumplings into the waters to throw great fish off his scent, and to this day, Singaporeans eat rice dumplings wrapped in banana leaves in memory of their vain efforts.

Mooncakes and lanterns ▶

Singaporeans mark the **Mid-Autumn Festival** and the autumn full moon by eating mooncakes – sweet pastries traditionally filled with bean paste though now available in a range of flavours such as mocha and durian – and by parading through the Chinese Gardens at night carrying brightly coloured lanterns.

Festival City

Modern Singapore may have inherited many age-old religious festivals, but it has also created a few secular celebrations of its own. In April, the Singapore International Film Festival thrills cinephiles, while June's annual Arts Festival brings together hundreds of artists from across the world. July sees the nation's mania for eating and shopping celebrated in the Singapore Food Festival and the Great Singapore Sale, respectively. And, on August 9, the entire country comes to a standstill to celebrate National Day, an annual outburst of civic pride that is marked by pyrotechnics and parades.

Breaking fast, Malay-style ▶

The Muslim fasting month of **Ramadan** represents an annual test of faith through abstinence – a sort of detox for the soul – and for the whole of the ninth month of the Islamic calendar, Muslims forgo food, drink, tobacco and sex during the hours of daylight. Every evening, once darkness falls, they come together to break their fast in the food markets that spring up in Geylang and the Arab Quarter, where fried chicken, rich biryanis and delicious Malay cakes feature heavily, while the most lavish feast is saved until the night of **Hari Raya Puasa**, which marks the end of Ramadan.

Christmas ▼

For many Westerners, there's something deliciously incongruous about spending **Christmas** in the Tropics. But although the sun may be shining and the temperature up around 30°C, one element of the festive season will be reassuringly familiar – its commercialism. For shopping-mad Singaporeans, Christmas represents another excuse to hit the stores, and shopping centres spare no expense to court customers with tempting sales and extravagant displays and decorations. If you are determined to mark the occasion with a turkey roast, you'll find menus to accommodate you – but why not go for Christmas dinner Singaporean-style with a fish head curry or chilli crab?

Chinese New Year ▲ ▼

Some eighty percent of Singapore's population are ethnic Chinese, making **Chinese New Year** the biggest and most widely celebrated festival in the calendar. The Chinese celebrate the New Year's actual arrival at home with their families, but they spend the run up in busy and colourful

preparation. It's at this time of the year that **Chinatown** is at its most charismatic. Impromptu dragon- and lion-dances are a regular sight, and the streets are hemmed with stalls selling barbecued pork, pussy willow (signifying future prosperity) and mandarin oranges – considered auspicious gifts as the pronunciation for them is "gam", the same as for gold.

One of the highlights of Chinese New Year is the **Hong Bao Festival**, named after the red envelopes containing gifts of money that are given to children over the festive period. Held in Marina Bay, the festival is a riot of fireworks, amusements and performances, while the **Chingay Parade** sees a carnival wend its way through the downtown district.

13

Festivals

With so many ethnic groups and religions present in Singapore, you'll be unlucky if your trip doesn't coincide with some sort of **festival**, either secular or religious. Religious celebrations range from exuberant, family-oriented pageants to blood-curdlingly gory displays of devotion; secular events tend to comprise a carnival with a cast of thousands. Below is a chronological round-up of Singapore's major festivals, with suggestions of where best to enjoy them. Most have no fixed **dates**, but change annually according to the lunar calendar. We've listed rough timings, but for specific dates each year it's a good idea to check with the STB, which produces a monthly round-up of festivals in Singapore, or check out the calendar of events to be found on many Singapore tourism websites such as ⓦwww .visitsingapore.com.

Some, but by no means all, festivals are also **public holidays**, when many shops and restaurants may close. For a full list of public holidays, see p.43.

January–March

Thaiponggal

Mid-Jan A Tamil thanksgiving festival marking the end of the rainy season and the onset of spring. In Hindu homes, rice is cooked in a new pot and allowed to boil over, to symbolize prosperity. At the Sri Srinivasa Perumal Temple on Serangoon Road, food is prepared against a cacophony of drums, bells, conch shells and chanting, offered up to the gods, and then eaten by devotees as a symbol of cleansing.

Chinese New Year

Jan–Feb Singapore's Chinese community springs spectacularly to life to welcome in the new lunar year. The festival's origins lie in a Chinese legend telling of a horned monster that was awoken by the onset of spring, terrorizing nearby villagers until they discovered it could be held at bay by noise, light and the colour red. Essentially, Chinese

New Year is a family affair – old debts are settled, friends and relatives visited, mandarin oranges exchanged, red envelopes (*hong bao*) containing money given to children, and red scrolls and papers bearing the character *fu* pasted to front doors as a sign of good fortune. Even so, there's still plenty to see in Chinatown, whose streets are ablaze with lanterns and fairy lights. Chinese opera and lion and dragon dance troupes perform in the streets, while ad hoc markets sell sausages and waxed ducks, pussy willow, chrysanthemums, lanterns and mandarin oranges; particularly splendid is the flower market that sets up on open ground at the junction of Neil and Kreta Ayer roads. On and along the Singapore River, the Hong Bao Special takes place, an extravaganza of floats, fireworks, music, dance and stalls that lasts for a couple of weeks. SBC's annual televised Lunar New Year Countdown is broadcast live from an outdoor location in Chinatown, and is well worth looking out for in the press. Colourful parades of stilt-walkers, lion dancers and floats along Orchard Road celebrate the Chinese holiday. Nowadays, however, the parade is a multicultural affair. See p.213 for the Chinese calendar chart.

Thaipusam

Jan/Feb Not for the faint-hearted, this Hindu festival sees entranced penitents walking the three kilometres from Little India's Sri Perumal Srinivasa Temple to the Chettiar Temple on Tank Road, carrying *kavadis* – elaborate steel arches decorated with peacock feathers and attached to their skin by hooks and prongs – and with skewers spiked through their cheeks and tongues, to honour the Lord Murugan. Some join the procession to pray for assistance, others to give thanks for heavenly aid already granted. Coconuts are smashed at the feet of the penitents for good luck as they set off, and friends and relatives jig around them en route, singing and chanting to spur them on.

Hari Raya Haji

Feb/March An auspicious day for Singapore's Muslims, who gather at mosques to honour those who have completed the Haj, or pilgrimage to Mecca (birthplace of Muhammad); goats are sacrificed, and their meat given to the needy.

April–August

Qing Ming

April Ancestral graves are cleaned and restored, and prayers and offerings made of joss sticks, incense papers and food from Chinese families at the beginning of the third lunar month, to signal the onset of spring and a new farming year.

Singapore Film Festival

April Movies, shorts, animations, documentaries are shown with due focus given to local and Southeast Asian moviemakers. Ⓦwww.filmfest.org.sg

Vesak Day

May Saffron-robed monks chant sacred scriptures at packed Buddhist temples, and devotees release caged birds to commemorate the Buddha's birth (May), enlightenment and the attainment of Nirvana; in the evening, candle-lit processions are held at temples. Race Course Road's Temple of a Thousand Lights is a good place to view the proceedings.

Birthday of the Third Prince

May Entranced mediums cut themselves with swords to honour the birthday of the Buddhist child god Ne Zha, who is said to carry a magic bracelet and a spear, and to ride the wind; their blood is wiped on much sought-after paper charms at temples around the state.

Dumpling Festival

May/June Stalls along Albert Mall sell traditional pyramid-shaped Chinese dumplings in the run-up to the Dumpling Festival, celebrated on the fifth day of the fifth lunar month. The festival commemorates Qu Yuan, a Chinese scholar who drowned himself in protest against political corruption. Local people, it is said, tried to save him from sea creatures by beating drums, disturbing the waters with their oars, and throwing in rice dumplings to feed them, but to no avail.

Singapore Arts Festival

June Annual celebration of world dance, music, drama and art, utilizing venues around the state, with events lasting several weeks.

Dragon Boat Festival

June/July Rowing boats, bearing a dragon's head and tail, their crews spurred on by the pounding of a great drum in the prow, race across Marina Bay to commemorate Qu Yuan (see Festive Singapore colour insert).

Singapore National Day

August 9 Singapore's gaining of independence in 1965 is celebrated with a national holiday and a huge show at either the Padang or the National Stadium, featuring military parades and fireworks.

Festival of the Hungry Ghosts

August/September Sometimes called *Yue Lan*, this festival is held to appease the souls of the dead released from Purgatory during the thirty days of the seventh lunar month, and therby forestall unlucky events. Chinese street operas are held, and

joss sticks – som[...] candles and paper [...] Chinese homes. Pape[...] goods such as houses, [...] ants are sometimes burnt, [...] marquees are set up in the s[...] festive banquets, followed by a [...] pieces of charcoal, cake and flo[...] thought to be auspicious.

WOMAD

Aug/Sept Four-day celebration of international music, arts and culture on the lawns of Fort Canning Park. ⓦ www.womad.org

September–December

Birthday of the Monkey God

Sept (also Feb) To celebrate the birthday of one of the most popular deities in the Chinese pantheon, mediums possessed by the Monkey God's spirit pierce themselves with skewers and dispense charms written in their own blood at the Monkey God Temple on Seng Poh Road, while a sedan chair possessed by the god himself is carried by worshippers. Elsewhere, street operas and puppet shows are performed – look out for ad hoc canopies erected near Chinese temples.

Moon Cake Festival

Sept Also known as the Mid-Autumn Festival (held on the fifteenth day of the eighth lunar month), when Chinese people eat and exchange moon cakes (made from sesame and lotus seeds and stuffed with red bean paste or a duck egg) to honour the fall of the Mongol Empire – plotted, so legend has it, by means of messages secreted in cakes. Another, simpler explanation is that the cakes represent the full moon, at its brightest at this time of year. Moon cake stalls spring up across Singapore two weeks before the festival, but particularly in Chinatown.

Lantern Festival

Sept Strictly speaking a subset of the Moon Cake Festival (see Festive Singapore colour insert), the Lantern Festival is celebrated

over two weeks in the Chinese Gardens (see p.121), where children parade with gaily coloured lanterns, and cultural shows – lion and dragon dances in particular – are a common sight.

Navarathiri

Sept–Oct Hindu temples such as the Chettiar Temple on Tank Road, and Chinatown's Sri Mariamman Temple, devote nine nights to classical dance and music in honour of Durga, Lakshmi and Saraswathi, the consorts of the Hindu gods Shiva, Vishnu and Brahma. Visitors are welcome at the nightly performances that take place at temples across the island. On the tenth night, a silver horse is carried at the head of a procession from Tank Road, taking in River Valley, Killiney and Orchard roads and Clemenceau Avenue.

Thimithi

Sept–Nov Another dramatic Hindu ceremony, this one sees devotees proving the strength of their faith by running across a four-metre-long pit of hot coals at the Sri Mariamman Temple in Chinatown. Outside the temple, devotees in their hundreds line up awaiting their turn, and building up their courage by dancing, shouting and singing.

Festival of the Nine Emperor Gods

Oct The nine-day sojourn on earth of the Nine Emperor Gods, thought to cure ailments and bring good health and longevity, is celebrated

...an Temple on Upper Seran-
...u by Chinese opera and mediums
...orting in the streets. Capping the festival
is a procession, during which effigies of the
nine gods are carried in sedan chairs.

Pilgrimage to Kusu Island

Oct Locals visit Kusu Island (see p.128)
in their thousands to pray for good luck
and fertility at the Tua Pekong Temple and
the island's Muslim shrine. The pilgrimage
commemorates the ancient tale of a turtle
that turned itself into an island to save two
shipwrecked sailors.

Deepavali (Diwali)

Oct/Nov Serangoon Road is festooned with
fairy lights during this, the most auspicious
of Hindu festivals, celebrating the victory of
the Lord Krishna over Narakasura, and thus
of light over dark. Oil lamps are lit outside
homes to attract Lakshmi, the goddess of
prosperity, and prayers are offered at all
temples.

Ramadan

Sept–Nov Muslims spend the ninth month of
the Islamic calendar fasting in the daytime
in order to intensify awareness of the plight
of the poor and to identify with the hungry.
Many also abstain from drinking (anything),
smoking and sex. The fast is broken nightly
with delicious Malay sweetmeats served
at stalls outside mosques. The biggest
collection of stalls sets up along Bussorah
and Kandahar streets, outside the Arab
Quarter's Sultan Mosque, though the
lights, bustling bazaar and Malay Village of
Geylang (see p.109) also warrant a visit.
Muslims mark Hari Raya Puasa (Eid) the
end of Ramadan, by feasting, donning their
best traditional clothes and visiting family
and friends.

Christmas

December 25 Singapore's central shopping centres vie annually for the best
decorations in town, making Christmas a
particularly colourful and atmospheric time
for shopping.

Shopping

F or many stopover visitors, Singapore is synonymous with shopping, though – contrary to popular belief – prices are not rock bottom across the board, owing to the consistently strong Singaporean dollar and a rising cost of living. Good deals can be found on watches, cameras, electrical and computer equipment, fabrics and antiques; cut-price imitations (Rolexes, Lacoste polo shirts, and so on) are rife, but many other articles offer no substantial saving. Choice and convenience, though, make the Singapore shopping experience a rewarding one, with scores of shopping centres and department stores meaning that you're rarely more than an air-conditioned escalator ride away from what you want to buy. What's more, come during the annual Great Singapore Sale (from late May to late July; Ⓦwww .greatsingaporesale.com.sg), and you'll find seriously marked-down prices in many outlets across the island.

The art of shopping in Singapore

Unless you're in a department store, prices are negotiable, so be prepared to **haggle**. If you're planning to buy something pricey – a camera, say, or a stereo – it's a good idea to pay a visit to a reputable department store and arm yourself with the correct retail price, so you'll know if you're being ripped off. Asking for the "best price" is always a good start to negotiations; from there, it's a question of technique, but be realistic – shopkeepers will soon lose interest if you offer an unreasonably low price. Moving towards the door of the shop often pays dividends: it's surprising how often you'll be called back. And don't be hurried into a purchase, but shop around until you're content with the deal you've secured.

Usual **shopping hours** are daily 10am–9pm, though some shopping centres, especially along Orchard Road, stay open until 10pm. Mustafa Centre, on the northern edge of Little India, is known all over the island for being open 24/7.

Deposits, guarantees and refunds

Deposits shouldn't be required unless you're having clothes made up by a tailor – don't trust any other shops if they ask you to part with cash before you receive your purchase. If you buy any electrical goods, make sure you get an international, not a national, **guarantee**, and that it's dated and endorsed by the shop. Guarantees should detail the model and serial number of your purchase. It's also important to check that the product's **voltage** and cycle is compatible with that of your home country – especially if you're from

Canada or the USA. Even if you are not buying something that warrants a guarantee, make sure you leave with a **receipt** – larger stores will produce one as a matter of course, though in small outlets you may have to ask for itemized proof of purchase. **Refunds**, while often possible in department stores for faulty goods, are unusual in small shops, but if you wish to make an official complaint, a receipt will be required.

Singapore's goods and services **tax** (GST) adds a five percent sales tax to all goods and services, but tourists can claim a refund on purchases over a certain amount at retailers displaying a **Tax Refund** or **Tax Free Shopping** sticker. It's fairly complicated and only really worth the trouble if you are going to spend a large amount of money on electronics or something similar. For detailed information have a look at ⓦ www.customs.gov .sg/travel2.html.

Should you have a complaint that you can't resolve with a particular store, contact the Retail Promotions Centre at ⓣ 64502114. Or you can go to Singapore's Small Claims Tribunal, Subordinate Courts, 5th floor, Apollo Centre, 2 Havelock Road ⓣ 65356922, ⓦ www.smallclaims.gov .sg, which has a fast-track system for tourists; it costs $10 to have your case heard.

Customs, shipping and insurance

If you are buying in bulk, or purchasing products made of materials such as crocodile skin or ivory, be aware of **customs** regulations back home – your nation's consulate should be able to tell you what you can and can't import. Any weapons (including the *keris*, or Malay ceremonial sword) going through Singapore customs must have an export permit issued by the Arms and Explosives Licensing Division, 02-701 Police Cantonment Complex, 391 New Bridge Road (ⓣ 68350000). Larger stores will usually pack and ship items home for you, or you can go to the General Post Office (see p.44); either way, be sure to arrange **insurance** with your shipping.

Antiques and crafts

Singapore bulges with stores selling Asian antiques and crafts, ranging from Bornean wooden effigies to Korean chests, and from Chinese snuff bottles to Malaysian pewterware. If it's **antiques** you're after, trawling through Tanglin Shopping Centre and Tudor Court at the western end of Orchard Road, or Holland Road Shopping Centre in Holland Village (see p.120), is your best bet.

Crafts can be found everywhere, but again there are specific areas worth heading for. Chinatown boasts a glut of souvenir stores stocking interesting goods beside the usual tack, and is home to the Singapore Handicraft Centre (see p.184). Little India's shops stock all manner of Indian bangles, *bindis*, and music. At Marina Square there are daily demonstrations of traditional crafts, while Arab Street is good for robust basketware and leatherware.

Amida 219 South Bridge Rd. Emphasis on crafts from Nepal and Burma.

Antiques of the Orient 02-40 Tanglin Shopping Ctr, 19 Tanglin Rd. Specialists in antiquarian books, maps and prints.

China Mec 03-31/32 Raffles City Shopping Ctr, 252 North Bridge Rd. Vast selection of Beijing cloisonné goods – patterned bowls, statues and other articles decorated with copper inlays and enamel.

Cho Lon Galerie 43 Jln Merah Saga, Holland Village. Specializes in Chinese and Vietnamese furniture and crafts.

Eng Tiang Huat 284 River Valley Rd. Chinese musical instrument shop; also *wayang* (opera) costumes and props.

△ Leatherware shop, Arab Quarter

Far East Inspirations 33 Pagoda St. The classiest of several antique shops along Pagoda Street, offering Asian furniture, porcelain-based lamps, prints and watercolours.

Funan Stamp and Coin Agency 03-03 Funan the IT Mall, 109 North Bridge Rd. As you'd expect, a wealth of old coins and stamps from all over the world.

House of Zhen 252 South Bridge Rd. This expansive store at South Bridge's junction with Temple Street, matches the famous Katong Antiques House (see below), in its range of antiques, collectables and furniture. Members of staff are friendly and knowledgeable.

Katong Antiques House 208 East Coast Rd. Dark, cluttered Aladdin's cave of Asian collectables; through its swing doors are tiffin carriers, Peranakan slippers and clothes, and Chinese porcelain.

Lajeunesse Asian Art 94 Club St. Stock in this beguiling outlet spans all corners of Southeast Asia and beyond; Buddhist statuary a speciality.

Lim's Arts & Living 02-01 Holland Rd Shopping Ctr, 221 Holland Ave, Holland Village. Furniture and housewares with a Balinese accent.

Lopburi 01-04 Tanglin Place, 91 Tanglin Rd. Seriously fine – and seriously expensive – antique Buddhas and Khmer sculptures, as well as some old silk textiles.

National Museum Shop 53 Armenian St (the Substation); 71 Bras Basah Rd (the Singapore Art Museum). A potpourri of books, prints, souvenirs and artefacts homing in on Singapore's cultural heritage.

Ming Village 32 Pandan Rd. Jurong East MRT, then bus #78; free shuttle from Orchard Hotel daily 9.20am. Ming and Qing dynasty porcelain reproductions made by hand, according to traditional methods – most fascinating is the painstaking work of the painters. This is not a place to come unless you are dead set on buying some porcelain.

One Price Store 3 Emerald Hill Rd. This venerable old shop, fronted by a jungle of potted plants, carries everything from carved camphorwood chests to Chinese snuff bottles. Sadly not everything is one price.

Poh Hwa Stamp Maker 02-50 Hong Lim Complex, Blk 531 Upper Cross St. Handmade yet inexpensive rubber stamps.

Polar Arts of Asia 02-16 Far East Shopping Ctr. Thousands of Buddha statues of all shapes, sizes, poses and nationalities.

Red Peach Gallery 68 Pagoda St. A fragrant shop, thanks to its soaps, candles, aromatherapy oils and incense; there are also contemporary Asian arts, housewares, and reproduction Ming dynasty furniture.

Rishi Handicrafts 58 Arab St. Leather sandals, necklaces, briefcases, belts and knick-knacks.

Selangor Pewter 32 Pandan Rd; outlet at 03-33 Raffles City Shopping Ctr, 252 North Bridge Rd. The Pandan Road HQ (**Jurong East MRT, then bus #78**) is a store masquerading as something more cultural, with its "museum" of pewterware and free demonstrations all increasing the pressure to buy; unless you have an abiding interest in pewter, it's best to stick with the downtown branch.

Sin Chew Chinese Cultural Products Supermarket 01-00 Skyline Bldg, 192 Waterloo St. Sells images of Chinese Taoist and Buddhist deities, trinkets, necklaces, books and other Buddhism-related goods.

Sin Seng Huat Arts & Crafts 6 Ig Mambong, Holland Village. A large selection of reproduction Chinese and Vietnamese ceramics and porcelains.

Singapore Handicraft Centre Chinatown Point, 133 New Bridge Rd. This place gathers around fifty souvenir shops under one roof, making it a handy one-stop shopping point.

The Tatami Shop 02-10 Esplanade Mall, 8 Raffles Ave. Charming shop within the Theatres by the Bay, specializing in Japanese tatami mats, rugs and miscellanea.

TeaJoy 01-05 North Bridge Centre, 420 North Bridge Rd. A dandy collection of Chinese tea sets – with special attention paid to oolong accoutrements – and glazed porcelain ware.

Tong Mern Sern Antiques Blk D Clarke Quay. A potpourri of vintage bits and bobs – postcards, abacuses, lamps – from Singapore's past.

Zhen Lacquer Gallery 1a/b Trengganu St. Boxes, bowls, trays and paintings, whose exquisite polished finish is crafted from the resin of the lacquer tree.

Fine art

Sophisticated Singapore has become something of a sales hub for contemporary **Asian art** works of late, and a thriving number of galleries exist to feed off this fact. As elsewhere in the world, high-quality art doesn't come cheap here – but if your wallet can run to a classy painting or sculpture on a regional theme, you'll have yourself an Asian memento to last you a lifetime.

Artfolio 02-12/25 Raffles Hotel Arcade, 328 North Bridge Rd. The works of contemporary Asian artists are showcased here.

Galerie Dauphin 80 Cairnhill Rd. Located in an immaculately restored conservation building close to Scotts Road, Galerie Dauphin brings together paintings and sculpture by both regional and global artists.

Jasmine Fine Arts 05-25 Paragon, 290 Orchard Rd. Appealing art works by artists from all over the world. You never know who you will find exhibited at Jasmine. A permanent collection features works by Burmese artist Win Pemin.

Kwok Gallery 03-01 Far East Shopping Ctr, 545 Orchard Rd. The Kwoks have been amassing and selling antique Chinese art works for nearing a century; their inventory is accordingly broad and impressive.

MITA Building 140 Hill St. As good a selection of art galleries as you'll find in Singapore. Cape of Good Hope and Gajah galleries both carry a lot of Asian works, while Art-2 specializes in contemporary Burmese artists.

Singapore Tyler Print Institute 41 Robertson Quay. Housed in a nineteenth-century riverside godown, the STPI is a state-of-the-art print- and paper-making workshop-cum-art exhibition space-cum print shop.

Sun Craft 02-08 Tanglin Shopping Ctr, 19 Tanglin Rd. Work by well-known local artists, using a range of different media.

Bookshops

MPH bookshops stock a wide choice of titles, and crop up all over town, with branches at B1-26a Citylink Mall, 1 Raffles Link, and 02-24 Raffles City Shopping Centre, 252 North Bridge Road. **Times** shops are also well stocked; you'll find a central branch at 04-08/15 Centrepoint, 175 Orchard Road.

Most bookshops carry selections of Western magazines and newspapers of varying breadth – as do the newsagents you find in every hotel foyer. Books are good value in Singapore and generally cheaper than in Malaysia and Thailand.

Books Kinokuniya 03-10/15 Ngee Ann City, 391 Orchard Rd. Singapore's largest bookstore by a long way, with an excellent selection of novels and magazines; branch at Sogo Department Store, 3rd floor, Raffles City Shopping Centre, 250 North Bridge Rd.

Borders 01-00 Wheelock Place, 501 Orchard Rd. All-conquering US bookstore chain, with an in-house café.

Popular 04-23 Bras Basah Complex, Blk 231 Bain St; B1-02 Orchard MRT, 437 Orchard Rd. Cannot boast the stock of the bigger names, but this is still a safe bet for current bestsellers and local interest books.

Pro Saint Book Store 02-77 Bras Basah Complex, 231–233 Bain St. Books bought, sold and rented. Large collection of Japanese *manga* comic books.

Select Books 03-15 Tanglin Shopping Ctr, 19 Tanglin Rd. A huge array of specialist books on Southeast Asia.

Sunny Bookshop 03-02 Far East Plaza, 14 Scotts Rd. New and secondhand English- and Chinese-language books.

Electronic equipment

Electronic equipment remains reasonably priced in the duty-free city of Singapore, but don't expect huge bargains. What's more impressive than Singapore's prices is its range of goods – whether you want to buy an MP3 player, a laptop, a camera or even a karaoke machine, some or other store is bound to stock the model you're after. Singaporeans love all things high-tech, and entire shopping centres specialize in electronics, making comparing prices and models a breeze. Orchard Road's Lucky Plaza is the focal point for **cameras**, with nearby Orchard Plaza and Far East Plaza also crammed with stores. You'll find the galleries of Sim Lim Tower and Sim Lim Square, around the intersection of Bencoolen Street and Rochor Road, teeming with stores selling **electronic goods** galore, from transistor radios to state-of-the-art TVs, DVDs and handhelds. For **computers** and **software**, Funan the IT Mall, 109 North Bridge Road, boasts a choice second to none, though nearby Peninsula Plaza specializes in this field too. Haggling is the norm in electrical goods shops, and all the rules laid out on p.181 apply – as do the warnings about checking compatibility and ensuring you get an international guarantee.

Jewellery

Singapore's glut of stores selling precious stones and gold means that **jewellery** prices remain competitive. Goldsmiths, in particular, are abundant, and their **gold** is of a consistently high quality – usually 22 or 24 carat. Prices of gold jewellery are affected, to some extent, by the craftsmanship involved, though primarily it's the weight and current market rate that dictate cost. Goldsmiths aplenty are to be found in Chinatown's People's Park Complex, and at the Pidemco Centre, 95 South Bridge Road, where the entire first floor is a jewellery mart. Little India's Serangoon Road has a wide choice too, while in Orchard Road you'll find gold worked by international designers. Orchard Road is also the place to find high-quality **pearls**, **precious stones** and **jade**, or try Arab Street and Chinatown. As ever, bargaining is essential.

Chu's Jade Centre 01-53/54 Chinatown Point, 133 New Bridge Rd. Semiprecious stones, huge clusters of freshwater pearl necklaces, and exquisite jade sculptures.

CT Hoo 01-22 Tanglin Shopping Centre, 19 Tanglin Rd. Pearl specialists up at the western end of Orchard Road.

Famous Goldsmith & Jewelry 91 Serangoon Rd. Large range of gold chains and jewellery, on Little India's main drag.

Je T'aime 02-12 Ngee Ann City, 391 Orchard Rd. Specialists in gold jewelry for weddings and engagements.

Png Watch dealer 02-206 Golden Mile Food Centre, 505 Beach Rd. Buys and sells antique watches.

Richard Hung Jewellers 01-24 Lucky Plaza, 304 Orchard Rd. Well-regarded jewellers, based in central Orchard Road, where staff are all qualified gemologists.

Risis Botanic Gardens, Cluny Rd. Specializes in jewellery made by silver and gold-plating flora of all sorts – from ferns to orchids.

Music

CDs and tapes of all the latest mainstream and classical Western releases are universally available, as well as a surprising number of independent ones. In addition, most music stores stock a wide library of **Canto-pop** releases, though to check out some **Indian sounds** you'll have to go to Serangoon Road, and for Malay artists you'll want to make for the Joo Chiat Complex. **Thai pop** – often very good – is available at stores in the Golden Mile Complex on Beach Road. CDs cost around $20–25, but one or two smaller stores slash prices considerably.

Disc Planet 03-123 Far East Plaza, 14 Scotts Rd. Electronic music specialists.

Flux Us 04-34 Peninsula Shopping Centre, 3 Coleman St. Shop selling music, books and DVDs of a more indie nature.

HMV Singapore 01-11 The Heeren Shops, 260 Orchard Rd. Global music chain, now in Singapore, and offering good deals on latest releases.

Roxy Records 03-36 Funan the IT Mall, 109 North Bridge Rd. Discerning CD store with a good collection of indie and dance sounds, plus Singaporean artists.

Sembawang 03-04 Raffles City Shopping Ctr, 252 North Bridge Rd. One of nearly two dozen

branches, Sembawang has prices that are consistently a dollar or two below those in the major chains.

Supreme Record Centre 03-28 Centrepoint, 175 Orchard Rd. One of the widest pop music selections in Singapore, plus a selection of imports from England and the USA.

That CD Shop 01-17 Tanglin Mall, 163 Tanglin Rd. Excellent collection of new age, Acid jazz and classical CDs that draws discerning musos in droves.

Tower Records 2nd floor Suntec City Mall, 3 Temasek Blvd. Wide choice of CDs and DVDs.

Fashion and textiles

There is a vibrant **fashion scene** in Singapore, and several of the city's eminent designers have their own boutiques. Inevitably, their works lean heavily upon Asian textiles and motifs. Up-and-coming local designers' collections are best witnessed during Singapore Fashion Week (Ⓦwww.singaporefashionweek.com .sg), when there are daily shows in central shopping malls.

Having a suit made up at one of the scores of **tailors** operating in Singapore, while not as cheap as in Bangkok, is still a money-saving exercise. The trick is to have a very clear idea of the style you want, and several days in hand for having alterations made. At the measuring stage, ensure the tailor knows exactly what design you want – it helps if you have a photo or catalogue clipping of the sort of suit you have in mind. A **deposit** is required at this stage, but don't be persuaded into paying the full cost until you've had as many fitting sessions as are necessary for the suit to be tailored to your satisfaction. Orchard Road's shopping centres boast the greatest number of tailors – try Far East Plaza, Far East Shopping Centre, Lucky Plaza or Orchard Plaza; otherwise, Peninsula Plaza has several options, or check out the pricier hotel-arcade tailors.

For something a little more ethnic, you'll find Singapore is exactly the hotbed of Asian **fabrics** you'd expect it to be. The streets of the Arab Quarter, and the markets of Geylang Serai stock the greatest choice of fabrics, including vast selections of Malaysian and Indonesian **batik**. Batik is produced by applying hot wax to a piece of cloth with either a pen or cotton stamp; when the cloth is dyed, the wax resists the dye and a pattern appears, a process that can be repeated many times to build up colours. The traditional way to wear batik is as a **sarong** – a rectangular length of cloth wrapped around the waist and legs to form a sort of skirt, worn by both males and females. The exquisite style of fabric known as **songket** is a step up in price from batik. Made by handweaving gold and silver thread into plain cloth, songket is used to make sarongs, headscarves and the like. Silk, too, is abundant: Chinese, Japanese and Thai silks are all available, or there are the multi-hued silk **sarees** of Little India's fabric stores.

As well as ethnic fabrics, Singapore is also a great place to stock up on cheap and cheerful **travelling gear** such as T-shirts and shorts. Finally, **carpets** – both new and antique – from all over the world are competitively priced in Singapore.

Aljunied Brothers 91 Arab St; 04-75 Lucky Plaza, 304 Orchard Rd. Batik lengths as well as ready-made clothes.

Amir & Sons 03-01/7 Lucky Plaza, 304 Orchard Rd. Fine carpets from Persia, Pakistan, Turkey and China. Said to be the oldest carpet seller in Singapore – since 1921.

Dakshaini Silks 164 Serangoon Rd. Premier Indian embroidered silks. Some of the best pieces are shot with gold or silver thread and sold by weight.

Far East Plaza 14 Scotts Rd. The basement level yields alley after alley of tiny local boutique outlets, such as Series, Barcode and Red 2, catering for Singapore's young urban fashionistas.

Goodwill Trading Co 56 Arab St. Indonesian batik sarongs heaped on varnished wood shelves.

Heeren: Annex 4th floor, The Heeren, 260 Orchard Rd. A whole floor of street and club wear by local designers such as Solid Fuel, Cloud Nine and Forward Statement.

House of Etiquette 86 Tanjong Pagar Rd. Breathtaking, sumptuous traditional Chinese wedding robes to buy or rent.

Jim Thompson Silk Shop 01-07 Raffles Hotel Arcade, 328 North Bridge Rd. Though businessman Jim Thompson disappeared under mysterious circumstances in Malaysia's Cameron Highlands in 1967, his name is still a byword for quality silk.

Marks and Spencer B1/B2 Wheelock Place, 501 Orchard Rd. Fashions and underwear for men and women, as well as toiletries and food.

M)phosis B1-09 Ngee Ann City, 391 Orchard Rd. Chic, glamorous women's eveningwear and shoes by Singaporean designer, Colin Koh.

The Orientalist 10 Tanglin Rd. Imposing address at western end of Orchard Road, offering absolutely vast range of carpets from Persia, Pakistan, India and Turkey.

Projectshopbloodbros 01-42 Wisma Atria, 435 Orchard Rd. Laid-back, cocktail-bar chic for women.

Shanghai Tang 02-09 Ngee Ann City, 391 Orchard Rd. Exotic silk tunics and other high-fashion Chinoiserie by a Hong Kong designer.

Sithi Vinayagar Co 69 Serangoon Rd. Raw Thai and embroidered silks and sarees.

Song+Kelly21 1st floor, Forum Shopping Mall, 583 Orchard Rd. Understated men's and women's casual wear in muted colours.

S.S. Bobby Traders 57 Arab St. Indian, Chinese and Thai silks, linen and lace.

Sports

Singapore may be the gastronomic capital of Southeast Asia, but its range of affordable **sports facilities** means there is no excuse for running to fat during your stay. Whether your recreational leaning is towards racquet sports, watersports, golf, or less energetic pastimes such as snooker and darts, you'll find ample opportunities. We've listed alphabetically the main possibilities below, along with advice on whom to contact. Armchair sports fans will find some scope too for **spectator sports**, but don't expect your fixture list to be as congested as it is back home. Should sporting activities not be your idea of a holiday, you might consider a day's pampering at one of Singapore's many **spas**.

International events do crop up periodically, some even attracting the odd household name, but on the whole, you'll have a simple choice between horse racing and soccer. The listings magazine, *8 Days*, details all forthcoming events, big and small, while the STB will fill you in on all major events in the Singaporean sporting calendar. Online, the best resources are ⓦwww .singaporesport.com.sg and the Singapore Sports Council's site ⓦwww.ssc.gov .sg. The online version of *8 Days* sometimes carries news of upcoming sporting events ⓦwww.8days.sg/thisweekissue/index.htm.

Bowling

A game of **tenpin bowling** in one of the centres listed below costs around $3.50 before 6pm on a weekday, and around $4 after 6pm and through the weekend.

Cathay Bowl Leisure Court, 1018 East Coast Parkway ☎64440118.
Orchard Bowl Level 9, Cathay Cineleisure Orchard, 8 Grange Rd ☎62382088.

Plaza Bowl 08-11 Textile Centre, 200 Jalan Sultan ☎62924821.
Super Bowl 03-200 Marina Square, 6 Raffles Boulevard ☎63346334.

Cricket

The Singapore Cricket Club hosts **cricket** matches, from March through October, on Saturday afternoons and Sunday mornings; spectators are welcome to watch from the Padang (see p.53), though entry into the club itself is restricted to members only.

Cycling and rollerblading

For cycling opportunities and bike rental in Singapore, see "Getting around", p.42. It's also possible to try rollerblading along the tracks of the East Coast Park. Again, see p.42, for rental outlets.

Golf

Singapore boasts a number of **golf** courses quite disproportionate to its size, and several of them are truly world-class. All the clubs listed below allow non-members to play upon payment of a green fee, though all will be bulging with members at the weekend. Green fees start from around $80 for eighteen holes, but you'll pay far more than this at the island's poshest country clubs; caddies' fees are around the $25 mark. Most clubs have their own driving range, but a cheaper option is the Parkland Golf Driving Range, 920 East Coast Parkway (☎64406726), where a good, long session won't run to more than $10.

If you just want to watch golf, the **Singapore Open Golf Championship** is an annual event that usually attracts some big names. The Johnnie Walker Classic, Southeast Asia's most prestigious golf tournament, was staged here in 1996, and is likely to return in the future.

Changi Golf Club 20 Netheravon Rd ☎65455133.
Jurong Country Club 9 Science Centre Rd ☎65685188.
Keppel Club 10 Bukit Chermin Rd ☎62735522.
Raffles Country Club 450 Jalan Ahmad Ibrahim ☎68617655.

Seletar Country Club 101 Seletar Club Rd ☎64860801.
Sentosa Golf Club 27 Bukit Manis Rd, Sentosa Island ☎62750022.

Horse racing, riding and polo

Besides on-course **horse racing** at the Singapore Turf Club, 1 Turf Club Avenue, there is also live coverage of Malaysian, Hong Kong and Western Australian meetings that are shown here on a giant screen. For more information, see p.107, call ☎68791000 or visit Ⓦwww.turfclub.com.sg. Otherwise, the Singapore Polo Club, 80 Mount Pleasant Road (☎62564530), hosts regular **polo** matches; call ahead for a current fixture list.

When the urge to saddle up becomes too great, there are several organizations offering **horse-riding** sessions. One is the Singapore Polo Club (see above), another, the **Bukit Timah Saddle Club**, 51 Fairway Drive (☎64662782). Riding sessions at these two places will set you back around $150.

Martial arts

Martial arts are not as evident as you would imagine in a country of such predominantly Chinese stock as Singapore. The best chance of catching any sort of performance is to watch locals practising **T'ai chi** – a series of slow, balletic exercises designed to stimulate mind and body – early in the morning at the Singapore Botanic Gardens. You'll find details of Singaporean T'ai chi schools and instructors at Ⓦwww.singapore-taiji.com.

Skiing

Strange though it may sound, **skiing** – along with snowman-building and snowball fighting – is possible at *Snow City*, an indoor snow centre in western Singapore. See p.120 for more details.

Snooker, pool and darts

Snooker and **pool** are hugely popular in Singapore, and there are heaps of clubs from which to choose; all are listed in Singapore's Yellow Pages. **The Billiard Rooms**, 03-01 20 Trengganu Street (☎62242997), is centrally located in the heart of Chinatown. At **Monstercue**, 02-42 Meridien Shopping Centre, 100 Orchard Road (☎62381689), there are twelve pool tables. **Pool Room**, attached to *DBL-O* nightclub at 02-20 Robertson Walk, 11 Unity Street (☎67352008; see p.170), is another central option. Clubs typically open between 10am and 2am, and an hour's play costs around $10, with rates increasing in the evening. While their dress code doesn't run to bow ties and waistcoats, you may find you are stopped at the door unless you are wearing long trousers, a collar and closed footwear.

As is only proper, a game of **darts** entails a trip to a pub – locals at both the *Leisure Pub* (p.168) and the *Yard* (p.169) take the game very seriously.

Soccer

The number of column inches set aside for **soccer**, both local and international, in the *Straits Times* and *New Paper*, testifies to the huge interest taken in the sport over here. English and European league and cup matches are shown weekly on TV, and there are occasional visits from world-famous teams such as Liverpool and Arsenal. Many pubs and bars (see p.166) advertise live sports screenings via satellite – those based on traditional British and Irish pubs are your best bet.

Singapore's national side draws crowds large enough to fill the 55,000-capacity National Stadium in Kallang. Until 1995, the team played in the Malaysia Premier League and the Malaysia Cup, but in 1995, the Football Association of Singapore (FAS) pulled out of both, possibly motivated by a desire to disassociate itself from the bribes scandal that rocked Malaysian soccer in 1994. Since then, the FAS has set up the S.League, Singapore's first ever professional league, which features twelve teams, including Chinese club Sinchi FC, and the Singaporean national under-23 team. The S.League season runs from February to October and a game is shown live on Singaporean TV's Channel i every Saturday night. In addition, the league's twelve teams battle for the Singapore Cup every year. For a current fixture list and ticketing details, check out the local press or go to ⓦwww.sleague.com.

Tickets for **national fixtures** normally go on sale in the week before match days, at the National Stadium's FAS box office (☎63457111). Again, check the local press or ⓦwww.fas.org.sg for details.

Spas

Singaporeans have gone health-treatment-crazy over the last few years, and a raft of luxury **spas** have opened up to cater for them. All offer a combination of whirlpools, pools, aromatherapy and beauty treatments, massages, saunas and body scrubs – but at a price. In Amrita Spa, for instance, treatments range from $155 to $365.

Amrita Spa 06-01 Raffles City Convention
Centre, 2 Stamford Rd ☎63364477.
Essence Vale 02-07 Orchard Emerald, 218
Orchard Rd ☎67358082.

Esthetica 04-17 Takashimaya Shopping Centre,
291a Orchard Rd ☎67337000.

Swimming

All hotels of a certain size in Singapore have **swimming** pools, but if you're in budget accommodation, you will have to opt either for the beach or for a public pool. The island's longest stretch of beach lies along the East Coast Park, but you'll find the waters off Sentosa's sands much cleaner. Singapore's twenty or so **public pools** are listed in the Yellow Pages. The most central of these is the River Valley Swimming Complex across the road from Clarke Quay, on River Valley Road. Out east, there's the Katong Swimming Complex at 111 Wilkinson Road; while in the west of the island in Holland Village, there's the Buona Vista Swimming Complex, at 76 Holland Drive.

Tennis, squash and badminton

Though a number of venues across Singapore offer facilities for racket sports, their popularity means it pays to book well in advance. On average, halls are open daily 7am–10pm, and an hour's **badminton**, **squash** or **tennis** in them costs between $7 and $10. Many will rent out rackets for two or three dollars, but phone ahead to check first.

Kallang Squash & Tennis Centre 52 Stadium Rd
☎64406839.
Singapore Badminton Hall 100 Guillemard Rd
☎63457554 or 63441773.

Singapore Tennis Centre 1020 East Coast Parkway ☎64199034.

Watersports

Sea-locked Singapore Island offers extensive scope for **watersports**. The **Pasta Fresca Sea Sports Centre** offers affordable introductory courses for newcomers to **windsurfing** and **sailing**, while proficient non-members can rent windsurfing boards by the hour or half day.

 Canoeing is possible at Changi Point, East Coast Park and Sentosa Island, and costs around $10 an hour, and a couple of dollars more for a double-seater. For **waterskiing** and wakeboarding, head for the Kallang River, northeast of the downtown area, or for either Sembawang or Ponngol, in the north of the island. You can expect to pay upwards of $100 an hour. Finally, several **scuba** outfits operate out of Singapore; however, for one of their trips into local, Indonesian or Malaysian waters, you'll pay several hundred dollars.

Cowabunga Ski Centre Kallang Stadium Lane
☎63348813. Offers a course of four water-
skiing lessons for beginners.

Living Seas 01-36 The Riverwalk, 20
Upper Circular Rd ☎64350436. Arranges
PADI courses and regional diving

trips, as well as renting and selling equipment.

Pasta Fresca Sea Sports Centre 1210 East Coast Parkway ☏**64495118.** A range of watersports for all levels. Also has a good beachfront Italian restaurant.

Ponggol Sea-Sports Ponngol Marina, 600 Ponngol 17th Ave ☏**63864736.** Wakeboarding and waterskiing in the far north of the island.

ProAir Watersports SAF Yacht Club, 43 Admiralty Rd West, Sembawang Camp ☏**67568012.** Wakeboarding specialists, with a Jacuzzi in which to relax, after a strenuous day's boarding.

William Water Sports Centre 35 Ponngol 24th Ave, Ponngol Point ☏**62575859.** Water-skiing and wakeboarding courses and sessions.

Kids' Singapore

Y ou needn't have any reservations about bringing your children to Singapore. Just walking around the streets unearths enough of interest to keep even the most active imagination on the boil for a while, and when the prospect of traipsing through the umpteenth camera shop induces murmurings of rebellion among your kids, you'll find plenty of activities to amuse them. Singapore's efforts to craft itself into a fully fledged holiday destination have resulted in an array of theme parks and attractions, some geared specifically to children, others with more general family appeal; otherwise, beaches and open spaces abound. You'll find there are significant reductions on admission prices for children to Singapore's various attractions, often more than fifty percent. The suggestions on pp.194–195 should give you some ideas for whiling away time; most places have been covered in the text, so you'll find further information by turning to the relevant page.

Taking in the spectacle of one of Singapore's many local **festivals** (see p.177) is another sure-fire way of keeping kids entertained, but be selective: some are wholesome – Chinese New Year, with its puppet shows, street operas and dragon and lion dances is one – but others, such as Thaipusam (see "Festivals" p.178), could prove disturbing for children. For details of watching and playing **sport**, see Chapter 15.

Eating needn't be a problem with children in tow. The listings in Chapter 10 cover a wide range of cuisines, ranging from the exotic to the familiar, so if your children aren't great culinary adventurers, you can always track down a burger bar or pizza joint nearby. In Southeast Asia, dining out is a family affair and shown little of the reverence it enjoys in the West, so unless you're going really upmarket, don't be shy of taking the kids with you.

Most mid-range and upmarket **hotels** in Singapore make no charge for children under 12 if they are occupying existing spare beds in hotel rooms. However, if you require an extra bed to be put in your room, ten to fifteen percent of the room rate is usually charged. Cots are almost invariably provided free. When you need time to yourself, **babysitting** is easy to arrange, either through a hotel or a private agency (see the *Singapore Buying Guide*, Singapore's telephone directory).

Parks, gardens and outings

The following parks, attractions and activities should all carry particular appeal for kids. Some – but by no means all – require payment of an entry fee.

Bukit Timah Nature Reserve Hiking and biking tracks through primary rainforest, under the watchful eyes of inquisitive macaques. See p.99.

Cable cars These whisk you from the HarbourFront (see p.116) to Mount Faber, which affords tremendous views of Keppel Harbour and the city.

Dizzee World 01-01/2 The Foundry, Clarke Quay. Loud, cavernous arcade, full of video games and other amusements.

East Coast Parkway Kilometres of clean sand, biking and rollerblading tracks and barbecue pits. Camping is also possible See p.109.

Fort Canning Park Pleasant strolls and underground bunkers dating from World War II to explore in the park, plus the River Valley Swimming Complex on the southern slope. See p.191.

Jurong BirdPark Residents, which include penguins, birds of prey and hornbills, are accessed by hopping on a sci-fi panorail. Kids will love the simulated tropical storm, daily at noon. See p.122.

Marina South Spacious park featuring an imaginative playground, kite-flying locals and great views of the city. See p.86.

Pan Pacific Hotel lifts Running up and down the outside of the hotel; the most exhilarating way to take in a bird's-eye view of the city.

Pulau Ubin (see p.113) and **southern isles** (see p.128). Biking, beaches and boats there and back.

Sea and river cruises (see p.43). Cruises around the Singapore River and the southern isles. Best of all for kids is the Wacky Duck tour (see p.43), taken on a Vietnam War-era amphibious craft that drives around the city before launching into Singapore Harbour.

Singapore Botanic Gardens Beautifully peaceful gardens, with oodles of space for kids to explore. See p.67.

Singapore Zoological Gardens (see p.105). Singapore's zoo, acclaimed for its humane conditions, complete with tram, animal shows and interactive children's zone, besides opportunities to breakfast with assorted animals (see p.144). For a late-night treat, the post-dusk Night Safari (see p.106), adjoining the zoo, opens a window on the animals' nocturnal habits.

Sungei Buloh Wetland Reserve A charming reserve, home to kingfishers, mudskippers, herons and eagles. See p.108 .

Museums and theme parks

When your kids tire of rampaging around parks, gardens and islands, you may want to introduce them to some of the rather more cerebral attractions Singapore

Shops

The shops and shopping centres below all cater for children. For nappies and other toiletries, see "Pharmacies" in the Directory (p.197).

Borders 01-00 Wheelock Place, 501 Orchard Rd ☏62357146. A healthy selection of books for the young, and a laissez-faire attitude that allows kids to plonk themselves down on the ground and have a good browse before buying.

Comics World B1-22 Parklane Shopping Mall, 35 Selegie Rd ☏63396413. Stocks current American titles, figurines and collectables, from Batman to the X-Men.

Computer Games are sold in the Funan Centre and Peninsula Plaza, both on North Bridge Road. For **electrical goods**, make for either Sim Lim Tower or nearby Sim Lim Square, at the junction of Bencoolen Street and Jalan Besar.

Mothercare 01-34/39 Centrepoint, 176 Orchard Rd ☏67327566. Worldwide chain stocking everything your child could ever need, from romper suits to buggies.

My Little Wardrobe 01-18/19 Forum the Shopping Mall, 583 Orchard Rd ☏67326167. Boutique carrying colourful and fashionable kiddies' wear from pre-eminent designers, including Oshkosh B'Gosh, Boboli and Mickey for Kids. One of numerous kids' clothes stores in this shopping centre.

Toys "R" Us 03-04 Forum the Shopping Mall, 583 Orchard Rd ☏662354322. Kids will think they have died and gone to heaven in this, Singapore's largest toy shop.

has to offer. All the listings below will provide them with plenty of historical or cultural food for thought.

Chinatown Heritage Centre If any museum is capable of grabbing kids' attention, it is this, with its faithful reconstruction of the appalling conditions endured by early Chinese settlers in Singapore. See p.81.

Escape Theme Park No Disneyland, but still a selection of enjoyable rides. See p.115.

Haw Par Villa Hundreds of lurid statues, murals and dioramas offering imaginative retellings of Chinese myths – some of which are rather gory and risqué. See p.118.

Sentosa Island Extensive pleasure island with enough attractions to fill a whole day, as well as beaches and wildlife. See p.124.

Singapore History Museum Hit-and-miss, though the dioramas telling Singapore's history may well appeal to children, as might the 3D glasses you don before viewing the story of Singapore in the "theatrette". See p.62.

Singapore Discovery Centre Motion simulators and virtual reality rides. See p.122.

Singapore Science Centre Scores of hands-on science exhibits targeted at children, as well as an omni-theatre screening educative films on a wraparound screen. See p.120.

Snow City Skiing, tobogganing and snowman making. Jackets and boots are provided free of charge for everybody. See p.120.

Temples

All of the temples listed below are colourful, arresting and eventful enough to interest an open-minded child. Some feature fortune-tellers, turtle ponds and caged snakes.

Kuan Yim Temple Waterloo St. See p.60.

Phor Kark See Temple Bright Hill Drive. See p.105.

Lian Shan Shuang Lin Temple Jalan Toa Payoh. See p.104.

Sakaya Muni Budha Gaya Temple Race Course Rd. See p.94.

Sasanaramsi Burmese Buddhist Temple Tai Gin Rd. See p.104.

Sri Mariamman Temple South Bridge Rd. See p.77.

Sri Srinivasa Perumal Temple Serangoon Rd. See p.93.

Thian Hock Keng Temple Telok Ayer St. See p.74.

Directory

Airlines The main airlines are listed below. You'll find any others in the phone directory. Aeroflot 01-02/02-00 Tan Chong Tower, 15 Queen St ☎63361757; Air Canada, 02-43/46 Meridien Shopping Centre, 100 Orchard Rd ☎62561198; Air India, 17-01 UIC Building, 5 Shenton Way ☎62259411; Air New Zealand, 24-08 Ocean Building, 10 Collyer Quay ☎65358266; American Airlines, 06-05 Cairnhill Place, 15 Cairnhill Rd ☎67370900; Berjaya Air, 67 Tanjong Pagar Rd ☎62273688; British Airways, 06-05 Cairnhill Place, 15 Cairnhill Rd ☎65897000; Cathay Pacific, 16-01 Ocean Building, 10 Collyer Quay ☎65331333; Garuda, 12-03 United Square, 101 Thomson Rd ☎62505666; KLM, 12-06 Ngee Ann City Tower A, 391a Orchard Rd ☎67377622; Lufthansa, 05-07 Palais Renaissance, 390 Orchard Rd ☎68355912; MAS, 02-09 Singapore Shopping Centre, 190 Clemenceau Ave ☎63366777; Philippine Airlines, 01-10 Parklane Shopping Mall, 35 Selegie Rd ☎63361611; Qantas, 06-05 Cairnhill Place, 15 Cairnhill Rd ☎65897000; Royal Brunei 03-11 UE Shopping Mall, 81 Clemenceau Ave ☎62354672; Royal Nepal Airlines, 03-09 Peninsula Shopping Centre, 3 Coleman St ☎3395535; Silkair, 08-01 Temasek Tower, 8 Shenton Way ☎62238888; Singapore Airlines, 02-26 The Paragon, 290 Orchard Rd ☎62236666; SriLankan Airlines, 13-02 Keck Seng Tower, 133 Cecil St ☎62257233 Thai Airways, 02-00 The Globe, 100 Cecil St ☎62249977; United Airlines, 44-02 Hong Leong Building, 16 Raffles Quay ☎68733533.

Airport enquiries The toll-free Changi airport flight information number is ☎1-800/5424422.

British Council West of Orchard Rd at 30 Napier Rd ☎64731111.

Car rental Avis, 01-0 Waterfront Plaza, 392 Havelock Rd ☎67371668 and Terminal 1 and 2, Changi airport ☎65450800, ☎65428855; Hertz, 01-01 Thong Teck Building, 15 Scotts Rd ☎1800-734 4646 and Terminal 2 Changi airport, ☎65425300; Sintat, 8 Kim Keat Lane ☎62952211 and Terminal 1, Changi airport ☎65427288.

Credit card helplines American Express ☎1800-299 1997; Diners Club ☎62944222; Mastercard ☎65332888; Visa ☎64375800.

Dentists Listed in the *Singapore Buying Guide* (equivalent to the Yellow Pages) under "Dental Surgeons" and "Dentist Emergency Service".

Departure tax A $15 tax is levied on all flights out of Singapore.

Doctors There are clinics in most shopping centres – there are scores in both the Tanglin Shopping Centre and the Specialists Shopping Centre; for A&E listings, see "Hospitals" below.

Electricity Singapore's mains electricity is 220–240 volts, 50 Hertz.

Embassies and consulates Australia ☎68364100; Brunei ☎67339055; Canada ☎63253240; France ☎68807800; Germany ☎67371355; India ☎67376777; Indonesia ☎67377422; Ireland ☎62387616; Malaysia ☎62350111; New Zealand ☎62359966; Philippines ☎67373977; Sri Lanka ☎62544595; Thailand ☎67372644; UK ☎64739333; USA ☎64769100; Vietnam ☎64625938.

Emergencies Police ☎999; Ambulance and Fire Brigade ☎995 (all toll-free); larger hotels have doctors on call at all times.

Hospitals Singapore General, Outram Rd ☎62223322, Alexandra Hospital, Alexandra Rd ☎64722000, and National University Hospital, Kent Ridge ☎67795555 are all state hospitals and all have outpatient/A&E departments. Raffles Hospital ☏63111555 is private, but very central.

Immigration department For visa extension enquiries, contact the Singapore Immigration and Registration Department, 10 Kallang Rd (Mon–Fri 9am–5pm; ☏63916100).

Laundry DryClean Express offers a pick-up and delivery service, ☏68615933/62860811; Washy Washy, 01-18 Cuppage Plaza, 5 Koek Rd (Mon–Sat 10am–7pm).

Left luggage A 24-hr luggage storage service is available in both terminals at Changi airport. Charges range from a dollar upwards, depending on size. Call ☏62140628 or 62141683.

Library The National Library, also known as the Lee Kong Chian Reference Library, is located at 100 Victoria St (daily 10am–9pm).

Pharmacies Guardian pharmacy has over forty outlets, including ones at Centrepoint, 176 Orchard Rd; Raffles City Shopping Contro, 252 North Bridge Rd; and Clifford Centre, 24 Raffles Place. Usual hours are 9am–6pm, but some stay open until 10pm. There are also around fifty outlets of Watson's pharmacy. For out-of-hours medication, you will need to go to one of the hospitals listed above.

Police In an emergency, dial ☏999; otherwise call the freephone police hotline, ☏1800-255 0000.

Taxis CityCab ☏64520220 or 65522222; Comfort ☏65521111; TIBS ☏65558888.

Time Singapore is eight hours ahead of GMT, sixteen hours ahead of US Pacific Standard Time, thirteen hours ahead of Eastern Standard Time, and two hours behind Sydney.

Tipping Tipping is not customary in Singapore. Restaurants, however, automatically add a service charge and government tax (around fifteen percent) to bills.

Travel agents All the following are good for discounted air fares and buying bus tickets to Malaysia and Thailand: Airpower Travel, 131a Bencoolen St ☏63346571; E & O Services (for the Eastern & Oriental Express), 32-01 Shaw Tower, 100 Beach Rd ☏63923500; Harharah Travel, 1st floor, 171a Bencoolen St ☏63372633; STA Travel, 400 Orchard Rd 07-02 Orchard Towers ☏67377188, ⍟www.statravel.com.sg; Sunny Holidays, 01-70 Parco Bugis Junction, 200 Victoria St ☏63345545.

Vaccinations Travellers' Health & Vaccination Clinic, Tan Tock Seng Hospital Medical Centre, 11 Jalan Tan Tock Seng ☏63572222.

Women's helpline Women's helpline AWARE ☏1-800/7745935, ⍟www.aware.org.sg.

⑰

DIRECTORY

Contexts

Contexts

A brief history of Singapore

hat little is known of Singapore's **ancient history** relies heavily upon legend and supposition. Third-century Chinese sailors could have been referring to Singapore in their account of a place called Pu-Luo-Chung, or "island at the end of a peninsula". In the late thirteenth century, **Marco Polo** reported seeing a place called Chiamassie, which could also have been Singapore: by then the island was known locally as Temasek – "sea town" – and was a minor trading outpost of the Sumatran Srivijaya empire. The island's present name comes from the Sanskrit *Singapura*, meaning "Lion City", and was first recorded in the sixteenth century. A legend narrated in the Malay annals (the *Sejarah Melayu*) told how a Sumatran prince saw a lion while sheltering on the island from a storm; the annals reported that the name had been in common use since the end of the fourteenth century.

Throughout the fourteenth century, Singapura felt the squeeze as the Ayuthaya and Majapahit empires of Thailand and Java struggled for control of the Malay peninsula. Around 1390, a Sumatran prince called **Paramesvara** threw off his allegiance to the Javanese Majapahit empire and fled from Palembang to present-day Singapore. There, he murdered his host and ruled the island until a Javanese offensive forced him to flee north, up the peninsula, where he and his son, **Iskandar Shah,** subsequently founded the Melaka sultanate. A grave on Fort Canning Hill (see p.62) is said to be that of Iskandar Shah, though its authenticity is doubtful. With the rise of the Melaka sultanate, Singapore devolved into an inconsequential fishing settlement; a century or so later, the arrival of the Portuguese in Melaka forced Malay leaders to flee southwards to modern-day Johor Bahru for sanctuary, and a Portuguese account, in 1613, of the razing of an unnamed Malay outpost at the mouth of Sungei Johor marked the beginning of two centuries of historical limbo for Singapore.

Sir Stamford Raffles and the founding of Singapore

By the late eighteenth century, with China opening up for trade with the West, the **British East India Company** felt the need to establish outposts along the Straits of Melaka to protect its interests. Penang was secured in 1786, but with the Dutch expanding their rule in the East Indies (Indonesia), a port was needed further south. Enter visionary colonial administrator **Thomas Stamford Raffles** (see p.54 full biography). In 1818, the governor-general of India authorized Raffles, then lieutenant-governor of Bencoolen (in Sumatra), to establish a British colony at the southern tip of the Malay Peninsula; early the next year, he stepped ashore on the northern bank of the Singapore River, accompanied by Colonel William Farquhar, who was a former Resident of Melaka and was fluent in Malay.

At the time, inhospitable swampland and tiger-infested jungle covered Singapore, and its population is generally thought to have numbered around 150, although some historians suggest it could have been as high as a thousand.

Raffles recognized the island's potential as a deep-water harbour, and immediately struck a treaty with **Abdul Rahman**, *temenggong* (chieftain) of Singapore, establishing a British trading station there. The Dutch were furious at this British invasion of what they considered was their territory, but Raffles – who still needed the approval of the sultan of Riau-Johor for his outpost, as Abdul Rahman was only an underling – disregarded Dutch sensibilities. Realizing that the sultan's loyalties to the Dutch would make such approval impossible, Raffles approached the sultan's brother, Hussein, recognizing him as the true sultan, and concluded a second treaty with both the *temenggong* and His Highness the **sultan Hussein Mohammed Shah**. The Union Jack was raised, and Singapore's future as a free trading post was set.

Strategically positioned at the foot of the Straits of Melaka, and with no customs duties levied on imported or exported goods, Singapore's expansion was meteoric. The population had reached ten thousand by the time of the first census in 1824, with Malays, Chinese, Indians and Europeans arriving in search of work as coolies and merchants. In 1822, Raffles set about drawing up the demarcation lines that divide present-day Singapore. The area south of the Singapore River was earmarked for the Chinese; a swamp at the mouth of the river was filled and the commercial district established there, while Muslims were settled around the Sultan's Palace in today's Arab Quarter. The Singapore of those times was a far cry from the pristine city of the early twenty-first century. "There were thousands of rats all over the district," wrote Abdullah bin Kadir, scribe to Stamford Raffles, "some almost as large as cats. They were so big that they used to attack us if we went out walking at night and many people were knocked over."

The early boom years

In 1824, Sultan Hussein and the *temenggong* were bought out, and Singapore ceded outright to the British. Three years later, the fledgling state united with Penang and Melaka (by now under British rule) to form the Straits Settlements, which became a British crown colony in 1867. For forty years the laissez-faire economy boomed, though life was chaotic and disease was rife. More and more immigrants poured onto the island and by 1860 the population had reached eighty thousand, with each arriving ethnic community bringing its attendant cuisines, languages and architecture. **Arabs, Indians, Javanese** and **Bugis** (from Sulawesi) all came, but most populous of all were the **Chinese**, who arrived in numbers from the southern provinces of China and settled quickly, helped by the clan societies (*kongsis*) already establishing footholds on the island. The British, for their part, erected impressive Neoclassical theatres, courts and assembly halls, and in 1887 Singapore's most quintessentially British establishment – the **Raffles Hotel** – opened for business.

By the end of the nineteenth century, the opening of the Suez Canal and the advent of steamships had consolidated Singapore's position at the hub of international trade in the region, with the port becoming a major staging post on the Europe–East Asia route. In 1877, **Henry Ridley** began his one-man crusade to introduce the rubber plant into Southeast Asia, a move which further bolstered Singapore's importance: the island soon became the world centre of rubber exporting. This status was further enhanced by the slow but steady drawing of the Malay Peninsula under British control – a process begun with the Treaty of

Pangkor in 1874 and completed in 1914 – which meant that Singapore gained further still from the mainland's tin- and rubber-based economy. Between 1873 and 1913, trade increased eightfold, a trend which continued well into the twentieth century.

Singapore's Asian communities found their political voice in the 1920s: in 1926, the **Singapore Malay Union** was established, and four years later, the Chinese-supported **Malayan Communist Party (MCP)** appeared. But pro-independence activity had still not achieved its goal when the spectre of war reared its head in 1942.

The Japanese invasion and occupation

In 1942, the bubble burst. In December 1941, the **Japanese** had bombed Pearl Harbor and invaded the Malay Peninsula. Less than two months later they were at the top of the causeway, safe from the guns of "Fortress Singapore", which pointed south from what is now Sentosa island. The inhabitants of Singapore had not been prepared for an attack from this direction and on February 15, 1942, the fall of Singapore (which the Japanese then renamed Syonan, or "Light of the South") was complete.

Three and a half years of brutal Japanese rule ensued, during which thousands of civilians were executed in vicious anti-Chinese purges, and Europeans were either herded into **Changi Prison**, or marched up the peninsula to work on Thailand's infamous "Death Railway". Less well known is the vicious campaign, known as **Operation Sook Ching**, mounted by the military police force, or *Kempeitai*, during which upwards of twenty-five thousand Chinese males between 18 and 50 years of age were shot dead at Punggol and Changi beaches as enemies of the Japanese.

The postwar years

In 1945, Singapore passed back into British hands, but things were never to be the same. Singaporeans now wanted a say in the governing of their island. A year later, the Straits Settlements were dissolved, and Singapore became a crown colony in its own right. Island politics, though, remained closely linked with those of the Peninsula for the next nineteen years.

Across the causeway, Malay nationalists set up the **United Malays National Organization (UNMO)** in 1946, whose main tenet was that Malays should retain special privileges over Chinese and Indians in Malaya. The pressure they brought to bear on the British government resulted, in February 1948, in the establishment of the Federation of Malaya, which brought together all the states of Peninsular Malaya, but not Singapore, whose inclusion would have led to ethnic Malays being in a minority. Protests erupted in Singapore at this exclusion, with the **Malayan Democratic Union (MDU)** calling for integration with Malaya – a position that commanded little support among the Chinese population. Singapore's first ever elections, a month later, were boycotted by the MDU.

> The possibility of Singapore having no landward defences no more entered my mind than that of a battleship being launched without a bottom.
>
> Sir Winston Churchill.

The hills and jungles of northern and western Singapore were the setting of the battle for "the strongest British bastion east of Suez". Popular wisdom had it that a Japanese attack could come only from the sea: the view of one British intelligence officer, that "the Japanese are very small and short-sighted and thus totally unsuited physically to tropical warfare", embodied the complacency and self-delusion of the Allied Command under **Lieutenant-General Arthur Percival**.

Events were to prove the British wrong. On December 8, 1941, Japanese forces led by **General Tomoyuki Yamashita** – the "Tiger of Malaya" – landed on Malaya's northeastern coast at Kota Bahru. By the end of January they had reached Johor Bahru, a kilometre away from Singapore. Judging that the Japanese attack would focus on the northeast coast of Singapore, Percival deployed what few defences were at his disposal there, leaving the scant Australian presence guarding the northwest stretched to breaking point.

From his command room in JB's istana, Yamashita oversaw a week's bombing of Singapore. Then, on February 7, 1942, the **invasion** began, with Japanese Imperial Guards mounting an attack on Pulau Ubin, northeast of Singapore. On the following day, Yamashita ordered intensive bombing of the coastline west of the causeway. Having softened up their point of invasion, the Japanese used collapsible launches and the cover of darkness to attack the area west of what is now Sungei Buloh Reserve. Allied troops quickly withdrew in disarray, and by the following morning the Japanese had probed eight kilometres inland. After another landing a day later, this time at the mouth of the Kranji River, the Imperial Army began its two-pronged offensive.

Tengah Airfield (then 5km north of Jurong Lake) fell on February 9, and the following day saw Yamashita take his first steps on Singaporean soil and **establish command** near the airfield, as his troops pushed towards MacRitchie and Peirce reservoirs, the city's only sources of water.

Between February 11 and 14, **decisive victories** were won by the Japanese at Bukit Timah Hill and a few hundred metres from today's Haw Par Villa at Pasir Panjang Village, where a brigade of Malays made a heroic 48-hour stand before being all but wiped out. By February 14, Singapore was as good as lost – a fact that made the massacre of two hundred patients and staff at the Alexandra Hospital (northwest of Mount Faber) all the more appalling. Faced with further loss of life – and unaware to what extent Japanese supplies were stretched – Percival travelled up Dunearn Road to the Ford Motor Factory at Bukit Timah Village, where Yamashita was now based, and **surrendered** on Sunday, February 15. Winston Churchill called the British surrender "the worst disaster and the largest capitulation in British history"; it later transpired that the Japanese forces had been outnumbered and their supplies hopelessly stretched immediately prior to the surrender.

Chinese opposition to the Federation of Malaya on the mainland ignited the **Communist Emergency**, an MCP-led guerrilla struggle lasting from 1948 until 1960, whose aim was to turn Singapore and Malaysia into a republic; in Singapore, the MCP was outlawed, and a state of emergency declared.

In the 1950s Singapore's progress towards independence slowly gathered momentum. In 1953 the British government appointed a commission to review the island's constitution, and though still flawed (only 25 of a legislative assembly of 32 were voted in), the elections of April 1955 were the most representative seen so far on the island. **David Marshall**, leader of the victorious **Labour Front**, became chief minister.

By 1957, the Federation of Malaya had achieved independence, and that same year, the British government agreed to the establishment of an elected, 51-member legislative assembly in Singapore. Full internal self-government was achieved in May 1959, when the **People's Action Party (PAP)**, led by Cambridge law graduate **Lee Kuan Yew**, won 43 of the 51 seats. Lee became Singapore's first prime minister, and quickly looked for the security of a merger with neighbouring Malaya. For its part – and despite reservations about aligning itself with Singapore's predominantly Chinese population – anti-Communist Malaya feared that extremists within the PAP would turn Singapore into a Communist base, and accordingly preferred to have the state under its wing.

In 1963, Singapore combined with Malaya, Sarawak and British North Borneo (modern-day Sabah), to form the **Federation of Malaysia**. The alliance, though, was an uneasy one. Differences soon developed between Lee Kuan Yew and the mainland's Malay-dominated **Alliance Party** over the lack of egalitarian policies. Although the PAP had dominated recent elections, many Chinese were concerned that Malays exercised too great a control over the federation. Tensions rose on the island and ugly racial incidents developed into full scale riots, in which several people were killed. Within two years Singapore was asked to leave the federation, in the face of outrage in Kuala Lumpur at the PAP's attempts to break into Peninsular politics in 1964.

Hours after announcing Singapore's full independence, on August 9, 1965, a tearful Lee Kuan Yew described the event, on national TV, as "a moment of anguish". One hundred and forty-six years after Sir Stamford Raffles had set Singapore on the world map, the tiny island, with no natural resources of its own, faced the prospect of being consigned to history's bottom drawer of crumbling colonial ports.

Independence

Against all the odds, Lee's personal vision and drive transformed Singapore into an Asian economic heavyweight. Political alignments were made to maximize business opportunities, and the economy grew fast: per capita income increased an astonishing fourfold between 1965 and 1977, with huge profits being made in financial services, high-tech manufacture, information technology and the petroleum industry. The high taxes these boom areas produced were used to bolster the island's infrastructure and housing, and by 1980, the impossible had been achieved: Singapore stood on the verge of becoming a **Newly Industrialized Economy (NIE)**, along with Hong Kong, Taiwan and South Korea.

But these developments were achieved at a price. Heavy-handed **censorship of the media** was introduced, and offences such as dropping litter were punished in a draconian style, with offenders submitted to the public humiliation of forced litter duty. Most disturbing of all was the government's attitude towards political opposition. When the opposition **Worker's Party** won a by-election in 1981, the candidate, J.B. Jeyaretnam, found himself charged with several criminal offences, and chased through the Singaporean law courts for the next decade. The archaic **Internal Security Act** still grants the power to detain without trial anyone the government deems a threat to the nation – a law which kept political prisoner **Chia Thye Poh** under lock and key from 1966 until 1998 for allegedly advocating violence. Population policies, too, have brought criticism from abroad. These began in the early 1970s, with a **birth control campaign** which proved so successful that it had to be reversed: the 1980s saw the introduction of the "Go For Three" project, which offered tax incentives for those having more than two children in an attempt to boost the national – and, some say, more specifically the Chinese Singaporean – birth rate. Lee Kuan Yew also made clear his conviction that Singapore's educated elite should intermarry, thereby breeding the sort of babies that would serve the country well in the future.

At times, Singapore tries so hard to reshape itself that it falls into self-parody. "We have to pursue this subject of fun very seriously if we want to stay competitive in the twenty-first century", was the reaction of government minister, George Yeo, when challenged on the fact that some foreigners found Singapore dull. Whether Singaporeans will continue to suffer their government's foibles remains to be seen. Adults beyond a certain age remember how things were before independence, and, more importantly, before the existence of the MRT system, housing projects and savings schemes. Their children and grandchildren have no such perspective, however, and telltale signs – presently nothing more extreme than feet up on MRT seats, or jaywalking – suggest that the government can expect more dissent in future years. Already a substantial brain drain is afflicting the country, as Singaporeans with skills to offer choose to move abroad in the pursuit of a more liberal environment.

Singapore today

As Singapore entered the new millennium, the man at the helm was **Goh Chok Tong**. Goh became prime minister upon Lee's retirement from that post in 1990. At the start of his tenure, Goh made it clear that he favoured a more open form of government. In April 2001, he even allowed an unprecedented anti-government rally to take place, which raised funds for veteran opposition leader, J.B. Jeyaretnam. Though, in the 1991 elections, Goh had suffered the relative setback of seeing an unprecedented four opposition members voted into parliament, by the time of the elections of January 1997 (which the PAP had won even before the polling stations opened, as opposition candidates contested fewer than half of the seats), he clawed back two of these seats, partly thanks to insinuations that constituencies failing to return their PAP candidate would drop down the waiting list for housing estate renovations. In the **November 2001 elections**, he again won all but two of the 84 seats being contested. Yet throughout Goh's tenure, Lee still loomed over the political scene in his role as senior minister. When Lee's eldest son, **Brigadier-General Lee Hsien Loong**, took over as Prime Minister in a planned handover of power in 2004, the continuation of the Lee dynasty was assured. Brigadier Lee has vowed to continue Goh's policy of opening up Singaporean society, but true democracy and inclusiveness still elude Singapore. When Chee Soon Juan, the leader of the tiny opposition Singapore Democratic Party, was briefly imprisoned for contempt of court in March 2006, after he accused the Singapore judiciary of pro-government, the PAP's continued refusal to brook criticism was plain to see. And the decision, in 2005, to call a halt to Nation (check), the gay festival that had been tolerated for three years, revealed a government unprepared to embrace minority groups. As this guide went to press, Singaporeans were awaiting a confirmed date for the 2006 elections.

Politics apart, Singapore has had a tough time, economically, over the past decade. The state was able to weather the **financial crisis** that struck first Thailand, and then the rest of Southeast Asia in the late 1990s. Though the economy slowed – and unemployment rose – it emerged from the crisis dented but intact. However, the global downturn that followed the events of September 11, 2001 took a further economic toll. After achieving ten percent growth in 2000, the economy had contracted two percent by the end of 2001; and by late 2002, the *Straits Times* was warning of a possible recession if GDP growth continued to contract. Happily this recession never materialized, and by 2006 record tourism revenues, booming pharmaceutical and biotechnology industries and other advantageous economic factors had combined to push Singapore well into growth once again. The impact of 9/11 was not confined to economics. In September 2002, the authorities arrested 21 suspected terrorists. And in early 2003, a report from the Ministry of Home Affairs detailed a series of alleged plots by Jemaah Islamiah, a regional group of radical Muslims, to attack Western interests in Singapore.

In February 2003, Singapore's first cases of Severe Acute Respiratory Syndrome, or **SARS**, came to light, adding another problem to those of the economy and terrorism. Within weeks, the island was one of the global hotspots for SARS, with an official death toll that had risen to 31 by the end of May 2003. The Singaporean government moved decisively to counter the threat posed by SARS to its population and its tourism trade, earning praise from the World Health Organization for surpassing the WHO's recommended measures.

Religion

T otal **freedom of worship** is enjoyed in Singapore, whose multicultural society is reflected in the wide range of creeds that it supports. Over half of the population of 3.87 million follow Chinese religions – mostly Buddhism, but with elements of Taoism and Confucianism. Malays, who make up fourteen percent of the population, are predominantly Muslim, while the nation's Indians are either Hindu, Muslim or Sikh. In addition, one in ten Singaporeans are Christians: most are Protestants, though all denominations are represented, and there's a large enough Jewish community to support two synagogues.

Below are overviews of the three main strands of belief in Singapore today: Chinese religions, Islam and Hinduism.

Chinese religions

Singaporean Chinese are mainly either **Buddhist**, **Taoist** or **Confucianist**, although in practice they are often a mixture of all three. These different strands of Chinese religion ostensibly lean in very different directions, but in practice the combination of the three comprises a system of belief which is first and foremost pragmatic. The Chinese use religion to ease their passage through life, whether in the spheres of work or family, while temples double as social centres, where people meet and exchange views.

Buddhism

Buddhism states that the suffering of the world can only be achieved by attaining a state of personal enlightenment, or nirvana, through meditation. The founder of Buddhism, **Siddhartha Gautama**, was born a prince in Lumbini in present-day Nepal, around 500 BC. Shielded from knowledge of suffering and death for the first decades of his life, he subsequently renounced his pampered life and spent years in meditation, before finding enlightenment under a bodhi tree. At this point he became the Buddha or "Awakened One". (In Singapore and Southeast Asia he is called *Sakyamuni*, or "Holy Man of the Sakya tribe".) In his first sermon, Buddha taught the four noble truths: that suffering exists; that its source should be recognized; that one should strive for a cessation of suffering; and that this can be achieved by following the **Eightfold Path** – practising right views, intentions, speech, action, livelihood, effort, mindfulness and concentration. The Buddhist faith is split into two schisms: **Hinayana** (Lesser Vehicle) Buddhism, which teaches individuals how to attain enlightenment for themselves, and **Mahayana** (Greater Vehicle) Buddhism – favoured in Singapore – which teaches that, having reached enlightenment, followers should help others to do the same.

Taoism

Unity with nature is the chief tenet of Taoism, a philosophical movement dating from the sixth century BC, and propounded by the Chinese scholar **Lao Tze**. Taoism advocates that people follow a central path or truth, known as *Tao* or "The Way", and cultivate an understanding of the nature of things. This search for truth has often expressed itself in Taoism by way of superstition on the part of its devotees, who engage in fortune-telling and the like. The Taoist gods are mainly legendary figures – warriors, statesmen, scholars – with specific powers that can generally be determined by their form; others represent incarnations of the forces of nature.

Confucianism

Confucianism began as a philosophy based on piety, loyalty, humanitarianism and familial devotion. In the 2500 years since **Confucius**, its founder, died, it has transmuted into a set of principles that permeate every aspect of Chinese life. A blueprint for social and moral harmony, the Confucian ideology stresses one's obligation to family, community and the state, hinging on the individual's need to recognize his or her position in the social hierarchy and act accordingly – son must obey father, student must obey teacher, subject must obey ruler. Little wonder that Lee Kuan Yew has long advocated Confucian values in Singapore.

Chinese temples

The rules of **geomancy**, or **feng shui** (wind and water), are rigorously applied to the construction of **Chinese temples**, so that the buildings are placed to render them free from evil influences. Visitors wishing to cross the threshold of a temple have to step over a kerb that's intended to trip up evil spirits, and walk through doors painted with fearsome door gods; fronting the doors are two stone lions, providing yet another defence. Larger temples typically consist of a front entrance hall opening onto a walled-in courtyard, beyond which is the hall of worship, where joss (luck) sticks are burned below images of the deities. The most important and striking element of a Chinese temple is its roof. They are grand, multi-tiered affairs, with low, overhanging eaves, the ridges alive with auspicious creatures such as dragons and phoenixes and, less often, with miniature scenes from traditional Chinese life and legend. Temples are also normally constructed around a framework of huge, lacquered timber beams, adorned with intricately carved warriors, animals and flowers. More figures are moulded onto outer walls, which are dotted with octagonal, hexagonal or round grille-worked windows. Feng shui comes into play again inside the temple, with auspicious room numbers and sizes, colour and sequence of construction. Elsewhere in the temple grounds, you'll see sizeable ovens stuffed constantly with slowly burning fake money, prayer books and other offerings. Pagodas – tall, thin towers thought to keep out evil spirits – are common too.

Chinese temples play an important part in Chinese community life, and some hold occasional musical and theatrical performances, which can be enjoyed by visitors as well as locals. Temples are open from early morning to early evening and devotees go in when they like, to make offerings or to pray; there are no set prayer times. Visitors are welcome and larger temples have janitors who will show you round, though few speak good English.

Islam

Islam ("submission to God") was founded in Mecca in present-day Saudi Arabia by **Muhammad** (570–632 AD), the last in a long line of prophets that included Abraham, Moses and Jesus. Muhammad transmitted Allah's final and perfected revelation to mankind through the writings of the divinely revealed "recitation", the **Koran**. The official beginning of Islam is dated as 622 AD, when Muhammad and his followers, exiled from Mecca, made the **hijra**, or migration, north to Yathrib, later known as Medina, "City of the Prophet". The *hijra* marks the start of the Islamic calendar, 1 AH (Anno Hijra). All the central tenets of Islam are embodied in the Koran, with the most important known as the **Five Pillars of Islam**. The first pillar is *shahada* – the confession of faith, "There is no god but God, and Muhammad is his messenger." The *shahada* is recited at the *salat*, the second pillar, which enjoins the faithful to kneel five times daily and pray in the direction of Mecca. The other three tenets are: alms-giving to the local Muslim community (*zakat*); fasting during the ninth month of the Muslim lunar calendar, **Ramadan** (*saum* – see p.180); and the pilgrim-age (**haj**) to Mecca, money and health allowing.

The first firm foothold made by Islam in Southeast Asia was the conversion of the court of Melaka, in modern-day Malaysia, in the early fifteenth century. One after another, the powerful Malay court rulers took to Islam, adopting the title sultan (ruler); nearby Singapore couldn't help but feel its influence. Today, almost all of Singapore's Malays are Muslims, as well as a proportion of its Indian population. The form of Islam practised is fairly liberal. Some, but not all, women wear long dress and headscarves, and certain taboos – like not drinking alcohol – are ignored by a growing number of Muslims.

Mosques

While only a small proportion attend the mosque every day, all Muslims converge on their nearest **mosque** on Friday – the day of prayer. Once there, the men wash their hands, feet and faces three times in the outer chambers, before entering the prayer hall to recite sections of the Koran. After this initial period, an **Imam** will lead prayers and, on occasions, deliver a sermon, in which the teachings of Muhammad will be applied to a contemporary context. Women cannot enter the main prayer hall during prayers and must congregate in a chamber to the side of the hall.

Visitors are welcome at certain times, provided that their shoulders and legs are covered. No non-Muslim is allowed to enter a mosque during prayer time or go into the prayer hall at any time, although it's possible to stand just outside and look in.

Hinduism

Hinduism reached the Malay Peninsula and Singapore long before Islam, brought by Indian traders more than a thousand years ago. Its base of support grew in the nineteenth century, when large numbers of indentured workers and convicts arrived from the subcontinent to labour on rubber estates and in construction.

Hinduism had no founder, but grew slowly over thousands of years. Its central tenet is the belief that life is a series of rebirths and reincarnations (*samsara*) that eventually leads to spiritual release (*moksha*). An individual's progress is determined by his or her *karma*, very much a law of cause and effect, in which negative decisions and actions slow up the process of upward reincarnation and positive ones accelerate it.

A whole variety of deities are worshipped, which on the surface makes Hinduism appear complex, but with only a loose understanding of the **Vedas** (the religion's holy books) the characters and roles of the main gods quickly become apparent. The deities you'll come across most often are the three manifestations of the faith's Supreme Divine Being: **Brahma the Creator, Vishnu the Preserver** and **Shiva the Destroyer**. Other enduring favourites among Hindus include: elephant-headed Ganesh, the son of Shiva, who is evoked before every undertaking except funerals; Vishnu's consort, the comely Lakshmi, worshipped as goddess of prosperity and wealth; and Saraswati, wife to Brahma, and seen as a goddess of purification, fertility and learning.

Hindu temples

Visitors are welcome to explore **Hindu temples**, but are expected to remove their shoes before entering. Step over the threshold and you enter a veritable Disneyland of colourful gods and fanciful creatures. The style is typically **Dravidian** (South Indian), as befits the largely Tamil population, with a soaring *gopuram*, or entrance tower, teeming with sculptures, and a central courtyard leading to an inner sanctum (off-limits to tourists) dedicated to the presiding deity. In the temple precinct, there are always busy scenes – incense burning, the application of sandalwood paste, and the *puja* (ritual act of worship).

Chinese astrology

Most people are interested to find out what sign they are in the Chinese zodiac system, particularly since – like the Western system – each person is supposed to have characteristics similar to those of the sign that related to their birth date.

There are twelve Chinese zodiac signs, corresponding to twelve types of animals, whose characteristics you'll find listed below. These animal signs have existed in Chinese folk tradition since the sixth century BC, though it wasn't until the third century BC that they were incorporated into a formal study of astrology and astronomy, based around the lunar calendar. Quite why animals emerged as the vehicle for Chinese horoscopy is unclear: one story has it that the animals used are the twelve that appeared before the command of Buddha, who named the years in the order in which the animals arrived.

Each lunar year (which starts in late January/early February) is represented by one of the twelve animal symbols. Your sign depends on the year you were born – check the calendar chart below – rather than the month as in Western systems.

The details below will tell you the basic facts about your character and personality, though it's only a rough guide: to explore your real Chinese astrological self, you need to be equipped with your precise date and time of birth as well as a specialist textbook that can cast light on all your horoscopical idiosyncrasies. The animals always appear in the same order so that if you know the current year you can always work out which one is to influence the coming Chinese New Year.

The Rat

Characteristics: usually generous, intelligent and hard-working, but can be petty and idle; has lots of friends but few close ones; may be successful, like challenges and be good at business, but is insecure; generally diplomatic; tends to get into emotional entanglements.

Partners: best suited to Dragon, Monkey and Ox; doesn't get on with Horse and Goat.

Famous Rats: Wolfgang Amadeus Mozart, William Shakespeare, Marlon Brando, Doris Day, Yves St Laurent, Leo Tolstoy, Jimmy Carter, Prince Charles, Ozzy Osbourne, Gwyneth Paltrow, Ben Affleck, Eminem, Prince Harry, Bono.

The Ox

Characteristics: healthy; obstinate; independent; usually calm and cool, but can get stroppy at times; shy and conservative; likes the outdoors and old-fashioned things; always finishes a task.

Partners: best suited to Snake, Rat or Rooster; doesn't get on with Tiger, Goat or Monkey.

Famous Oxen: Walt Disney, Adolf Hitler, Napoleon Bonaparte, Richard Nixon, Vincent Van Gogh, Peter Sellers, Dustin Hoffman, Robert Redford, Margaret Thatcher, Shirley Bassey, Jane Fonda, Jack Nicholson, George Clooney, Saddam Hussein.

Date of Birth

1/2/1900	–	18/2/1901 Rat
19/2/1901	–	7/2/1902 Ox
8/2/1902	–	28/1/1903 Tiger
29/1/1903	–	15/2/1904 Rabbit
16/2/1904	–	3/2/1905 Dragon
4/2/1905	–	24/1/1906 Snake
25/1/1906	–	12/2/1907 Horse
13/2/1907	–	1/2/1908 Goat
2/2/1908	–	21/1/1909 Monkey
22/1/1909	–	9/2/1910 Rooster
10/2/1910	–	29/1/1911 Dog
30/1/1911	–	17/2/1912 Pig
18/2/1912	–	5/2/1913 Rat
6/2/1913	–	25/1/1914 Ox
26/1/1914	–	13/2/1915 Tiger
14/2/1915	–	13/2/1916 Rabbit
14/2/1916	–	22/1/1917 Dragon
23/1/1917	–	10/2/1918 Snake
11/2/1918	–	31/1/1919 Horse
1/2/1919	–	19/2/1920 Goat
20/2/1920	–	7/2/1921 Monkey
8/2/1921	–	27/1/1922 Rooster
28/1/1922	–	15/2/1923 Dog
16/2/1923	–	4/2/1924 Pig
5/2/1924	–	23/1/1925 Rat
24/1/1925	–	12/2/1926 Ox
13/2/1926	–	1/2/1927 Tiger
2/2/1927	–	22/1/1928 Rabbit
23/1/1928	–	9/2/1929 Dragon
10/2/1929	–	29/1/1930 Snake
30/1/1930	–	10/2/1931 Horse
17/2/1931	–	5/2/1932 Goat
6/2/1932	–	25/1/1933 Monkey
26/1/1933	–	13/2/1934 Rooster
14/2/1934	–	3/2/1935 Dog
4/2/1935	–	23/1/1936 Pig
24/1/1936	–	10/2/1937 Rat
11/2/1937	–	30/1/1938 Ox
31/1/1938	–	18/2/1939 Tiger
19/2/1939	–	7/2/1940 Rabbit
8/2/1940	–	26/1/1941 Dragon
27/1/1941	–	14/2/1942 Snake
15/2/1942	–	4/2/1943 Horse
5/2/1943	–	24/1/1944 Goat
25/1/1944	–	12/2/1945 Monkey
13/2/1945	–	1/2/1946 Rooster
2/2/1946	–	21/1/1947 Dog
22/1/1947	–	9/2/1948 Pig
10/2/1948	–	28/1/1949 Rat
29/1/1949	–	16/2/1950 Ox
17/2/1950	–	5/2/1951 Tiger
6/2/1951	–	26/1/1952 Rabbit
27/1/1952	–	13/2/1953 Dragon
14/2/1953	–	2/2/1954 Snake
3/2/1954	–	23/1/1955 Horse
26/1/1955	–	11/2/1956 Goat
12/2/1956	–	30/1/1957 Monkey
31/1/1957	–	17/2/1958 Rooster
18/2/1958	–	7/2/1959 Dog
8/2/1959	–	27/1/1960 Pig
28/1/1960	–	14/2/1961 Rat
15/2/1961	–	4/2/1962 Ox
5/2/1962	–	24/1/1963 Tiger
25/1/1963	–	12/2/1964 Rabbit
13/2/1964	–	1/2/1965 Dragon
2/2/1965	–	20/1/1966 Snake
21/1/1966	–	8/2/1967 Horse
9/2/1967	–	29/1/1968 Goat
30/1/1968	–	16/2/1969 Monkey
17/2/1969	–	5/2/1970 Rooster
6/2/1970	–	26/1/1971 Dog
27/1/1971	–	14/2/1972 Pig
15/2/1972	–	2/2/1973 Rat
3/2/1973	–	22/1/1974 Ox
23/1/1974	–	10/2/1975 Tiger
11/2/1975	–	30/1/1976 Rabbit
31/1/1976	–	17/2/1977 Dragon
18/2/1977	–	6/2/1978 Snake
7/2/1978	–	27/1/1979 Horse
28/1/1979	–	15/2/1980 Goat
16/2/1980	–	4/2/1981 Monkey
5/2/1981	–	24/1/1982 Rooster
25/1/1982	–	12/2/1983 Dog
13/2/1983	–	1/2/1984 Pig
2/2/1984	–	19/2/1985 Rat
20/2/1985	–	8/2/1986 Ox
9/2/1986	–	28/1/1987 Tiger
29/1/1987	–	16/2/1988 Rabbit
17/2/1988	–	5/2/1989 Dragon
6/2/1989	–	26/1/1990 Snake
27/1/1990	–	14/2/1991 Horse
15/2/1991	–	3/2/1992 Goat
4/2/1992	–	22/1/1993 Monkey
23/1/1993	–	9/2/1994 Rooster
10/2/1994	–	30/1/1995 Dog
31/1/1995	–	18/2/1996 Pig
19/2/1996	–	6/2/1997 Rat
7/2/1997	–	27/1/1998 Ox
28/1/1998	–	15/2/1999 Tiger
16/2/1999	–	4/2/2000 Rabbit
5/2/2000	–	23/1/2001 Dragon
24/1/2001	–	11/2/2002 Snake
12/2/2002	–	31/1/2003 Horse
1/2/2003	–	21/1/2004 Goat
22/1/2004	–	8/2/2005 Monkey
9/2/2005	–	28/1/2006 Rooster
29/1/2006	–	17/2/2007 Dog
18/2/2007	–	6/2/2008 Pig
7/2/2008	–	25/1/2009 Rat

C

213

The Tiger

Characteristics: adventurous; creative and idealistic; confident and enthusiastic; can be diplomatic and practical; fearless and forward, aiming at impossible goals, though a realist with a forceful personality.

Partners: best suited to Horse for marriage; gets on with Dragon, Pig and Dog; should avoid Snake, Monkey and Ox.

Famous Tigers: Karl Marx, Queen Elizabeth II, Alec Guinness, Stevie Wonder, Ludvig Van Beethoven, Marilyn Monroe, Princess Anne, Charles de Gaulle, Rudolf Nureyev, John Coltrane, Tom Cruise.

The Rabbit

Characteristics: peace-loving; sociable but quiet; devoted to family and friends; timid but can be good at business; needs reassurance and affection to avoid being upset; can be vain; long-lived.

Partners: best suited to Pig, Dog and Goat; not friendly with Tiger and Rooster.

Famous Rabbits: Fidel Castro, Bob Hope, Harry Belafonte, David Frost, Martin Luther King, Josef Stalin, Queen Victoria, Albert Einstein, Brad Pitt, Tiger Woods.

The Dragon

Characteristics: strong, commanding, a leader; popular; athletic; bright, chivalrous and idealistic, though not always consistent; likely to be a believer in equality.

Partners: best suited to Snake, Rat, Monkey, Tiger and Rooster; should avoid Dog.

Famous Dragons: Joan of Arc, Ringo Starr, Mae West, John Lennon, Frank Sinatra, Salvador Dali, Kirk Douglas, Che Guevara, Yehudi Menuhin, Maya Angelou, Pierce Brosnan, Russell Crowe.

The Snake

Characteristics: charming, but possessive and selfish; private and secretive; strange sense of humour; mysterious and inquisitive; ruthless; likes the fine things in life; a thoughtful person, but superstitious.

Partners: best suited for marriage to Dragon, Rooster and Ox; avoid Snake, Pig and Tiger.

Famous Snakes: J.F. Kennedy, Abraham Lincoln, Edgar Allan Poe, Mao Zedong, Pablo Picasso, Johannes Brahms, Franz Schubert, Lennox Lewis, J.K. Rowling, Tony Blair, Bob Dylan, Stephen Hawking.

The Horse

Characteristics: nice appearance and deft; ambitious and quick-witted; favours bold colours; popular, with a sense of humour; gracious and gentle; can be good at business; fickle and emotional.

Partners: best suited to Tiger, Dog and Goat; doesn't get on with Rabbit and Rat.

Famous Horses: Neil Armstrong, Babara Streisand, Paul McCartney, Theodore Roosevelt, Rembrandt, Raquel Welch, Leonid Brezhnev and Igor Stravinsky.

The Goat

Characteristics: a charmer and a lucky person who likes money; unpunctual and hesitant; too fond of complaining; interested in the supernatural.

Partners: best suited to Horse, Pig and Rabbit; should avoid Ox and Dog.

Famous Goats: Andy Warhol, Liberace, Michelangelo, Laurence Olivier, James Michener, Diana Dors, Nicole Kidman, John Major, Michael Owen, Keith Richards, Pamela Anderson, Robert De Niro, Noel Gallagher, Bill Gates, Mick Jagger.

The Monkey

Characteristics: very intelligent and sharp, an opportunist; daring and confident, but unstable and egoistic; entertaining and very attractive to others; inventive; has a sense of humour but with little respect for reputations.

Partners: best suited to Dragon and Rat; doesn't get on with Tiger and Ox.

Famous Monkeys: Leonardo da Vinci, Mick Jagger, Bette Davis, Charles Dickens, Julius Caesar, Paul Gauguin, Rene Descartes, Kylie Minogue, Michael Schumacher, Christine Aguilera, Halle Berry.

The Rooster

Characteristics: frank and reckless, and can be tactless; free with advice; punctual and a hard worker; imaginative to the point of dreaming; likes to be noticed; emotional.

Partners: best suited to Snake, Dragon and Ox; doesn't get on with Pig, Rabbit and Rooster.

Famous Roosters: Michael Caine, Prince Philip, Charles Darwin, Peter Ustinov, Elton John, Katharine Hepburn, Peter O'Toole, Anna Kournikova, Renee Zellweger, Osama bin Laden.

The Dog

Characteristics: alert, watchful and defensive; can be generous and is patient; very responsible and has good organizational skills; spiritual, home-loving and non-materialistic.

Partners: best suited to Rabbit, Pig, Tiger and Horse; should avoid Dragon and Goat.

Famous Dogs: David Niven, Henry Moore, Brigitte Bardot, Liza Minnelli, Zsa Zsa Gabor, Winston Churchill, Elvis Presley, Sophia Loren, Voltaire, Madonna, George W. Bush, Naomi Campbell, Bill Clinton, Michael Jackson.

The Pig

Characteristics: honest; vulnerable and not good at business, but still materialistic and ambitious; outgoing and outspoken, but naïve; kind and helpful to the point of being taken advantage of; calm and genial.

Partners: best suited to Dog, Goat, Tiger and Rabbit; should avoid Snake and Rooster.

Famous Pigs: Alfred Hitchcock, Ronald Reagan, Maria Callas, Henry Kissinger, Woody Allen, Julie Andrews, Humphrey Bogart, Al Capone, Ernest Hemingway, Ewan McGregor, Iggy Pop.

Singaporean recipes

The most profound pleasures of a stay in Singapore revolve around meal times; eating is a national mania, and locals have some fifty thousand establishments from which to choose. Of course, swanky restaurants abound for gourmands intent on exploring the exclusive end of Asian cooking, but it's far more rewarding to visit a hawker stall, eating house or coffee shop, and sample everyday food as eaten by the Singaporeans.

We can't re-create for you the sensory overload of a busy hawker centre, but **recipes** for three of the island's most popular dishes are given below, representing Singapore's major ethnic groups, the Chinese, Malays and Indians. For the vast majority of visitors, these are a much better reflection of local food than bird's nests and shark's fins.

None of the **ingredients** used should be difficult to find in your local stores, and they don't require specialist equipment to cook.

Hainanese Chicken Rice

You can't walk far in Singapore without stumbling across a coffee shop or stall that serves **Hainanese Chicken Rice**, a deceptively unassuming dish of succulent **boiled chicken** laid on **aromatic rice** that's regarded by many as Singapore's unofficial national dish. The first giveaway is the row of ghostly pale chickens hanging on butcher's hooks along the shop front, the second the ringing noise of metal on butcher's block as the apron-ed Chinese cook hacks away unceremoniously with his meat cleaver at the chicken carcasses.

Part of the appeal of the dish (which was imported by immigrants from the Chinese island of Hainan, south of China off the north coast of Vietnam) lies in its simplicity and its completeness. Nothing is wasted, with the stock created by boiling the chicken being used to cook rice before finally ending up as a light broth. Hainanese Chicken Rice is traditionally served with chilli and ginger sauce, soya sauce and minced garlic.

Serves 4 people

1.7l or 3 pints chicken stock
Whole 1.5kg or 3lb chicken, giblets removed
1 red chilli, finely sliced
2 cloves garlic, crushed
1cm or half inch piece ginger, finely grated
1 teaspoon salt
Half teaspoon freshly ground black pepper
400g or 13oz long grain rice
Half cucumber, sliced
3 tomatoes, sliced
2 tablespoons soya sauce

For the chilli and ginger sauce:
8 fresh red chillies, chopped
4cm or 1.5 inch piece ginger, grated
2 cloves garlic, chopped
1 tablespoon vinegar
Sugar and salt to taste

Bring the stock to the boil in a large pan, add the whole chicken, along with the chilli, garlic, ginger, salt and pepper. Cover the pan, and boil the chicken for 45 minutes or until tender. Remove the chicken from the stock and set to one side, reserving the stock. While the chicken is cooling, rinse the rice thoroughly, and cook in the chicken stock. Meanwhile, make the sauce. Pound together the chillies, ginger and garlic in a pestle and mortar. Transfer to a bowl and add the vinegar.

When the rice is cooked, drain, reserving the stock. Pack the rice into cups, and upturn them onto individual plates to form domes.

Cut the chicken into slices, lightly baste them with soya sauce, and lay them around the rice. Garnish with cucumber and tomato. Finally, bring the remaining stock to the boil, season to taste, and serve as a soup.

Satay

If any one Malaysian dish has caught the world's culinary imagination it's surely **satay**, an aromatic snack comprising marinated strips of meat skewered on small sticks, grilled and dipped in a spicy peanut sauce. The sight of the Muslim Malay satay man, sporting a *songkok* and fanning the flames of his charcoal barbecue pit with a woven fan, is a reassuringly traditional one in today's high-tech Singapore. **Beef** and **chicken** are the two classic ingredients for Malay satay, though oddities such as fish, seafood and vegetarian satays often crop up on Singaporean menus. The pork satay of the Nonya cook is a variation of the traditional Malay satay, reflecting the Chinese predilection for pork.

There are two styles of satay: **satay terkan**, for which the meat is finely minced and wrapped around a skewer, and the far tastier **satay chochok**, for which whole pieces of meat are used. Nowadays, satay is sold in bunches of five or ten; in days gone by, customers would accumulate skewers during an evening, and the satay man would tally the bill by counting these up at the end of the night.

Makes approximately 20–30 sticks of satay

400g or 13oz beef or chicken, cut into thin strips
Oil for basting

For the marinade:
1 lemon grass stalk, sliced and crushed
8 shallots, finely sliced
2 cloves garlic, chopped
1 teaspoon cumin
1 teaspoon coriander
1 teaspoon turmeric
1 teaspoon sugar
Pinch of salt
2 tablespoons peanut oil

For the sauce:
1 lemon grass stalk, finely grated
2.5cm or 1 inch piece ginger, finely grated
1 onion, finely sliced
10 dried red chillies, soaked and finely chopped
2 cloves garlic

3 tablespoons tamarind juice
250g or 8oz unsalted peanuts, finely chopped
2 tablespoons sugar
Salt to taste
Oil for frying

To make the marinade, mix the lemon grass, shallots, garlic, cumin, coriander, turmeric, sugar and salt in the oil. Mix the strips of meat into the paste and leave for a couple of hours.

Meanwhile, prepare the sauce. Pound the lemon grass and ginger in a pestle and mortar. Fry the onion over a moderate heat for five minutes or until soft, stirring occasionally. Add the lemon grass, ginger, chillies and garlic and mix. Cook for a further two minutes. Now add the tamarind juice, peanuts, sugar, salt and 200ml or 7fl oz water, and simmer for 15 minutes or until thickened.

Skewer the strips of marinated meat onto small skewers and grill on a barbecue or under a preheated hot grill until crisp, regularly brushing the meat with oil.

Satay is best served hot, dipped in the sauce, with generous chunks of raw cucumber and onion.

Murtabak

The **murtabak** is a thick pancake stuffed with meat, fried onion and egg, and loved by Singapore's Indian population. Half the fun of ordering a murtabak is watching it being made: murtabak cooks have made an art out of spinning their dough dramatically up in the air to stretch it paper-thin, and perhaps it's this process that has earned the dish the otherwise misleading title of Singapore's answer to the pizza. The spectacle is best viewed at one of the Muslim Indian restaurants behind the Sultan Mosque, on North Bridge Road: the *Zam Zam* even boasts a champion in the field. Murtabaks can be made out of chicken or beef, but more often, they feature **minced mutton**. In Singapore, they are cooked on wide griddles, but a frying pan will do. A saucer of curry sauce or **daal** perfectly complements the dish.

Makes 6 murtabaks

For the dough:
300g or 10oz plain flour
Half teaspoon salt
1 tablespoon ghee (or butter)
Oil to coat dough balls
Flour for rolling

For the filling:
2 tablespoons ghee (or vegetable oil)
2 medium-sized onions, finely sliced
4 green chillies, finely sliced
3 garlic cloves, crushed
5 eggs
400g or 13oz minced meat
1 teaspoon garam masala
Salt and pepper to taste

To make the dough, place the flour, salt and ghee in a mixing bowl and slowly add approximately 8 tablespoons of warm water, mixing together until a stiff dough is formed. Knead until soft. Divide the dough into six balls and leave standing in a covered dish for at least an hour, turning once or twice.

Next, make the filling. Heat the ghee in a pan over moderate heat, add the onion, chilli and garlic, and fry for 5 minutes stirring occasionally. Meanwhile, beat the eggs in a bowl. When the onions are soft, add the meat and garam masala and season. Cook for 20 minutes or until cooked through.

To assemble a murtabak, lift a ball of dough out of the oil and roll out as thinly as possible on a floured surface. Transfer the dough to a greased and pre-heated griddle, or frying pan.

As the dough begins to cook, baste it with beaten egg, and then heap a mound of filling in the middle. Fold in the four corners of the dough to form a parcel, and cook for a couple of minutes on each side, basting with egg to secure the flaps. Serve at once.

Singapore in literature

Since its foundation in 1819, Singapore has provided rich pickings for travel writers, novelists and historians. However, due to the scarcity of indigenous written material, we have to rely almost exclusively on writings by foreign visitors for early depictions of the island.

The one notable exception is the historian **Abdullah bin Kadir**, born in Melaka in 1797 of Malay and Tamil stock, and later employed as a scribe by Sir Stamford Raffles. The first excerpt below comes from his autobiography, the *Hikayat Abdullah*. Published in Malay in 1849, it remains, despite factual inaccuracies, a fascinating social and historic document. It is interesting to contrast Abdullah's squalid portrayal of early Singapore with the altogether more civilized picture painted by spunky English traveller **Isabella Bird** thirty years later. By the time of her five-week tour of Singapore and the Malay states in 1879, recorded in *The Golden Chersonese*, Bird had already seen Amenca, Canada, Hawaii, Australia and New Zealand. Subsequent travels took her to Armenia, Persia, Kurdistan, Kashmir and Tibet and saw her honoured as the first woman fellow of the Royal Geographical Sociey in 1892.

Singapore's contemporary writers are represented first by Lee Tzu Pheng, a lecturer at the National University of Singapore, whose poem *My Country and My People* reflects the cultural disorientation inherent in the establishment of a new nationhood. Finally, R. Rajaram's short story *Hurry* is played out against a Singapore completely remoulded since the days of Abdullah, though the nineteenth-century scribe would surely have recognized the hustle and bustle that Rajaram evokes in his story.

Hikayat Abdullah

It was Colonel Farquhar's habit to go for a walk every morning looking round the district. It was all covered with thick scrub. Only in the middle of the open space already mentioned were there no thick bushes, but only myrtle, rhododendron and eugenia trees. On the side nearest the shore were many kinds of trees, *ambong-ambong*, *melpari*, *bulangan* and scattered tree trunks. On the opposite side of the river there was nothing to be seen except mangrove trees, *bakau*, *api-api*, *buta-buta*, *jeruju* and strewn branches. There was no good piece of ground even as much as sixty yards wide, the whole place being covered in deep mud, except only on the hills where the soil was clay. There was a large rise, of moderate elevation, near the point of the headland at the estuary of Singapore River.

In the Singapore River estuary there were many large rocks, with little rivulets running between the fissures, moving like a snake that has been struck. Among these many rocks there was a sharp-pointed one shaped like the snout of a swordfish. The Sea Gypsies used to call it the Swordfish's Head and believed it to be the abode of spirits. To this rock they all made propitiatory offerings in their fear of it, placing bunting on it and treating it with reverence. "If we do not pay our respects to it," they said, "when we go in and out of the shallows it will send us to destruction." Every day they brought offerings and placed them on the rock. All along the shore there were hundreds of human skulls rolling about on the sand; some old, some new, some with hair still sticking to them, some with the teeth filed and others without. News of these skulls was brought to Colonel Farquhar and when he had seen them he ordered them to be gathered up and cast into the sea. So the people collected them in sacks and threw them into the sea. The Sea Gypsies were asked, "Whose are all these skulls?" and they replied, "These are the skulls of men who were robbed at sea. They were slaughtered here. Wherever a fleet of boats or a ship is plundered it is brought to this place for a division of the spoils. Sometimes there is wholesale slaughter among the crews when the cargo is grabbed. Sometimes the pirates tie people up and try out their weapons here along the sea shore." Here-too-was the place where they went in for cockfighting and gambling.

One day Colonel Farquhar wanted to ascend the Forbidden Hill, as it was called by the *temenggong*. The *temenggong*'s men said, "None of us has the courage to go up the hill because there are many ghosts on it. Every day one can hear on it sounds as of hundreds of men. Sometimes one hears the sound of heavy drums and of people shouting." Colonel Farquhar laughed and said, "I should like to see your ghosts," and turning to his Malacca men, "Draw this gun to the top of the hill." Among them there were several who were frightened, but having no option they pulled the gun up. All who went up were Malacca men, none of the Singapore men daring to approach the hill. On the hill there was not much forest and not many large trees, only a few shrubs here and there. Although the men were frightened they were shamed by the presence of Colonel Farquhar and went up whether they wanted to or not. When they reached the top Colonel Farquhar ordered the gun to be loaded and then he himself fired twelve rounds in succession over the top of the hill in front of them. Then he ordered a pole to be erected on which he hoisted the English flag. He said, "Cut down all these bushes." He also ordered them to make a path for people to go up and down the hill. Every day there was this work being done, the undergrowth being slashed down and a pathway cleared.

At that time there were few animals, wild or tame on the Island of Singapore, except rats. There were thousands of rats all over the district, some almost as large as cats. They were so big that they used to attack us if we went out walking at night and many people were knocked over. In the house where I was living we used to keep a cat. One night at about midnight we heard the cat mewing and my friend went out carrying a light to see why the cat was making such a noise. He saw six or seven rats crowding round and biting the cat; some bit its ears, some its paws, some its nose so that it could no longer move but only utter cry after cry. When my companion saw what was happening he shouted to me and I ran out at the back to have a look. Six or seven men came pressing round to watch but did nothing to release the cat which only cried the louder at the sight of so many men, like a person beseeching help. Then someone fetched a stick and struck at the rats, killing the two which were biting the cat's ears. Its ears freed, the cat then pounced on another rat and killed it. Another was hit by the man with a stick and the rest ran away. The cat's face and nose were lacerated and covered with blood. This was the state of affairs in all the houses, which were full of rats. They could hardly be kept under control, and the time had come when they took notice of people. Colonel Farquhar's place was also in the same state and he made an order saying, "To anyone who kills a rat I will give one *wang*." When people heard of this they devised all manner of instruments for killing rats. Some made spring-traps, some pincer traps, some cage-traps, some traps with running nooses, some traps with closing doors, others laid poison or put down lime. I had never in my life before seen rats caught by liming; only now for the first time. Some searched for rat-holes, some speared the rats or killed them in various other ways. Every day crowds of people brought the dead bodies to Colonel Farquhar's place, some having fifty or sixty, others only six or seven. At first the rats brought in every morning were counted almost in thousands, and Colonel Farquhar paid out according to his promise. After six or seven days a multitude of rats were still to be seen, and he promised five *duit* for each rat caught. They were still brought in thousands and

Colonel Farquhar ordered a very deep trench to be dug and the dead bodies to be buried. So the numbers began to dwindle, until people were bringing in only some ten or twenty a day. Finally the uproar and the campaign against the rats in Singapore came to an end, the infestation having completely subsided.

Some time later a great many centipedes appeared, people being bitten by them all over the place. In every dwelling, if one sat for any length of time, two or three centipedes would drop from the attap roof. Rising in the morning from a night's sleep one would be sure to find two or three very large centipedes under one's mat and they caused people much annoyance. When the news reached Colonel Farquhar he made an order saying that to anyone who killed a centipede he would give one *wang*. Hearing this, people searched high and low for centipedes, and every day they brought in hundreds which they had caught by methods of their own devising. So the numbers dwindled until once in two or three days some twenty or thirty centipedes were brought in. Finally the campaign and furore caused by the centipedes came to an end, and people no longer cried out because of the pain when they got bitten.

The above extract is taken from the *Hikayat Abdullah*, by Abdullah bin Kadir, translated by A.H. Hill (1969), with kind permission of Oxford University Press/Penerbit Fajar Bakti.

The Golden Chersonese

Singapore, January 19, 1879.

It is hot — so hot! — but not stifling and all the rich-flavoured, coloured fruits of the tropics are here — fruits whose generous juices are drawn from the moist and heated earth, and whose flavours are the imprisoned rays of the fierce sun of the tropics. Such cartloads and piles of bananas and pineapples, such heaps of gold and green giving off fragrance! Here, too, are treasures of the heated crystal seas — things that one has dreamed of after reading Jules Verne's romances. Big canoes, manned by dark-skinned men in white turbans and loin-cloths, floated round our ship, or lay poised on the clear depths of aquamarine water, with fairy freights — forests of coral white as snow, or red, pink, violet, in massive branches or fernlike sprays, fresh from their warm homes beneath the clear warm waves, where fish as bright-tinted as themselves flash through them "living light". There were displays of wonderful shells, too, of pale rose-pink, and others with rainbow tints which, like rainbows, came and went — nothing scanty, feeble, or pale!

It is a drive of two miles from the pier to Singapore, and to eyes which have only seen the yellow skins and non-vividness of the Far East, a world of wonders opens at every step. It is intensely tropical; there are mangrove swamps, and fringes of coco-palms, and banana groves, date, sago and travellers' palms, tree ferns, india-rubber, mango, custard-apple, jack-fruit, durian, lime, pomegranate, pineapples, and orchids, and all kinds of strangling and parrot-blossomed trailers. Vegetation rich, profuse, endless, rapid, smothering in all shades of vivid green, from the pea-green of spring and the dark velvety green of endless summer to the yellow-green of the plumage of the palm, riots in a heavy shower every night and the heat of a perennial sunblaze every day, while monkeys of various kinds and bright-winged birds skip and flit through the jungle shades. There is a perpetual battle between man and the jungle, and the latter, in fact, is only brought to bay within a short distance of Singapore.

I had scarcely finished breakfast at the hotel, a shady, straggling building much infested by ants, when Mr Cecil Smith, the Colonial Secretary, and his wife called, full of kind thoughts and plans of furtherance; and a little later a resident, to whom I had not even a letter of introduction, took me and my luggage to his bungalow. All the European houses seem to have very deep verandahs, large, lofty rooms, punkahs everywhere, windows without glass, brick floors, and jalousies and "tatties" (blinds made of grass or finely split bamboo) to keep out the light and the flies. This equatorial heat is neither as exhausting or depressing as the damp summer heat of Japan, though one does long "to take off one's flesh and sit in one's bones…"

It is all fascinating. Here is none of the indolence and apathy which one associates with Oriental life, and which I have seen in Polynesia. These yellow, brown, tawny, swarthy, olive-tinted men are all intent on gain; busy, industrious, frugal, striving and, no matter what their creed is, all paying homage to Daikoku. In spite of the activity, rapidity, and earnestness, the movements of all but the Chinese are graceful, gliding stealthy, the swarthy faces have no expression that I can read, and the dark liquid eyes are no more intelligible to me than the eyes of oxen. It is the "Asian mystery" all over.

It is only the European part of Singapore which is dull and sleepy looking. No life and movement congregate round the shops. The merchants, hidden away behind jalousies in their offices, or dashing down the streets in covered buggies, make but a poor show. Their houses are mostly pale, roomy, detached bungalows, almost altogether hidden by the bountiful vegetation of the climate. In these their wives, growing paler every week, lead half-expiring lives, kept alive by the efforts of ubiquitous "punkah-wallahs", writing for the mail, the one active occupation. At a given hour they emerge, and drive in given directions, specially round the esplanade, where for two hours at a time a double row of handsome and showy equipages moves continuously in opposite directions. The number of carriages and the style of dress of their occupants are surprising, and yet people say that large fortunes are not made nowadays in Singapore! Besides the daily drive, the ladies, the officers, and any men who may be described as of "no occupation", divert themselves with kettle-drums, dances, lawn tennis, and various other devices for killing time, and this with the mercury at 80°! Just now the Maharajah of Johore, sovereign of a small state on the nearest part of the mainland, a man much petted and decorated by the British Government for unswerving fidelity to British interests, has a house here, and his receptions and dinner parties vary the monotonous round of gaieties.

The native streets monopolise the picturesqueness of Singapore with their bizarre crowds, but more interesting still are the bazaars or continuous rows of open shops which create for themselves a perpetual twilight by hanging tatties or other screens outside the side walks, forming long shady alleys, in which crowds of buyers and sellers chaffer over their goods, the Chinese shopkeepers asking a little more than they mean to take, and the Kings always asking double. The bustle and noise of this quarter are considerable, and the vociferation mingles with the ringing of bells and the rapid beating of drums and tom-toms, an intensely heathenish sound. And heathenish this great city is. Chinese joss-houses, Hindu temples, and Mohammedan mosques almost jostle each other, and the indescribable clamour of the temples and the din of the joss-houses are faintly pierced by the shrill cry from the minarets calling the faithful to prayer, and proclaiming the divine unity and the mission of Mahomet in one breath.

How I wish I could convey an idea, however faint, of this huge, mingled, coloured, busy, Oriental population; of the old King and Chinese bazaars; of the itinerant sellers of seaweed jelly, water, vegetables, soup, fruit and cooked fish, whose unintelligible street cries are heard above the din of the crowds of coolies, boatmen and gharriemen waiting for hire; of the far-stretching suburbs of Malay and Chinese cottages; of the sheet of water, by no means clean, round which hundreds of Bengalis are to be seen at all hours of daylight unmercifully

beating on great stones the delicate laces, gauzy silks, and elaborate flouncings
of the European ladies; of the ceaseless rush and hum of industry, and of the
resistless, overpowering, astonishing Chinese element, which is gradually turning Singapore into a Chinese city! I must conclude abruptly, or lose the mail.
I.L.B.

Letter VII (Beauties of the Tropics),
extracted from *The Golden Chersonese*, by Isabella Bird.

My Country and My People

My country and my people
are neither here nor there, nor
in the comfort of my preferences,
if I could even choose.
At any rate, to fancy is to cheat;
and worse than being alien, or
subversive without cause,
is being a patriot
of the will.

I came in the boom of babies, not guns,
a 'daughter of a better age';
I held a pencil in a school
while the 'age' was quelling riots
in the street, or cutting down
those foreign 'devils',
(whose books I was being taught to read).
Thus privileged I entered early
the Lion City's jaws.
But they sent me back as fast
to my shy, forbearing family.

So I stayed in my parents' house,
and had only household cares.
The city remained a distant way,
but I had no land to till;
only a duck that would not lay,
and a runt of a papaya tree,
(which also turned out to be male).

Then I learnt to drive instead
and praise the highways till
I saw them chop the great trees down,
and plant the little ones;
impound the hungry buffalo
(the big ones and the little ones)
because the cars could not be curbed.
Nor could the population.
They built milli–mini–flats
for a multi–mini–society.
The chiselled profile in the sky
took on a lofty attitude,
but modestly, at any rate
it made the tourist feel 'at home'.

My country and my people
I never understood.
I grew up in China's mighty shadow,
with my gentle, brown-skinned neighbours;
but I keep diaries in English.
I sought to grow
in humanity's rich soil,
and started digging on the banks, then saw
life carrying my friends downstream.

Yet, careful tending of the human heart
may make a hundred flowers bloom;
and perhaps, fence-sitting neighbour,
I claim citizenship in your recognition
of our kind,
my people, and my country,
are you, and you my home.

My Country and My People by Lee Tzu Pheng,
reprinted by kind permission of Heinemann

Hurry

I was running. In the centre of the road. True, I wasn't running like the wind,
but my speed was fast enough for beads of perspiration to run down my body
and my breath to come in short gasps.

Cars and lorries flashed past me either way. Still I kept running. Somehow it
seemed appropriate that I should be running on the white centre line separating
the dual carriageway.

Where were the vehicles heading to? I didn't know. Did the drivers in them
know where I was running to? No, but there was a possibility that they would
think I was a lunatic. So I should not continue to run in this manner.

I would have to cross the road, walk or run the short distance to the MRT
station to board a train to Orchard Road. Then I would have to disembark and
cross the road to Dynasty Hotel to meet my friend Kamal staying there.

The train would arrive at the station in two minutes' time and I must be in it.
I was running in this wild manner all for this. I had crossed half the road. Now
running along the white line, I tried desperately to find a way through the thick
of the moving traffic to find an opening to make my dash across. Suddenly I
spied an opening and lashed across, leaving behind two drivers screeching to
a halt as they tried to avoid the collision. One driver even made an obscene
gesture with his hands.

I felt a sense of regret. Not at his gesture, but that I had cut his speed of travel.
Anyway, there was no time to apologise to him. I had to catch that train or I
would really be late.

I must buy a car, I thought to myself. It would be so convenient considering
the amount of travelling I have to do. The convenience was more than that. A
motorist dares to use foul language and rude gestures because he knows he is
safe from the poor pedestrian out on the road. Yes, a car is definitely a convenience in more ways than one.

Miraculously I arrived at the Jurong Station with thirty seconds to spare.
From the third level of the station, I could see the sun had half-disappeared in
the horizon. When I had left my home in the morning, he had also been half-
hidden, but that was the dawn.

Passengers on the platform suddenly moved forward with some standing in the yellow safety line. I could see the train in the distance. This wasn't a bus. There would be ample time for all to board the train before it pulled out. Then why the rush? To ensure that they could get seats? But even if one pushed his way through not everyone could get a seat. I wasn't going to be left out however. I, too, rushed with the crowd and pushed my way to the front.

As the train ground to a halt and the doors slid open we rushed in. I was lucky enough to grab the only seat in my compartment and sank down gladly.

My eyes scanned the passengers. Young, old, middle-aged, they all seemed lost in some thoughts. What were they thinking about, or were they just staring blankly, I wondered.

As the train pulled up at the next station, another human wave entered the train. I noticed my friend Ravi among them in the next compartment. Ravi is a very close friend. Well, at least during our school days. But I still considered him as one. Unfortunately, we had not had many opportunities to meet as often as we used to. As he was staying in the Jurong area, occasionally we met like this in the train.

He had not noticed me. "Hello, Ravi!" I shouted across. He turned, saw me and waved. My voice, however, had shattered the silence in the train and several dozen pairs of eyes bored into me. I turned pink with embarrassment.

Ravi could not come any nearer, the crowd was that thick. No one appeared willing to allow Ravi to walk through to me.

"How is father?" I gestured with my hands. His father had been ill for some time. Ravi answered in a similar manner, giving me the thumbs down sign. His normally cheerful face was tinged with sadness.

As the train sped on, I wondered what I could do. I attempted to convey how I felt with expressions. He was about to say something but changed his mind, pulled out a paper from his pocket and started to scribble something.

The train reached Raffles Place Interchange. Most of us, including me, had to change trains here. In no time, three quarters of the train had emptied. Ravi made his way through the crowd and as I was about to disembark, thrust the paper into my hands. As he didn't need to change trains, I didn't have the time to even exchange a few words.

As the train pulled away my train pulled into the opposite tunnel. Running with the others, I crossed over the platform and boarded it.

Eagerly I opened his note. "We have finalised marriage plans for Chitra. Father insists that he wants to see the marriage before he dies. I'll phone you later."

Chitra marrying. I sat stunned. How could she marry someone when she was my girlfriend…?

Why not? No one, not even Chitra, knew of my love. That's a joke isn't it!

I had wanted to tell Ravi of my love. But the opportunity had never arisen, and being the coward I am I had kept postponing the discussion. Now it was too late. Who could I blame but myself? Anyway, where did I have the time for courtship when I never returned from work till eleven in the night every day.

I crumpled the note and threw it on the floor and looked up. The passenger opposite looked meaningfully at me and the note on the floor. I had littered. Sheepishly I picked up the note and shoved it in my shirt pocket.

Irritated, I reached for a cigarette. My eyes fell on the warning note directly opposite. "No smoking! $500 fine." My hand dropped to the side. I, more than anyone else, knew that every mistake had its penalty.

The train sped on through the tunnels. It was pitch dark outside. I wasn't aware where we were. This is the drawback in travelling by train. A minute's inattention, and one loses track completely of one's whereabouts. The speed with which one was travelling was the only consolation.

Some light pierced the darkness. Instantly the passengers came to life. Orchard Station. I would have to get out here. I glanced at my watch – 7.26pm. I was pleased. Had I come by bus I would not have made it in this short time to keep my 7.30pm appointment with Kamal at Dynasty Hotel's lobby.

I crossed glittering Orchard Road and walked briskly into the hotel. But Kamal was not there. Maybe he was still up in the room. Reception should be able to help.

"Can you give me Kamal's room number?"

"Mr Kamal just vacated his room. His flight was brought forward and he's left for the airport."

If he had just left, he must be waiting for a cab outside the hotel. In my hurry, I must have missed him outside. Maybe, just maybe, I could catch him before he caught a cab, I thought as I dashed out.

Hurry, by R. Rajaram, translated by K. Sulosana.

Books

The majority of books about Singapore tend to be penned by Western visitors to the region, rather than by local writers. Only in the last few decades has writing about Singapore by Singaporeans themselves begun to gather momentum.

The best selection of local writing is available on the island itself, though Skoob Books of London is doing much to introduce Singaporean literature to the West. Some of the titles below are ostensibly concerned with Malaya or Malaysia, but all cast some light on Singapore, as the island's fortunes have always been closely linked with those of the Peninsula.

In the reviews below, books marked ⅉ are particularly recommended; o/p signifies out of print.

Travel writing and exploration

ⅉ **John Bastin** (ed) *Travellers' Singapore*. Singapore-related vignettes from as early as 1819 and as late as the Japanese conquest of 1942.

Isabella Bird *The Golden Chersonese*. Delightful epistolary romp through old Southeast Asia, penned by the intrepid Bird, whose adventures in the Malay states in 1879 ranged from strolls through Singapore's streets to elephant-back rides and encounters with alligators.

G.M. Gullick *They Came To Malaya*. A cornucopia of accounts of people, places and events, written by the governors, planters and explorers who tamed Malaya and Singapore.

Rev G.M. Reith *1907 Handbook to Singapore* (o/p). Intriguing period piece which illuminates early-twentieth-century colonial attitudes

in Singapore: drill hall, gaol and docks are detailed, while the list of useful Malay phrases includes such essentials as "harness the horse" and "off with you".

ⅉ **Michael Wise** (ed) *Travellers' Tales of Old Singapore*. Identical in theme to Bastin's *Travellers' Singapore* (see above), though Wise's selection of tales is the more catholic and engrossing of the two.

Gavin Young *In Search of Conrad*. Young plays detective and historian, tracing Joseph Conrad's footsteps around Southeast Asia in search of the stories and locations that inspired him. Young's time in Singapore takes him from the National Library to Bidadari cemetery in search of A.P. Williams – Conrad's Lord Jim.

History and politics

Abdullah bin Kadir *The Hikayat Abdullah* (o/p). Raffles' one-time clerk, Melakan-born Abdullah later turned diarist of some of the most formative years of Southeast Asian history; his first-hand account is crammed with illuminating vignettes and character portraits.

Barbara Watson Andaya and Leonard Andaya *The History of Malaysia*. Unlike more paternalistic histories, written by former colonists, this standard text on the region takes a more even-handed view, and finds time for cultural coverage.

David Brazil *Street Smart Singapore*. An Aladdin's cave of Singaporean history and trivia that remains fascinating throughout. Published by Times Editions, Singapore.

Maurice Collis *Raffles* (o/p). The most accessible and enjoyable biography of Sir Stamford Raffles: very readable.

Images of Asia series: Maya Jayapal's *Old Singapore*. Concise volume which charts the growth of the city-state, drawing on contemporary maps, sketches and photographs to engrossing effect.

Lee Kuan Yew *The Singapore Story*. Spanning the 42 years from his birth to Singapore's separation from Malaysia in 1965, the Granddaddy of contemporary Singapore's first volume of memoirs has drawn plaudits from the likes of Thatcher and Chirac, Keating and Kissinger. Essential reading for anyone wanting the inside track on Singapore's huge expansion over the past fifty years.

Nick Leeson *Rogue Trader*. Leeson's own account of his beginnings, his ambitions and of the whirlpool of deceit in which he floundered as the result of his covert trading in Singapore. The inadequacies of Barings' systems and controls are revealed as contributing factors, though Leeson's apparent lack of penitence wins him little sympathy.

James Minchin *No Man Is An Island*. A well-researched and at times critical study of Lee Kuan Yew, which refuses to kowtow to Singapore's ex-PM and is hence unavailable in Singapore itself, but gleefully sold in shops throughout Malaysia.

C. Mary Turnbull *A Short History of Malaysia, Singapore and Brunei* Published by Graham Brash in Singapore, this is an informed introduction to the region, touching on the major issues that have shaped it. Its big brother, Turnbull's *History of Singapore 1819–1988* (o/p), is, in contrast, as scholarly an approach to Singapore as you could wish for.

C.E. Wurtzburg *Raffles of the Eastern Isles*. A weighty and learned tome that's the definitive study of the man who founded modern Singapore; not for the marginally interested.

WWII and the Japanese Occupation

Noel Barber *Sinister Twilight*. Documents the fall of Singapore to the Japanese, by re-imagining the crucial events of the period.

Russell Braddon *The Naked Island*. Southeast Asia under the Japanese: Braddon's disturbing and moving first-hand account of the POW camps of Malaya, Singapore and Siam displays courage in the face of appalling conditions and treatment. Worth scouring secondhand stores for.

Peter Elphick *Singapore: The Pregnable Fortress*. Drawing on documents made available only in 1993, Elphick has produced the definitive history of the fall of Singapore, showing the gaffes, low morale and desertion that led to it; a scholarly *tour de force*.

Culture and society

Culture Shock! Singapore. Cultural dos and don'ts for the leisure and business traveller to the region, spanning subjects as diverse as handing over business cards and belching after a fine meal.

Leslie Layton *Songbirds in Singapore* (o/p). A delightful examination of songbird-keeping in Singapore, detailing all facets of the pastime, from its growth in the nineteenth century to its most popular birds.

Tan Kok Seng *Son of Singapore* (o/p). Tan Kok Seng's candid and sobering autobiography unearths the underside of the Singaporean success story, telling of hard times spent as a coolie.

Literature

Charles Allen *Tales from the South China Seas*. Memoirs of the last generation of British colonists, in which predictable Raj attitudes prevail, though some of the drama of everyday lives, often in inhospitable conditions, is evinced with considerable pathos.

Gopal Baratham *Moonrise*; *Sunset*. When How Kum Menon's fiancée is murdered while sleeping by his side in Singapore's East Coast Park, it seems everyone he knows has a motive. How Kum turns detective, and an engaging whodunnit emerges. In *A Candle or the Sun*, Baratham swallows hard and tackles the thorny issue of political corruption.

Noel Barber *Tanamera*. Romantic saga based in mid-twentieth-century Singapore.

Anthony Burgess *The Long Day Wanes*. Burgess's Malayan trilogy – *Time for a Tiger*, *The Enemy in the Blanket* and *Beds in the East* – published in one volume, provides a witty and acutely observed vision of 1950s Malaya, underscoring the racial prejudices of the period. *Time for a Tiger*, the first novel, is worth reading for the Falstaffian Nabby Adams alone.

James Clavell *King Rat*. Set in Japanese-occupied Singapore, a gripping tale of survival in the notorious Changi Prison.

Joseph Conrad *Lord Jim*. Southeast Asia provides the backdrop to the story of Jim's desertion of an apparently sinking ship and subsequent efforts to redeem himself; modelled upon the sailor A.P. Williams, who lived and died in Singapore.

Alastair Dingwall (ed) *Southeast Asia Traveller's Literary Companion*. Among the bite-sized essays in this gem of a book are enlightening segments on Malaysia and Singapore, into which are crammed biographies, a recommended reading list, historical, linguistic and literary backgrounds. Excerpts range from classical Malayan literature to the nations' leading contemporary lights.

J.G. Farrell *The Singapore Grip*. Lengthy novel – the last of Farrell's empire trilogy – of World War II Singapore in which real and fictitious characters flit from tennis to dinner party as the countdown to the Japanese occupation begins.

W. Somerset Maugham *Short Stories Volume 4*. Peopled by hoary sailors, bored plantation-dwellers and colonials with mutton-chop whiskers and topees, Maugham's short stories resuscitate the Malaya of a century ago; quintessential colonial literature graced by an easy style and a steady eye for a story.

Skoob Pacifica Anthology No. 1 and No. 2. These two thorough compendia of writings from the Pacific Rim together comprise an invaluable introduction to the contemporary literatures of Singapore and Malaysia.

Southeast Asia Writes Back! Anthology. A thorough compendium of writings from the Pacific Rim, published by Skoob, that provides a useful introduction to the contemporary literature of Singapore.

Paul Theroux *Saint Jack.* The compulsively bawdy tale of Jack Flowers, an ageing American who supplements his earnings at a Singapore ship's chandlers by pimping for Westerners; Jack's jaundiced eye and Theroux's rich prose open windows on Singapore's past.

Wildlife

G.W.H. Davison and Chew Yen Fook *A Photographic Guide to Birds of Peninsular Malaysia and Singapore.* Well-keyed and user-friendly, these slender volumes carry oodles of glossy plates that make positive identifying a breeze.

Chua Ee Kiam *Chek Jawa: Discovering Singapore's Biodiversity.* The shallow tidal flats of Chek Jawa, on Pula Ubin's east coast, were saved from the redevelopers in 2001. This beautiful book, published by Select Books, traces its salvation, and features stunning photography of its rich wildlife.

Glossary

Baba Straits-born Chinese (male).

Bukit Hill.

Bumboat Small cargo boat.

Cheongsam Chinese dress with long slit up the side.

Chunam Plaster made from eggs, lime, sugar and coconut husks.

Expressway Motorway/freeway.

Five-foot way Covered verandah outside a shophouse.

Godown Riverside warehouse.

Gopuram Bank of sculpted deities over entrance to a Hindu temple.

Haj Trip to Mecca.

Halal Something that's permissible by Islam.

Hawker centre A cluster of food stalls gathered under one roof and sharing common tables.

Istana Palace.

Jalan Road.

Kampung Village.

Kavadi Steel frames hung from the bodies of Hindu devotees during Thaipusam.

Keramat Auspicious Malay site.

Kongsi Chinese clan association.

Kris Wavy-bladed dagger.

Lorong Lane.

Mahjong A Chinese game with similarities to dominoes.

Mandi Asian method of bathing by dousing with water from a tank using a small bucket.

Masjid Mosque.

Nonya Straits-born Chinese (female); sometimes *Nyonya*.

Padang Field or square.

Peranakan Straits-born Chinese.

Pulau Island.

Ramadan Muslim fasting month.

Rotan Rattan cane; used in the infliction of corporal punishment.

Saree Traditional Indian woman's garment, worn in conjunction with a *choli* (short-sleeved blouse).

Singlish Singaporean English.

Shophouse Shuttered building with living space upstairs and shop space on ground floor.

Songkok Hat worn by Muslim males.

Sultan Ruler.

T'ai chi Chinese martial art; commonly performed as an early-morning exercise.

Temenggong Chieftain.

Tiffin Lunch.

Tongkang Chinese sailing boat.

Trishaw Three-wheeled bicycles with a carriage for passengers.

Wayang Chinese opera.

Acronyms

CBD Central Business District.

JB Johor Bahru.

KL Kuala Lumpur.

MCP Malayan Communist Party.

MDU Malayan Democratic Union.

MRT Mass Rapid Transit system.

PAP People's Action Party.

SIA Singapore International Airline.

STB Singapore Tourist Board.

UNMO Malaysia's United Malays National Organization.

WTC World Trade Centre.

Travel store

UK & Ireland
Britain
Devon & Cornwall
Dublin **D**
Edinburgh **D**
England
Ireland
The Lake District
London
London **D**
London Mini Guide
Scotland
Scottish Highlands &
  Islands
Wales

Europe
Algarve **D**
Amsterdam
Amsterdam **D**
Andalucía
Athens **D**
Austria
The Baltic States
Barcelona
Barcelona **D**
Belgium &
  Luxembourg
Berlin
Brittany & Normandy
Bruges **D**
Brussels
Budapest
Bulgaria
Copenhagen
Corfu
Corsica
Costa Brava **D**
Crete
Croatia
Cyprus
Czech & Slovak
  Republics
Dodecanese & East
  Aegean
Dordogne & The Lot
Europe
Florence & Siena
Florence **D**
France
Germany
Gran Canaria **D**
Greece
Greek Islands
Hungary
Ibiza & Formentera **D**

Iceland
Ionian Islands
Italy
The Italian Lakes
Languedoc &
  Roussillon
Lanzarote **D**
Lisbon **D**
The Loire
Madeira **D**
Madrid **D**
Mallorca **D**
Mallorca & Menorca
Malta & Gozo **D**
Menorca
Moscow
The Netherlands
Norway
Paris
Paris **D**
Paris Mini Guide
Poland
Portugal
Prague
Prague **D**
Provence & the Côte
  D'Azur
Pyrenees
Romania
Rome
Rome **D**
Sardinia
Scandinavia
Sicily
Slovenia
Spain
St Petersburg
Sweden
Switzerland
Tenerife &
  La Gomera **D**
Turkey
Tuscany & Umbria
Venice & The Veneto
Venice **D**
Vienna

Asia
Bali & Lombok
Bangkok
Beijing
Cambodia
China
Goa
Hong Kong & Macau
India

Indonesia
Japan
Laos
Malaysia, Singapore
  & Brunei
Nepal
The Philippines
Singapore
South India
Southeast Asia
Sri Lanka
Thailand
Thailand's Beaches &
  Islands
Tokyo
Vietnam

Australasia
Australia
Melbourne
New Zealand
Sydney

North America
Alaska
Baja California
Boston
California
Canada
Chicago
Colorado
Florida
The Grand Canyon
Hawaii
Las Vegas **D**
Los Angeles
Maui **D**
Miami & South Florida
Montréal
New England
New Orleans **D**
New York City
New York City **D**
New York City Mini
  Guide
Orlando & Walt
  Disney World® **D**
Pacific Northwest
San Francisco
San Francisco **D**
Seattle
Southwest USA
Toronto
USA
Vancouver

Washington DC
Washington DC **D**
Yosemite

Caribbean
& Latin America
Antigua & Barbuda **D**
Argentina
Bahamas
Barbados **D**
Belize
Bolivia
Brazil
Cancún & Cozumel **D**
Caribbean
Central America
Chile
Costa Rica
Cuba
Dominican Republic
Dominican Republic **D**
Ecuador
Guatemala
Jamaica
Mexico
Peru
St Lucia **D**
South America
Trinidad & Tobago
Yúcatan

Africa & Middle East
Cape Town & the
  Garden Route
Egypt
The Gambia
Jordan
Kenya
Marrakesh **D**
Morocco
South Africa, Lesotho
  & Swaziland
Syria
Tanzania
Tunisia
West Africa
Zanzibar

D: Rough Guide
DIRECTIONS for
short breaks

Available from all good bookstores

ROUGH GUIDES Complete Listing

For more information go to www.roughguides.com

ROUGH GUIDES

Visit us online

www.roughguides.com

Information on over 25,000 destinations around the world

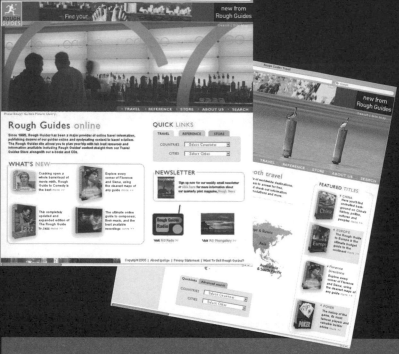

- **Read** Rough Guides' trusted travel info
- **Access** exclusive articles from Rough Guides authors
- **Update** yourself on new books, maps, CDs and other products
- **Enter** our competitions and win travel prizes
- **Share** ideas, journals, photos & travel advice with other users
- **Earn** points every time you contribute to the Rough Guide community and get rewards

BROADEN YOUR HORIZONS

NOTES

NOTES

NOTES

NOTES

NOTES

NOTES

NOTES

Small print and

Index

A Rough Guide to Rough Guides

Published in 1982, the first Rough Guide – to Greece – was a student scheme that became a publishing phenomenon. Mark Ellingham, a recent graduate in English from Bristol University, had been travelling in Greece the previous summer and couldn't find the right guidebook. With a small group of friends he wrote his own guide, combining a highly contemporary, journalistic style with a thoroughly practical approach to travellers' needs.

The immediate success of the book spawned a series that rapidly covered dozens of destinations. And, in addition to impecunious backpackers, Rough Guides soon acquired a much broader and older readership that relished the guides' wit and inquisitiveness as much as their enthusiastic, critical approach and value-for-money ethos.

These days, Rough Guides include recommendations from shoestring to luxury and cover more than 200 destinations around the globe, including almost every country in the Americas and Europe, more than half of Africa and most of Asia and Australasia. Our ever-growing team of authors and photographers is spread all over the world, particularly in Europe, the USA and Australia.

In the early 1990s, Rough Guides branched out of travel, with the publication of Rough Guides to World Music, Classical Music and the Internet. All three have become benchmark titles in their fields, spearheading the publication of a wide range of books under the Rough Guide name.

Including the travel series, Rough Guides now number more than 350 titles, covering: phrasebooks, waterproof maps, music guides from Opera to Heavy Metal, reference works as diverse as Conspiracy Theories and Shakespeare, and popular culture books from iPods to Poker. Rough Guides also produce a series of more than 120 World Music CDs in partnership with World Music Network.

Visit www.roughguides.com to see our latest publications.

Rough Guide travel images are available for commercial licensing at www.roughguidespictures.com

Rough Guide credits

Text editor: Alison Murchie
Layout: Pradeep Thapliyal
Cartography: Katie Lloyd-Jones
Picture editor: Harriet Mills
Production: Aimee Hampson
Proofreader: Madhulita Mohapatra
Photographer: Simon Bracken
Cover design: Chloë Roberts
Editorial: London Kate Berens, Claire Saunders, Geoff Howard, Ruth Blackmore, Polly Thomas, Richard Lim, Karoline Densley, Andy Turner, Keith Drew, Edward Aves, Nikki Birrell, Helen Marsden, Alice Park, Sarah Eno, David Paul, Lucy White, Joe Staines, Duncan Clark, Peter Buckley, Matthew Milton, Tracy Hopkins, Ruth Tidball; **New York** Andrew Rosenberg, Steven Horak, April Isaacs, AnneLise Sorensen, Amy Hegarty, Hunter Slaton, Sean Mahoney, Ella Steim
Design & Pictures: London Simon Bracken, Dan May, Diana Jarvis, Mark Thomas, Jj Luck; **Delhi** Umesh Aggarwal, Ajay Verma, Jessica Subramanian, Ankur Guha, Sachin Tanwar, Anita Singh

Production: Sophie Hewat, Katherine Owers
Cartography: London Maxine Repath, Ed Wright; **Delhi** Manish Chandra, Rajesh Chhibber, Jai Prakash Mishra, Ashutosh Bharti, Rajesh Mishra, Animesh Pathak, Jasbir Sandhu, Karobi Gogoi, Amod Singh
Online: New York Jennifer Gold, Suzanne Welles, Kristin Mingrone; **Delhi** Manik Chauhan, Narender Kumar, Shekhar Jha, Rakesh Kumar, Chhandita Chakravarty, Amit Verma
Marketing & Publicity: London Richard Trillo, Niki Hanmer, David Wearn, Demelza Dallow, Louise Maher, Jess Carter; **New York** Geoff Colquitt, Megan Kennedy, Katy Ball; **Delhi** Reem Khokhar
Custom publishing and foreign rights: Philippa Hopkins
Manager India: Punita Singh
Series editor: Mark Ellingham
Reference Director: Andrew Lockett
PA to Managing and Publishing Directors: Megan McIntyre
Publishing Director: Martin Dunford

Publishing information

This fifth edition published October 2006 by **Rough Guides Ltd**,
80 Strand, London WC2R 0RL UK
345 Hudson St, 4th Floor,
New York, NY 10014, USA
14 Local Shopping Centre, Panchsheel Park, New Delhi 110017, India
Distributed by the Penguin Group
Penguin Books Ltd,
80 Strand, London WC2R 0RL
Penguin Putnam, Inc.
375 Hudson Street, NY 10014, USA
Penguin Group (Australia)
250 Camberwell Road, Camberwell,
Victoria 3124, Australia
Penguin Books Canada Ltd,
10 Alcorn Avenue, Toronto, Ontario,
Canada M4V 1E4
Penguin Group (New Zealand)
Cnr Rosedale and Airborne Roads
Albany, Auckland, New Zealand
Cover concept by Peter Dyer.

Typeset in Bembo and Helvetica to an original design by Henry Iles.
Printed and bound in China
© Mark Lewis 2006

No part of this book may be reproduced in any form without permission from the publisher except for the quotation of brief passages in reviews.
256pp includes index
A catalogue record for this book is available from the British Library
ISBN 1-84353-705-2
ISBN 13: 9-78184-353-705-2
The publishers and authors have done their best to ensure the accuracy and currency of all the information in **The Rough Guide to Singapore**, however, they can accept no responsibility for any loss, injury, or inconvenience sustained by any traveller as a result of information or advice contained in the guide.

1   3   5   7   9   8   6   4   2

Help us update

We've gone to a lot of effort to ensure that the fifth edition of **The Rough Guide to Singapore** is accurate and up to date. However, things change – places get "discovered", opening hours are notoriously fickle, restaurants and rooms raise prices or lower standards. If you feel we've got it wrong or left something out, we'd like to know, and if you can remember the address, the price, the time and the phone number, so much the better. We'll credit all contributions, and send a copy of the next edition (or any other Rough Guide if you prefer) for the best letters. Everyone who writes to us and isn't already a subscriber will receive a copy of our full-colour thrice-yearly newsletter. Please mark letters: "**Rough Guide to Singapore Update**" and send to: Rough Guides, 80 Strand, London WC2R 0RL, or Rough Guides, 4th Floor, 345 Hudson St, New York, NY 10014. Or send an email to **mail@roughguides.com**
Have your questions answered and tell others about your trip at
www.roughguides.atinfopop.com

Acknowledgements

Mark Lewis would like to extend huge thanks to Hamid at the Singapore tourist board and to Suzy Lewis. At Rough Guides he would like to thank Alison Murchie for editing, Pradeep Thapliyal for typesetting, Katie Lloyd Jones for map work, Harriet Mills for photo research and Madhu Mohapatra for proofreading.

Steve Martin proffers special thanks to Benjamin Sirirat, Jack Barton, Karishma Vyas, Michael Newbill, Angeline Thangaperakasam, Dr. Zheng Yangwen, Ronni Pinsler, Yishane Lee, Eric & Jennifer Ho, Wilfred Hong, and the lovely Loog sisters.

Readers' letters

Thanks to all those readers of the fourth edition who took the trouble to write in with their amendments and additions. Apologies for any misspellings or omissions.

Tan HongBoon; Patrick Major; David Stevens; Ilene Africk; Ken and Hazel Ferguson; Timmy Williams; John and Maggie Coaton; Bill and Sandra Martin; Tor Brendeford; Andy and Claire Brice; Ian Hawker; Rosalind Hoffer; Rob Beaty; Susan Booth

Photo credits

All photos © Rough Guides except the following:

Things not to miss
02 Chinese New Year celebrations in old Singapore © G P Bowater/Alamy
04 Tropical lowland rainforest in Bukit Timah Nature Reserve © Nigel Hick/Alamy
17 Dancers at the Zouk night club © Yadid Levy/Alamy
20 Running over red-hot coals at Sri Mariamman Temple during Thimithi Festival © How Hwee Young/Corbis

Colour insert – Festive Singapore
Kumquat trees for sale during Chinese New Year celebrations, Chinatown © John Voos/Reuters

Chinatown, Singapore, at Chinese New Year © Glen Allison/Stone/Getty
Dragon dancers during Chinese New Year celebrations © Wong Maye-E/AP/Empics
Christmas decorations outside a shopping mall, downtown Singapore © Ben Lynn/Reuters
Dragon boat race in Singapore © Tim Chong/Reuters/Corbis
Market near the Sultan Mosque © Bob Krist/CORBIS
Mid-Autumn Festival lanterns © Singapore Tourist Board
Hindu devotee carries a "kavadi" during Thaipusam © David Loh/Reuters

Index

Map entries are in colour.

INDEX

INDEX

Map symbols

maps are listed in the full index using coloured text

----	Chapter division boundary	🏺	Museum
▬▬▬▬	International border	ⓘ	Tourist office
▬▬▬	Expressway	⊠	Post office
═══	Main road	ⓒ	Telephone office
══	Minor road	@	Internet access
▬▬	Pedestrianized road	⊞	Hospital/clinic
⫿⫿⫿⫿	Steps	⊝	MRT station
▬●▬	Railway	▮	Building
------	Footpath	▦	Underground mall
— —	Ferry route	⬭	Stadium
●---●	Cable car	→	Church
○—○	Tramway/monorail	✡	Synagogue
═══	Waterway	🕌	Mosque
✈	Airport	✿	Buddhist temple
)(	Bridge/tunnel	▲	Hindu temple
▲	Peak	⛩	Chinese temple
ⵣ	Public gardens	⟇+⚏	Christian cemetery
◉	Accommodation	⟇⚏	Muslim cemetery
▣	Restaurant/café/bar	▦	Park
◆	General point of interest		

THE MRT SYSTEM

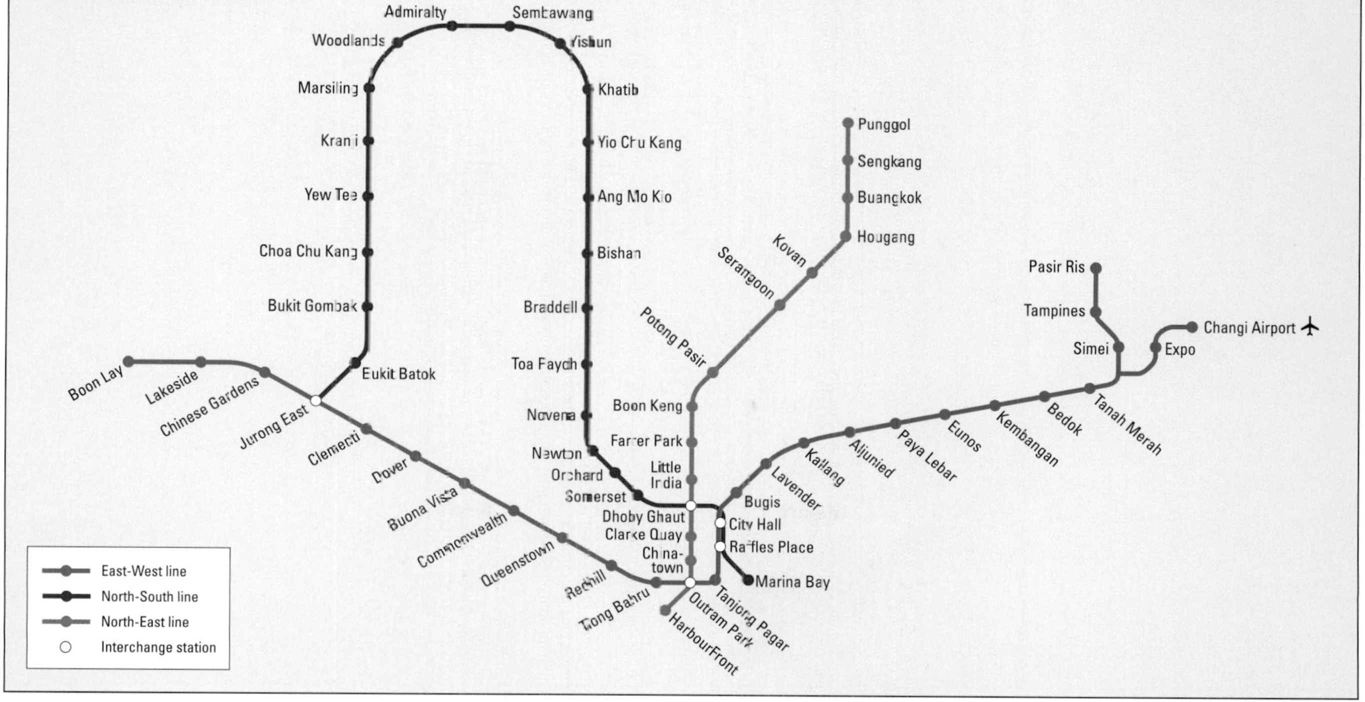

Legend:
- East-West line
- North-South line
- North-East line
- ○ Interchange station

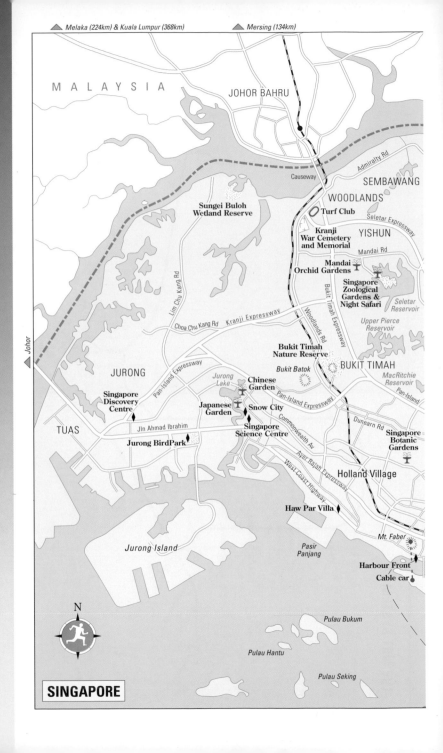

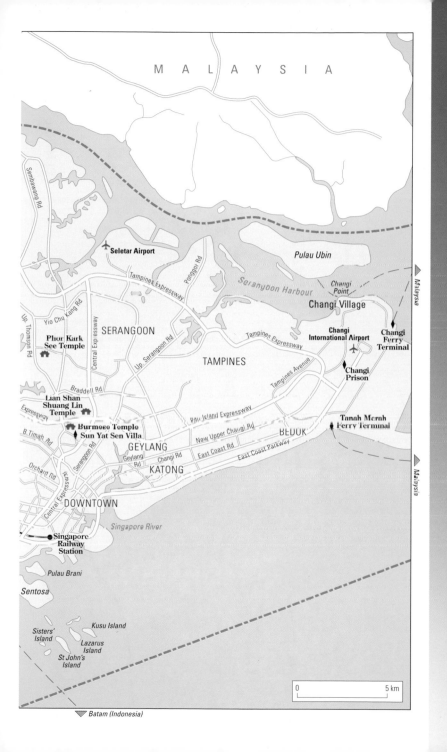

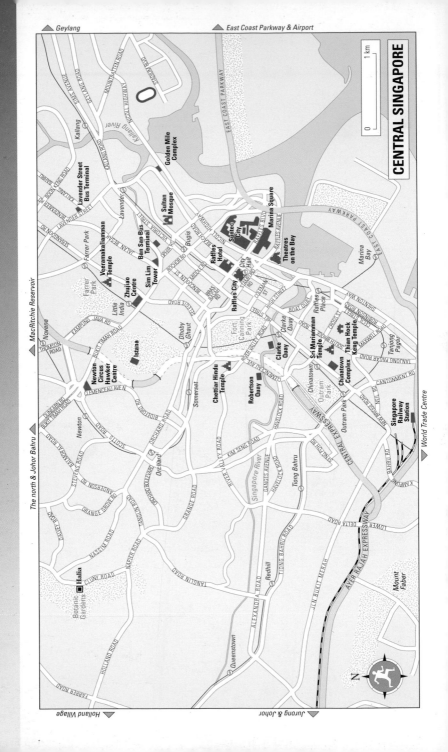

CENTRAL SINGAPORE

Geylang

East Coast Parkway & Airport

The north & Johor Bahru

MacRitchie Reservoir

0   1 km

N

Holland Village

Jurong & Johor

World Trade Centre

Golden Mile Complex
Sultan Mosque
Lavender Street Bus Terminal
Veeramakaliamman Temple
Ban San Bus Terminal
Sim Lim Tower
Zhujiao Centre
Marina Square
Suntec City
Raffles Hotel
Raffles City
Theatres on the Bay
Raffles Place
Istana
Newton Circus Hawker Centre
Chettiar Hindu Temple
Robertson Quay
Clarke Quay
Sri Mariamman Temple
Thian Hock Keng Temple
Chinatown Complex
Singapore Railway Station
Halia
Botanic Gardens
Mount Faber